SECOND EDITION

HOW TO DO YOUR

RESEARCH PROJECT

A GUIDE FOR STUDENTS IN EDUCATION AND APPLIED SOCIAL SCIENCES

GARY THOMAS

⊘SAGE

Los Angeles | London | New Delhi
Singapore | Washington DC

Los Angeles | London | New Delhi
Singapore | Washington DC

SAGE Publications Ltd
1 Oliver's Yard
55 City Road
London EC1Y 1SP

SAGE Publications Inc.
2455 Teller Road
Thousand Oaks, California 91320

SAGE Publications India Pvt Ltd
B 1/I 1 Mohan Cooperative Industrial Area
Mathura Road
New Delhi 110 044

SAGE Publications Asia-Pacific Pte Ltd
3 Church Street
#10-04 Samsung Hub
Singapore 049483

Editor: Jai Seaman
Development editor: Amy Jarrold
Production editor: Katherine Haw
Copyeditor: Richard Leigh
Marketing manager: Ben Sherwood
Cover design: Lisa Harper
Typeset by: C&M Digitals (P) Ltd, Chennai, India
Printed in Great Britain by
Ashford Colour Press Ltd

Library of Congress Control Number: 2013930449

British Library Cataloguing in Publication data

A catalogue record for this book is available from
the British Library

MIX
Paper from
responsible sources
FSC® C011748

ISBN 978-1-4462-5886-6
ISBN 978-1-4462-5887-3 (pbk)

CONTENTS

ABOUT THE AUTHOR

Being of a nervous disposition as a child, Gary Thomas failed to write anything on his 11-plus examination paper, which inaction took him to secondary modern school. His subsequent zigzag through the education system gave him broad experience of its good and bad sides.

He eventually became a teacher, then an educational psychologist, then a professor of education at the University of Birmingham, where his teaching, research and writing now focus on inclusive education and the methods used in social science research. He has led a wide range of research projects and has received awards from the AHRC, the ESRC, the Nuffield Foundation, the Leverhulme Trust, the Department for Education, charities such as Barnardo's and the Cadmean Trust, local authorities and a range of other organisations. He has written or edited 20 books and lots of boring academic articles.

People tell him he looks far too young to be a grandparent, but, believe it or not, he is the proud grandfather of a little boy called Nicholas. He likes, in alphabetical order, cats, chess, cycling, dogs and writing. He dislikes 4x4 cars, pomposity and people who try to make things sound more complicated than they are (in that order).

Despite supporting Aston Villa football club, he maintains an optimistic outlook on life.

PREFACE

I was delighted when SAGE asked me to write a second edition of this book, and I was especially pleased on reading students', tutors' and reviewers' comments on the first edition. These made it clear that something I had tried to achieve with the first edition – to write a book about doing research that communicated easily and without jargon – had come off. In the second edition I resolved to update the book, to include more material and, crucially, to write in the same style, always striving to use a conversational approach and, where there was a choice between a simple word and a hard one, to use the simple one.

Research is useful and it is exciting to do, and the expectation for students to do a research project is becoming more and more common in almost every area of applied social science: education, health sciences, social work, criminology, and so on. And this is happening at every stage in higher education: foundation, undergraduate and postgraduate. It is right that this should be the case – that students should be learning by doing – for the research project teaches skills that no lecture can teach. Not only does it enable learning about the particular topic chosen for research but it also teaches students about having a questioning disposition, about evidence and about the frailty of knowledge, about methods of research and their strengths and weaknesses. It helps you to learn independently and to organise your time. With the skills and the awarenesses that it fosters, research provides an almost tangible platform for personal and professional development.

I don't like to think too long about how many hundreds of projects – undergraduate, postgraduate and doctoral – I have supervised because it reminds me of my age. But the more I supervise the more I realise that whether you are doing an undergraduate project, a master's, a PhD or a major piece of research for a government department, you always go through much the same sequence of activity. All research contains the same basic ingredients – having a question, discovering what others have done, refining your question in the light of that discovery and then going out to answer the question yourself. That's the basic framework, and beyond that there are better and worse ways of going about doing it. In this book I wanted to show the better ways, using examples (of mistakes as well as successes) from my own experience wherever possible, to those who are inexperienced in doing research: the ways that avoid pain and encourage satisfaction and pleasure. Yes, pleasure: research really can give you a buzz. There's an immense satisfaction that comes from finding out something new and presenting it in a form that other people can understand.

On the assumption that the basic ground rules for research are similar at whatever stage, I haven't attempted to pitch this book at one particular group: undergraduate or postgraduate. I've tried to keep it simple and straightforward in a way that I hope will appeal to all students in education and the social sciences, and whether you are an undergraduate or just beginning doctoral work I hope it will be relevant. While I realise that what emerges is inevitably a bit of a cookbook, I hope it is more of an Elizabeth David cookbook than any other – in other words, telling a story or set of stories, and containing opinions as well as recipes.

At several points in the book I discuss the importance of critical reflection, and I hope that I have given a taster of this in my own writing. So, where there is methodological controversy I say so. Where the academic community seems to me to be pretentious, pompous or unsure of itself, I also say so, and try to explain why. To my mind, there is no purpose to be had in papering over the frailties of an academic area with verbosity, pretend-clarity or pseudo-scientific jargon, and where the academic community in applied social science seems to me to do this I say so. I hope that in communicating a critical disposition I have presented the book more as a series of conversations than as a set of lectures.

I've wanted to write this book also because in my experience students undertaking projects often don't think hard enough about the questions that they want to answer. As a result, those projects are less interesting than they might have been, looking at a question that is much too hard to answer given the time available, or restricting the focus to something perceived to be easy to measure. Often certain approaches to research are completely sidestepped: numbers or anything to do with statistics may be studiously avoided, and this is partly because of the backgrounds of many students in education and the social sciences. They are cautious of using numbers, even though they have the ability and the wherewithal.

It seemed to me that many of the introductory textbooks didn't really help very much, focusing heavily on research methods rather than research processes, with too little information on how to knit together a story. Methods are not the end of research – they are simply ways of doing it, and it's more important that a piece of research has integrity, coherence and meaning than it is that a particular method is properly used. And those methods are sometimes described in scope and levels of detail that are of no interest to undergraduate or master's students. There is, in the modern phrase, too much information. Stanislav Andreski, the perceptive commentator on social science, said that social scientists in the academy display an 'adulation of formulae and scientific-sounding terms, exemplify[ing] the common tendency ... to displace value from the end to the means' (Andreski, 1972: 108–9). I think he was correct back then in 1972, and he is still correct now: we can become hypnotised by the elegance of our shiny instruments and forget the integrity of the whole – the story we are telling.

Much of the literature on research method seems to me to be dipped into by students, who emerge from their dip sometimes with inappropriate and half-digested notions (e.g. about reliability and validity), with little in the way of glue to stick the bits together. It seems to me that many of these readers have not been guided by the literature to understand what good research is – how it bonds together and why it is important for there to be a sense of integrity and narrative to the whole. I attribute students' hurried forays into the literature partly to that literature's emphasis on method and technique rather than on the balance of the whole research project.

The following is a note to tutors. I have adopted what I think is a novel approach to the way that research methodology and design are discussed and handled, and I hope that you agree with me that this will be helpful to students. Everywhere I have looked I have found tensions about how to explain research design and method to students, with some quite serious ambiguities raised by overlapping vocabularies. This confusion was noted more than twenty years ago by Smith and Heshusius (1986), but textbook writers seem to have paid little heed. The confusion is not too troubling for you and me because we have a gestalt that lets us re-slot and reconfigure things when they are presented differently. What is an interview? Is it a method or a data-gathering technique? (You'll find it handled in both ways in the textbooks.) Are case studies, action research and experiments designs or methods? Again, you'll find them described as both. I think the reason for this ambiguity is apparent in this quotation from distinguished sociologists Schatzman and Strauss, where it seems to me they are unclear about what they mean by 'method':

> Field method is not an exclusive method in the same sense, say, that experimentation is. Field method is more like an umbrella of activity beneath which any technique may be used for gaining the desired information, and for processes of thinking about this information. (Cited in Burgess, 1982: 2)

Well, I'd venture that experimentation is not a method, except in the vernacular sense of the word: it is a design framework of such proportions that there is even a discrete branch of study dedicated to it, namely experimental design. And I have no idea what Schatzman and Strauss mean by an 'exclusive method'. They imply in 'exclusive method' that a discrete and limited range of techniques is used in experimentation (by contrast with field method). But this is clearly wrong, since experimentation may employ a wide range of data-gathering techniques, just as field study does. It's how the design frames handle the data that is different, and what I guess they are getting at is that this design (i.e. experiment) prescribes particular, well-defined processes – processes about, for example, control.

Though I differ with them on their explication of field method I do like the idea of the 'umbrella': much of our design rationale in social research, when you think about it, incorporates the umbrella. As they rightly note, field method is an umbrella, but so are action research, case study and evaluation – all use a range of methods and data-gathering techniques, and even envelop each other.

Before the metaphor of umbrellas and envelopment becomes over-extended, I'll just lay out my thesis about research design for this book, which is that it proceeds from *purposes* to *questions* to *decision about approach*, then *design frame*, then *data-gathering methods*, then *analytical methods*. All of these elements, considered together, constitute the design route. Sometimes this design route will be straightforward, since certain methods almost always go with certain approaches, but usually in educational and social research it isn't simple (for umbrellas and other things interfere with the simplicity), and this is why I have taken time to outline paths of decision-making in design (e.g. in Figures 5.10 and 5.11 on pp. 126 and 129).

This orientation has influenced also my attitude to what my colleague Stephen Gorard calls 'the Q words': qualitative and quantitative. The division here sometimes seems to dazzle students in the QQ headlights so that they can't see beyond it. As Richard Pring (2000) has pointed out, while there is a *distinction* between these two types of research, they are not in *opposition* to one another, and it seems to be becoming clearer to all concerned with the teaching of research methods that they should not sit on either side of a fulcrum, dividing the whole world of social research into the one or the other. For this reason, I have tried to avoid using them, and thereby avoid the dichotomy they engender. Instead, I prefer to look first and foremost at the design frames – then at whether these use words or numbers in data collection and analysis (and of course sometimes they use both).

Back to students, and a word of advice. Every tutor has different expectations about what a research project should be about and look like. Some prefer the emphasis here, others there. One will want this kind of project, another will prefer something different. I've tried always in this book to indicate that there is no absolutely right way, that there are different avenues to follow. However, if I seem to be giving different advice from that given by your tutor (and there are places in social scientific study where there are real differences and unresolved issues, as I make clear in the book), listen to your tutor: your tutor is always right.

Look forward to your research project. When you have completed it you will have learned so much. You will have learned how to organise a major piece of work, how to get hold of information, and how to analyse and synthesise it. You will have learned sophisticated presentation skills and all the basics and more of the most common data-management software. It is one of the most significant and productive things you will do in your time at university.

ACKNOWLEDGEMENTS

I'd like to thank all those who have helped in the reading of drafts and for encouraging and/or corrective comments of one kind or another. Special thanks go to my colleagues at the Schools of Education at the University of Birmingham and the University of Leeds, and especially Catherine Robertson, library subject adviser at the University of Birmingham, for her guidance through the maze of new databases.

This book grew partly out of a seminar series that I led on quality in social research which was funded by the ESRC Teaching and Learning Research Programme. I'd like to thank the ESRC and particularly Andrew Pollard, director of that programme, for his support before, during and after the series. I'm grateful to all of those who have taken the time and trouble to write such gratifyingly positive things about the first edition.

Many thanks to Helen Fairlie, who kept encouraging me to write a book that might be useful to students, rather than an academic one that 'only three people and a dog read' (I paraphrase Helen's actual comments, but this was the gist). Many thanks to Patrick Brindle and Jai Seaman at SAGE for stimulating this second edition, and huge thanks to Amy Jarrold for the massive task of coordinating readers' comments on the first edition and writing a coherent plan of action for this second edition. Thanks also to Katherine Haw and her colleagues in production at SAGE for transforming the presentation of the book for this second edition.

Thanks to all my students (some of whom are mentioned in the book) whose ideas I have stolen and some of which have led to the examples used here. And of course I am grateful to all of those in our wider community of inquiry whose ideas I have borrowed and used. Any errors of fact or judgement, though, are of course entirely down to me.

ABOUT THE COMPANION WEBSITE

This book is supported by a wealth of material online to help both lecturers and students. You can access it by visiting www.sagepub.co.uk/thomas. Here you will find:

- **Videos** of Gary answering the most frequently asked questions and talking about common problems with research projects.

- **Annotated examples of research projects** highlighting the different sections of a piece of research (to show you how it really looks) and pose some points to get you thinking.

- **Links to websites** where you can find more guidance on specific parts of your project or how to manage your time.

- **Journal articles** which go into more depth about parts of the research process and are available as full text.

- **Worksheets** to help you get on with your project and manage your time.

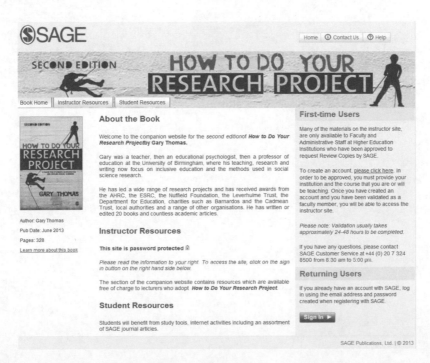

ROAD MAP – HOW TO USE THIS BOOK

There are many metaphors for the research project – a journey, a voyage, or, as the cover of this book suggests, a mountaineering trek. All imply that there is effort involved, that there is a beginning and an end, that you may meet unexpected problems and delights on the way.

In Figure 0.1, I suggest that the research project is like a marathon – but it is a very special kind of marathon, with some well-defined tasks along the way, and certain places where you have to pause for thought and reflection. It gives a 'road map' for your marathon where I have flagged up these tasks and stopping-points and given each of them numbers, and I have organised the chapters of the book so that they correspond to those numbers. Thus, Chapter 1 is about starting off and asking a sensible question and Chapter 9 is about drawing your conclusion. Figure 0.2 'rolls out' the road map and shows the itinerary of your project in a little more detail.

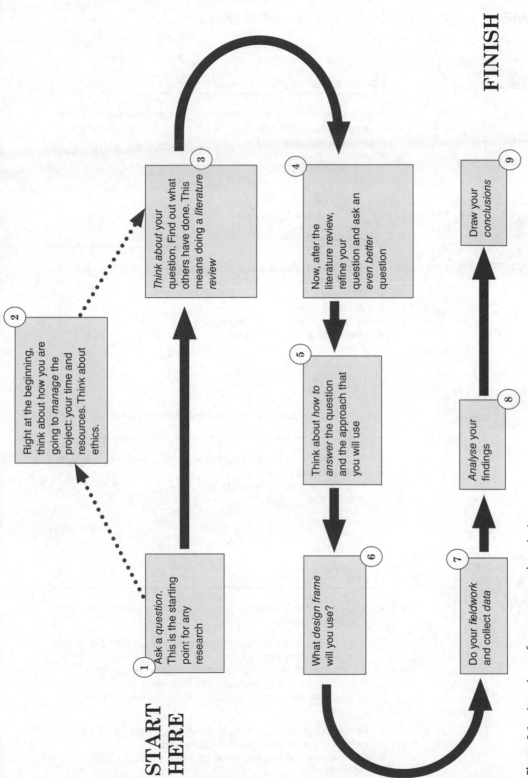

START HERE

1 Ask a *question*. This is the starting point for any research

2 Right at the beginning, think about how you are going to *manage* the project: your time and resources. Think about ethics.

3 *Think about* your question. Find out what others have done. This means doing a *literature review*

4 Now, after the literature review, refine your question and ask an *even better* question

5 Think about *how to answer* the question and the approach that you will use

6 What *design frame* will you use?

7 Do your *fieldwork* and collect data

8 *Analyse* your findings

9 Draw your *conclusions*

FINISH

Figure 0.1 A road map for your research project

Introduction

①

Decide on your purposes, ideas and questions

- What takes you to this research area? Is it personal interest? Or is it your reading of the literature, which makes you feel that there are unanswered questions?
- Get your research question right. This is the foundation stone for the whole project.

How are you going to *manage* the project?

②

Project management

- Make a rough plan of how you want to proceed. Use the guide here to help you plan in this first stage.
- Managing the project.
- Managing your time.
- Getting clearance and getting access.
- Being ethical.

Think about your question

③

What have other people done about this or similar questions? – the literature review

- Finding out how – the easy way (Google, Web of Science, Amazon).
- Keeping records of your searches.
- Writing a coherent story – not a list.
- Drawing a storyboard.

Ask an *even better* question

④

Decide on your question – again

- In the light of your search in stage 2, how does your question from stage 1 look now?
  - ○ Have you in fact found out that many other people have already done what you were going to do?
  - ○ Is the question more complicated than you had thought?
  - ○ Will you be able to get hold of the information you need?
  - ○ Will there be ethical problems in getting the information you need?

- Refine your question, making sure that it is not too broad, not too difficult, in the context of your literature search.
- Establish a storyline – this will form the clear plan for your research.
- Think about how you will develop theory.

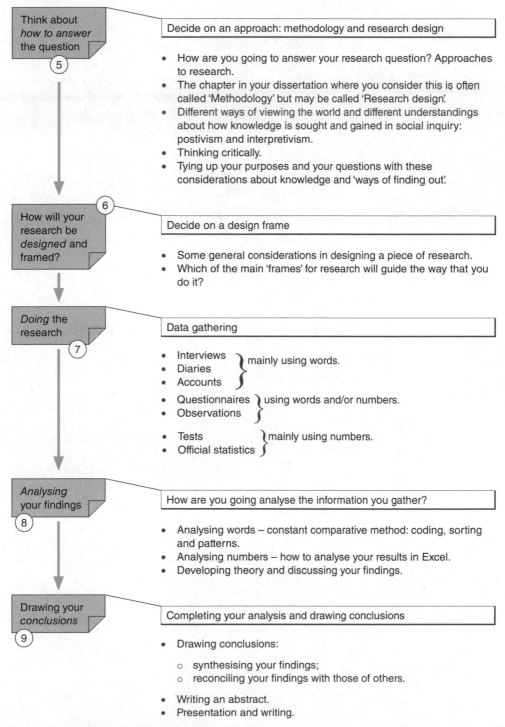

Think about *how to answer* the question
(5)

Decide on an approach: methodology and research design

- How are you going to answer your research question? Approaches to research.
- The chapter in your dissertation where you consider this is often called 'Methodology' but may be called 'Research design'.
- Different ways of viewing the world and different understandings about how knowledge is sought and gained in social inquiry: postivism and interpretivism.
- Thinking critically.
- Tying up your purposes and your questions with these considerations about knowledge and 'ways of finding out'.

(6)
How will your research be *designed* and framed?

Decide on a design frame

- Some general considerations in designing a piece of research.
- Which of the main 'frames' for research will guide the way that you do it?

***Doing* the research**
(7)

Data gathering

- Interviews } mainly using words.
- Diaries
- Accounts

- Questionnaires } using words and/or numbers.
- Observations

- Tests } mainly using numbers.
- Official statistics

***Analysing* your findings**
(8)

How are you going analyse the information you gather?

- Analysing words – constant comparative method: coding, sorting and patterns.
- Analysing numbers – how to analyse your results in Excel.
- Developing theory and discussing your findings.

Drawing your *conclusions*
(9)

Completing your analysis and drawing conclusions

- Drawing conclusions:
  o synthesising your findings;
  o reconciling your findings with those of others.

- Writing an abstract.
- Presentation and writing.

Figure 0.2   Rolling out the road map

1

YOUR INTRODUCTION: STARTING POINTS

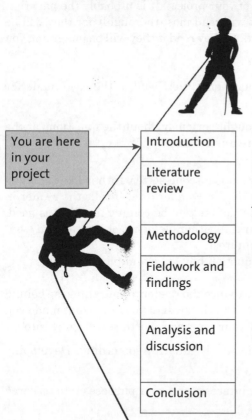

You are here in your project	→	Introduction
		Literature review
		Methodology
		Fieldwork and findings
		Analysis and discussion
		Conclusion

Your introduction says why you have chosen to do your research project in this area. In it, you explain what you want to inquire into and why you want to do it, and you justify your research question. This chapter considers:

- what takes you to this research area? Is it personal interest? Or is it your reading of the literature, which makes you feel that there are unanswered questions, uncertainty or ambiguity?

- getting your research question right – this is the foundation stone for the whole project. Different kinds of questions will lead you to different kinds of projects.

- what sort of evidence will you seek to answer your research question?

Question: Where do I begin? Answer: Begin at the beginning, with an introduction

'Begin at the beginning,' the King said gravely, 'and go on till you come to the end: then stop.' (*Alice in Wonderland*)

The King of Hearts' advice to Alice is wise not just for Alice, but for any storyteller. And your research project is like a story. Like a story, it has to hang together, so it needs to have a beginning, a middle and an end. So, as the beginning, your introduction is especially important: it needs to set the scene and outline the case for the whole project. While it is relatively short (just a few pages usually), it is vitally important for it sets the tone for the whole write-up of your project. It is probably the part that the people who read and mark your work will read most thoroughly for they will be looking for the rationale behind the project. As they read it they will be imagining you doing your research and asking:

- Was this project worth doing? In other words, how well is the case made for research into this issue?

- Has the author (that is to say, *you*) thought seriously about the questions at the centre of the project – whether they are answerable?

The introduction is a scene-setter, rather like the illustration from *Alice in Wonderland*. It tells the reader in summary what is likely to be coming and, if it is good, manages to knit together elements of the story to whet the reader's interest.

Your introduction has to do a number of things.

- It has to introduce the reader to your thinking behind the project: what interested you, and what made you think that your topic was worth researching into?

- It has to outline the *purpose*: Pure curiosity? Evaluating something? Developing your practice?

- It has to translate your thinking, your interests and your purposes into *research questions*.

- And it has to summarise the ways that you are likely to go about *finding evidence and answering* these questions.

However, your introduction is not a summary of the whole project. Students often make the mistake of limiting their introduction to a list: 'Chapter 1 is about … Chapter 2 is about … Chapter 3 is about …, etc.' Leave this kind of summary for the abstract (see pp. 288–9). Instead of this, the introduction should be the beginning of a story: it should capture the reader's interest. Most of all, it should say *why* you are doing it.

Doing the BIS

Here in the introduction you have to communicate to the reader (that is to say, your marker) why you think this is a good topic to research. What is the problem you are trying to solve? There has to be a problem there, or at least an issue – something that needs to be found out – which your research promises throw light on. In other words, why are you doing this research? Your research should not simply launch off into some exploration without a reason for that exploration. There has to be, as Booth et al. (2003: 228) put it, 'some condition of incomplete knowledge or understanding' which you are promising in your research project to throw light on. You must let the reader know what this condition of incomplete knowledge or understanding is.

Maybe it's only going to be a little bit of light, a chink, but it is light nonetheless – and more important than the *amount* of light you manage to throw is the relationship of this light to some issue, problem or dilemma. You have to make it clear what this issue, problem or dilemma is. Not making this clear is one of the commonest weaknesses in both undergraduate and postgraduate research. If you don't make it clear, the reader is quite justified in asking 'So what? What is the *point* of the research?' Indeed, this is one of the commonest weaknesses in professionally done research as well: when I was the editor of an education research journal I would ask myself, when reading an article that had been submitted, 'Why is this research being done?' If the author didn't make that clear, the article did not stand much chance of being accepted. However experienced or inexperienced, a researcher always has to be able to answer the question, 'Why should anyone care?'

I like to frame the answer to the 'Who cares?' question in a mnemonic that captures the relationship between what it is that needs to be explained and the explanation that will hopefully be forthcoming from your research: it's about **doing the BIS** – about the relationship between the **background,** the **issue**, and the promised **solution**. The BIS is the core of your introduction.

Can you state the 'BIS' in your introduction?

- Background (the general area which gives rise to the issue)

- Issue (or problem, or question)

- Solution (you promise to throw some light on the issue through your research)

Let's look at this in a little more detail. The **background** will contain some common ground on which everyone can agree; it's the context within which your issue is seated. The **issue** or 'angle' contains two parts: (i) some missing evidence or contradictory reasoning or some paradox or dilemma in the existing literature; and (ii) the consequences of not being able to resolve this lack of information or this dilemma. The **solution** concerns your promise of elucidation. (See Figure 1.1.)

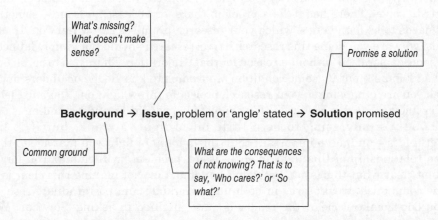

Figure 1.1 Doing the BIS: making it clear how your research will address an issue of importance

I give an example of the BIS in Table 1.1. It's from a research project that I undertook for the children's charity Barnardo's (Thomas et al., 1998). The case to be studied was of one special school closing and moving all of its staff and students to continue in the local secondary and primary schools. Politicians and educators mainly agreed that moves such as these were to be welcomed. The issue, though, which the research promised to address was 'How did the move to inclusion actually have an impact upon the affected children?'

You will notice in this discussion of the *background* and the *issue* that consideration of these comes *before* deliberation about the *methods* to be used in the research. A common mistake made by inexperienced researchers is to do this the

other way round – to think first about methods, almost before they have thought about the issue to be addressed by the research. They will say 'I want to do a questionnaire' or 'I want to do a piece of qualitative research' before they have even worked out the principal focus of the research. Doing this is, as the illustration suggests, like putting the cart before the horse. Always let the issue and your research questions take centre-stage, for, as we shall see in Chapter 5, different kinds of issue will lead to different approaches and different methods.

Table 1.1 The BIS in practice

Background ...	Inclusion of children with special needs into mainstream schools is happening increasingly. The move to inclusion, backed by anti-discrimination legislation, is occurring principally in response to concerns over the loss of social and educational opportunities for those who are segregated in special schools ...
Issue, problem or 'angle' stated ... *What's missing from the available information? What are the consequences of not having this information?*	While the push to inclusion means that more children are being included in mainstream schools, little is known about the experiences of students who make this transfer to the mainstream from special schools. Concerns have been expressed about (a) the ability of mainstream teachers adequately to meet the needs of young people with serious difficulties, and (b) the readiness of mainstream students to help accommodate special school students ...
	Much comparative research has been undertaken [*brief outline of what it is prior to full explanation in the literature review*] but little work has been undertaken to examine the quality and 'texture' of students' experiences in the new environment and how this changes over time – improving or deteriorating – as the process of inclusion becomes 'bedded in' ...
	Without information on these issues the policy to include children with special needs risks failure in practice ...
Solution, or response ... *promise of a solution*	A case study focusing intensively on the experiences of the students of a recently closed special school promises to add to knowledge about students' social and educational adaptation over time, and will offer insight into the means by which such closures are effected.

Thinking of a research idea

Once you know that a research project is part of the expectation for your course, you have to think of an idea for it – the 'issue' or problem that I have just spoken about; the 'I' of the BIS – and this can be one of the hardest parts. The right idea can lead to a good project, and the wrong idea will almost certainly lead to a poor project.

A research project begins with your curiosity – with an issue or an uncertainty, and this issue or uncertainty is reframed into the *research question* (which we shall come to in a moment). You may want to know whether something is the case,

or why it is the case. You may want to know what the consequences are of doing something. Your interest may stem from personal experience, from a discussion with a friend or colleague, from a lecturer's comment in a lecture, or from having read an article in the newspaper. There may be an 'angle' that needs investigating: you may, for example, want to resolve an apparent discrepancy between your own observation of the world and the situation that is reported by others. But whatever the inspiration, you should feel curious; you should feel that you want to know the answer.

Remember, though, that you are not out to prove something or to demonstrate that something is the case. Rather, you are looking to find the answer to a genuine question. It's a great privilege being able to research into a question of this kind with the guidance of a university tutor, and as you progress toward the end of your project you will realise that there is great satisfaction that comes from the analysis of your findings.

Purposes of research

Of course, the purpose of your research is to fulfil the requirements of your degree, but let's put that aside for a moment. Why are you doing it? The idea that you have for your research (if you have one yet) does not exist in a vacuum. It exists as part of your curiosity, and your curiosity in turn depends on your own circumstances. Your circumstances affect the purposes of your research. They may mean that you want to:

> Other words for a project are thesis and dissertation. They all mean more or less the same, though 'thesis' usually applies to a longer piece of work.

- *Find something out for its own sake.* Here you may just have an idea that you want to pursue. It is not related to anything other than your own curiosity. For example, you may have relatives who work in a social services department who may have mentioned disapprovingly how young and inexperienced in life all the social workers seem to be nowadays. This may lead you to look at (a) whether the perception is correct by examining the age profiles of social workers over the last 20 years, and (b) the possible reasons and potential consequences of any changes that seem to be occurring.

- *Evaluate something.* Here, there may be a programme or an innovation that is being introduced or that has already been introduced, and you want to see what its impact has been. What are its outcomes? In short, 'Did x work?' For example, an 'Active Kids' programme may have been started by a supermarket chain, with the provision of extra sports and PE equipment for schools if parents collect the supermarket's vouchers. You may choose to evaluate the project's take-up in schools local to you. As a follow-on (depending on the length of your project) you may wish to see what the impact has been locally and try to make some assessment of the costs and benefits of schools' involvement in the programme.

> There are different purposes to research. Ask yourself what your purposes are.

- *Find out if something works.* Here you may be interested in the consequences of bringing in a particular innovation and you may choose systematically to test this. For example, a publisher may have brought out a new series of reading books, which your school has decided to buy. You may choose to look at how effective these are by using them with half of your class while the other half use the existing scheme.

- *Improve your own or others' practice.* The aim here is to look in detail at your own practice or an element of it to see if it can be improved. Or, in your research, you may be helping others to do this – to examine their own practice. It will involve introducing new ways of working, thinking and talking about events and incidents as they happen, and collecting information about how these changes and this thinking and talking seem to be influencing things. This kind of research is often called 'action research'. Its main aim is to change practice – for the better.

Moving on to research questions

When you have thought of an issue which your research will throw light on, and you have decided what kind of purpose your research will meet, you will need to shape your ideas into a more specific question, or set of questions, which will lie at the heart of your research. Different kinds of questions will lead to different kinds of projects. This may sound obvious, but failure to recognise this represents one of the main problems for those beginning to undertake research: too often students get into trouble because they set off with a question that is not right and by the time they realise that this is the case it is too late.

Remember the question asked of the supercomputer in *The Hitch-Hiker's Guide to the Galaxy*: 'What's the answer to the question of Life, the Universe and Everything?' After seven and a half million years the computer comes up with the answer: forty-two.

'Forty-two!' yelled Loonquawl. 'Is that all you've got to show for seven and a half million years' work?'

(Continued)

(Continued)

'I checked it very thoroughly,' said the computer, 'and that quite definitely is the answer. I think the problem, to be quite honest with you, is that you've never actually known what the question is.'

Maybe social scientists' questions will never actually be posed as simplistically as this, but the story is a salutary warning to us all. It warns us that we should be aware of the complexities of the subjects we are studying.

The questions that educational and social researchers pose and try to answer aren't simple. And simplistic – that is to say, over-simple – questions lead to silly answers. It's very important in any inquiry concerned with people, how they behave and interrelate, that we think about the *nature* of the questions we want to ask.

How, then, do you think of a good question? First you have to understand that there are many *kinds of questions*, and that these will lead you off into different lines of inquiry and different kinds of research. Some questions have fairly simple answers. For example, if you ask whether there are more men teachers than women teachers, and whether the proportions of each have changed over the years, the answer will be quite easy to discover. However, if you ask a question such as 'Why do girls tend to do better than boys in literacy?' an answer – or a route to finding an answer – will not be so readily evident. In fact, to this question several possible answers immediately suggest themselves. It may be that girls' brains are better 'hard-wired' for language. Or the answer may be nothing to do with brains and hard-wiring: it may be because parents, friends and family of baby girls talk more to them than they do to boys. Eventually schools repeat the process. More is expected of girls in the way of language, and so girls get more feedback and training in the way that language is used. They therefore get better at it.

Each of these possible answers to this question comes with a perfectly valid train of reasoning behind it, and you might think that we should be able dispassionately to work out which is correct. But that isn't possible. It isn't possible because …

a these answers aren't either/or – in other words, it is not one cause *or* the other. Both may be contributing to the phenomenon of girls' superior literacy;

b there are measurement issues involved – it may be that girls merely look as though they are better because of the nature of the tests that we use to assess performance;

c we have no definitive way of answering the question – even if (a) and (b) didn't apply, there is no research design that could be set up which would enable an answer to be given once and for all.

Just because a question is difficult, though, it doesn't mean that we should not try to answer it, but we should be aware of the difficulties and, possibly, frame different, additional or more tentative questions.

So, if getting the right research question is vital, how can we decide on it? It is first necessary to acknowledge that there are different kinds of questions and it might be helpful to spend a moment categorising them. Broadly speaking, there are four kinds of questions involved in social research, all of them perfectly valid as starting points for a project, but each of them involving different kinds and degrees of complexity and each of them leading to different kinds of inquiry.

Four kinds of question ...

1 *What's the situation ...?* You're a business studies student and have noticed the increase in number of 'assistant' professions developing in the public services – community support officers in the police force, teaching assistants in schools, healthcare assistants in hospitals. This may lead you to be interested in the growth in the number of these kinds of staff over the last 20 years. It would lead to the first kind of question: *What's the situation ...?* The actual question may be something like: 'How have numbers of ancillary professionals grown as a consequence of ideas about workforce reform over the last 20 years?'

> **Four kinds of question**
>
> 1 What's the situation ...?
>
> 2 What's going on here ...?
>
> 3 What happens when ...?
>
> 4 What is related to what ...?

2 *What's going on here ...?* You may be a teaching assistant and note that a group of students in a class persistently flouts the rules and engages in more difficult behaviour than others in the class. Or you may note that one child in the class is always putting up her hand but has no idea what the answer is when the teacher asks her. These are specific instances that emerge from your own observation, and in each case you may ask yourself why this is happening. You want to make an exploration into the issue. This leads then to the question: *What's going on here ...?* The actual question may be something like: 'Why does Jade put up her hand when she doesn't know the answer?'

3 *What happens when ...?* You're a teacher and your school plans to introduce a new policy on bullying. You decide to try and see whether it has any effect. This leads to a third kind of question: *What happens when ...?* The actual question may be something like: 'What are the consequences of implementing an anti-bullying policy in Tower Hill Primary School?'

4 *What is related to what ...?* As a student in education and taking a 'wild' module in economics, you notice from the latter that there seems to be a relationship between a country's gross domestic product and the amount it spends on education. Looking further, you see that while the relationship seems to be strong, there are interesting variations that seem to exist in the

amounts spent on different phases of education (nursery, primary, secondary, tertiary and higher education). You decide to explore these relationships further, to see whether there are cultural or historical reasons that might explain them.

Though these four categories may seem similar – they are all questions, after all – in fact they offer very different kinds of starting points and will lead to very different lines of inquiry. And within one study it may be appropriate to ask more than one kind of question, with several lines of inquiry, each intertwining with the others. Let's look at them in a little more detail.

Kinds of question – and some nutshell-sized studies and their implications

What's the situation?

'How have numbers of ancillary professionals grown as a consequence of workforce reform over the last 20 years?'

Here you are looking to *describe* something that is happening. When you are describing, you are not trying to do anything much more complicated than saying 'This is the case.' Nor are you trying to find the *cause* of something – you are not, in other words, trying to see if *x* causes *y*.

But the researcher understands that to say 'this is the case', while relatively simple if compared with saying *x* causes *y*, is nevertheless not straightforward. Like an artist or a photographer, you are trying to present a faithful representation of the facts that you find, and this is harder than it seems.

Like an artist, you will be more or less successful at representing the world that you are trying to describe, depending on what you choose to focus on and depending on the techniques you use. The first problem the researcher faces compared with an artist is that, while artists literally try to draw a picture, in research you are making your picture with words or numbers, and we all know (e.g. from the way that politicians present their cases) that words and numbers are unreliable messengers of truth. We select the words and numbers that we use. Also like an artist or a photographer, your portrait will be vulnerable to pressures and prejudices of one kind or another and the picture you paint will be

susceptible to distortion because of this. Artists' subjects want to look beautiful or handsome, and the subjects of research tend to be the same: they want to look good.

Like an artist or a photographer, you will also be exposed to the risk of things going wrong: a photographer may have the picture go fuzzy or blurred or underexposed, or may have the wrong part of a portrait focused, or may make a beautiful person look ugly. A skilled photographer will know how to avoid these problems. Likewise, the photographer may be able to magnify the relevance of a particular facet of a scene by using a special lens. These kinds of problems and opportunities are possible also when you are using words or pictures, and in the same way that skilled photographers can avoid problems, well-prepared researchers can circumvent the traps that confront them when doing research.

> **Fieldwork:** The process of collecting data – so a place where data is being collected is called 'the field'. The field could be a classroom, a playground, a street, a hospital ward, someone's home – anywhere that you are collecting data.

While this represents a simple kind of question, it is perfectly acceptable and valid as a basis – a platform – for an undergraduate or master's degree and can lead to a first-rate project or dissertation. But description on its own will not be sufficient for a project. You will be expected to make some sort of *analysis* of the increase in ancillary professionals as well, and this may depend on further reading or on certain kinds of *fieldwork* – perhaps asking informed people (such as police officers, nurses and teachers) for their opinion on the growth of this group of personnel.

What's going on here?

'Why does Jade put up her hand when she doesn't know the answer?'

How could you answer this question? You can't climb inside Jade's head. And asking her why she does it probably will not reveal very much. To try to answer it without recourse to a map of Jade's mind, you have to use your own knowledge of situations like this, and your own knowledge of people (including your knowledge of yourself) to make informed guesses. All of this is of course subjective, but it is none the worse for this, as long as you realise and acknowledge the boundaries that surround this kind of inquiry – and, as in all research, we must be sure that we do not make inappropriate claims for it. Deciding to judge the situation as a person makes this a particular kind of research: it is about two people – the observed and the observer, and we must be careful not to generalise from this very particular situation to others. You are trying to *interpret* the situation in order to *illuminate* what is going on. That is why a study of this kind may be called *interpretative* or *illuminative*.

When you are *illuminating*, you are shining a light on something. This implies that the subject currently is in the dark (or at least is badly lit): it's impossible to see what is going on. (If the sun were shining brightly, there would be no need for illumination – no need for research.) So you shine a light. What does this metaphor mean here?

First, it means that you are expecting to see something that you couldn't see before. Second, it implies also that you will be able to see because you are looking in a way that you weren't able to previously. Third, it implies that you are giving time and energy to looking hard (i.e. shining the light) and using *your own self* – your intelligence and experience – to make sense of the subject under study.

There's nothing 'unscientific' about this use of your own self, as some people who prefer more structured research proclaim: the famous mathematician George Pólya (1945/2004: 172) said that all kinds of discovery, in research or elsewhere, are determined by having 'brains and good luck' and by 'sitting tight until you get a bright idea'. In other words, the main part of research is not the cleverness or the specialness of the methods that you use, but rather your willingness to use your own head to look at something intelligently.

Don't, in other words, ignore your own ability to reflect on a problem, and don't minimise its significance in helping you to understand the problem. This is the case in all kinds of research, but particularly in illuminative inquiry you will be drawing on your own resources – your own knowledge of people and social situations – to make sense of what you find.

Extending the metaphor about illumination, remember that the object will look different when the light shines from different angles, and will appear different from various viewpoints and to different people. In remembering all of this, you will realise that you are doing something more than describing. In doing this kind of study, your aim will not be simply to describe the facts, because you will be interested in a social situation that is not usefully explicable simply within a framework of description. You will be involved in the kind of study that is about feelings, perceptions and understandings, and to get at these you will need to be listening to people and interpreting what they are saying, observing what they are doing and trying to understand their actions.

What happens when?

'What are the consequences of implementing an anti-bullying policy in Tower Hill Primary School?'

This 'What happens when?' question is accompanied by a particular kind of structure. This structure usually involves taking two or more observations or measures (e.g. before and after an imposed change) and then trying to deduce what any difference between those observations or measures may mean. So, in this example, you would need a measure of the amount of bullying that took place before the policy and after the policy to see whether there had been a drop – which you might *infer* was due to the implementation of the policy. Clearly, the measures that would be taken about the subject under study, namely bullying, could be taken in a multitude of ways, and it is these different forms – and their satisfactoriness – that will be examined in Chapter 5.

Usually in this kind of study you are asking 'Does *this* seem to be causing *that*?' You are asking questions of the variety: 'Does *x* cause *y*?'

The situations here may have been engineered by you, for example by your setting up an experiment, or they may be naturally occurring situations where you want to examine the influence of one phenomenon on another. Your observations of them may be more or less structured and your inferences more or less particular on the basis of this structuring.

Another example: you may be interested in changing the way that you, as a year tutor in a secondary school, address your Year 8s when you meet them in the morning. You may choose to be in class half an hour early, not take a formal register and instead ask the youngsters to sign in as they arrive. What effects does this seem to have? You will be making deductions about any possible consequences. You could make this observation informally by just watching and taking notes, or in a much more structured way by precisely adjusting the conditions (down to the length of time you are making the change) and also the outcome you are choosing to measure, and comparing the behaviour under the original condition and the new one. You might also compare what happens in a colleague's class where no such changes are made. Whether your observations are informal or formal, you will be making inferences about the cause and effect.

A particular kind of research design emerges from this sort of question, a design that promises an indication about the causative link. But, just as was the case in the consideration of 'What's going on here?' questions, we have to acknowledge the potential frailty of this kind of inquiry, and we must be sure that we do not make inappropriate claims for it. We'll discuss some of the things that might go wrong in Chapters 6 and 8.

What is related to what?

I gave earlier an example of the seeking of relationships – what is related to what – in the relationship between a country's gross domestic product and the amount it spends on education. Such relationships could easily be explored by examining official statistics.

These relationships can also be sought in questions that lead to empirical study 'in the field'. For example:

'What are the relationships between reading attainment, exclusion and non-attendance at Harley Green Comprehensive School?'

This is a question raised by a master's degree student, having noted in the educational press that children designated as having special needs were far more likely to be excluded than other children. Her study involved the collection of data in the school and inspection of school records. My interest in her comment on the press stories centred on the implication in those stories that in some way schools were picking on children with special needs to exclude – that special needs in some way or another 'caused' the exclusion. In fact, what seemed more likely to me was that 'special needs' as a category 'picked up' young people who are failing for a host of reasons, and this generic failure ultimately led to disaffection and exclusion. One did not lead to the other. Rather, the young people in each group were essentially being drawn from the same pool.

This inappropriate attribution of causation highlights the main challenge to the interpretation of a question that seeks relationships of any kind, as I shall discuss further in Chapter 8.

All of these four types of questions lead to their own routes of inquiry and will cause you to lean lightly or heavily toward a particular kind of approach and design for your research. Approach and design are facets of the research process that we shall examine

> **Data**: This is a rather confusing word when you first come to social research, since you will probably associate 'data' with numbers. In social research, however, the term 'data' means any source of raw information – 'raw' in the sense that no one has worked on it. So it may indeed be numbers (test scores, say) but it may also be the transcript of an interview, questionnaire responses, photographs, documents, videos, etc. All of these constitute data. By the way, 'data' is a plural noun (it's the plural of 'datum') so whenever you refer to **data** you should use the plural form, for example 'These data show …' and 'The data support the view that …' (not 'This data shows …', etc.).

in more detail in Chapter 5, but you should be aware at this stage where your initial questions are likely to take you.

Descriptive or explanatory questions?

You can probably see from the four kinds of question that I have just outlined that the nature of your question can be more or less complex. At their simplest, questions are descriptive, such as:

- What are the principal means by which students at this university arrive on campus?
- What are some of the main ways in which anti-MRSA measures are being ignored at Gotham General Hospital?
- What are consumers' most trusted commercial websites?

By contrast, questions which promise some kind of explanation are always going to be more complex. These might be questions such as:

- What factors are determining students' choices concerning travel to campus?
- Why has there been resistance to anti-MRSA measures being implemented in Gotham General Hospital?
- Are there factors associated with consumers' trust of commercial websites?

The second set of questions is about more than just description since they more conspicuously seek to offer an explanation of an issue or a problem. Such questions will usually be asked by students who have more time and resources at their disposal – that is to say, those at master's or doctoral level. For an undergraduate project a question that leads to description is quite acceptable, although those which seek some kind of explanation, if only in conjecture or theorisation in the discussion, will always be looked upon favourably (see 'theory' pp. 96–99).

It may be the case that one kind of question will emerge out of another, so that description precedes and explanation follows. Let's imagine an important issue in applied social science – one that concerns child abuse. Here, the question about child protection may be followed by another one, thus:

- Who are the professionals centrally involved in child protection?

will be followed by:

- Why did these professionals fail to communicate effectively in the case of Baby X?

So, to a question that students often ask, 'Can I have more than one research question?', the answer is 'Yes, though these will need to be related to one another, and you shouldn't start off with too many.' It is best to start with fewer, simpler questions and see what these lead to as your project progresses. Questions that demand description may precede ones that demand explanation.

A research question – or a hypothesis?

You may come across the term *hypothesis* and it may be suggested to you that your research should be framed around a hypothesis rather than a question. Research in the social sciences is framed less around hypotheses now than it was ten or twenty years ago for several reasons which are too knotty to go into here. However, if your question is of a particular kind it may well be appropriate to structure your research around a hypothesis – especially if you have been encouraged to do this by your tutor. Hypotheses are framed around 'what happens when … ?' questions. The difference between a research question and a hypothesis is that the expectation surrounding the hypothesis is that the hypothesis is *precisely* testable. The emphasis is on 'precisely'. You have to be able to specify the conditions under which your hypothesis will be tested, and the expectation is that you will be able at the end of your research project to say: 'Yes, this is the case' or 'No, that is not the case.' (In fact, you can never say these kinds of things definitively in social research, and hypotheses are problematic for this reason.)

But let's forget about the problems with hypotheses for a moment and assume that we can use them unproblematically. In order to be able to say 'Yes' or 'No' you have to be able to measure two or more features of a situation precisely and set up experimental conditions that will enable you to test the hypothesis. I'll explain further how you can test a hypothesis using an experiment in Chapter 6.

Coming up with a question

Your question will emerge from your interests and your observations. If you are having difficulty coming up with a question …

- Think of the situation in which you are working or the subject you are studying. Is there something novel, perplexing or unusual about it? If so, think about how you might look into it further.

- Ask a colleague, friend or relative who works in the field about a particular issue or problem in their working day. How might this lead on to research questions?

- Think of a story in the media about education, the media, healthcare, probation, business or the field in which you are studying. Are there aspects of it that seem interesting or puzzling? What aspects of it could be followed up?

- Try looking at some websites on the Internet, such as those of the big government departments (Department for Education, Department of Health, etc.). Find out what is topical. School meals? Children's happiness? How could a project be geared around these topics?

- Look at Emma Smith's website, www.secondarydataanalysis.com, which gives access to a broad range of UK, US and international data. Scan through some of the data. See if it gives you any ideas.

- Go to the Campbell Collaboration or Cochrane Collaboration websites (see p. 88) for information on important current issues.

If you are still left wondering what to do, try ...

- brainstorming (see box). From your brainstorming try to come up with three different research questions, preferably from a situation you know something about.
- doing an A to Z of topics – think of anything at all, and see what it sparks off in your mind. For example:

A – Adopted children – do they have special difficulties?

Academies – what do parents think of them?

B – 'Black history' – students' attitudes.

Barack Obama's health policy – contrasts with the UK system.

C – Criminal justice and the young person.

Computers in the primary classroom.

D – Diversity – how well are we doing?

Diary-keeping by business leaders.

E – Early years education internationally.

'Every Child Matters' – how aware are parents of it?

> **Brainstorming**: This is a technique that was developed in the advertising industry (but let's not hold that against it) for helping to produce interesting new ideas. Two or more people get together and say anything that comes into their heads on the topic in question. The ground rules are: (1) quantity (of ideas) rather than quality; (2) no criticism of the ideas of others; (3) unusual ideas are welcome.

Is it feasible? Problems with research questions

When you have thought of a question, and have thought about how it maps onto the four types of question I outlined above, consider it against two more important criteria: preciseness and 'doability'.

Is it precise?

The most common problems with research questions are that they are too *broad* or too *general*. 'What causes children to have reading difficulties?', for example, is a question that is almost impossible to answer. However, 'What are the characteristics of Sean's behaviour when he is reading?' is a question that *can* be answered in a small-scale study. Remember that you have time and material constraints and some questions will not be answerable in the time you have available.

Common problems with research questions

- They are too broad.
- There's no clear way to answer them.
- You can't get the information you need.

Is the research that will come from this question doable?

Sometimes there will be *ethical* problems about a research question. For example, if you were interested in how parents' arguing affected children at school, it would not be ethical to ask children (or parents) about these intimate matters. Or there may be problems of *access* to the kind of information that you want. If your question would require observation in classrooms, are you sure that any school is going to let you in to observe? These issues of ethics and access are addressed in Chapter 2.

Prima facie questions

Prima facie questions are questions that you start off with – the questions that you state here in your introduction. They change and become refined as your study progresses.

If you feel that your question is not quite right at this stage, don't worry. It is often the case – no, *nearly always* the case – that things won't be sorted out once and for all at the beginning of the study. Actually, I should state it even more strongly than that: *it is to be expected* that this (or these) will not be your final question(s). Especially in small-scale research of the kind that you are doing, and particularly where there is any kind of practitioner bent to it, it is very likely that you will not be able to specify your questions exactly at the outset.

You may feel that you don't know enough about the area to make definitive choices at this stage about your questions or your plan of attack on the subject. This is fine. Or you may feel that you wish

Your will revise and sharpen your ideas as your work progresses. For this reason, your early ideas and questions are prima facie questions. These can be refined after your literature review. And social research rarely follows a blueprint. Plan for change as you progress.

to do some practical groundwork that will in some way set the boundaries for the project, and in some way map out the channels down which your inquiry can run. Your reading of the literature will almost certainly enable you to refine your first questions.

The idea that you have to specify exactly and definitively your course of action at the beginning of your project is something of a hangover from the days when social research aped the methods of the natural sciences, with experiments in which a blueprint of questions, procedures and methods would be drawn up in detail at the outset and followed conscientiously. In fact, it is doubtful whether that is actually the way that natural science researchers ever operated in real life, but it's what they *said* they did. As the renowned biologist Sir Peter Medawar put it in debunking this idea of cleanly planned and executed research, the special methods and procedures that are supposed to be associated with scientists' work represent merely 'the postures we choose to be seen in when the curtain goes up and the public sees us' (Medawar, 1982: 88).

But social scientists, having a bit of an inferiority complex about their status as scientists, believed the natural scientists and tried to copy the folklore model of science that had been presented to the public. In the social sciences, though, it is nigh on impossible to set up a project of the kind you will be doing without stopping, rethinking, replanning, changing, starting again. And rethinking your *question* is the first part of this process of revisiting. It is to be expected, and is a necessary and integral part of the process of a research project such as yours.

All of this replanning and revisiting means that the kind of research that you do in investigating the social world is often called *recursive* or *iterative*. In other words, it turns back on itself and starts again, and a distinction is drawn between this pattern – involving reviewing and replanning – and what is sometimes called a 'linear' plan (see Figure 1.2).

So the idea that things won't go to plan is itself planned for. If the 'recursive' part of Figure 1.2 looks a bit of a mess, that's because that's what social research is often like. Your research in fact *may* follow an entirely different or simpler path, but most

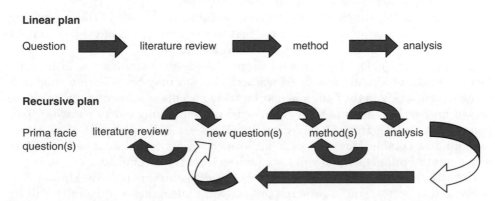

Figure 1.2 A linear or a recursive plan?

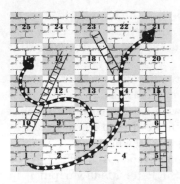

likely it won't be a straight, blinkered path from beginning to end. Importantly, your reading for your literature review will inform your question and help you to refine it. Beyond this, you will see things to the side of the path; you will notice something over there and decide that that is more interesting than the original topic; you will find that you can't talk to the people to whom you wanted to talk, and so on. What you discover and the way that the world treats you will always influence the way that you proceed: it's like a game of snakes and ladders – you'll get knock-backs and sudden boosts and insights. And both knock-backs and insights will make you do a lot of rethinking.

For this reason, the question or questions that you have at the beginning of your study are called *prima facie questions*. Prima facie means 'on its first appearance' or 'at first sight', so calling your questions *prima facie* is an acknowledgement of their status – an acknowledgement that they are tentative and will change. We will look at how you will revise your prima facie questions in Chapter 4.

Kinds of evidence and kinds of answer

I've concentrated so far on questions. When we want to answer a question we are going to have to rely on *evidence* of some kind, and it is worth at this stage thinking about the kinds of evidence that might help to answer particular kinds of questions. We talk of evidence being of varying kinds: strong, weak, circumstantial, primary, secondary, etc., but what do these mean and how are they likely to be related to your thesis? This is important to think about at this stage, since the assessment of your thesis by your marker will depend on your collection of evidence. If you have a question that leads to weak evidence, you will be marked down heavily for it. This is a good reason to get the question right at the outset.

Let's look at the simple questions given in Table 1.2 – none of them anything to do with education or social science – just to see what kinds of evidence might emerge and why you should be very careful at this stage.

Already from Table 1.2 you'll note several processes – you may be looking up facts in books or already published research. Or you may be collecting your own evidence 'out there' in the field: you may be asking people who are directly involved, or you may be making an observation, or trying something out to see what happens. What you get from each of these processes are different kinds of evidence, each kind acceptable. However, each has its own strengths and weaknesses and its own potential pitfalls, as you will have noticed from the examples.

Usually (but not always), there will be an expectation that the kind of evidence you collect during a research project you undertake at university will be *empirical*. That is to say, you will be expected to go out into the wide world and

Table 1.2 Questions and evidence

Question	Ways of answering it with evidence	Is the evidence reliable and robust? (Stars out of 5)	Why the star rating?
How many colours are there in the rainbow?	Look it up in a book.	★★★★	The book is almost sure to be right. However, books aren't always right. There's always room for interpretation (e.g. what do you mean by 'colour'? Does ultraviolet count?).
	Wait for the next rainbow and count the colours.	★★★★	It's good to rely on your own observations rather than someone else's (e.g. in a book). However, be aware that your answer may not agree with another person's – because, in the case of this example, you may disagree on what constitutes one colour (where do yellow and blue become fused, and does the merging constitute a separate colour?).
	Ask someone else.	★★★	They may know; they may not. They may not know, but not want to tell you that they don't know – and make something up.
What is my best friend's middle name?	Ask her/him.	★★★★	You'd think this should be pretty accurate. But what if your best friend is ashamed of their name? Might they claim not to have one, or make up a different one?
What is the meaning of life?	Reflect on it yourself, or ask others. Read books.	★	No clear answer (ever, no matter how much research you do).
How can I get to Edinburgh from here?	Look it up on a map, or go on the Internet.	★★★★★	The chances of a published map being wrong in directions of this simplicity are vanishingly small.
How many legs does a millipede have?	Look it up – e.g. a book, or via an Internet search.	★★★	Doing an Internet search reveals a suspiciously similar range of answers, giving 'between 80 and 400' rather too often for my liking, revealing that 'authorities' may just rely on each other rather than find out for themselves (see the danger of secondary sources, p. 58).
	Dig up some earth, find one and count.	★★★	There's a good chance you'll lose count or in some way be inaccurate. And if you decide to check by counting the legs of another millipede and you come up with a different number you are into further questions about the possibility of different species or variation within one species.
What does this button do?	Press it.	★★★★	You should be able to see what the button does when you press it, but it may be the case that nothing happens (imagine a car dashboard, or a microwave oven control panel). However, if something observable *does* happen you can be fairly sure that the button did it. (But not absolutely sure – it might have been coincidence of some kind.)

collect data yourself rather than relying on information marshalled by others – for example in a book. (In fact, a research project as a literature review – that is, *just* as a literature review – is sometimes acceptable, but if you want to do a research project that is based solely on the literature you should check with your tutor.)

Empirical: Strictly speaking this means something that has been found out from experience, from trial and error or from the evidence of your senses. 'Empirical' is often wrongly used, though, with the intimation of experiment of some kind, so when people talk of 'empirical evidence' they usually (incorrectly) mean evidence coming from some kind of trial or experimental study.

Because of the potential frailties and weaknesses of one kind or another in evidence, it is useful to gather it in different ways, so that one piece of evidence supports another. When the police gather evidence at a crime scene they talk about *corroborative evidence* when one piece of evidence supports another piece. One piece of evidence on its own is often taken to be not enough, since mistakes can be made by witnesses or police officers; equipment may be faulty; witnesses may not understand what has been asked of them, or may be making something up for any of a host of reasons. So, if Mr Dorrit says that he saw his neighbour Mrs Nickleby go into her house at 10.30, he may be believed, but this on its own will not be taken to be satisfactory, for he could have been mistaken about the time, or may have confused Mrs Nickleby for someone else. But if another witness, independent of Mr Dorrit, says the same thing, you become surer about the fact that Mrs Nickleby indeed entered the house at that time. And if the video camera across the road catches a good likeness of Mrs Nickleby, timed 10.31, we're almost home and dry.

It's good to look for different sources of evidence, e.g. reading, observing, interviewing people.

The same kind of thing applies in a social research project. It is much better to rely on several kinds of evidence rather than just one. There are many ways in which evidence can be sourced: from

- personal experience
- the testimony of others
- documents or archives
- artefacts
- observation

and so on. In social research, using more than one kind of evidence is sometimes called **triangulation** (see p. 145). Having noted the importance of corroboration (or triangulation), though, it is important to say that you will never in social research get conclusive evidence of something being the case. However, the more evidence there is – each piece corroborating the other – the surer you will be. This is why the noun 'evidence' is so often qualified with adjectives – prima facie evidence, inconclusive evidence, weak evidence, strong evidence, conclusive evidence, and so on.

I have spoken about these issues of evidence in general, but it is important to think about them in particular in relation to the social sciences and your own thesis. Will you be able to collect evidence that will enable you to answer your question? Think about the evidence you are likely to collect when you answer a question. Suppose your question were something to do with the problems children have with maths. What kind of evidence could you collect? You could:

- Ask the teacher directly about the problems.

- Ask children what their problems are.

- Get children to talk to you while they are doing a problem.

- Get children to complete diagnostic tests.

All of these would garner evidence of some kind, and each would have its own strengths and weaknesses.

A final word about evidence: it is the way that you view, scrutinise and use evidence that is important. It is a matter always of looking at evidence, thinking about it *critically* and *assessing* it. The great philosopher John Dewey (1920/2004), in reviewing several kinds of thinking, argued that it is only 'reflective thought … [that] is truly educative in value' (p. 3). He distinguished this *reflective thought*, where there is a deliberate self-questioning about the grounds for a belief, from other kinds of thought where there is slight or no acknowledgement of the strength of the evidence or grounds on which it is held. He proceeded:

> [Some thoughts] are picked up – we know not how. From obscure sources and by unnoticed channels they insinuate themselves into acceptance and become unconsciously a part of our mental furniture. Tradition, instruction, imitation – all of which depend upon authority in some form, or appeal to our own advantage, or fall in with a strong passion – are responsible for them. Such thoughts are prejudices, that is, prejudgments, not judgments proper that rest upon a survey of evidence. (pp. 4–5)

Dewey makes the important point here that we should be suspicious of certain kinds of thinking, particularly those arising from *tradition* and *authority*. We should think for ourselves. And we should be wary of any line of reasoning (in others or in ourselves) that comes from

> Show that you can think critically. When you seek evidence always be questioning about its value.

a vested interest or a strongly held opinion (a 'passion'). The *reflective thought* that he favours is about being sceptical about our thoughts and about always looking for evidence for a line of reasoning. He suggests that we should try to be almost instinctively critical. Such reflective thought is the hallmark of a good research project.

A title

You may want to have a precise title for your thesis right from the start, and while this may seem like good planning, in fact this is one place (that is to say, the beginning) where it is probably good to be a little imprecise. In fact it is more important to be thinking about your *question* than your *title*. This isn't to say that a title is unimportant. It *is* important. It is vitally important, because your work will be assessed by reference to your title – in other words, the examiners will ask themselves 'Does this thesis address the title?'

But when you are doing a project in the social sciences, large or small, you will realise that the world isn't quite as you thought it was going to be. You can't get access to this place, there are ethical problems there, or better questions occur to you as you begin to read about the issue. (These changes will be addressed in Chapter 4.) The important fact to realise is that these changes will inevitably occur and that if you stick rigidly to a premeditated title you will be missing many opportunities to make your project more interesting or more manageable.

Or you might take notice of the necessary changes, but still stick unthinkingly to the title even though the project has changed substantially in practice. After all, *you* know what you are doing, and as your research gathers momentum the title may slip to a cobwebby corner of your reptile brain, never to be re-examined. But remember that while your tutors are reading your project they will be asking themselves if it is addressing the title. So if you have a title that doesn't match up to what is actually in the write-up of your project the marker will be disappointed and wonder why. One of the commonest causes of low marks is when a piece of work – essay or project – doesn't match the title.

So the best plan is to have a *working title* – something that captures what you originally set out to do – which you can then change once you have finished the dissertation. It may just need a tweak or perhaps a substantial modification. But the new title – the one you decide on after you have finished – will match the completed product exactly. Always use the working title, though, to remind yourself of what you set out to do, because you will always find when you are doing research that you will be tempted to follow a hundred different paths. It might be worth following one of them, but do you really want to? Always examine your motives for potential change and your likely outcomes. This is where the storyboard in Figure 3.1 (p. 65) will help. It will help you to decide which are the likely main routes that will emerge from your working title and what avenues of investigation may be opened up by each main route.

> Be prepared to change your title. But do this at the end of your project.

What research is – and what it isn't

It is worth closing this chapter with a word about what research is and what it isn't. Research is about curiosity and inquiry, as for example journalism is. However, it differs from journalism in that it is governed by a number of expectations. There is the expectation that research will:

- aim to find new knowledge
- be thorough
- be balanced
- be fair
- be ethical.

These are some ground rules, and we'll look at them in more detail in later chapters. But it is worth reinforcing the fact that research is not journalism and it is not about campaigning for an issue. It's not about being committed to a position. Nor is it about 'knowing' something and trying to find 'proof' for it. You cannot assume that you already know the answer.

Research *is* about disciplined, balanced inquiry, conducted in a critical spirit.

Overview

Your introduction is important: it sets the scene for the reader. It should interest readers and make them want to read further. It tells them why you are interested in an area and why you think it is worth researching. It outlines what your first research questions are. You should have taken time thinking about the kinds of questions you will ask because your whole project will be geared around the way that they are constructed and the kinds of evidence you will need to address them. As you think about your questions, you should consider their nature and the likely paths of inquiry down which they will lead you. But you shouldn't become paralysed with fear about these early questions. At this stage they are prima facie questions – questions that will be refined as you undertake preliminary work and as you do your literature review. They are working questions, in the same way that your title at this stage is a working title.

In fact, the whole of your introduction is really a working document, to be revised as your work progresses. It should not, however, attempt to airbrush out difficult aspects of your journey or places where you have decided to change direction. These are all part of your story. If you say where you started and where you have altered course it will help readers to understand why you went where you did. Do tell them about what you intended to do originally and how things have progressed as you have worked on your project.

Checklist ✔

You may find it helpful to copy this table and write down the answers to the questions.

Have you …

	Notes	
1 … done the BIS?		☐
• **considered the** *background*?	Write a sentence or two on the background	
• **thought about the** *issue* **or** *problem* **you specifically want to address?**	Outline the specific problem in a sentence or two	
• **reflected on the kind of** *solution* **that may be forthcoming – the kind of research that will address your issue?**	Don't write anything down yet – just think about it at this stage. You can be more definite only after considering different research approaches and methods (Chapter 5)	
2 … thought about your *purpose* **in doing your research?**	Write down a couple of sentences	☐
3 … had an *idea* **to focus on?**	Say how your issue or problem (above) translates into an idea for research	☐
4 … got a *prima facie* **question?**	Write this down. Remember that it will change as you read around the area (see Chapter 4)	☐
5 … thought of a working title?	Keep it short	☐

Further reading

Becker, H.S. (2008) *Writing for Social Scientists: How to Start and Finish Your Thesis, Book, or Article*. Chicago: Chicago University Press.
More for advanced students than undergraduates. Really gets you to think about research and what it is you are trying to do. A nice antidote to recipe-driven research.

Booth, W.C., Colomb, G.C. and Williams, J.M. (2003) *The Craft of Research* (2nd edn). Chicago: University of Chicago Press.

This excellent book is about research right across the spectrum, from the sciences to the humanities, and gets its readers to examine the relationship of research question to research approach.

Laws, S. (2003) *Research for Development.* London: SAGE.
Focused particularly on development work, Chapter 5 is good on research questions and focus.

Luker, K. (2010) *Salsa Dancing into the Social Sciences.* Cambridge, MA: Harvard University Press.
Written less as a manual and more as a story or a series of anecdotes about supervising research, this is an unusual book. Luker interestingly and very helpfully teases out the problems students experience in formulating a problem to be solved in their research. She does this by distinguishing between the 'explanandum' (the thing being explained) and the 'explanans' (the explaining thing) – which is rather like my BIS, above, but more fully and technically covered.

OECD (2002) *Frascati Manual: Proposed Standard Practice for Surveys on Research and Experimental Development.* Paris: OECD. Available at: http://browse.oecd bookshop.org/oecd/pdfs/browseit/9202081E.PDF
This provides a technical discussion of what research is – for the advanced student.

Thomas, G. and Pring, R. (2004) *Evidence-Based Practice in Education.* Maidenhead: Open University Press.
A compilation looking especially at evidence and evidence-based policy and practice in medicine as well as in education. See Chapter 1 for my discussion of evidence, what it is and how it is used.

Thomson, A. (2005) *Critical Reasoning: A Practical Introduction.* London: Routledge.
This contains some good discussion and advice on evidence.

White, P. (2008) *Developing Research Questions: A Guide for Social Scientists.* London: Palgrave Macmillan.
This book concentrates, as the title suggests, on the research question in social science, its importance and how it can be developed.

2

PREPARING: PROJECT MANAGEMENT, ETHICS AND GETTING CLEARANCE

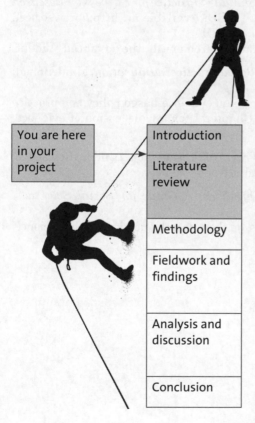

You are here in your project	Introduction
	Literature review
	Methodology
	Fieldwork and findings
	Analysis and discussion
	Conclusion

Most projects conform to a similar structure, but this is quite complex, involving several different kinds of activity on your part. Your work therefore needs to be well planned and organised. And your research can only proceed if you can gain access to the people and situations you are interested in, and if you can conduct your work respecting your participants' interests and wishes. This chapter considers:

- managing the project – the main elements and how they fit together;

- making a rough plan of how you want to proceed;

- working with your supervisor;

- ethics, and getting ethical clearance to do your research;

- managing your time;

- access – getting hold of the information you need.

Management is especially important for a project – even more important than it is for an essay or some other kind of assignment – because the project is such a large piece of work. It may comprise one, two or three modules' worth of effort, with direction from a supervisor which may not amount to more than a few hours. All of the onus is on you to be organising your own work. So it's a good idea to recognise this and prepare for it. It's not like an essay, where if the worst comes to the worst you can burn the midnight oil and polish it off (not very well) in a night or two. You really do need to 'project-manage'.

Understanding the structure of your dissertation or thesis

Once you have had an idea and decided on your question(s) you will have some notion about the sort of project you will be doing. You can now begin to project-manage it. Whatever kind of research project you do, you should know that there are several elements that will almost certainly be included in its composition:

The introduction explains your interest in the topic of the study and says why it is important

The literature review organises and explains what other research has been done in the area. The review can comprise more than one chapter if you feel that there are areas of focus which divide themselves cleanly enough for separation into two or more chapters.

A methodology chapter (sometimes called 'Research design') explains why you have chosen to do your research in the way that you have chosen. You will say why you have done, for example, an action research project using a questionnaire.

Chapter 5
Analysis and
discussion

You'll say what you actually found here. Often this chapter is combined with the next one, since in many kinds of research it is difficult to separate the report of the findings from the analysis.

Chapter 5
Analysis and
discussion

Here, you'll be analysing your findings using the tools outlined in Chapter 8 of this book. You will go on to discuss your analysis in the context of your research questions and in the light of any issues raised in the literature review. The analysis and the discussion may be separated into two chapters if this seems appropriate.

Chapter 6
Conclusion

In the conclusion you will draw together the threads and offer the reader an assessment of how well your questions have been answered.

We'll deal with each of these in more detail as the book proceeds. For now, you just need to know that they exist and what proportion of the total dissertation each usually occupies. A very rough guide (and it is very rough – you shouldn't take it as 'gospel') is given in Figure 2.1.

Thinking in terms of words and pages, the proportions in Figure 2.1 translate roughly (and again I would emphasise *roughly*) to the numbers given in Table 2.1, with each A4 page taken to be written double-spaced and to contain around 300 words.

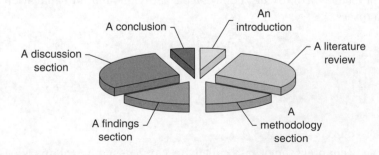

Figure 2.1   Elements of a dissertation

Table 2.1 Rough proportions of words and pages

Element	Proportion of words (very roughly)	In an undergraduate thesis of 10,000 words		In a postgraduate thesis of 20,000 words	
		Words	Pages	Words	Pages
Introduction	5%	500	2	1,000	4
Literature review	30%	3,000	12	6,000	24
Design and methodology	15%	1,500	6	3,000	12
Findings	15%	1,500	6	3,000	12
Analysis and discussion	30%	3,000	12	6,000	24
Conclusion	5%	500	2	1,000	4
Total		10,000	40	20,000	80

These can now be divided up into the time you have available. Suppose you have in total two semesters (or three terms) to complete a 10,000-word project – a piece of work that is sometimes said to be a double module's worth. Subtracting holidays and weekends, this probably amounts to around 80–90 days on which you can be putting some time towards the project.

You'll need to decide how to apportion time to each element of the project. It's helpful to plot this on a graph in some way. Suppose you decide as shown in Table 2.2.

Table 2.2 Apportionment of time

	Days
Read around the area	10
Write literature review	14
Examine methodology	7
Write methodology section	4
Do fieldwork	21
Analyse and write up results	21
Write conclusion	3
Finalise presentation	2
Total	82

Drawing a timeline

This can, for the sake of clarity, be presented as a timeline (sometimes called a *Gantt chart*), as in Figure 2.2.

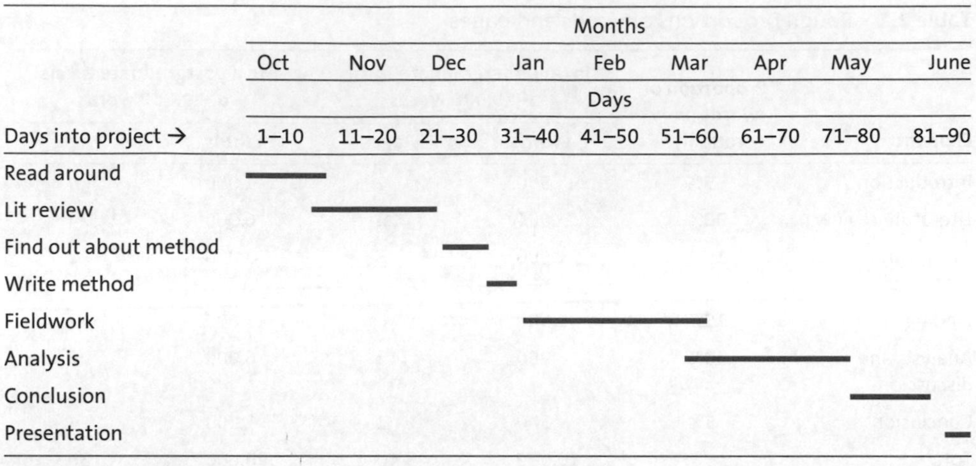

		Months							
Oct	Nov	Dec	Jan	Feb	Mar	Apr	May	June
				Days				
1–10	11–20	21–30	31–40	41–50	51–60	61–70	71–80	81–90

Days into project →

Task									
Read around	▬								
Lit review		▬							
Find out about method			▬						
Write method				▬					
Fieldwork					▬▬				
Analysis						▬▬			
Conclusion								▬	
Presentation									▬

Figure 2.2 Timeline or Gantt chart

If you can see the time available and the time needed for the various elements of your project it will be easier to make sure that you have enough time for each. The last thing you want is to get to a month or a week from submission date only to discover that you still have to do most of the literature review and the data collection.

How to draw a timeline using Word 2007

1 From the menu at the top of the Word screen, click on 'Insert'.

2 Click on 'Table'.

3 Click on 'Draw Table' – a little pencil ✐ should take the place of your cursor.

4 With the pencil, draw the shape of the table and draw in the numbers of rows and columns that you need.

5 Double click on the table so that the 'pencil' changes back to a cursor.

6 Click where you want to write in the table and start entering information about months, days and tasks to be fulfilled. *Hint*: for the tasks, you can probably copy the left-hand column of Figure 2.2.

7 From the menu at the top of the Word screen, click on 'Insert' again and then click on 'Shapes'. A list of all the different possible shapes will appear. Left-click on the simple 'line'. Now take your cursor back to the table and it will appear as a horizontal cross +. 'Stretch' the cross across the rows of the table one by one to show the length of time you want for each phase of the project.

You don't have to use a Word table. You can just draw one in freehand. However, it's worth persevering with the Word chart because it is a useful presentation skill, and clear presentation of your findings is one of the skills on which you will be assessed – not just in the project but also in the rest of your degree. Show your timeline to your supervisor and discuss it with them: not only will they be able to offer useful advice, they will also be impressed.

It is worth remembering that the dissertation proportions given here are a guideline only – they are not set in concrete, and you can vary these proportions depending on the needs of your research. For example, one piece of research may contain a much longer findings section than another. Another may have a longer literature review. In yet another, it may be that there is very little need for a conclusion, which can be assimilated into the discussion. Don't feel as though you have to keep to a rigid formula in this regard. Look, for example, at the varying proportions between two dissertations in Figure 2.3.

I have said that you should be prepared to be flexible on the structure, but all other things being equal I personally like the balance of dissertations which are similar to Project 1 in Figure 2.3. If you adopt this as a guide – and you are prepared to be flexible – you won't go far wrong.

You may wonder whether this degree of preparation is worth it. It is. Preparation is a key skill and you are being assessed in part on your ability to organise, prepare, think ahead and manage your work.

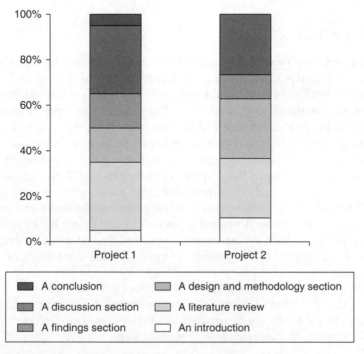

Figure 2.3   Not all dissertations are the same

Just look at those fingernails! Time management

We all know we should manage our time better, because there is always a reason for not doing it effectively. I know the syndrome only too well: I sit down at the keyboard, but nothing happens. I gaze at my fingers hopefully, but then … 'Just look at those nails!' Another half hour is wasted looking for some nail scissors and then eventually getting round to carefully trimming the offending claws. Then I have to file off the rough bits. And by then of course it's time for a cup of tea, and then 'Oh, there's the postman', and the two hours I have carefully reserved for my work are gone.

If this sounds familiar, here are some things you can try …

Make a schedule

On the basis of the timeline you have drawn, and the apportioning of days to elements of the project, decide which days you are going to work during a week. Will it be just weekdays, just weekends, both, or what? Fit your timetable around your life, decide which days and hours you are going to work, and then keep to the plan (the last bit is important).

> The Rolling Stones were wrong: time is not on your side. Be systematic.

Little and often

Do a little every day. One of the commonest excuses for not being able to get on with work is 'I just don't get the extended periods of time I need to do the work.' Well, extended periods of time would be lovely, but they are difficult for anyone to find, and it is unrealistic to expect that a fairy godmother will present you with them. Modern life is chaotic and full of demands. It's more realistic to knuckle down to the understanding that you are going to have to compromise, and just do little and often. If it is often enough (that is, once every day or every other day) you will find that you are able to keep up the continuity – you'll be able to remember where you were. If it is less often than this (say, missing three or four days at a time) you'll find that you have forgotten what you were thinking and you will lose momentum and interest. So it is good to reconnect with your books and computer every day, even if you don't actually write anything. Even if it is 11.00 p.m. and you are absolutely exhausted, force yourself to turn on your computer and read what you were doing yesterday.

On the issue of little and often, and at the risk of getting whimsical, I'll offer my 'principle of the laburnum', to which I often refer when I want to prompt myself into working. Outside my study window is a laburnum tree. In May I notice that small buds appear on the branches. The next time I notice them, perhaps two or three weeks later, they are magnificent long racemes of golden flowers. How did they do this without me noticing? They grew a tiny bit every day, and they carried on doing it. Little and often ...

Negotiate time

Set aside a time every weekday which you reserve for your work and which you and friends and family treat as sacred. Negotiate a time with them which is your research time. Make sure friends and family respect this: tell them your future depends on it, and tell them how guilty they will feel if you fail your dissertation. Tell them that if you fail you will probably descend into a depression from which you will never recover, and it will be their fault.

Set yourself targets

Keeping to your schedule, target yourself to write 250 words a day as a minimum for the days that you are working. Don't leave your desk until the 250 words are complete.

Decide on a time period

You could get up early at 6 o'clock and work from 6 until 7. Or you can tell yourself that you will not watch TV between 8 and 9. Reward yourself with a little treat *after* your work period – a coffee or a glass of wine, or listening to some music, or going out or whatever, but keep these goodies for *after* the work, rather than *during* it.

Use a structured technique

You may find that it helps to use a specific technique for organising those periods of time. Try the 'Pomodoro technique' at www.pomodorotechnique.com (called Pomodoro after a tomato-shaped egg-timer). In brief, this involves:

- choosing a manageable task that can be done in 25 minutes (say, writing 100 words);
- writing down what the task is and your target (e.g. the 100 words);
- setting a timer – on your computer, or your phone, on the cooker or wherever – to ring after 25 minutes;
- *not* responding to any distractions (fire alarms and screams for help excepted) during the 25-minute period – so you don't respond to emails, you don't search the Internet, you don't answer phone calls during the period;
- taking a 5-minute break before the next 25-minute period.

At www.pomodorotechnique.com you can download a PDF that explains this in more detail.

If you still can't find the time

If you are still stymied for time, draw up a blank timetable of a couple of days which shows every hour of every day. Then fill in the timetable with how you have actually been using your time over these days. Even if you have a busy life, you will be surprised at the time spent doing very little, pottering around or watching nothing very interesting on the TV. It's a salutary experience.

Stresses in doing research

Isolation

Research can be a lonely business, especially as you only get to see your supervisor every few weeks. Loneliness, feeling you are doing everything wrong, not being able to see the light at the end of the tunnel – these are all symptoms of research isolation stress syndrome. Personally, I am mildly socially phobic, so I don't get lonely, but I am told by people who like people that it's helpful to have a support group amongst your fellow students to discuss where you're up to, good sources of information, where you are going wrong, and so on. A problem shared is a problem halved.

Things going wrong

Unless you are a very lucky person, things will go wrong. Bad things happen: participants withdraw; there's a ridiculously low return rate for your questionnaire; you can't get access to the people you want. So it's a good idea to build in some degree of *contingency planning* at the outset. This is less complicated than it sounds. It just means that at the beginning of your research you should try to assess which are the riskiest bits (in terms of things potentially going wrong) and devise a 'plan B' for them. For example: you plan to send out 100 questionnaires by email, but you realise that this is a risky business, given that people are notoriously unreliable about responding. So you build in a contingency to send reminder emails after one month, and then phone non-responders after another two weeks, as shown in Table 2.3.

Table 2.3 Contingency planning for a questionnaire

Plan	Contingency 1	Contingency 2
Jan 6th	If 20% have not been returned by Feb 6th	If 20% have not been returned by Feb 20th
Send out 100 questionnaires	Send reminder letters	Phone non-responders

Working with your supervisor

You will be allocated a supervisor (or 'tutor') before your project begins and she or he will be the key person guiding you through your work. Working with your supervisor is different from working with your tutor in taught modules: the relationship is much more personal, with one-to-one meetings in which your supervisor will give you guidance and advice. It's important to remember, though, that supervisors 'stand back' in offering this guidance. They will not tell you what to do: the ideas have to come from you. They will then:

- talk these ideas over with you;
- point you in the direction of appropriate reading;
- recommend ways of structuring your work;
- make you aware of appropriate approaches and methods;
- suggest how you should write up your work;
- set objectives with you about what you need to do before your next meeting;
- read drafts of your work.

You will be expected to meet your supervisor even before your project starts in order to begin the process of planning. You may find it helpful to agree with your supervisor the ways that they want to be approached. Some supervisors will not be able to give time outside the periods scheduled in your dissertation handbook; others may be happy for you to knock on their door on the off-chance. It's best to find out their preference from the word go.

A couple of things to remember for your first – indeed for every – meeting with your supervisor:

- Before the meeting, draw up a list of queries. This means that you will not suffer the syndrome of the patient at the doctor's surgery, when you immediately forget all those things you had been meaning to ask.

- Do some reading about your topic before the first meeting. Your supervisor won't expect you to be an expert, but will expect you to understand something of the background to the topic so that you can work on issues to be addressed and questions to be answered.

- Keep notes in the meeting; and it's a good idea to provide a copy of these for the supervisor afterwards.

The importance of being ethical

One of the first things that you will have to think about at the first meeting with your supervisor is ethical clearance. We'll look at the forms and the procedure for ethical clearance in a moment, but it is important to remember that ethics is much more than a practical matter – it is about the conduct of your work: it is about how you think about inquiry, how you think about this research project; it is about your respect for others. To put these concerns into a box called 'ethics', as university procedures are sometimes apt to encourage us to do, is to minimise considerations about conduct and respect, so I shall leave the practical matters for a moment and discuss some wider issues about the conduct of inquiry.

A university is a place where inquiry is put to the fore. Inquiry is taken to be not just a necessity, but almost a thing of beauty – and, as such, universities give special privileges to academics to inquire and research without constraint, summed up in the term 'academic freedom'. This is a cherished freedom and it is one that is accompanied by important responsibilities.

Our freedoms in the academic world – freedom of inquiry and freedom to disseminate the findings of that inquiry – have at their centre expectations about the importance of the freedom – the *need* even – to challenge conventional wisdom, thoughts and ideas without fear of censorship or interference. A century and a half ago John Henry Newman put it this way in his seminal paper, *The Idea of a University*:

> A university is a place … in which the intellect may safely range and speculate, sure to find its equal in some antagonistic activity and its judge in the tribunal of truth. It is a place where inquiry is pushed forward, and discoveries verified and proved, and rashness rendered innocuous, and error exposed, by the collision of mind with mind and knowledge with knowledge. (Newman, 1852/1960: 15–16)

A university is a place where ideas are challenged. It is a community of inquiry where it is expected that there will be not just critical reflection, but controversy, gloves-off critique and argument – the 'collision of mind with mind'. As a member of a university – and this includes students as well as staff – you are part of this community of critical inquiry, and by being part of it you have conferred upon you some important privileges. Those privileges, though, are balanced with responsibilities, and it is in the balancing of the one with the other that ethics come in.

Ethics are principles of conduct about what is right and wrong. When applied to research, ethical principles encompass some decisions and dilemmas that not just pit right against wrong, but balance one right action against another right action, taking into account the possibly conflicting interests of the parties involved. What is right for me may not be right for you. What is right for the researcher may not be right for the participant. Or they may force us to examine what is potentially wrong, hidden dangers – force us to look at the nature of what we are doing in the name of furthering knowledge.

Clearly, we want to do what is right and avoid what is wrong. The matter seems simple, yet there are many examples in social research where a questionable action may have been taken in the name of doing right. In other words, researchers have had as the purpose for doing their research the idea that they are promoting knowledge or alleviating suffering or helping humankind in some other way and have used this as a reason for employing intrusive or distressing procedures in their research. Two case studies serve to illustrate some issues.

Ethics case study 1

The Milgram experiments

One of the most celebrated examples of the ethical dilemmas that emerge in social research happened in the 1960s in experiments about the power of personal authority. Stanley Milgram, a social psychologist working at Yale University, was concerned about the effects of authority on people's good judgement. If people were told to do something by someone in authority, even if went against their better judgement, would they do it? He invited ordinary people off the street to take part in an experiment about learning. They were told to give increasingly severe shocks to another person, using a dial marked from 'Slight Shock' to 'Danger: Severe Shock'. The person to whom the shocks were being given was actually an actor, and the 'electric shocks' were not real. As the 'shocks' increased in intensity, screams for mercy could be heard coming from the room where the 'victim' was situated. If the subject showed reluctance in continuing to increase the shocks, the researcher would first say 'Please continue'. If reluctance was still shown the experimenter would say 'The experiment requires that you continue', then 'It is absolutely essential that you continue' followed by 'You have no other choice, you *must* go on.' How far would these ordinary folk proceed with these electric shocks before refusing to comply with the researcher's instructions? Two-thirds of them administered the highest level of 'shocks'. This is from the abstract of the experiment ('S' refers to 'Subject'):

> 26 Ss obeyed the experimental commands fully, and administered the highest shock on the generator. 14 Ss broke off the experiment at some point after the victim protested and refused to provide further answers. The procedure created extreme levels of nervous tension in some Ss. Profuse sweating, trembling, and stuttering were typical expressions of this emotional disturbance. One unexpected sign of tension – yet to be explained – was the regular occurrence of nervous laughter, which in some Ss developed into uncontrollable seizures. The variety of interesting behavioral dynamics observed in the experiment, the reality of the situation for the S, and the possibility of parametric variation within the framework of the procedure, point to the fruitfulness of further study. (Milgram, 1963: 371)

One of the interesting things about this paper is that several major journals rejected it on ethical grounds. Yet ultimately the work was awarded the annual Socio-Psychological Award of the American Association for the Advancement of Science.

Clearly opinions differ as to the ethics of the experiment here, and there is a whole branch of academic study devoted to exploring ethical issues of the kind that it presents.

(Continued)

(Continued)

In the case of this experiment and many others the issue is, in short, 'Does the end justify the means?' The end purpose was the better understanding of obedience to authority. Coming quite soon after the Second World War, when many had justified their actions in perpetrating appalling crimes by saying that they were only obeying orders, the experiment could be said to be defensible. It was warranted if it helped an understanding of why it seems to be so easy for people to do this to others in the name of obeying authority.

But deception was used and people were distressed, some of them quite seriously, by the experience. Was *this* justifiable ethically, even if it advanced knowledge about obedience to authority? Could this knowledge have been found any other way than by deception? It is unlikely: if we were asked what we would do hypothetically in such a situation, how many of us would be able to be honest, even with ourselves?

Ethics case study 2

The Tuskegee syphilis experiment

Another renowned case, in which the issues were rather more clear-cut, was the Tuskegee syphilis experiment conducted between 1932 and 1972 in Tuskegee, Alabama, by the US Public Health Service. Here, 600 poor, rural, black men – some with syphilis, some without – were recruited to a study about the progression of untreated syphilis. The problem, though, was that the men were not told that this was the purpose of the study: they thought they were receiving free healthcare. Even though a cure for syphilis (penicillin) became available during the 1940s, soon after the start of the study, the men with syphilis were not appropriately treated – because to do so would have completely undone the study's purpose (in looking at the progression of untreated syphilis) and it would have had to close down.

In fact the study was ultimately closed down when there were leaks to the press about what was happening. This shameful episode in the history of research with human participants led to the US government setting up a National Commission for the Protection of Human Subjects of Biomedical and Behavioral Research, which gave its findings in the *Belmont Report* (National Commission, 1978). The report emerged with three basic ethical principles:

1 Respect for persons.
2 Beneficence: persons are treated in an ethical manner not only by respecting their decisions and protecting them from harm, but also by making efforts to secure their well-being.

3   Justice: depending on the 'riskiness' of the research, you shouldn't research on people if they are unlikely to benefit.

The report also gave three applications of those principles to the conduct of research:

1   Informed consent, thinking especially about comprehension (the manner in which information is conveyed is as important as the information itself) and voluntariness.

2   Assessment of risks and benefits.

3   Selection of subjects: researchers should avoid selecting vulnerable or 'easy to persuade' persons for risky research.

You are most unlikely to be contemplating anything as dramatic as the Milgram experiments or as egregiously disrespectful and harmful as the Tuskegee experiments. However, there may be ethical issues lurking of which you were not aware or which you had not considered. Many of these will present questions of the kind that confront us now looking back at Milgram, albeit on a smaller scale. Who is the research benefiting? Do you have the right to take up people's time and energy? Is there any possible discomfort that participants will have to experience? Are you invading their privacy? Is it justifiable to have a control group if you feel that the experimental group is getting something worthwhile?

There may be more mundane motivation than promoting the good of humankind for using procedures that do not fully respect the wishes, the privacy or the integrity of the people with whom you are working. You may be in a hurry; you may think it is obvious that participants would not mind taking part in your research. But there are many reasons why participants may mind: they may be embarrassed; they may, if they are children, not want to lose respect amongst their peers; they may, if they are professionals, not want to be seen taking part in a project that has the endorsement of management or, conversely, not want to be seen to be critical of management, and so on. The potential reasons for not wanting to participate in a research project are legion, and you should be aware of this. And they may feel pressurised, just by being asked – however nice, however gentle you are in your request for participation.

Most research in the social sciences involves some kind of direct or indirect involvement with people, and will need some kind of ethical consideration. Whether your involvement with those people is direct, for example through interviews, questionnaires or direct observation, or indirect through interviews about someone else, or looking at documentary records, you will need to consider the ethics of what you are doing. However, ethics will not be a matter of concern if you are looking at matters that do not involve individual people – such as policy issues or data that are in the public domain.

Getting clearance – ethical review

A key element in starting your project is in getting ethical or institutional clearance. This goes under different names in different places, but may be referred to as *ethical review* or *institutional review*. You will have to write an outline of your proposed research which will be looked at by a group known as the 'ethics committee' or, more commonly in the USA, the 'institutional review board' (IRB).

The use of these formal procedures by universities for ensuring ethical practice in social science research projects is relatively recent and still regarded by many researchers, both student and professional, as a bit of a chore. However, this is not the right attitude, and it stems – I speak only for myself – from a less than self-critical belief that I could not possibly be doing anything that would harm anyone with whom I researched. It stems from a belief that my own judgement about the balance of rights and wrongs is naturally the best judgement and that it is an attack on my integrity to question this. But the passage of time and experience has shown me how delicately balanced these matters can be and how necessary it is to have ethical concerns explicitly articulated and systematically checked. In fact, the systematic checking of these concerns with another person often will add insights beyond ethics to the design and conduct of the research.

Potential risks include:

- causing psychological or physical harm to participants or others;
- damaging the standing or reputation of participants or others;
- infringing the privacy of participants or others;
- breaking the law;
- harming a community in some way (e.g. by drawing attention to differences within it).

If there is considered to be any significant risk concerning any of these matters you should consider its extent and duration. You may need to consider also the extent to which any risk can be 'undone', either naturally or through steps taken by you. You will need to weigh any risks against benefits or scholarly merit, which may include particular advantages to participants or others or any potential advance in knowledge. You should be prepared to expand on all of these and make a good case for your research.

Your university will have a code of conduct for research, and it will have a helpful webpage outlining procedures for gaining ethical clearance. The relevant professional organisations also have policies and guidelines on ethical research. Those for the British Educational Research Association (BERA), for example, can be found by Googling 'BERA ethical guidelines'. Others are given below. All are very helpful, though some (e.g. those for the American Psychological Association) are so long that you may lose to will to live if you embark on them. A very good, well-written one is the Social Policy Association's *Guidelines on Research Ethics*.

Codes of conduct and other guidelines

For the codes of conduct or guidelines issued by these professional bodies or government agencies, just enter the words below into your favourite search engine:

- American Psychological Association Ethical Principles of Psychologists and Code of Conduct

- American Sociological Association Code of Ethics

- British Educational Research Association Ethical Guidelines

- British Psychological Society Code of Ethics

- ESRC The Research Ethics Guidebook

- General Medical Council Good Practice in Research and Consent to Research

- Social Policy Association Guidelines on Research Ethics

- US Department of Health and Human Services Office for Human Research Protections

- World Health Organization Informed Consent Form Templates

The key thing to remember in looking at any of these protocols is that it is the consideration of ethics that is important – not the protocols themselves, helpful though these can be. A reflection on ethics should be integral, and not seen as a bolt-on or a chore to be squeezed into your timeframe.

Undergraduate-level ethical clearance

For undergraduate research, ethical review usually happens at school or department level. Getting clearance will involve completing a form which gives, in a nutshell, details of your plans. You will need to think about this right at the beginning of your project, as soon as you have decided what to focus on and have discussed the topic with your supervisor. In other words, once you are at the stage of being able to complete the checklist at the end of Chapter 1, you should be in a position to get the relevant form filled in.

Don't be intimidated by this form or by the procedure surrounding it. It shouldn't take too long, and it may help you to get down your early thoughts on paper to give structure to your work. To give you an idea of the kind of thing that has to be done, I have copied in Table 2.4 an abbreviated version of one that is used in my own university, along with my own comments on what is expected.

Table 2.4 A typical ethical review form at undergraduate level

Form heading	Details required on the form	*My comment*
Your name and supervisor's name		
Purpose of the research	in 300 words, giving key references.	*You may find it helpful to write this in the context of the Issue and Solution of the BIS (see p. 3).*
Participants	Specify the target sample, including sample size, age, gender, etc. Also include method(s) of recruitment and any inclusion/exclusion criteria.	*A rough idea is all that is needed here. Your tutors realise that circumstances change.*
Design of the study	State the proposed methodology, including research design, duration of the project, and approximate contact time with each subject or research participant. Also include where the study will take place, any relevant access arrangements (names of gatekeepers, etc.), and how confidentiality will be ensured. If appropriate, also include details of any discomfort involved in the research.	*A lot is required here by this form for this early stage of your project. As much may change, just give an idea of your thinking so far on these questions. This should be sufficient. It may change later on, but changes will be monitored by your supervisor.*
Consent	How will you ensure that all participants have given their consent? How will you seek consent from vulnerable individuals (e.g. children)?	*It's good to think about this at this early stage (see 'Consent' on p. 48). An indication of what you think you will do is all that is required.*
Finance	Identify any costs involved in the study and how these will be met.	*There will probably be no significant costs, in which case say so.*
Data storage		*Say that any data relating to persons or institutions will be anonymised (see p. 47), kept on a passworded personal computer and destroyed after your project is completed.*
Key references		*Include your reading so far (in Harvard style – see p. 83). May be just three or four references at this stage.*

So, this is the kind of thing that is expected in undergraduate research, and it will usually be looked at in-house – that is, in your department or school – for approval.

Postgraduate-level ethical clearance

For postgraduate research projects there are more complex arrangements. These usually entail a process which will involve completing an online form first in which you are asked various questions about your research. Your answers to these determine whether the research is 'low risk' or otherwise. If you have been able to answer 'no' to a series of questions, the project is taken to be 'low risk' – and that, for you, is then happily the end of the procedure. You can proceed on your way.

However, if you have not been able to answer 'no' to all the questions you will have to proceed to the second stage which involves scrutiny of your plans by a university-wide committee. The itinerary is summarised in Figure 2.4.

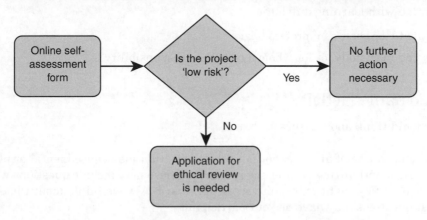

Figure 2.4   The procedure usually required for postgraduate ethical review

The process of ethical review must happen before the start of any active empirical work, including any pilot studies.

For your own university's exact procedure, take guidance from your department, or just Google 'University of [name of your university] ethical review', or, in the US, 'University of [name of your university] IRB review'.

What to think about in considering ethics

Your participants

In the bad old days, social scientists used to do 'experiments' with people whom they called 'subjects'. Now, especially in *applied* social science, we think of the people with whom we research as 'participants' or even 'partners' rather than 'subjects'. There are several reasons for this change, some of which we will explore in this book. The main thing, though, is a recognition that participants have rights and they should have a stake in the process of research: it shouldn't be a question of simply 'using' people and then waving goodbye. To be genuine participants they have to be involved to some extent in the planning, execution and write-up of your work.

You will need to think about their particular kinds of contributions and their particular needs. Consider especially the needs of

- children/legal minors (anyone under 16)
- people from non-English-speaking backgrounds
- anyone with a physical disability
- anyone with learning difficulties
- patients, or clients, of professionals
- anyone in custody, or for whom a court has responsibility.

Participants' activity

You should think about issues such as:

- Administration of any questions or procedures that may cause mental or physical discomfort during or after the research – these may include questions which appear at first sight to be quite straightforward. Always think about the effect that questions may have on your participants.

- Performance of any acts (such as role play) that might diminish self-esteem or cause embarrassment. If you are outrageously extrovert you may not appreciate how mortifying and disabling procedures such as role play can be to those of us who are more introverted. Such procedures are not only questionable on ethical grounds, but also may give misleading findings.

- Involvement of participants in any illegal activity. Definitely a no-no.

- Whether the participants will be in receipt of any substance or agent – this is likely only in health-related research and there will be very strict professional codes of conduct on issues such as this.

Deception or concealment

The default position on doing research is that you should be honest and open in all your dealings with research participants. Sometimes, though, as in the Milgram experiment we looked at earlier, you will need to be less than 100 per cent open because you may be researching something where the participants' knowledge of your aims would invalidate any findings that you may make. If this is the case, you must be prepared to argue convincingly for the need for concealment and you must build into your plans a debriefing session with your participants after the research has finished wherein you explain what you were doing in your study and why you could not be fully open at the outset.

The codes of conduct from professional associations usually recognise that an element of concealment or even deception may sometimes be necessary. Indeed, the US government's *Belmont Report* (National Commission for the Protection of Human Subjects of Biomedical and Behavioral Research, 1978; see p. 40 (above http://www.nhs.gov/ohrp/humansubjects/guidance/belmont.html (accessed 16th April 2013)) recognises it, but says that:

> In all cases of research involving incomplete disclosure, such research is justified only if it is clear that (1) incomplete disclosure is truly necessary to accomplish the goals of the research, (2) there are no undisclosed risks to subjects that are more than minimal, and (3) there is an adequate plan for debriefing subjects.

So, if any degree of withholding or misrepresentation is involved, it will be important for you in your ethical clearance to:

- explicitly acknowledge what is being done;
- justify fully the reasons why it is being done;
- note that you will be explaining to participants following the research the purpose of the research and why it was necessary to withhold information from them.

If asked about risks and benefits, you should spell out:

- the physical, psychological, social, legal or economic risks that may be associated with the research and outline the arrangements that you have put in place to manage that risk;
- if there are likely to be any immediate benefits to participants;
- if there are any specific risks to researchers;
- how potential benefits to participants outweigh any risks;
- any arrangements that you have put in place for support after the study.

Confidentiality and anonymity

You should always treat any information provided to you as confidential, taking care at all times not to breach or compromise that confidentiality. Maintaining the anonymity of your participants is a key part of this both in your everyday dealings and conversations with others and in your storage of data and your reporting. Anonymity can be ensured by changing participants' names as well as the name of any institutions (such as schools) to which they are affiliated and the regions in which they are situated. You can either give pseudonyms or code numbers to achieve this. You'll need to be especially careful in working with participants whose identity may be hard to disguise, for example those in minority groups. Where appropriate, you should make it clear to participants that your commitment to confidentiality as a researcher may be overridden given your legal or moral duty to report incidents of harm. Circumstances such as these will be most unusual, but if you do come across them you should discuss them with your supervisor and/or the appropriate services (such as child protection services) immediately.

Data security and stewardship

You have a responsibility to keep the data you collect about people secure, especially in so far as it relates to individuals who can be identified. Various exemptions exist in the UK Data Protection Act to allow researchers to collect data without the need to inform the Data Commissioner, but this does not mean that you can ignore principles of good stewardship of data:

- Only use data for the purposes for which it was collected – not for other purposes.

- Keep data for an appropriate length of time. What counts as 'appropriate' varies according to the circumstances: for most undergraduate research it will be appropriate to destroy raw data immediately your project is completed and marked; however, for some research (e.g. that which is part of a clinical programme, which a postgraduate project may be part of) professional codes of conduct specify that data must be kept for several years following the close of a programme.

- Keep data secure – you should use passwords on any files that contain pre-anonymised names. For Microsoft Office documents, this means clicking the Office button (top left of the screen), clicking 'Prepare', then clicking 'Encrypt document'. (If this doesn't work, click the F1 button for help, and enter 'password'.) You'll be asked for a password, which you *must* remember. If you don't remember it, there is no way to get your data back short of taking Bill Gates hostage and demanding the keys to Microsoft Central. Seriously. You won't get it back without the password.

- Don't pass the data on to anyone else – obviously, since it wouldn't then be secure.

- Keep the data anonymous (see previous section).

Consent

Because of the harm that might be caused during research involving people, an important concept when considering the ethics of research is that of consent. Consent is about the agreement of people to take part in the study. More than simple agreement, however, is required, given the issues noted above. *Informed consent* is needed. In other words, potential participants should understand what they are agreeing to. Informed consent is based on the points in Table 2.5.

Table 2.5   Informed consent

(a) The information participants need to know, including:
  – the nature and purpose of the study, including its methods
  – expected benefits of the study
  – possible harm that may come from the study
  – information about confidentiality, anonymity, how data will be kept and for how long, with details of when data will be destroyed
  – ethics procedures being followed and appeals
  – your full name and full contact details
(b) The presentation of (a) in a meaningful and understandable way, explaining any unusual terms simply, in non-technical language
(c) The option for a potential participant to choose to take part or not

Opting-in versus implied consent

An important distinction exists between *opting-in* consent and *implied* consent:

- With *opting-in* consent, participants have to make an active choice about becoming involved and signal their willingness to take part in the research. You would have to offer an invitation to participants to become involved, preferably in writing, requesting that they return a form indicating willingness to participate. This could be done directly and orally if written communication is not possible. Alternatively, some other *active* choice of the participant would have to be involved, as would be the case in returning a questionnaire. It must be made clear that consent (from the participant) may be withdrawn at any time and that if this is the case there will be no further collection of additional data, no further analysis of data initially collected and removal of existing data from your records.

- With *implied* consent, you tell participants about the research and assume that they give their consent unless they tell you otherwise. Information about the research can be distributed by a range of means, for example by a letter from the school to all children who would be personally involved. The letter would include the information you would give as for opting in, but would be accompanied by a phrase such as 'I am assuming that unless I hear from you, you have no objections to Ellie's participation ...'. Depending on the degree of risk assumed to be involved, information might also be communicated by announcements or leaflets, as long as it can reasonably be assumed that the intended recipients will receive the information. There should, of course, in every case be a clear explanation of the provisions for opting out, and people should be given the easiest possible way of doing so – by letter, telephone or email, or personally to you.

There are pros and cons to opting-in versus implied consent. If there is any degree of significant risk, then opting-in procedures are clearly to be preferred. Opting-in consent involves more work for the researcher than does opting out (or implied consent). However, there is some evidence that samples may be skewed by the use of opting-in procedures (because only really willing people opt in, and this may exclude important subsections of the population). Junghans et al. (2005), working in a medical context, therefore suggest that: 'The opt-out approach should be the default recruitment strategy for studies that pose a low risk to patients.' The key phrase here is 'a low risk', and what constitutes low risk is a matter of judgement. This can be discussed with your supervisor and your local ethics representative if necessary.

Issues of consent are particularly important with children. There is an unequal power relationship between any adult and any child, and your position as a researcher heightens the perception of authority held by the child. Good discussions of the ethics of working with children are provided in Lewis and Lindsay (2000), Alderson (2004) and Kellett (2005).

When you write or talk to your potential research participants, you will have to do so after having thought about all of these issues. If it is a complex project you will need to produce an **information sheet** for participants which explains the details of your project and what you expect to come from it. If the project involves any degree of discomfort for participants, they should also be asked to sign a **consent form**. Either – information sheet or consent form – should include:

- the title of the project and the name(s) of researcher(s) and their institution;

- an explanation of what the research is about;

- confirmation that involvement in the project is voluntary and that participants are free to withdraw at any time and/or withdraw data supplied;

- an explanation about what involvement will be asked of participants and whether, for example, audio or visual recording will be involved;

- details of arrangements being made to provide for confidentiality, such as anonymisation;

- arrangements for data security, including when the data will be destroyed;

- arrangements for debriefing and feedback.

Where involvement is more uncomplicated, a simple *letter* may be all that is needed, as long as it covers these issues in an intelligible way. Figure 2.5 shows an example.

Vulnerable groups

For those who may not understand the ins and outs of consent or who may be susceptible to pressure to cooperate because of their social or economic position there will need to be special considerations. Some people are especially prone to

University College, Badlands
24th October 2015

Dear Parent

Invitation to participate in research

I am a student at University College, Badlands, and as part of my course I am doing a research project on parent involvement in reading. In my spare time I work as a volunteer helper at Badlands Primary School, and Mrs Tumbleweed, Headteacher, has kindly agreed to allow me to contact parents to ask for their participation in the project.

(Say something about you)

We know that when parents are involved in helping their children to read this can have great benefits. In my research I want to find out how much parents read with their children in an ordinary week and the kinds of things that are read. I hope this will contribute to our understanding of the ways in which parents can be helped by school to read with their children at home.

(Briefly explain your project)

I will be asking parents to fill in a short diary every day for a week. Each day's diary asks you to record any reading done with your child in the previous 24 hours. It should take only seconds to complete each day.

(Say what the participant is being asked to do)

Your participation in this research is entirely voluntary. If you choose not to participate, no questions will be asked and there will, of course, be no consequences for your child.

I will not be sharing the personal information I receive from you with anyone, even school staff, and the information I collect from my research project will be kept private. Any information about your diary will have a number on it instead of your name. After my write-up, all information I have collected will be destroyed. Each participant will receive a summary of the results.

(Explain anonymity, data security and feedback)

If you would like to take part in my project, please complete the tear-off slip below and return it with your daughter or son to give to their teacher.

Many thanks

Lucy Bloggs
Student in educational studies

✂———————————————————————————

Name of child _____

Name of teacher _____

Your name (parent/guardian) _____

I would like to be involved in your research project. Please contact me in the following way for further details (tick as many boxes as apply)…

☐   phone me on _____

☐   text me on _____

☐   email me on _____

I understand that my participation in this project is voluntary and that I may withdraw at any time.

Signed   _____

Figure 2.5   An example of a letter seeking participants' involvement

being involved in research because of their 'ready availability in settings where research is conducted', as the US government's *Belmont Report* put it. Careful thought should be given to questions about why and how they are being involved, and they should be protected against involvement solely for the sake of convenience, or because they may be easy to persuade or even manipulate.

Lewis and Porter (2004) urge that the following questions should always be asked with any kind of vulnerable group, including children and those with learning difficulties:

- Has the participant's ability to give fully informed consent been assessed and discussed with others such as parents, caregivers or teachers?

- Have ways of checking for understanding of confidentiality/research purposes been explored?

- Will participants, at appropriate intervals, be reminded of their right to withdraw?

- Have all possible steps been taken to ensure anonymity, given that this may be particularly difficult to achieve with minority populations?

- In giving feedback, have steps been taken to ensure the intelligibility of the information? This can be done through, for example, asking a familiar person to talk with the individual, or offering pictures with simplified text or case study material.

- How is the end of the research relationship with participants to be managed? It is easy for close relationships to be forged during research and these should not be terminated abruptly.

Contacting participants

Remember that each situation is different. You will need to assess how best to make contact with potential participants and how to explain to them the nuts and bolts of your research. A very good website is that of the World Health Organization (http://www.who.int/rpc/research_ethics/informed_consent/en/) which gives templates of letters, forms and information sheets covering:

- informed consent for clinical studies;

- informed consent for qualitative studies;

- informed assent for children/minors;

- informed parental consent for research involving children (qualitative).

In written communications with participants, always use straightforward language. Imagine that you are in a spoken conversation with them. So, for example, say 'the project *starts* on ...' rather than 'the project *commences* on ...', or 'Please *read through* this' instead of 'Please *peruse* this.' (When has anyone actually *said* the words 'commence' or 'peruse'? I've no idea why people who devise forms are so fond of words like this.) Use everyday terms such as 'information' rather than 'data'.

Care for your participants ... and for yourself

I have discussed the many things you will need to consider in order to avoid causing harm or discomfort to your research participants. If, despite your best endeavours, though, it happens that you uncover something distressing for your participants – or you trigger a response which is clearly painful for them, you should think about whether it is appropriate to offer information to them about relevant support services.

And you should consider, too, the potential for harm to yourself in doing social research. While most situations will not, of course, present any danger, some will. If you are meeting people who are strangers, for example, always take a mobile phone with you and let a friend or family member know where you will be going, whom you are meeting, and when you will be expected back.

Where do I put discussion about ethics in my dissertation?

It's a moot point. Your discussion of ethics can come right at the beginning, in your introduction, but if put there it can rather unbalance the narrative about the purpose of your study. It can have a chapter all on its own, but this seems almost to treat matters about ethics as a separate, special concern, distanced from the main body of your work. I think the best place for your discussion about ethics is in a separate section in your design and methodology chapter (see p.186 of this book). Here, you can discuss ethics alongside your deliberations about design and explanations about how you have gone about your work. You may also want to discuss ethics briefly as you actually report your findings and analysis, if this seems appropriate. Put sample copies of any forms, information sheets, letters to participants, guidelines, etc., in an appendix.

Access

Access is about getting hold of the data that you want, and where people are providing the information that you need this can present some dilemmas. Whether you are conducting a set of interviews or questionnaires or making some formal or informal observations, you will need to identify those people, contact them (and often their colleagues) and secure their agreement, attending to all of the issues we have just discussed about informed consent. Table 2.6 lists some possible forms of contact, with some considerations of which to be aware.

Table 2.6 Possible forms of contact

Through personal contact, or that of a colleague	You will be an insider in the organisation. This has advantages and disadvantages. You have easy access to people. Your knowledge gives you insights about the culture and the politics of the place. But on the downside, others in the organisation or system have expectations of you that may affect their opinions of you. This may or may not matter. If you are working as an interpretative researcher, these expectations are part of your place and context (see *positionality* on p. 144), but if you are expecting to achieve any sort of objectivity, you must examine your questions to see how your position may affect the answers you get from others.
Through the knowledge of a friend or relative	For undergraduates, this is often the best 'way in' to an organisation. However, it does not mean that you can avoid getting the permission of those in authority and other key stakeholders in the organisation. If in a school, for example, it is essential to involve the head teacher (or their delegated deputy) – and not just to get an 'OK', but also if possible to achieve their active support. You should therefore go through points (a) to (c) in Table 2.5, explaining the project as clearly as possible.
From your supervisor's lead	Your supervisor may well know of an organisation or group or individual that would provide a suitable base. However, you cannot expect your supervisor to do any more than give you the initial contact. Beyond this, the liaison and everything that comes after is your own work.
Random or other forms of sampling	You may simply be picking names from a hat – for example, a group of physiotherapists who work in a particular region to whom you send a postal questionnaire. Or your sample may be more purposive – you may know the individuals you need to contact. (See 'Sampling' on p. 135 for the various forms of sampling.)

Overview

A research project is a major undertaking. If you don't plan systematically you will end up trying to do everything at the last minute, and it will show. At this stage – that is to say, near the beginning of your project – you need to understand how your work will be structured and you need to discuss this with your supervisor. You have to look at the kind of project you expect to do, divide up the time available and plan out how your practical work will fit into the timetable.

While you are thinking about the shape of your inquiry, you must think about the ethical dimensions of what you intend to do and how you are going to get access to the people you intend to involve in the research. These issues, if not addressed at the planning stage, can easily derail the best strategy. It's important to think about them not just for practical reasons but because they raise questions about the nature of your inquiry, why you are doing it and whom it is going to benefit.

Checklist ✔

You may find it helpful to copy this table and write down the answers to the questions.

Have you …

	Notes	
1 … drawn a timeline?	Make sure you note the beginning and end of each element	☐
2 … met your supervisor and given an outline of your work?		☐
3 … consulted your subject's ethical code of conduct?		☐
4 … found and completed your university's ethical review form (or IRB form, in the USA)?		☐
5 … located the people to whom you will need access?		☐
6 … fully considered how you will gain access to your research participants?		☐
7 … prepared an information sheet and (if necessary) drafted letters inviting participation?		☐

Further reading

Alderson, P. (2004) *Ethics, Social Research and Consulting with Children and Young People* (2nd edn). London: Barnardo's.
A useful manual from a renowned expert.

Burgess, R. (ed.) (1989) *The Ethics of Educational Research*. Lewes: Falmer.
An authoritative collection of essays on ethics.

Burns, T. and Sinfield, S. (2012) *Essential Study Skills: The Complete Guide to Success at University* (3rd edn). London: SAGE.
This is a good guide to studying at university. Lots of practical advice.

Cottrell, S. (2003) *The Study Skills Handbook* (2nd edn). Basingstoke: Macmillan.
This hugely popular book provides very, very basic advice on study skills. When I say basic, I mean basic: don't say I didn't warn you.

Farrell, A. (2005) *Ethical Research with Children.* Maidenhead: Open University Press.
A good all-round review on working with children.
Covers the practicalities of researching with people with learning difficulties.

Gorard, S. (2002) Ethics and equity: pursuing the perspective of non-participants. *Social Research Update*, 39, 1–4.
The author provides a useful discussion of alternative dimensions of ethics.

Howard, K. and Sharp, J.A. (2002) *The Management of a Student Research Project* (3rd edn). London: Gower Publishing
Especially good on working with your supervisor.

Kellett, M. and Nind, M. (2001) Ethics in quasi-experimental research on people with severe learning disabilities: dilemmas and compromises. *British Journal of Learning Disabilities*, 29, 51–55.

Lewis, A. and Porter, J. (2004) Interviewing children and young people with learning disabilities: guidelines for researchers and multi-professional practice. *British Journal of Learning Disabilities*, 32 (4), 191–7.
A very useful overview.

Oliver, P. (2010) *The Student's Guide to Research Ethics* (2nd edn). Maidenhead: Open University Press.
An excellent book that covers just about everything you need to know on ethics.

Open University (2013) Skills for OU study. http://www.open.ac.uk/skillsforstudy/
Another basic guide on how to study.

Simons, H. (2009) *Case Study Research in Practice*. London: SAGE.
Simons is very good on ethical considerations in case study and other qualitative research.

Walliman, N. (2004) *Your Undergraduate Dissertation: The Essential Guide for Success*. London: SAGE.
Good for the planning process involved in doing a research project.

Ward, L. (1998) Practising partnership: Involving people with learning difficulties in research. *British Journal of Learning Disabilities*, 26, 128–32.
Useful on ideas of participation and partnership with people who have learning difficulties.

3
THE LITERATURE REVIEW

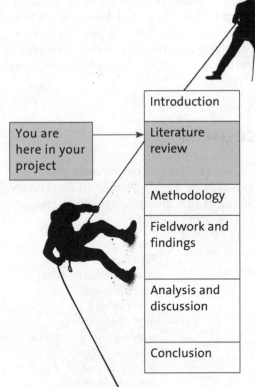

Introduction
Literature review
Methodology
Fieldwork and findings
Analysis and discussion
Conclusion

You are here in your project

You are not an island. Your work must occur in the context of what is already known. What have other people done about this or similar questions? In doing the literature review you find out, and in finding out you can focus and sharpen up your original research ideas. This chapter considers:

- that the literature is not all the same quality — there are different kinds of sources, each with strengths and weaknesses;

- keeping records of your searches;

- telling a coherent story — not writing a list;

- using the library, remembering it's the twenty-first century! — find out online through Google, Web of Knowledge, Amazon and others;

- beginning a storyboard;

- being critically aware.

Once you have outlined the problem or issue that you wish to examine and you are happy with the expression of this in the form of an initial question or questions, you will need to find out about what other people have accomplished in researching this topic. Assuming that you have done your work properly in making sure that your research question is precise and doable, this review of the literature should lead you down some paths that will help you to define more exactly what you wish to do. Ultimately, you will be able to refine your research questions.

In thinking about a literature review, you first need to establish what's meant by 'literature'. Literature can be almost anything that represents the results of research or scholarship on a subject. It is written material that may appear in books, articles, conference proceedings, dissertations, websites, and so on. The shorthand for these kinds of information is *sources*.

Just running through these sources, you will see, even at first glance, that they are of different kinds, and they will be viewed differently by your tutors. Some have more credibility than others, and you must be careful not to be taken in by something just because it is in print. Just because it is in written form doesn't mean that it is of unimpeachable quality as a piece of information. You will need to be clear about the status of the evidence that you are drawing on when you cite literature. You should ask yourself what kind of literature it is. Let's look at a few sources as shown in Table 3.1.

Primary and secondary sources

In Table 3.1, you'll notice that mention is made of primary and secondary sources, and I note that secondary sources are not usually as highly thought of as primary sources. It is worth spending some time looking at this distinction between primary and secondary, since tutors may place stress on using one (usually primary) rather than the other. Most of the sources mentioned in Table 3.1 will usually be primary (though textbooks are always secondary). Let's look at some others.

Examples of primary sources:

- autobiographies

- diaries

- government documents and statistics

- letters and correspondence (including electronic kinds such as email)

- original documents (such as birth certificates)

- photographs and audio or video recordings

A primary source is 'straight from the horse's mouth' – in other words, no other person has subsequently analysed or summarised it. A secondary source is a reworking of usually many primary sources, either in analysis or summary. Textbooks are the most common form of secondary source.

- reports from commercially produced surveys or other research (e.g. using focus groups)
- speeches
- technical reports.

Examples of secondary sources:

- biographies
- dictionaries and encyclopaedias
- review articles
- textbooks.

The main difference between a primary source and a secondary source is in the directness of the data or evidence being presented. Think of the primary source representing a first presentation or first analysis of the data, and the secondary source representing a second look, usually by someone other than the author of the primary source. In practice, it is difficult sometimes to distinguish between a primary and a secondary source, so you should not get too worried about strict demarcations between them. And one thing that Table 3.1 highlights is that there is no automatic correlation between the quality of a source and its 'primary-ness' or 'secondary-ness'. Some primary sources may be very suspect, while some secondary sources may be excellent.

You'll notice that I include *review articles* in secondary sources, and these are worth a special mention since they are taken to be rather more authoritative reviews of the literature than those that exist in encyclopaedias and textbooks. There are two kinds of review article: the *systematic* review and the *narrative* review. The systematic review uses particular methods to search for research on a topic in a wide range of peer review sources. Only studies of a predetermined type and/or quality are included in the ultimate review. A narrative review, by contrast, discusses and summarises the literature on a particular topic without conforming to a particular search formula. Narrative reviews often do not report on how they searched for literature or how they decided which studies were relevant to include. There are also *meta-analyses*. These are studies which use particular techniques for selecting and summarising the findings of many pieces of research.

Review articles and meta-analyses can be very valuable as sources, if you can find up-to-date ones which are relevant to your topic. While they appear in general academic journals, you can look especially for journal titles that contain 'Review' such as the *Review of Educational Research* or *Educational Review*.

A relatively new and increasingly important resource is the 'collaboration' that brings together high-quality evidence and then synthesises and summarises it for the reader. The most important of these for the social sciences is the Campbell Collaboration (www.campbellcollaboration.org/). This gives as its general purpose 'Improving decision-making through systematic reviews on the effects of interventions

Table 3.1　Sources of written information

Kind of source	What is it?	☺ Good things about this source	☹ Not so good things about this source
Article in a peer review journal Usually primary	This has been offered by the author to the journal to be judged. The peer reviewers (i.e. other academics in the same field) will ask themselves if it is good enough for publication. Only the best articles will be accepted, and for this reason the peer review journal is seen as the 'gold standard' for quality.	Only the best articles get published. You can therefore be sure of quality (in theory).	This material is published for the author's peers in the academic community, and may be difficult for anyone else to understand. Also, it will usually be on esoteric or cutting-edge matters and not necessarily straightforward issues. It may give little attention to explaining the wider context, or explaining in simple terms.
Article in a professional journal Usually primary	A professional journal is similar to a peer review journal, and may be reviewed by peers. However, criteria for judgement will be rather different. It will be judged principally on its practical usefulness to the professional, rather than on the satisfactoriness of the design of the study or the methods used.	Likely to be of practical relevance.	May be simply the view of the author. The work will not have been subject to such stringent scrutiny of research design, method, analysis, etc. It is difficult to assess the difference between a professional journal and a peer review journal, since both have elements of peer review. If in doubt, try to make an assessment of the article itself. Does it just seem to be a personal view? Is it well referenced? How thoroughly does it seem to have been done?
Authored book Usually primary	Books vary in their 'scholarliness'. They will usually have been written as a major presentation of the author's work – research work or academic study – but they may be explanations of other people's work (see 'Textbook').	Books written by a single author represent an extended academic treatment of a particular topic. Because they are by one person they have integrity: they tend to 'hang together'.	Tend to be personal representations of a topic, unmoderated by the comments or views of others. So be cautious: this may be a very particular 'take' on a subject, or a personal view.
Chapter in an edited book Primary or secondary	Edited compilations are books all on one theme brought together by an editor. These are like journals, but without the same degree of peer review.	Edited books are a good way of gathering related material on a topic. The editor will be an expert in the field, often taking an interesting slant.	Can be 'bitty', with some very weak chapters interspersed with good ones. The multiple authorial 'voice' may be confusing.

Kind of source	What is it?	☺ **Good things about this source**	☹ **Not so good things about this source**
Textbook Secondary	A textbook is a bringing together of much work on one theme. This is not original work by the author, but work that she or he has summarised for the particular purpose of meeting students' course needs.	Saves a lot of time searching sources. It may, if the textbook is good, provide a very effective summary.	Because an author is reporting on others' work it is susceptible to distortion or misunderstanding (think of 'Chinese Whispers'). It is referred to as a 'secondary source' for this reason. When other people's work is brought together in this way by a textbook author it has to be summarised, perhaps not very well. It can become out of date quickly. For all these reasons a textbook is not valued highly as a source.
Conference paper Usually primary	A paper that has been presented at an academic conference and that has then been printed in a collection of papers (called the 'proceedings' of the conference).	Usually right up to date, and often reporting on work that is still in progress.	Conferences vary in their status, and papers are often subject to only a minor form of peer review, if they are peer reviewed at all. Conference proceedings are therefore of very variable quality.
Thesis or dissertation Usually primary	The theses and dissertations that you will be able to gain access to are written by students who have written master's degrees or PhDs.	May be on a topic very similar to your own. May be very good (but may not – see the next column).	May be very weak. Do not use one as a model for your own. It may only have scraped a pass.
Research or technical report Usually primary	A report written by researchers and addressed directly to the people who funded the research.	Direct, to the point and well focused on the issue being researched.	Not peer reviewed, so no quality control. Also, since paid for by the funder ('contract research'), conclusions may have been influenced by those funders.
Magazine or newspaper article Usually secondary	Like other forms of publication, newspapers and magazines (periodicals) take various forms, though the differences are more marked. Some periodicals and newspapers are as 'respectable' as some journals. Others are not.	Right up to date, and can be used as a starting-point which leads you to a more reliable source.	Most of these publications depend on good sales and may be willing, even the 'high-quality' ones, to distort material to make it more interesting. Reporters are subject to none of the peer review checking used in academic journals. It is not unheard of for reporters simply to make up stories.
Website Usually secondary	These are as varied as the sources of information above. A website is really just a medium for carrying a range of sources and has no inherent strengths or weaknesses. It's up to you to judge.	Most websites carry reliable information, some, for example, taking you directly to a publisher's site, where you can download peer reviewed articles.	Some websites, even quite well-known ones, carry misleading information. Be particularly wary of those offering off-the-shelf answers to essay questions. Wikipedia can be helpful for giving you an impression of the breadth of the area, but is unreliable. Always verify from another source.

within the areas of education, crime and justice, and social welfare'. This is an example of one of its summaries on the impact of street lighting in the reduction of crime:

> This review of 13 studies of street lighting interventions in the United Kingdom and United States, spanning four decades, finds that crime decreased by 21% in areas that experienced street lighting improvements compared to similar areas that did not. The review also notes that street lighting appears more effective at reducing crime in the United Kingdom compared to the United States – a 38% reduction compared to 7%. In general, the American studies were older and several reported just nighttime crime, rather than both night-time and daytime crime.

A similar resource is the Evidence for Policy and Practice Information and Co-ordinating Centre (EPPI-Centre) at http://eppi.ioe.ac.uk/cms/.

Another of these banks of summaries is at the Cochrane Collaboration (www.cochrane.org/). This is a library of systematic reviews in healthcare. Also see the Educational Evidence Portal (www.eep.ac.uk/DNN2) and digests such as the Social Policy Digest Online (http://journals.cambridge.org/spd/action/home). This provides an easily accessible listing of new developments across the whole social policy field.

I'll finish this section on the quality of sources with a warning story. In 2007 BBC News, The *Guardian*, The *Independent*, *The Times* and Reuters all wrote obituaries of the composer Ronnie Hazlehurst. Unfortunately, they all contained an error that revealed that the obituary writers had all simply cut and pasted a phoney fact from Wikipedia. A joker had maliciously edited the Wikipedia entry for Hazlehurst to say that the composer had emerged from retirement to write a song called 'Reach' for the pop group S Club 7, and this strange and interesting 'fact' was duplicated by the journalists without bothering to check its veracity. Result: red faces all round.

However, the moral is about more than just Wikipedia, which can be (and usually is) an excellent resource. It's about all published material. Try to avoid using only one source, and wherever possible corroborate and verify from others. Use primary sources if you can. It's not just facts that can be wrong. Perhaps more of a problem is the impression that you can get from one source where matters of opinion are involved and varied interests at play. If interpretations of data or analysis are involved, be aware that these can take many shapes and hues. By reading from a variety of sources you will get an overview and a more rounded picture of the topic.

Quality of sources

Aside from your judgement about the source that is being used, make a more general assessment of the work that you are referencing. Ask the following questions of it:

- Is this literature written following a piece of research? If so, what kind of research was being undertaken? Was it a large-scale or small-scale study? What was being claimed of the research? Usually research authors are 'up-front' about the limitations and weaknesses of their research, and work that is published in a good journal should not have been accepted if it makes unrealistic claims. This is not to say that small-scale research is in any way inferior to large-scale research: each has its strengths and weaknesses. The main thing is to be aware of these and to show that you understand the limitations of any kind of research – to show that you are *critically aware* (see 'critical awareness' below).

- Or, if it is not a piece of research appearing in a journal, is it, by contrast, someone's opinion? Who is the person? What authority do they have? Do they have any vested interests that may have caused them to give the opinion or advice that they have given?

> Not all sources are equal. Think about the quality of the source. Is it primary or secondary? Is it based on research evidence? Has there been a peer review process?

Your literature review should tell a story – it should not be a list

Your aim is to examine the literature for material that is relevant to your research topic. What have other people done that is relevant to your research question? You don't, after all, want to be reinventing the wheel. Your search will take you up against some disparate ideas and some interesting information, but your principal aim here isn't simply to make a list of everything that has been written on a topic. Such *summarising* and listing is necessary but is by no means enough. To conduct a good literature review, you also need to *synthesise* and *analyse*.

Summary is not too difficult, and this is perhaps why it tends to dominate student literature reviews. Analysis and synthesis are more difficult ...

When you *analyse*, you see what is going on; you see how one part relates to another; you see the wood for the trees. For example, political journalists don't simply write down everything that is said in Parliament: they analyse how one statement relates to another; they remember what was said last month and note whether it is consistent with this; they look for the vested interests that might be held by those making a statement.

> Your literature review should be a story with a beginning, a middle and an end. It is a synthesis that links ideas or finds differences. It is not a list.

When you *synthesise*, you bring things together, relating one to another to form something new. When chemists synthesise a new molecule from two existing molecules, they don't simply glue one molecule to the next one. Rather, they put the molecules through some process that creates something entirely new and different, with different qualities from the two original molecules. This is what happens in the best literature reviews: there is an intelligent appraisal of a range of sources that in some way extracts the key messages and accounts for them in the context of an overarching statement or idea.

In the end, your literature review should make sense as a story with a beginning, a middle and an end, with lots of connections between one part and another. You outline the issues at the beginning; you provide the analysis and synthesis in the middle (always linking one bit with another: 'Sikes found more fluff in men's trouser pockets, while Cratchett discovered more in women's. The reasons for this may be found in …'); and you tie it up at the end by summarising the issues, differences, paradoxes, dilemmas and questions yet to be resolved.

Making it a story

I have stressed that your literature review should be more like a story than a list. The aim is to find themes – or, by contrast, discontinuities, breaks, disagreements – that run through the literature. When you have done a reasonable amount of searching you will be able to see these emerging and it is useful at this stage to draw a storyboard – a plan that sums up and brings together the ideas that are emerging from your literature review.

Let's look at the storyboard in Figure 3.1. The original question that has been posed is 'How do head teachers cope with difficult people?' This might be the sort of question posed by a head teacher or deputy head teacher undertaking a master's degree in education. To draw your storyboard you will need to have done some reading already, and it will help if you have thought about or brainstormed on this reading.

Think of this process of combining summary, analysis and synthesis as telling a story or a series of stories. A story makes sense: it is not simply a list. A story has a beginning a middle and an end, and you can make your literature review take this structure. Try to build an interest in the area, rather like a novelist does. Start by establishing what the great educator Jerome Bruner (1997: 142) calls the 'trouble' in the story – not literally 'trouble', of course, but rather the issue, question or uncertainty. A good novelist begins a story by capturing the reader's interest with this 'trouble', and this is what you should do when you begin your literature review. You could begin by saying, for example, that although your area of interest is clearly a matter of national concern, researchers have tended not to focus on it, or have focused on an aspect of it that is not relevant to the teacher in the classroom. Or you could establish some 'trouble' by pointing out a major area of controversy, which still exists even after decades of research. You then need the 'middle' of the story – the establishment of what people are actually saying, and how they are disagreeing or agreeing. The end will come with a summing up and a moving on to the reasons for doing your own thesis.

Do authors concentrate on a particular theme? Do they disagree? Are there areas of controversy? Are there surprising areas of agreement or similar findings? Are there gaps that no one seems to be looking at?

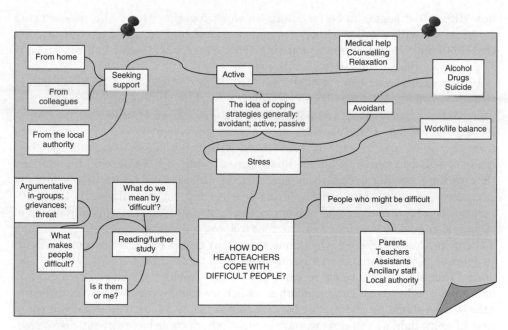

Figure 3.1 Storyboard

Table 3.2 Useful linking words

When there is a difference	When there is agreement	When one idea leads to another
however; but; notwithstanding this; although; yet; conversely; in spite of this; nevertheless; on the other hand; despite; then again; besides	moreover; indeed; further; furthermore; additionally; likewise; also; similarly; equally; and; what is more; again	hence; because of this; thus; for example; as a result; consequently; therefore; accordingly; so; for this reason; this is why; otherwise; then; finally

Use your words cleverly to tell the story

When writing your literature review, try to make links between different areas of work and make those links explicit with the words that you use at the beginning of sentences or paragraphs. For example, if Smith has found something different from Brown, don't simply list one after the other. Instead, show that you recognise the difference in their opinions by simply inserting a 'however', and relating one with the other: 'Smith (2006) found that boys in Year 9 were significantly below the level of girls in reading ability. However, Brown (2007) found no such difference.' Useful linking words are given in Table 3.2.

Figure 3.2 shows a few paragraphs from the literature review of my own PhD thesis, which was about additional adults in the classroom – people such as classroom assistants and parents. In this particular bit, I was looking at how difficult it seems to be for adults to work together there and was making connections with similar kinds of situations that had occurred earlier, during the 1960s and 1970s, in team teaching. This excerpt is useful, I think, since it shows how different ideas can be linked.

In this excerpt you can see that I was trying to do two things as far as telling a story is concerned. I was trying to *link* the work of the researchers (Geen and Cohen) that I had located, and I did this by using words and phrases such as 'similar' and 'like Geen'. I was also linking the ideas that seemed to be coming through from the literature, ideas that were linked with the kinds of observations I had made myself and which had made this an area I wanted to research. I had noticed that working together in classrooms seemed to be difficult, and here were researchers saying exactly the same, and proffering reasons for the difficulties. So those difficulties were a thread I could pull out of the review. It wasn't simply a question of summarising what was found by the researchers, but rather a question of finding a theme or themes. For me, the theme was about teams being much more difficult to operate in classrooms than anybody seemed to be assuming.

And this is where your own research fits into the review. Would you be aiming to add some weight to one view or another? It is here that your research will be beginning to take shape, since you may now see that original research question you posed in a different light as you start to uncover what other people have already discovered.

Joining the pieces

Being in a research area is a bit like being told to go into a room in which pieces of a jigsaw puzzle have been scattered around the furniture, with half of the pieces missing: not only do you have to find the pieces you have been given and how they fit together; you also have to understand what is missing. Doing the literature review is like being at that first stage; doing your own research is the second – filling in the bits that are missing. In the first stage you have to discover what is already

there and how one bit of the puzzle relates (or doesn't relate) to another. But when you embark on a literature review you are not only looking for pieces, you are also seeing how they fit together and interrelate. Does this piece go here, or there? What can we tell from these several pieces that seem to fit together? What do they tell us about the gaps that are in the area that is missing?

Speed reading and taking notes

You will not find a stock of books and articles that are on the precise subject of your project. You will, however, find literature that is related and you must do what you can to see the relevance of this.

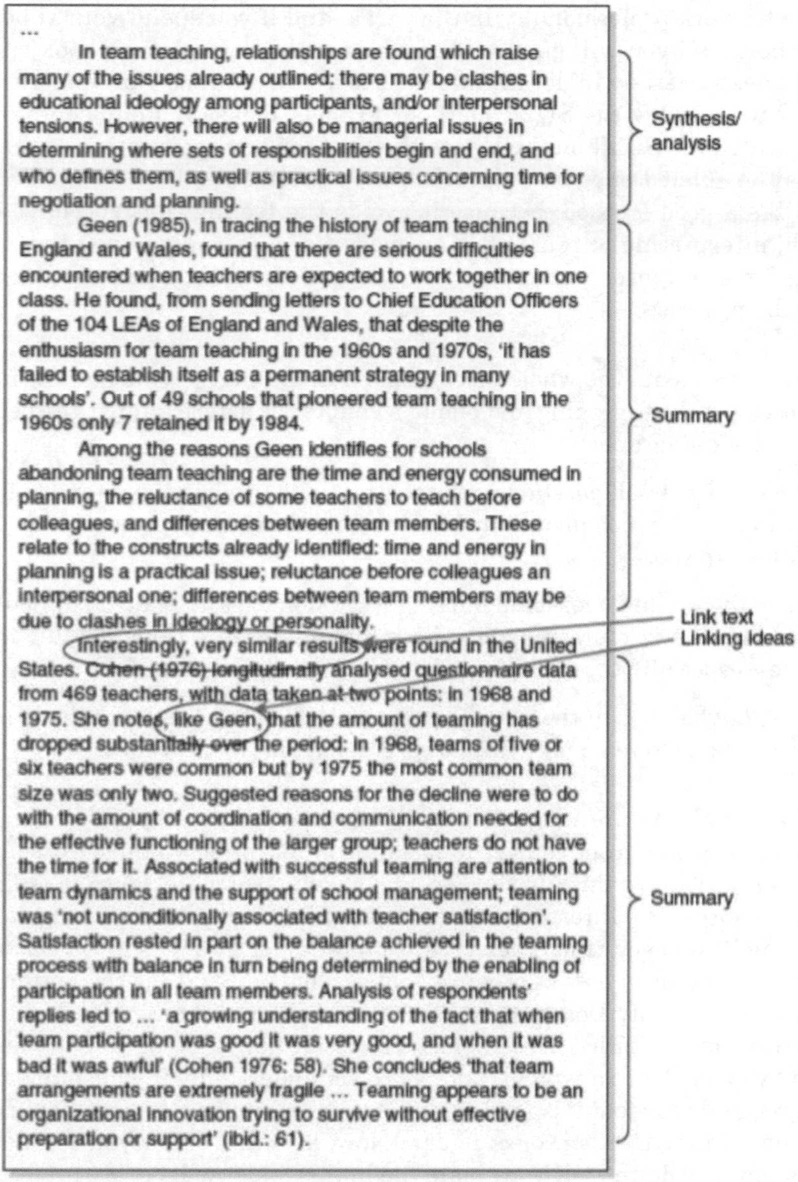

...

In team teaching, relationships are found which raise many of the issues already outlined: there may be clashes in educational ideology among participants, and/or interpersonal tensions. However, there will also be managerial issues in determining where sets of responsibilities begin and end, and who defines them, as well as practical issues concerning time for negotiation and planning.

Geen (1985), in tracing the history of team teaching in England and Wales, found that there are serious difficulties encountered when teachers are expected to work together in one class. He found, from sending letters to Chief Education Officers of the 104 LEAs of England and Wales, that despite the enthusiasm for team teaching in the 1960s and 1970s, 'it has failed to establish itself as a permanent strategy in many schools'. Out of 49 schools that pioneered team teaching in the 1960s only 7 retained it by 1984.

Among the reasons Geen identifies for schools abandoning team teaching are the time and energy consumed in planning, the reluctance of some teachers to teach before colleagues, and differences between team members. These relate to the constructs already identified: time and energy in planning is a practical issue; reluctance before colleagues an interpersonal one; differences between team members may be due to clashes in ideology or personality.

Interestingly, very similar results were found in the United States. Cohen (1976) longitudinally analysed questionnaire data from 469 teachers, with data taken at two points: in 1968 and 1975. She notes, like Geen, that the amount of teaming has dropped substantially over the period: in 1968, teams of five or six teachers were common but by 1975 the most common team size was only two. Suggested reasons for the decline were to do with the amount of coordination and communication needed for the effective functioning of the larger group; teachers do not have the time for it. Associated with successful teaming are attention to team dynamics and the support of school management; teaming was 'not unconditionally associated with teacher satisfaction'. Satisfaction rested in part on the balance achieved in the teaming process with balance in turn being determined by the enabling of participation in all team members. Analysis of respondents' replies led to ... 'a growing understanding of the fact that when team participation was good it was very good, and when it was bad it was awful' (Cohen 1976: 58). She concludes 'that team arrangements are extremely fragile ... Teaming appears to be an organizational innovation trying to survive without effective preparation or support' (ibid.: 61).

Synthesis/analysis

Summary

Link text
Linking ideas

Summary

Figure 3.2 Telling a story

When you are reading, try to develop the skill of speed reading, 'gutting' an article or book for the material that you need. Keep an eye out for key words or phrases and ignore what is irrelevant. You cannot read an academic book in the same way that you read a novel or even a newspaper. Academics write in strange prose that is sometimes meaningful only to the limited group of people who work professionally in that area, and if you spend your time trying to decipher it all you will go mad. For a particularly important book or article that you need to study in detail (maybe it is a key reference for your research), you may wish to try the SQ2R method. Francis Pleasant Robinson developed what is called the SQ3R method – see the 'further reading' section at the end of this chapter – but I suggest a variant which deletes the last 'R', so it becomes SQ2R.) It's a good method, because it avoids the feeling that you have to plod through, interpreting or remembering every word. It reminds you that you are reading for a purpose, summarised by the questions that you set yourself as part of the process.

- S – *survey* or skim the whole piece, remembering that key nuggets of information occur at the beginning and end of a chapter or article, and at the beginning and end of paragraphs.

- Q – now ask yourself *questions*, related especially to what you intend to find out. Don't worry too much about stuff that is irrelevant: stick to questions that are important to you.

- R – *read* the whole piece, again fairly quickly, don't get hung up on difficult bits – and, if the book is yours, mark it with a highlighter or a pencil for key words or phrases, especially those that are relevant to your questions.

- R – *recall* what was in the piece (having shut the book first). Jot down notes. If you aren't able to remember anything, start again with *survey*.

Whether or not you are using the SQ2R method for your speed reading, keep a Word file of notes from your reading. Call it 'My project notes' (or something more imaginative). To this file you can add downloaded material from online copy or from websites. The Internet material is easy to copy by cutting and pasting, so paste straight into your file. Then create a new folder into which you can put this file. If you don't know how to create a folder, click on Start (at the bottom left of your screen), then My Documents, File, New, Folder and a new box will appear in your Documents called 'New Folder'. You can now type in your name in the place of 'New Folder'. So type in 'Lucy's project folder' (only if your name is Lucy, obviously), and your folder is made – and it didn't cost you a penny. Now drag 'My project notes' into 'Lucy's project folder'. Now, into this folder you can add all of the files that you download. Your main file in this folder will be 'My project notes', but it will also comprise all of the files of articles and webpages that you have downloaded. It's worth noting that when you download a file from the Internet, it will be directed straight to 'My Documents' (or possibly 'Downloads'), so drag all of these downloads from My Documents (or Downloads) into 'Lucy's project folder'. A quick tip: if, like me, you tend to lose files on your computer (and, like me, you find the new Windows search facility incomprehensible) download a free program called 'Agent Ransack', which ferrets around wonderfully to find all your lost stuff.

Critical awareness: be your own Jeremy Paxman

Critical awareness is a key phrase that will come up again and again in your university work, and despite the efforts of tutors to instil it in their students, it remains a rare commodity. You will get good marks for having it, and you will be marked down for not demonstrating it.

What, then, is critical awareness? The key thing about study in higher education is your *attitude* to knowledge rather than the *amount* of knowledge that you can show you possess. While at school the key thing seems to be to learn as many facts as possible and then reproduce them in a more or less logical form for an assignment, the attitude at university is rather different. Certainly there may be issues and knowledge with which you will be expected to be familiar, but it is your attitude to such knowledge that is more important than your familiarity: your approach should always be of scepticism – of suspicion and doubt. You will be expected to be aware there will always be different ways of interpreting some observation, different ways of arguing a case, different interests at play in any argument. In short, you'll be expected to recognise, and to demonstrate that you recognise, that truth is hard to come by.

Why is this lying bastard lying to me?

You will usually be marked more for your *approach* to facts than for your knowledge of them. You should understand how someone comes to a decision, judgement or conclusion, and understand that there will always be other kinds of decision, judgement or conclusion that could have been drawn from data that have been gathered. As the great biologist J. B. S. Haldane put it, this is really about 'the duty of doubt'. Or as René Descartes (1647/1996) said: 'Doubt is the origin of wisdom.'

Or as Jeremy Paxman put it, less elegantly though perhaps more straightforwardly: 'Why is this lying bastard lying to me?' Actually, Jeremy Paxman claims that he never said this. He says of his reported use of this phrase:

> Do I think that everybody you talk to is lying? No I do not. Only a moron would think that. But do I think you should approach any spokesman for a vested interest with a degree of scepticism, asking 'why are they saying this' and 'is it likely to be true'? Yes of course I do. (Wells, 2005)

What Jeremy Paxman says is just about the best way of summing up critical awareness, and it applies not just to politicians and spokespersons. It applies to anyone who reports a finding or expresses an opinion, because everyone reports those findings and expresses those opinions in the context of their own experience. And this experience may be more or less valid, more or less loaded, more or less interested (where 'interested' means 'having a stake in'). You have to put out of your mind the idea that all researchers, indeed all people who write anything anywhere, are fair-minded, neutral observers. There may be any one of a thousand reasons why someone takes a particular slant on a research question, so they will go out and look for data in a particular way or analyse those data in particular ways to suit their purposes and end up with the sort of findings that they expect. They may simply start off with an involvement or personal investment in a particular area, or they may be sponsored by a particular company or government department which may have an interest in a particular finding being made. So, start with Paxman's axiom of 'Why are they saying this?'

Critical awareness, however, is not just about spotting bias or personal involvement of this kind. It is about an awareness that knowledge is frail, not fixed, and that you should approach everything you read and hear with a questioning mind, always asking yourself whether something could have been done differently.

For example, in August 2007 the respected survey research organisation ICM undertook a poll for the *Daily Mail* on the topic of the royal family (ICM, 2007). One of the questions asked: 'As far as you are aware, do you think that Camilla is carrying out too many royal duties, too few royal duties or about the right number?' The responses were: too many, 10 per cent; about the right number, 55 per cent; too few, 12 per cent; refused to answer, 1 per cent; don't know, 22 per cent. With an uncritical eye, this all looks pretty straightforward: most people thought Camilla was carrying out about the right number of royal duties.

But how could you approach these findings more critically? You might first ask whether the political or commercial interests of the newspaper in question might have had an unspoken effect on the polling organisation. Both newspaper and polling organisation would of course strenuously deny any such connection (their reputation, after all, rests on their being honest purveyors of the truth) but there is a symbiotic connection between them and neither will want to alienate the other if it can be avoided. The polling organisation will know what kind of response the newspaper wants.

Then look at the categories that people have to fit their opinion into – too many, about right, too few, don't know. What about 'don't care'? Why isn't that there? This is a serious omission: the categories chosen imply that everyone has an opinion on the topic of Camilla's royal duties – even 'don't know' implies that respondents have carefully weighed up the alternatives and have come down on the side of 'insufficient evidence' or abstention.

The reality may be very different. It may be that the substantial proportion of people who are neutral or hostile to Camilla say 'about right' or 'don't know' simply to provide an answer. 'Too many', to a republican or a Camilla-hater, might be seen as too strong an opinion, or it might be taken to imply 'She should have fewer to give her more of a chance to settle into her role – she should be eased in gently.' No person who thinks that the UK would be better off without a royal family would have wanted to give this impression, because it might be taken to imply some kind of generous endorsement of Camilla or the royal family.

So, however respectable the source, be questioning, be critical. Also, be tentative about any conclusions that you yourself feel you are able to make: avoid phrases such as 'this proves' and 'this shows' and instead use words such as 'this indicates' or 'the evidence suggests' or 'points towards' or 'implies'. Try to use moderating phrases such as 'tends to' or 'one might conclude that' instead of bolder ones. Academic writing is an area where it pays to be tentative: no one will give you high marks for making unwarranted claims about your own research, or for gullibly believing the reports of others. Doubt everyone's findings, even your own. Remember again 'the duty of doubt'.

That duty of doubt, of *critical thinking*, has a long and illustrious intellectual tradition. Socrates started the ball rolling 2,500 years ago, He emphasised that you cannot rely on the views and declarations of those in authority. Authorities – that is to say, people in positions of power and influence – may sound impressive but may in fact be irrational and confused. He said that we should always subject any claim to knowledge to rigorous questioning as to its validity. His system of questioning has become known as the 'Socratic method'. All our beliefs, all our knowledge, should be subjected to such questioning, so that we can separate reasonable beliefs from those which lack rational grounding or adequate evidence.

> Demonstrating critical awareness, critical thinking, reflective thought is as important as anything else in your work. It's about being instinctively sceptical about claims to knowledge and truth.

Perhaps the most important philosopher of education of the twentieth century, John Dewey, put it this way:

Men *thought* the world was flat until Columbus *thought* it to be round. The earlier thought was a belief held because men had not the energy or the courage to question what those about them accepted and taught, especially as it was suggested and seemingly confirmed by obvious sensible facts. The thought of Columbus was a *reasoned conclusion*. It marked the close study into facts, of scrutiny and revision of evidence, of working out the implications of various hypotheses, and of comparing these theoretical results with one another and with known facts. Because Columbus did not accept unhesitatingly the current traditional theory, because he doubted and inquired, he arrived at his thought. Skeptical of what, from long habit, seemed most certain, and credulous of what seemed impossible, he went on thinking until he could produce evidence for both his confidence and his disbelief. Even if his conclusion had finally turned out wrong, it would have been a different sort of belief from those it antagonized, because it was reached by a different method. *Active, persistent, and careful consideration of any belief or supposed form of knowledge in the light of the grounds that support it, and the further conclusions to which it tends*, constitutes reflective thought. (Dewey, 1920/2004: 6, original emphasis)

You can employ such critical thinking about sources that you encounter – any piece of research or any scholarly argument – in your literature review by asking yourself these questions:

- Are there any vested interests at play?

- Might the writers' objectives in undertaking the research sway their reasoning in some way?

- Would different methods have yielded different findings?

- What sources of information are being drawn upon – is there evidence of balance, or are sources being 'cherry picked'?

- What is the quality of the data being drawn upon – is it from good primary sources?

- Is the writer's reasoning sound – so, if you were arguing with them, what would you say? (But ask yourself also how much validity your own criticisms would have, and whether you yourself are likely to be swayed by tradition, sentiment or vested interest.)

Click on 'Search': finding information

Finding information is one of the areas that has changed most dramatically over the past few years. Before the mid-1990s, researchers had to rely on printed articles in paper journals and on abstracts and indices catalogued on paper, microfiches and cards. They had to go to the library to find these resources. Then at the end of the 1990s came the widespread use of the Internet, and researchers came to depend on big library databases, using keywords to search them.

But then came Google. I'll say this very quietly so not too many of my colleagues hear (and I'm hoping you won't tell them), but when I am doing my own research I rarely use any other means of starting my searches. There is no point being snobbish about Google. It works. Not only does it work, but it works better than all of the posh library databases. Somehow (and it remains a total mystery to me how it does it) it seems to know what I am thinking and what I am wanting. It is free, reliable and quick. Not only is there Google, but there are also Google Scholar and Google Books. If you don't already know how they work, here's how …

Google

Unless you have been residing on Mars for the last ten years you will know how to use Google. Just a few hints:

- Type as much or as little as you wish into Google's search box. For example, if you are interested in whether the Head Start programme produces beneficial consequences for primary school children, you could either type in the whole sentence (that is to say, just like this: *Does the Head Start programme produce beneficial consequences for primary school children?*) and click on 'Search', or you can pick out the key words (*primary Head Start benefits*). Try it different ways and see what emerges.

- Google searches for the words in your search in any order; it doesn't keep the words you type in as phrases. If you want to keep the words in the same order – as phrases – then put them in double quotation marks. So, for example, if you wanted Google to search for the phrase 'Head Start' among the other words, you would type in *primary "Head Start" benefits*. It will then search just for the phrase 'head start', leaving out all other occurrences of 'head' and 'start'.

- If you want to search for something and you want the search to become narrower, so that it leaves out references to certain subjects or areas, you can put in a minus sign before a word or term that you wish to omit. So, if I wanted to find out about primary Head Start benefits, but I wanted only to look at children above reception age, I could type in *primary "Head Start" benefits–reception*. It's good to practise with many different ways of phrasing a Google query.

Accessing material from home

You need access to a computer and the Internet to use resources such as this, and if you don't have them you will have to rely on your university or college computer terminals. It is much better to have your own, though, so that you can work at home at odd times.

If you use your computer from home you'll probably have restricted access to the range of facilities that your university library provides. There are clever ways around this if you want to be bothered with them. Ask your librarian about setting up a 'proxy service' on your home computer, which in effect makes your home computer browser into a monitor for your university system.

Google Scholar

Google Scholar works in much the same way as Google, but it is more targeted at the kinds of reading material you will be looking for in university life. You can access it either from a link on the main page of Google (at the top, click on 'More' and then click on 'Even more' and then find the link to 'Scholar') or from http://scholar.google.com/. Once you have accessed the Google Scholar main page you use it in the same way that you would have used Google. That is to say, you can type in a question or a more targeted inquiry based on a particular article that you have already identified.

For example, try typing in the same question that I used above for testing Google: *Does the Head Start programme produce beneficial consequences for primary school children?* When you do this and click on 'Search' you will get many thousands of responses, as you do on ordinary Google. However, these responses, rather than being general, will only be to books and articles. The 'best' ones will usually be at the beginning, but you will also find good ones lower down (though they will become progressively less relevant as you proceed downwards).

Figure 3.3 shows the first 'answer' I got when I typed that question into Google Scholar. The figure shows the various elements of the Google Scholar 'answer' page. As with all forms of electronic resource, the key is to keep playing with it: click on links to see what happens.

I am reliably informed by librarians that Google Scholar will not pick up all relevant references because the information released to it is sometimes restricted by publishers. I guess this may change with time. However, do be aware that you will need also to use the subject-specific databases I mention later in this chapter. You can start off with a Google Scholar search and then supplement it with the targeted databases.

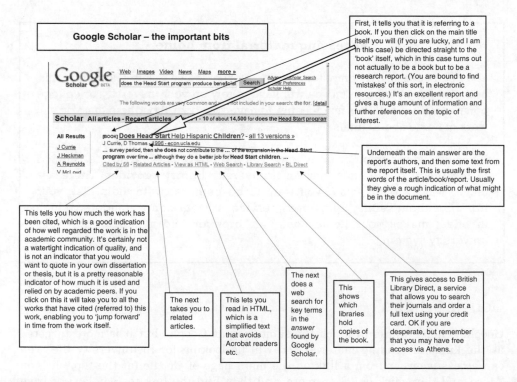

Figure 3.3   Google Scholar – the important bits

Google Book Search

As if Google Scholar weren't miraculous enough, there is also Google Book Search, which will find relevant books, point you to the page(s) relevant to your search inquiry, and even show you the page(s) themselves. From the Google main page, click on 'More' at the top, then click on 'Books'. Or you can type http://books.google.com directly into the address line. You will arrive at the familiar Google front page, but orientated to a book search.

Typing a general inquiry is less likely to be successful with Book Search than with a general Google search, so when I type *Does the Head Start programme produce beneficial consequences for primary school children?* as I did with Google and Google Scholar, it comes up with a dead end. So I have to open up the search by using fewer words. Remember that when you are asking Google just to look for books it is searching a far narrower range of resources, so keep your options open by reducing the number of words in your search.

Shibboleth and Athens

Some of the sources that you access using Google will be journal articles. You will emerge with a publisher's journal page which provides an abstract and an invitation to buy a full download of the article. Don't be tempted to buy it, because you will probably have access to the journal through your university library and something called 'Shibboleth' (this replaces 'Athens' which is still used in some places, particularly in America, and is used in NHS-based systems). If, on your introductory tour of the library, you haven't been told about Shibboleth or Athens, go along to one of the librarians and ask to be introduced to it. Don't be frightened to do this: in an information age this is what librarians are expected to do – to help you gain access to all kinds of information sources. It's what they get paid for. Remind them of this. (That's a joke, by the way.) Actually, most librarians I know don't conform to the frosty stereotype at all; they are friendly and helpful. And Shibboleth and Athens are easy to use: just be prepared to invest an hour or two playing with whichever system your library uses and seeing what it can do for you.

You will be given a username and a password for Shibboleth or Athens. Usually this is from your library or e-library access. Once you have entered your username and password details you will have access to an array of databases that carry the journal. Figure 3.4 shows the sort of page that emerges when you have done this. It is from my own university library, and yours will be similar.

Type in the name of the journal that came up from your Google inquiry and press 'Go' (or the equivalent in your library's system) and you will come up with a page like the one in Figure 3.5. My library's system here gives information about which databases hold access to the journal, and when I press 'Find It!' at the bottom of the page it gives me the choice of locating the article I want in one of several databases. It doesn't matter which one you use, but just check that the particular

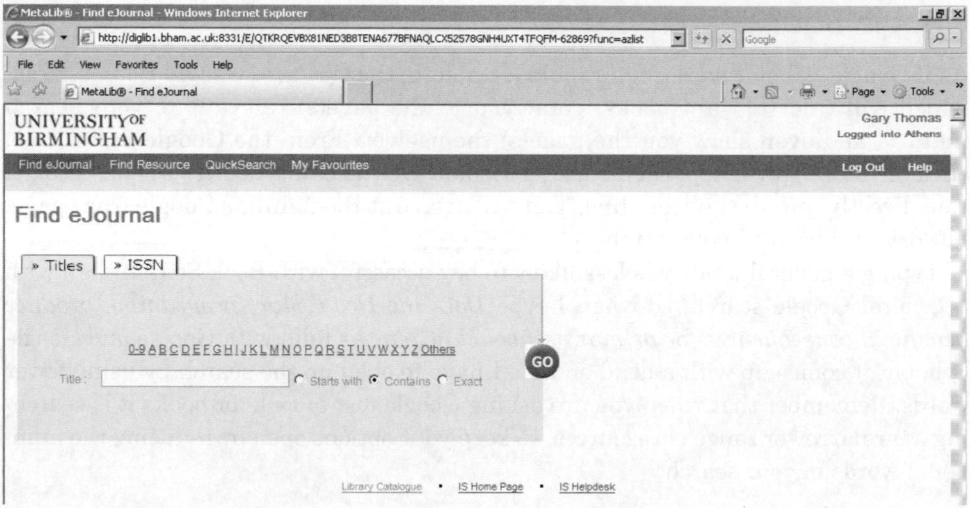

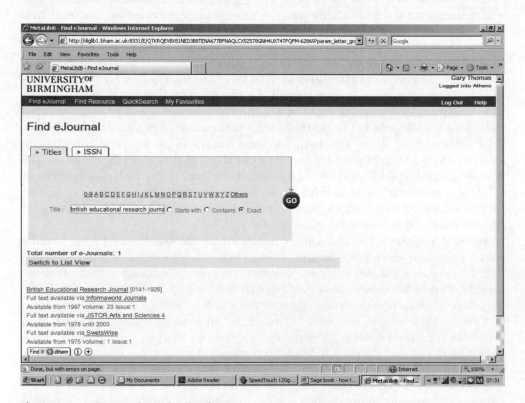

Figure 3.4 Searching for an e-Journal

Figure 3.5 Selecting from the databases

database (such as SwetsWise, which is the one I prefer) carries the journal for the year that you want.

Because every university's system is different, giving you more exact information from this point on in the process will not be of much use to you. So the next step is to make that library visit. Before you start asking librarians lots of questions, though, ask for the library's various leaflets and sheets on electronic access and try to make sense of them. Play around for a while on the computer and find what you can and can't do – what you can and can't access. Make a list of what will hopefully be more targeted questions and then go and see the librarian.

The Web of Knowledge

Your library should give you access to the Web of Knowledge (also called the Web of Science). Type http://portal.isiknowledge.com/portal.cgi. At the homepage click on 'Social Sciences Citation Index' and follow the instructions on what to do. You can search by topic or author or a range of other criteria. Web of Knowledge provides the gold standard on *citation* information.

Zetoc

> **Citation:** A reference to a particular piece of work, usually by using the Harvard system (e.g. 'Smith, 2002').

Your university library will provide a way for you to use to Zetoc, which gives access to the British Library's 20,000 journals and 16,000 conference proceedings published every year. Type http://zetoc.mimas.ac.uk/ and fill in your university's details. Zetoc is particularly useful as it includes an email alerting service to help you to keep up to date with relevant new articles and papers – in other words, Zetoc will automatically send you an email when a new article appears that 'hits the spot' as far as certain criteria that you specify are concerned. You could, for example, tell it to send you all articles by a certain author, or all articles with certain keywords in the title, or all articles in each new issue of a certain journal.

Zetoc will give you:

- a *search* facility, for citations of journal articles and conference proceedings – a bit like Google Scholar;

- the *alert* facility, to send you email alerts of new articles that may be of interest to you;

- *facilitated access* to full texts of articles and papers – Zetoc itself provides access to the table of contents rather than the full text. However, once you have found an article of interest, the full record page provides links to help you access the full text;

- *feeds* (also called RSS feeds – RSS stands for Really Simple Syndication), which help you to keep automatically up to date with what is happening in a journal. Click on 'Zetoc RSS' in Zetoc, and then click on the feed you want to see. In the example in Figure 3.6, I've clicked on the feed for the *American Educational Research*

Journal. When you subscribe to the feed, it will be added to your 'Favorites Center' in your browser, which will automatically check the website and download new content so you can see what is new since you last visited the feed.

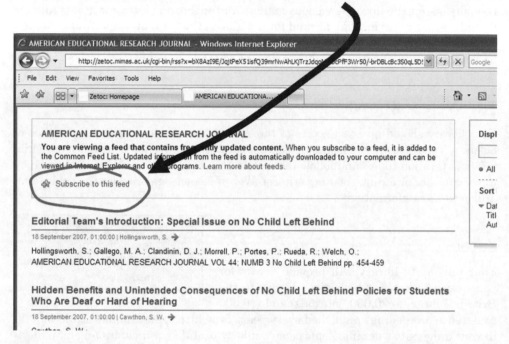

Figure 3.6 Example of a feed

Amazon

The Amazon website is a useful resource for seeking out related information about books (but not articles). Type www.amazon.co.uk (or www.amazon.com for the US version). It's not as good as Google Book Search but it does have some useful features such as 'Search Inside!'™ which allows you to look at the contents pages and to read the first chapter, the index and some other information about the book. Also, it gives you information about what other customers who have bought the book have also bought – surprisingly useful, since many will, inexplicably, seem to be on much the same train of thought as you. There will also be a publisher's synopsis of the book and, if you are lucky, some reasonably informative reviews (but often also some spectacularly uninformative ones). Clearly, this is not data disinterestedly given by Amazon out of the love of knowledge – they want to sell you books, so be wary.

Something that the Amazon website is particularly useful for is when you are compiling your reference list. Unless you are absolutely perfect, you will have lost certain references, or you will have somehow missed off a key bit of the reference when making your notes. The Amazon website has co-authors, the publisher, the date of publication and dates of various editions, and this is often all you need to enable you to plug the holes.

EThOS

EThOS is the British Library's digital repository of all doctoral theses completed at UK institutions. Such work can provide invaluable help on precisely targeted subjects, though I should re-state the point I made earlier – don't use such work as a model for your own, since it is of highly variable quality.

Inter-library loan

I've been at pains to point out that you should be very wary about clicking on any link that asks you to part with money for a download of the article. This is partly because there is a very good chance that you will be able to access the article or book completely free through your university Shibboleth or Athens account. Or you will be able to see enough of it to gain a sufficient impression of what it is about. If the worst comes to the worst and you decide that you simply must have a copy of the article and you are not able to access it by one of the means already explained here, you can get the article via inter-library loan, either electronically or as a photocopy. Ask your librarian about this. There will probably be a charge, but it won't be nearly as much as it would be from a publisher's website.

Specific subject databases

Aside from the generic databases I have just mentioned, there are also specific databases for particular subjects.

ERIC

ERIC stands for the *Education Resources Information Center*, which is an online digital library of education research and other information. (I'm not actually sure how an 'online digital library' is different from a database, but never mind, I'll give it its Sunday-best name since that's what its publishers call it.) ERIC is paid for by the United States Department of Education, and, as you would guess given these credentials, it is a pretty hefty piece of kit. It provides access to over 1 million records, including the 'grey literature' of, for example, fact sheets, information briefs, research syntheses, conference papers and policy reports. The latter are difficult to get hold of from any other source, and ERIC is worth consulting for this alone. It is updated continuously. With a move to open-access publishing of scientific findings now, many of the records are available in full text.

To search on ERIC, Google 'ERIC basic search', and try their Thesaurus for key terms that will take you to the area in which you are interested. Also try 'My

ERIC', which enables you to join a community of people interested in the same subject as you, lets you save searches, get alerts and even submit your own material for inclusion in the database.

BEI

The BEI is the British Education Index, which is the British equivalent of ERIC. It is rather smaller than ERIC, with, at the time of writing, 175,000 references to journal articles. The database grows by over 8,000 records per year. One particularly interesting feature of the BEI is the access it gives to Education-*line*, which offers a collection of over 6,000 full-length texts, most of them conference papers.

PubMed

If you work in healthcare, including medicine, you will almost certainly want access to PubMed, which is the repository for biomedical literature. It is truly enormous, containing 2 million citations for biomedical literature from life science journals and online books.

CINAHL

Even more enormous, and for students of nursing, CINAHL offers, as the producers put it, 'the world's most comprehensive nursing & allied health research database'. It indexes more than 5,000 journals, with full text for more than 700. The topics included cover nursing, biomedicine, health sciences librarianship, alternative/complementary medicine, consumer health and 17 allied health disciplines. It also gives access to healthcare books, nursing dissertations, conference proceedings, educational software, audiovisuals and book chapters.

PsycINFO

Primarily for psychologists, PsycINFO is run by the American Psychological Association and contains 3 million records in the behavioural sciences and mental health. It ranges over the literature in psychology and allied disciplines such as education, linguistics, medicine, nursing, pharmacology, physiology, psychiatry and sociology.

Other databases

There are dozens of other subject-specific databases. To review these to see which would be useful for you, go to your appropriate library webpage. Most university libraries nowadays will provide a page which is a bit like Google, which lets you search the vast expanse of the whole library. My library's (open to everyone) is at http://findit.bham.ac.uk/. From here, you go to the top right of the page and click on 'Find Databases', then click on 'Search by Subject', then choose a category, such as 'Healthcare' and then a subcategory (if you wish), such as nursing, and the webpage will list all relevant subject-specific databases.

It's worth finishing this section on the world of subject-specific databases, gateways and other online resources by saying that some of them offer remarkable resources, while others don't seem to last very long. In fact, I wonder how some of them last even as long as they do, given the power of the competition in big search engines such as Google Scholar. How should you judge which to look into? I think that you should look to see if these resources offer some value-added over Google, such as the ability to connect with other like-minded people or the facility to export citations or help you to organise and format those that you export. These latter features can be really useful.

Reference managers

One of the advantages of using databases such as ERIC, PubMed and Web of Science is that they enable you to export citations directly into reference management programs such as *EndNote*, *Reference Manager* or *ProCite*. Your university library will have a webpage which explains how to use these. The reference management software will organise all of your references for you and even format them appropriately. For undergraduates, I think that probably the easiest to use is a web-based system called *RefWorks*, to which you will have free access if your university subscribes. (If it doesn't, you have to pay, but 1,200 universities across the world do subscribe so there's a fair chance yours will.) It enables you to gather, manage, store and share all types of information, as well as generate citations and bibliographies. Once you have been a member, you stay a member, even when you leave your university.

Similar to RefWorks are WorldCat, which finds books and articles in the collections of 10,000 libraries worldwide and lets you export the citations that you find into your own bibliography or references list, and CiteULike, which offers reference to 6.5 million articles and enables you to receive automated article recommendations and to share references with your fellow students.

Hints on searching – separating the wheat from the chaff

Two common problems students come up with on doing a literature review are (1) that they can find no information, and (2) that there is just too much information.

Let's look at the first one: you can find absolutely no information at all on your topic of interest. The thing is, it is most unlikely to be the case in reality that there is no information to find on your topic, so if you are finding nothing in your various searches you should examine where you may be going wrong. It may be the case that you are not using enough search facilities, or, more likely, that you are making your search too narrow. You are pinpointing your search terms too finely, or throwing away related information that is not on the precise subject of your interest, but is connected and therefore useful. Remember that your literature review ultimately will not be on the exact topic of your research, but rather it will be on the more general subject *surrounding* your research. So, if you wanted to look, for example, at how head teachers cope with difficult people and you are coming up with nothing, it may be that you are searching too specifically. Your searches may need to concentrate on something broader, such as teacher stress, and you may wish to think about what 'difficult people' means. This will in turn suggest that you think about the 'people' with whom head teachers come into contact: there are the other teachers in the school, other head teachers in the area, parents, pupils, teaching assistants, administrators, support staff, etc. Were you thinking of all of these when you posed your question, or just certain categories? So, think about the broader ways that your question may be framed. Think about alternative search terms.

You'll see in Figure 3.7 that the original question about how head teachers cope with difficult people has been reformulated into a range of terms that you might not have thought of originally, and you might, for example, ask why 'drugs' and 'suicide' are included as alternatives to 'coping'. The key is to try to think like a search engine. The search engine is sorting through words and phrases in an unimaginably large set of websites, a tiny fraction of which will contain, in some sense or other, 'stories' about head teachers and difficult people. But these 'stories' are hardly likely to be framed in these exact terms. They are more likely to contain words that are associated with the words you have identified. What are difficult people likely to do to a head teacher? To cause stress. What does stress lead to? Possibly drinking excess alcohol, taking drugs or even suicide. These may not be the coping strategies you were thinking of, but they will lead into stories that address the topic, perhaps comparing these routes out of stress with more positive

> Think like a search engine. Find alternative ways of formulating ideas connected to your research question.

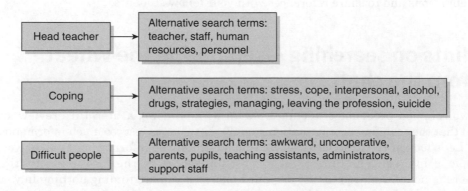

Figure 3.7   Turning your question into alternative search terms

ones. So the key is, if you don't at first succeed, try thinking like the search engine and formulating your question in a number of different ways using a range of related words.

And remember that your literature review is a general contextualisation. So stress in *teachers* as a *general* group is likely to be of relevance when you are thinking about stress in *head* teachers. Don't limit your search by a very precise word when you may find some very interesting information that relates to broader issues.

Now the second one: you are swamped with information on the topic. Suppose you are interested in the attainment of black boys and you enter *black boys attainment*. The search emerges with three quarters of a million 'answers'. If you now put in a term that is related to your interests – say *14–19* – it will reduce the number dramatically. Or you can put in a name of a key academic or a key commentator to delimit the search. Ask your tutor for key names. For example, if I put in the name of someone who I know is an expert here – *"Gus John"* – (in double quote marks because I want Google to find *only* references to Gus John, not to all the Johns and all the Guses in the world), it reduces the three quarters of a million to 155.

So, the key is to imagine that in your literature review the process is like sieving: with too coarse a mesh you let through too much; with too fine a mesh you don't get enough. Or imagine that you are trying to separate the wheat from the chaff. If you blow too hard you get rid of the wheat as well as the chaff. If you don't blow hard enough you don't get rid of the chaff.

Understanding how sources are cited: the Harvard referencing system

You need to understand the Harvard referencing system for two reasons. First, when you are reading, you need to understand the way that sources are referenced by authors in books and journal articles. Second, when you are writing, you need to know how to provide references yourself when you write up your literature review – in other words, how to give the full details of where others can find the work when you refer to a book or article. There are various ways in which referencing can be done, but the overwhelmingly preferred method in the social sciences is the Harvard system. (It has several variants, and you will find that the Harvard system may be called one of these variants, notably 'APA', or American Psychological Association. Don't worry too much about the variations unless you want to submit something for publication: just go for bog-standard Harvard.)

This is how it works. You find a source – let's say an article written by Jane Brown. If you then want to refer to the article in the literature review of your project you do so by using the author's surname, followed by the year of the publication in brackets – for example, by saying 'In a large study, Brown (2004) discovered that little bits of fluff accumulate in people's pockets.' You will then give the full details of Brown's publication in a list headed 'References' at the end of your report (not 'Bibliography', incidentally, which has the meaning of 'here are some interesting books that are related to my thesis' – by contrast, 'References' applies only to the works you have actually referred to in your text). We'll come on to how to compile the list in a moment, but first let's look at how you make reference to various kinds of sources in the text, since these will take a variety of forms.

How you make reference *in the text*:

- For a single author of a book or a journal article, use the author's name followed by the date of the publication in brackets, e.g. 'Sweedlepipe (2005) found that the fluff referred to by Brown (2004) is composed mainly of cotton fibre and dead skin.'

- Where a work is by two authors, use both authors' names followed by the date in brackets: 'Sweedlepipe and Sikes (2007), in later work, showed that the ratio of cotton fibre to dead skin (by weight) is between 3:1 and 5:1.'

- For more authors, use the first author's name, followed just by 'et al.' (which means 'and others'), e.g. 'Sweedlepipe et al. (2008) illustrated the mechanism by which cotton fibre bonds to dead skin.'

- If you actually quote from the author, you must give the page number from which the quotation comes, putting the page number after a colon after the publication date: 'Sweedlepipe (2005: 134) sums up the importance of the topic this way: "The precise mechanism involved in the accumulation of fluff in the pockets is one of the greatest mysteries remaining for science to solve."'

- In the unlikely case of an author having two outputs in 2005 that you are referencing in the text, this is indicated by 'a', 'b', 'c', etc., after the date: 'Sikes (2005a) found that trouser pockets of male students contained significantly more fluff than those of female students, and in later work (2005b) hypothesised that the lower amounts of fluff in female pockets were due to a higher frequency of personal hygiene measures (principally by washing and clothes laundering) among females.'

- A book that has been republished long after the original publication may be cited with the author's name as usual, but followed by both the first publication and republication dates, e.g. Ryle (1949/1990).

Then, at the end of your dissertation, you will have a *reference section*, headed 'References', which contains the full details of all the material to which you have referred. This is how you set out your 'References' section:

- For a book: name(s) and initial(s) of author(s) followed by year in brackets, followed by book title in italics, followed by place of publication and publisher. For example:

Sweedlepipe, P. (2005) *The Fluff in People's Pockets*. London: SAGE.

- For a journal article: name and initial(s) of author(s) followed by year in brackets, followed by article title, followed by name of journal in italics, followed by volume number, issue number and page numbers. For example:

Sweedlepipe, P. and Sikes, B. (2007) Ratios of cotton fibres to exfoliated skin in trouser pockets of US males. *International Journal of Fluff and Allied Detritus*, 31, 1, 252–7.

- For a downloadable Internet source: name and initial(s) of author(s) followed by year in brackets, followed by article title, followed by the words 'Available at' and the Internet source, followed by the date you accessed it. For example:

Wells, M. (2005) Paxman answers the questions. *Guardian Unlimited*. Availableat:http://politics.guardian.co.uk/media/2005/jan/31/mondaymediasection. politicsandthemedia (accessed 16 April 2013).

When formatting the reference list, it looks good if each reference has a hanging indent – in other words, the first line is formatted to the left, as normal, and the subsequent lines are indented. You can produce the hanging indent in Word by putting the cursor anywhere in the reference and pressing 'Ctrl+T'. Or do the whole lot together by selecting all the references (with your mouse, left-click at the beginning and drag down to the end) and then pressing 'Ctrl+T'.

The list should be in alphabetical order. To alphabetise a list automatically in Word (pre-2007), select the whole list with your mouse, then click on 'Table', then click on 'Sort', and click on 'OK'. In Word 2007 (and after) look for the 'Sort' button. You will find this under the 'Home' tab, in the 'Paragraph' group. The list will miraculously appear in order. (If it doesn't, the settings on your copy of Word may have been changed and you will need to look at the particular instructions under 'Sort' more carefully.)

As I mentioned in relation to subject-specific databases, there are now several software systems for organising your references automatically, such as EndNote, Reference Manager and RefWorks, and your library will almost certainly offer support in using these through leaflets, courses and email query and will provide a weblink on this and related issues. My own library's (open to everybody), which also offers detailed advice on the use of the Harvard method, is at www.i-cite.bham.ac.uk/. This excellent website provides all you need to know and more. Click on 'How to reference correctly' and on the next page click 'Harvard (author-date)'. It's most likely that you will be asked by your tutors to use Harvard referencing, but it may be the case in some subjects that you will be asked to use Numbering (Vancouver) or Footnotes or OSCOLA (for law students). The website also gives guidance on all of these.

Taking notes and quotes

There used to be a time when people had to take careful notes of every source they consulted on small cards that would be filed alphabetically. (For people like me, who suffer from a mild variant of Asperger's syndrome, this was enormously satisfying.) Researchers had to be meticulous about everything that they did, punctiliously keeping records of references – because if you lost one or forgot to record it, it would take hours or even days to track it down again. Things aren't like that any more: you can now find a lost reference on the Internet in seconds. And note-taking is different too: you can now be a lot more creative and idiosyncratic in the way that you keep notes on your word-processor. The problem with the old card index file systems was that they almost encouraged you to think of the literature review as a collection of names and notes. Now, though, if you take notes more fluidly – as I suggest in the next section – you can add observations, make connections and link one source with another through the notes that you take as you are reading.

A notes file in Word

The software packages I have just mentioned (EndNote, etc.) seem to work for some people. However, I find a simpler system is just to paste everything that would conceivably be of interest into a Word file which I can then search for the keywords that I want. When I say 'keywords' I don't mean anything very technical. I just mean that I use Word's search facility (Ctrl+F) to look for a word or part of a word that will find the topic I am looking for. So, for example, if I were interested in finding anything mentioning *science* or *scientists* I would ask the program to find 'scie'.

As I am reading I copy quotations (and, importantly, the references from which they come) willy-nilly into the file. I always make a point of recording the reference as exactly as possible, and then the notes as I see fit at the time. I make it clear with the use of quotation marks which are my own words and which are the author's. This may not have the satisfying tidiness of the old card index, but the question arises how far that alphabetical imperative is still necessary. When you can now simply find what you need to find in a file, why does it need to be in alphabetical order? You simply need to type a search word or phrase into the 'Find' box and the machine will do the rest. When you can easily fillet and sort a list alphabetically (see p. 85), why bother putting them in alphabetical order at the outset?

Many of the notes I take are copied directly from the Internet by cutting and pasting. This is particularly useful in copying reference details. However, you should always be very clear in your recording which are the author's words and which are your own. Whenever you quote someone else's words you must always *make full and clear attribution to the author in question.*

Plagiarism

Occasionally students are tempted to try to pass off the work and the words of others as their own. Your university will almost certainly have a policy on plagiarism, how it is defined, why you should not do it, how you can avoid it and the penalties for doing it. My own university defines plagiarism as:

the submission for formal assessment of an assignment that incorporates, without proper citation or acknowledgement by means of an accepted referencing standard, the intellectual property or work of a third party.

Its policy, which is fairly typical of all, is given at https://intranet.birmingham. ac.uk/as/studentservices/conduct/misconduct/plagiarism/index.aspx.

Having had the sense to read my book, you are not of course the sort of person who plagiarises. However, just speaking generally for a moment, plagiarism is a pity for a number of reasons.

- First, it is against the spirit of the thing: the aim is to learn, develop and improve – not just to get a certificate. So why pretend?

- Second, there is a real risk of being caught, as the likelihood of being found out is increasing as plagiarism software improves, and the penalties at any university are serious for those who are found plagiarising. Indeed, most universities are now demanding that all work must pass through plagiarism software such as *Turnitin* at submission and students may be deducted marks, made to resubmit or even failed if they are deemed to have plagiarised.

- Third, there is no penalty for drawing from others or using their ideas and words, as long as these are acknowledged. In fact, your marker will be pleased to see evidence of wide reading and the intelligent synthesis of this.

Although I have said that a marker will be pleased to see evidence of wide reading in quotations, you should avoid overdoing quotations. Generally, one short quotation per page would be the maximum I would want to see, with perhaps the occasional extended quotation. The aim in a literature review is to outline and demonstrate interconnections, not to present a list of other people's verbatim words. The key is analysis and synthesis, and quotations do not really play a role in either, unless you are using them to provide an excellent illustration of a point that an authority is making.

Overview

Your literature review is not an add-on: it should be a major contributor to the development of your project. It should help you to shape your questions by enabling you to find out what has already been done. The literature exists in many shapes and forms and you should be discriminating in what you choose to include – even seemingly unimpeachable sources can be wrong. This is where critical awareness begins: show that you understand that there is always room for interpretation in the reading of any piece of work. Interpret and understand what others have done, and weave their contributions into a narrative. The literature review should be a narrative – a story – not a list.

Checklist   ✔

Have you ...

	Notes	
1 ... used the main databases in your field of applied social science to locate relevant literature?		☐
2 ... secured some relevant and high-quality sources from which to draw?	What are the main themes, agreements and disagreements? Write them down here	☐
3 ... mapped out the main issues?		☐
4 ... drawn a storyboard?	What are 'stories' that emerge? Which will you follow?	☐
5 ... understood how the Harvard referencing system works?		☐

Further reading

Arksey, H. and O'Malley, L. (2005) Scoping studies: towards a methodological frame-work. *International Journal of Social Research Methodology*, 8 (1), 19–32. Available at: http://eprints.whiterose.ac.uk/1618/1/Scopingstudies.pdf.
Defines, describes and discusses the use of detailed literature reviews, which are sometimes called 'scoping studies'.

Campbell Collaboration http://www.campbellcollaboration.org/.
This contains systematic reviews in education, crime and justice, and social welfare. Useful not just for the analysis and synthesis of studies, but also for examples of the way that evidence is balanced.

Cochrane Collaboration http://www.cochrane.org/.
This is a library of systematic reviews in healthcare.

Evidence for Policy and Practice Information and Co-ordinating Centre (EPPI-Centre) http://eppi.ioe.ac.uk/cms/.
This is similar to Campbell, but tends to focus more on education.

Fink, A. (2005) *Conducting Research Literature Reviews: From the Internet to Paper*. London: SAGE.
Systematic, with good examples on searching in health, education and business domains. Not just the process, but also good on evaluating the articles you select to review.

Hart, C. (1998) *Doing a Literature Review: Releasing the Social Science Research Imagination*. London: SAGE.
This detailed book goes far beyond the mechanics of the literature review to discuss the organisation of ideas, the development of argument and the liberation of what the author calls 'the research imagination'. Oriented toward the postgraduate rather than the undergraduate.

Ridley, D. (2008) *The Literature Review: A Step-by-Step Guide for Students*. London: SAGE.

Robinson, F.P. (1970) *Effective Study* (4th edn). New York: Harper & Row.
Good for advice on speed reading.

Williams, K. and Carroll, J. (2009) *Referencing and Understanding Plagiarism*. London: Palgrave.
A useful little book that tells you all you need to know about the subjects of the title.

4

DECIDE ON YOUR QUESTION – AGAIN

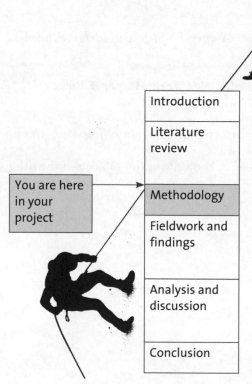

| Introduction |
| Literature review |
| Methodology |
| Fieldwork and findings |
| Analysis and discussion |
| Conclusion |

You are here in your project

The literature review will have helped you to sharpen your research question. Your refined question enables you to proceed confidently. This chapter considers:

- how, in the light of your literature search in Chapter 3, does your question – your prima facie question – from Chapter 1 look now?

  o Have you in fact found out that many other people have already done what you were planning to do?

  o Is the question more complicated than you had thought?

  o Will you be able to get hold of the information you need?

- refining your original questions and ideas, making sure that the new, refined questions are not too broad, not too difficult, in the context of your literature search;

- moving from your storyboard to a more definite storyline – this will form the clear plan for your research;

- how to use the process of refining your question to state a final research question;

- thinking about how you will develop theory.

Seeing the wood for the trees

When you came up with your first question after Chapter 1, it was from an idea in your head. It probably won't have been informed by much more than a feeling or an observation, or perhaps by a spark of inspiration that came from a lecture or an article in a newspaper. Because this was a question that came from this sort of 'top of the head' idea it is sometimes called a *prima facie* question, as I discussed in Chapter 1. It's now time to transform this prima facie question into a more refined, targeted question – a better question or set of questions. This new question (or questions) will be your *final* question(s).

The literature review will have given you avenues to follow, pockets of similar ideas from different authors or clashing ideas from others. If you have done it right you may be feeling at the end of your literature review more confused than you were when you started out, because you will have uncovered lots of new information and will have been set running on many new leads. Don't despair: this is normal. In fact, it *should* happen. These disparate ideas will form the basis both for a reorganisation of your literature review, for new ideas about how the project can proceed and for a reworking of your question.

You have to remember that the literature review is not simply a justification for your question. It is much more than this. It is a way of helping you to see your question from a distance – seeing the wood for the trees – and shaping it to something more meaningful. *Without* it, it's as if you are wearing blinkers, and walking straight down the first road you see. *With* the literature review, you can say, 'Shall I go this way or that way?'

So now you should be prepared to change your first question. Now that you have found what others have done you will very probably see your research question in a quite different light. I've mentioned that your literature review will give you a lot of information that will start you off on different lines of thinking. But there are also other reasons for rethinking your question: you may find out, for example, that someone has already done what you wanted to do – they have found the answer already. You may find that the research that has been undertaken in a certain area surrounds a particular controversy, and you may feel that you want to contribute to one aspect or another of the debate, rather than pursuing your original question. You may discover a particular gap in the literature that you feel needs filling. You will have got a feel of the area, where the most important lines of inquiry are and which are most interesting to you.

Perhaps even more importantly, the literature review will enable you to highlight areas that are irrelevant or too difficult to research ethically or in terms of getting access to relevant information. Remember one of the issues you had to face at the outset: 'Is it doable?'

So the first thing to do in reviewing your literature review is to go back to your storyboard (Figure 3.1 p. 65). Let's think about that now.

> Your literature review has allowed you to refine your initial questions. Now they can be sharper. Ask yourself what your purposes are.

From storyboard to storyline

The first thing that your storyboard will have done is to show you how broad the initial question could be. It will have shown you the directions that your research could take. More importantly, it will show you which of these directions you can now eliminate for any of a variety of reasons.

Figure 4.1 shows the redrawn storyboard shown in Figure 3.1 You'll see that I have taken out most of the brainstorming ideas from the bottom of the original storyboard and I have focused on the ideas from the top of the storyboard which related to the idea of stress. So the original question, namely 'How do headteachers cope with difficult people?', is already becoming more focused. Stress seems to be a key idea, and in examining it I will have looked at how stress is dealt with by people and the coping strategies that they adopt to manage it. In doing this I will have examined the concept of coping strategies generally, and I will have considered that psychologists claim that there are avoidant, active and passive coping strategies. All of this will have been discussed in my literature review.

On the basis of this literature review I now know a lot more about difficult people, who they are assumed to be, how they are defined by the individual who finds them difficult and what that individual does about dealing with them. Does that individual avoid the problem and turn to drink (the top right-hand side of the storyboard)? Or do they do something constructive and seek support (the top left-hand side)? And if they seek support, where do they get the support from?

Here we have the bones of a much more *targeted* project. From a fairly unspecific question about head teachers and difficult people we have something that travels along a clearly defined path. You have begun to get a more precise question about difficult people and how they may be described and defined, and you have the beginnings of a thesis about the connection of 'difficulty' with stress, and coping strategies around this. You understand that the coping strategies can be of various kinds.

The original topic has, then, developed many branches and you will have explored many of these in the literature review. The first thing you need to do now is to ask yourself which you want to pursue. This will be determined principally by your interest. You may not be attracted by certain lines of inquiry because they lead you along avenues that have no interest for you. On the storyboard it may be the case that you have no interest in the connections that head teachers have with the local authority. If, like me, you begin to feel yourself nodding off at the mere mention of local authorities then this is probably not a good line to pursue. It helps to be interested in the subject that you are researching.

Now you can also be asking yourself questions about 'doability'. If you have been led in your thinking towards the issue of coping strategies, will you actually be able to get information from head teachers about some of the avoidance phenomena that are flagged up in the storyboard? For instance, are head teachers likely to tell you honestly that they have turned to drink? The short answer is 'no', unless you are in a very particular position – perhaps as a headteacher yourself with the kinds of relationships with colleagues that would enable you to ask them about this kind

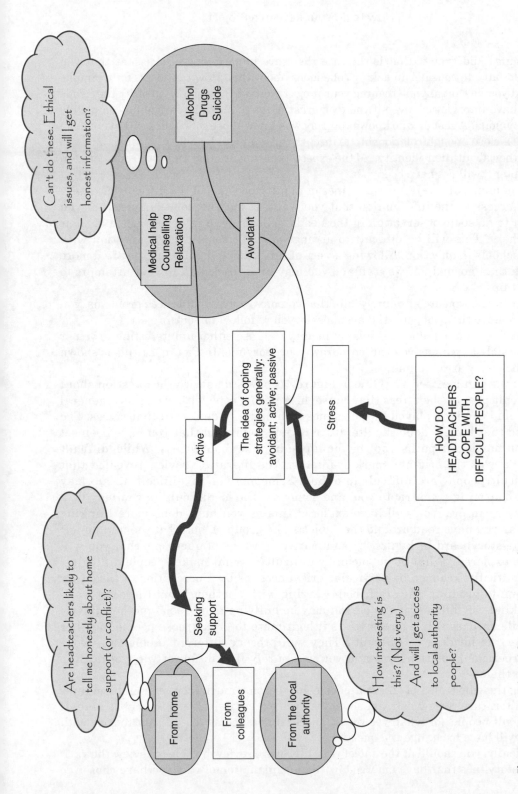

Figure 4.1 Storyboard from Figure 3.1 redrawn

of thing. And even if that is the case there are important ethical issues that you would have to consider in asking colleagues about this. How confident, for example, could you be that anyone reading your project would not be able to identify the heads you have interviewed, even if you took great pains to make any write-up completely anonymous? A reader who knows you may well know those colleagues with whom you have a close enough relationship to discuss this and will be able to put two and two together about their identity. So the expectations about anonymity we considered in Chapter 2 will not have been met.

You might also reject certain lines of inquiry because of the difficulties of getting access to the information that you want. It may be, for example, that you wish to do some observation in the heads' schools or to interview some of their teachers. This will be difficult to arrange without some prior connection with the schools in question. Allowing access of this kind will entail a great deal more work than normal for the staff and you may hit a brick wall in your attempts to set it up.

So, unless you are absolutely sure that you have ways round these problems, you can remove them as potential avenues for you to follow in your project.

Having eliminated all the lines of inquiry that are either uninteresting to you or impossible to pursue, you can now draw your storyline. In Figure 4.1 this is shown by the heavy arrowed line.

So the summarised storyline in Figure 4.1 now starts with the question about difficult people, the stress they cause, how people cope with stress as a general rule and the part played by colleagues in helping to deal with that stress. I've noted that having done the literature review you'll find that you have been set off on particular paths and the main one here is about stress. While 'difficult people' was the original spark of interest, the literature review revealed that 'difficult people' are difficult to define. Someone who is 'difficult' to me may be a charming eccentric to you, and someone who is 'difficult' to you may be a pussycat to me. You will have explored this as you have done more thinking and as you have read around the subject. The group of 'notes' at the middle-left of the storyboard in Figure 3.1 summarises a range of questions that you will have explored: 'What do we mean by difficult?', 'What makes people difficult?', 'Is "difficulty" caused by particular grievances, or by a perception of threat, or by one in-group in the staff room warring with another?' And there are various kinds of 'difficulty': one person may be bullying and brash; another quietly hostile or 'passively aggressive'. Is it legitimate to group those people together under the heading of 'difficult'? They will present different problems in your interpersonal relationships and you will surely find different ways of dealing with them.

So, the whole idea of 'difficult people' has become much more of a problem after the literature review and you should be brave enough to grasp the nettle here. If 'difficult people' (or whatever your subject is) now seems too difficult to cope with you will have to change the question.

Ideally, you should at the end of your literature review be able to review the various storylines that have emerged, with an explanation of why you have chosen to take the route that you have. Your refined question will, in this example, be something like:

> 'How do head teachers use support from colleagues in coping with stress arising from interpersonal relations?'

This has grown out of 'How do head teachers cope with difficult people?'

There are a number of points to remember in this development, principally that the new question

- is more specific on the issue of 'coping', specifying a method of coping, namely using support from colleagues;

- drops the mention of 'difficult people' which is impossible to define adequately – instead, it brings in the idea of interpersonal relations;

- brings in the concept of stress, noting implicitly that 'coping' is about dealing with a situation that is difficult to resolve – we tend to see such difficulties as stressful.

Reassessing your original question

- What has your literature review told you about the main issues in the area? Do you want to follow one of these instead of your original focus?

- Was your original idea 'doable' – would there have been ethical or practical problems?

- Can you sharpen your focus and/or redefine your terms to state your new research question more precisely?

You should still be aware with this question, though, that it is appropriate only for a certain kind of project, or, rather, a certain kind of researcher. To research it you will need access to head teachers who are willing to talk to you about personal issues, and this is most unlikely to be the case if you do not know the individuals personally, either as a close colleague or as a personal friend or family member. The more head teachers you want to talk to, the more difficult the issue becomes, so do be aware of the access issue right at the start.

Your final question

So now, after all of this deliberation, at the end of your literature review – after all of your thinking and rethinking – it is time to rewrite your original, prima facie question. Given that you have thought carefully about how your original question fits in with all of the other work in the area, you can sharpen your focus and even structure your new question so that it suggests a particular kind of research design.

We have seen how 'How do head teachers cope with difficult people?' grew into 'How do head teachers use support from colleagues in coping with stress arising from interpersonal relations?' Let's imagine how some other prima facie questions might morph into different kinds of more targeted questions: Figure 4.2 shows some prima facie questions sharpened into final questions.

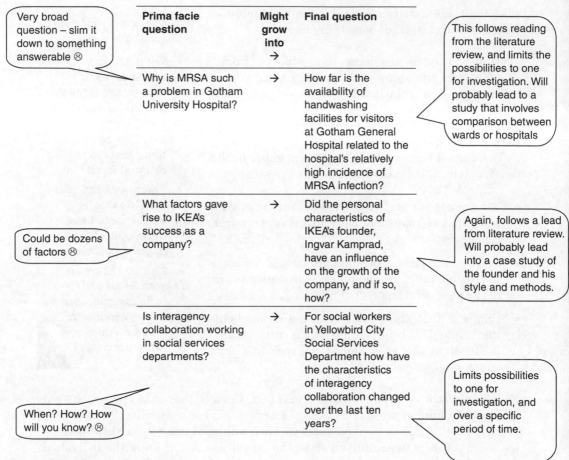

Figure 4.2 Final questions

Your final question can come at the end of your literature review chapter, with a special subheading such as 'Revised research question(s) in the context of the literature review'. Always explain things fully for your reader. So, note that you began with question X, but say that with the benefit of the contextual information you have gathered (and give a little summary) you have revised this into a more targeted question which more precisely addresses the issues in the area. Say that the work is further focused on the specific area in which you work (or the institution of your placement, or whatever).

Theory

During and after the literature review you will also have a chance to think about **theory**. I'll discuss the various meanings of theory in a moment, but in essence 'theory' is about the ability to get above your reading and your findings to see a shape in them – to devise, metaphorically, some sort of organising template through which you can look at your reading and findings. It's about seeing the interconnections and trying to understand how and why they exist. It's about going beyond mere description to explanation.

Theory is a key issue in educational and social research and many millions of words have been spent discussing its meaning. I personally spent the first twenty years of my academic life trying to work out what 'theory' was supposed to mean in social research and came up with some not very clear conclusions. If you are interested in my deliberations you can read my book *Education and Theory: Strangers in Paradigms* (Thomas, 2007). So, don't feel alone if theory perplexes you.

One thing is clear: everyone in academic life thinks theory – or at least the thinking that surrounds it – is vitally important, and 'He/she hasn't located his/her work in theory' is one of the most common reasons for a research project being marked down. So I'll get down from my hobbyhorse for a moment to explain to you why theory is thought to be important.

Five main meanings of theory

The first thing to be aware of when people talk about theory in the social sciences is that there is no *one* meaning. People mean different things when they talk about it. Perhaps the clearest statement that can be made is that it refers to thinking, abstraction and generalising. Having said this, the thinking, abstraction and generalising are different in different kinds of inquiry.

Theory can mean …	*A generalising or explanatory model.* Theory tries to distil a range of specific findings or observations into general propositions that explain these findings.
Theory can mean …	*The 'thinking side' of practice.* Especially in the applied side of the social sciences (such as teaching and social work), theory or 'theorising' means thinking and reflecting on practice. It is sometimes called 'reflective practice'. It has also been called 'personal theory' or 'practical theory'. When people talk about this 'personal theory' they mean conjectures, personal thoughts and insights that help practitioners to make sense of the practical world. Many people suggest that in practical fields (such as teaching, nursing or social work) the enhancement of this practical theorisation, coming from our own experience, is what professional development should ultimately be about. The idea is not new: the Greeks had words for this kind of practical theory: *phronesis* and *techne*.

(Continued)

(Continued)

Theory can mean …	*A developing body of explanation.* Here theory means the broadening bodies of knowledge developing in particular fields. A body of knowledge may be wide (e.g. 'management theory' or 'learning theory'), or tight, based around a particular set of ideas (e.g. 'Piagetian theory').
Theory can mean …	*Scientific theory.* Theory here is modelled on the idea of theory in the natural sciences. It may ultimately exist in the form of ideas formally expressed in a series of statements. With these statements you are able to predict and explain. As social science progresses it seems less hopeful of discovering this kind of theory.
Theory can mean …	*Grand Theory.* 'Grand Theory' is a term used mockingly by the great sociologist C. Wright Mills (1959/1970) to describe social scientists' expectation that their disciplines should attempt to build a systematic theory of 'the nature of man and society' (p. 23). The theories of Marx and Freud are examples. Wright Mills saw this effort as an obstacle to progress in the human sciences. I take it as given that Grand Theory is not what is generally wanted in social and educational research nowadays. You certainly will not be aiming to develop Grand Theory in your own research, though you may use Grand Theory as a framework or stimulus for it.

Theory: tool or product?

One of the great debates of social science has been about whether theory should be a *tool* or a *product*. In other words:

- Should theory be the *aim* of our endeavours, on the assumption that it will enable us to explain and predict more? Should we be trying to develop more and better theory with this aim in mind?

- Or should it be a tool, devised and used simply for the purpose of helping to explain something that we are currently researching?

Theory is about:

- seeing links;
- generalising;
- abstracting ideas from your data and offering explanations;
- connecting your own findings with those of others;
- having insights.

As the latter it will be fashioned and used for the purpose in hand. It will have been manufactured merely to explain a particular phenomenon. The sociologist Pierre Bourdieu favours this latter kind of theory. He says:

> There is no doubt a theory in my work, or, better, a set of *thinking tools* visible through the

results they yield, but it is not built as such … It is a temporary construct which takes shape for and by empirical work. (Bourdieu, in Wacquant, 1989:50

So, for Bourdieu, theory emerges and disappears in order to help us do our research and explain the findings we are making. And it is *temporary*, like a shooting star. It should not, in other words, be the *aim* of research. Another great sociologist, Howard Becker (1998: 3), talking of his highly respected tutor Everett C. Hughes, explains Hughes's 'take' on theory, which is similar to Bourdieu's:

His [Hughes's] theory was not designed to provide all the conceptual boxes into which the world had to fit. It consisted, instead, of a collection of generalizing tricks he used to think about society, tricks that helped him interpret and make general sense of the data.

This idea of *generalising tricks* is a key one in the theory of educational and social research. It is about your ability to suggest meaningful explanations concerning your findings and how these fit in with the other research that you have reviewed in your literature review. How does it all fit together? What insights can you come up with? What explanations can you offer? 'Generalising' here means 'finding the essence of', 'finding links between', and it is often what is meant by theory in social science.

Unfortunately, when you are at the beginning of an academic career and have little in the way of a broad resource of alternative viewpoints and ideas to make links *between*, this can be the hardest of all tasks. But you *can* show that you have done reading, that you have weighed up ideas, that you have looked at them critically, that you have seen links and themes. Often students make the mistake of undertaking this process only in the last few lines of an essay or the last page or two of a dissertation. Try to extend the process of thinking about what you have done and what you are finding beyond this minimal synthesis so that it becomes not just the concluding lines or paragraphs. If you can do this – if you can also put it at the centre of what you do throughout the process – you will have demonstrated something important to the reader. You will have demonstrated something not only about what you have discovered in your research and why you think it is important, but also about how you think about knowledge, and how you think knowledge can be used.

Overview

After your literature review you will have had an opportunity to climb the hill, look down and see the wood from the trees. You can look down on all of the other research and commentary and see where your prima facie questions stand next to all of this. Have those prima facie questions been answered already? Are there agreements or arguments in the literature? Now you can think about the area in detail, using the storyboard to emerge with a fairly definitive storyline for your research. If necessary you can rewrite your questions and you can think about how these new questions might be answered. This will form the backdrop while you consider the different approaches and methods that may be used to answer the kind of question you are posing. This is also a good time to be thinking about theory – about the ways in which ideas can be drawn together, links made, explanations offered. In doing this, in 'theorising', you are showing that you are more than a copy typist – rather, you are analysing and synthesising and already constructing potential explanations for your forthcoming findings.

Checklist ✔

You may find it helpful to copy this table and write down the answers to the questions.

Have you …

	Notes	
1 … drawn a storyboard that summarises the main themes and issues you found in your literature review?	If not, draw one	☐
2 … tracked a central theme which you will follow for your project?	What is it?	☐
3 … written your revised, final question?		☐
4 … considered how you will use and develop theory in your work?		☐

Further reading

Becker, H.S. (2008) *Writing for Social Scientists: How to Start and Finish your Thesis, Book, or Article* (2nd edn). Chicago: Chicago University Press.

Quite advanced, but can be read with pleasure, as is the case with all of Becker's writing.

Capital Community College Foundation produces a 'Guide to Grammar and Writing', which contains a useful page at http://grammar.ccc.commnet.edu/grammar/composition/thesis.htm#

This discusses what the authors call the 'thesis statement', which is an alternative to the research question.

Thomas, G. (2007) *Education and Theory: Strangers in Paradigms*. Maidenhead: Open University Press.
Detailed, critical discussion on the meaning of theory and how work can progress without recourse to 'formal' theory. I didn't really write this for beginners, though, so you may find it hard going if you don't have some sort of background in the area.

5

METHODOLOGY PART 1: DECIDING ON AN APPROACH

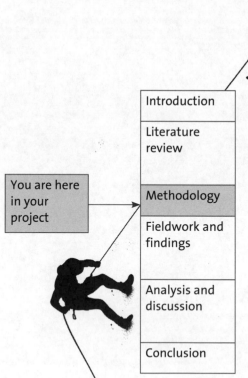

Introduction
Literature review
Methodology
Fieldwork and findings
Analysis and discussion
Conclusion

You are here in your project

Your literature review and your storyboard will have enabled you to sharpen your research question(s) and understand what they involve. You can now think about the means of answering them. This chapter considers:

- how are you going to answer your research question? Approaches to inquiry;
- different ways of viewing the world and different understandings about how knowledge is sought and gained in social inquiry – postivism and interpretivism;
- thinking critically;
- tying up your purposes and your questions with these considerations about knowledge and 'ways of finding out';
- deciding on a 'design route' that takes account of your purposes, questions, approach and methods.

The chapter in your dissertation where you consider this is often called 'Methodology' but may be called 'Research design';

Once you have decided on your question you have to think of the best way of answering it. This is an important point in the project, for the question you have decided to ask will determine the whole approach that you take in your work. It is now, at this point, that you will make decisions about the form that your research will take. How will your purposes, research questions and methods for collecting and analysing data all knit together? A successful research project depends upon the integration of all of these elements (purpose, questions, approach and methods), and you will be marked up or down on the way that you demonstrate your understanding of the need for this integration.

This chapter in your dissertation or thesis is often called your 'methodology' or your 'research design' chapter, and it is important to be clear what methodology is and why methodology and research design are often bracketed together. Methodology is *the study of* method ('-ology' simply means the study of something). So you must be aware that your methodology chapter is not simply the presentation of the method that you are going to be using in your research. Rather, it is a *discussion* of the methods that you will be using and, more importantly, why you are using them. This 'why' will relate back to the purposes of your inquiry and the choices you have made about the approach you intend to take to your research. This is also the reason why this chapter is often called 'research design': it is about thinking about why you are doing this research, how you intend to go about it and the 'shape' it will therefore ultimately take.

> In your methodology chapter you present the methods you will be using. More importantly, though, you say why you are using them to answer your research questions.

Research design

The research design is the plan for the research. In being a plan, it has to take into account your expectations and your context. If the idea of research design is unfamiliar, imagine another kind of design: that of a new kitchen. In designing your kitchen you will not (if you are sensible) just draw a plan completely off the top of your head and stick to it rigidly, come what may. You will first think about what you want a kitchen for – whether you have a large family and are always cooking, or whether you rarely cook; whether you have gas in your property; the position of the drains, water, electricity, natural light. How much money do you want to spend? What sort of 'feel' are you comfortable with – traditional or modern? Will you want to eat in the kitchen as well as cook there? You will want to look at friends' kitchens to see what has and hasn't worked. You will want to consult catalogues and kitchen design specialists. And so on – you get the idea.

Once all of these questions have been answered and you have done all of your fact-finding you will be able to draft out a sketch of your plan. The first few drafts will have to be discarded as you realise things that you didn't include in your plan – the units are 600 mm wide and don't fit in the space, so you have to rejig things and move them around on the design. Finally, you get to build the kitchen, but even now, as you are building it, you will come up against snags – the tap you

wanted is out of stock so you have to order another, or you discover when the electrician arrives that it's against building regulations to put an electricity socket so close to the water. Eventually, the kitchen is made, and you're pleased with it, but it will have involved a great deal of planning and re-planning.

The design for a research project has to bear in mind similar considerations:

- What is it you are trying to achieve? Will you want any findings to be used practically? If so, how?

- What resources – time, money – do you have available?

- What kind of access do you have to the people or the situations you will focus on?

- What kind of expertise can be called on to support you?

- What are your own strengths and skills, and could you realistically develop these in ways that will enable you to do a certain kind of research?

- What kinds of formal and informal regulations will you have to adhere to?

All of these questions will lead you ultimately to the kind of design route shown towards the end of this chapter in Figure 5.10, taking into account the possibility of using a number of *design frames* that are examined in more detail in the next chapter. Importantly, they will also lead you to consider the approach that you take to your research.

It's worth saying that in educational research and in research in the applied social sciences, research design is taken to mean something broader than that in 'pure' social science, for example in psychology. In psychology, research design is often taken simply to be a part of the method, and is often just a synonym for 'experimental design'. In applied social research it means something much wider and it is this broader vista that we shall look at in this chapter.

Research approach

When I talk about the *approach* that you adopt in your work I mean something quite fundamental, and something about which social scientists continually agonise and argue. The *approach* isn't just about whether you use this method or that method, but rather about how you think about the social world. The issue here is that education and the social sciences are hugely varied and complex, with our interests ranging across all kinds of individual and social behaviour. One of the main difficulties is that we are not sure what to focus on in this broad vista. Should it be individuals or groups? Should we measure closely defined variables (things that can be counted) – or should we forget about variables and try to understand the meanings that people invest in the encounters they have with one another? These are big issues to disentangle. By contrast, rocket science seems straightforward.

In this chapter I will talk about frameworks for thinking about these issues, about the difficulties of knowing anything, and about the need to be cautious in any claim to knowledge. In the light of this I will revisit questions about the different kinds of research that we might do.

Scientist or spy?

The way social scientists react to the complexity of social research differs. Some have suggested that it should be like the research of natural scientists – people such as chemists and physicists – asking very precise questions, identifying relevant variables (like gender, class, school funding or reading age), coming up with ideas and hypotheses about how these might (or might not) be related to one another and experimenting to discover the answers. They use their inquiries to try and explain and predict the social world.

Others have said that we should behave more like spies, infiltrating ourselves into the social worlds of those in whom we are interested to observe and describe in rich detail what happens there, behaving as naturally as possible while doing this.

> **Eclectic:** taking a broad view; using a variety of methods; taking the best of many methods; not following one tradition; using complementary insights.

Yet others have suggested that we might behave more like historians, listening to the accounts and narratives of the people with whom we are concerned and constructing explanations of events on the basis of these.

A common view now is that social researchers should be eclectic and do all of these things, depending on the kinds of questions that we pose.

Frameworks for thinking about the social world – paradigms

I have talked about scientists and spies, and while this will do as a simple metaphor for different frameworks about thinking and researching, it is something of an oversimplification.

The technical word used to describe the ways that we think about and research the world is *paradigm*. In common parlance (as distinct from technical parlance), paradigm has come to have several meanings. For example, it may mean 'an example of the best', as in 'David Beckham is the paradigm of a midfielder', or it may mean a particular kind of mindset. But you should forget these uses of the word, for when it is used in the social sciences it refers technically to two particular approaches to knowledge – how we seek knowledge and how we use it. These two approaches – these paradigms – are *positivism* and *interpretivism* and I'll discuss them more in a moment, but it is useful for you to know a little more about what 'paradigm' means before explaining them.

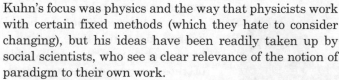

Paradigms ...

- are shared ideas in a particular community of inquiry;
- are 'thinking habits' of researchers;
- are 'rules' of procedure;
- *shift*, as the old one proves to be inappropriate.

The word comes from the Greek *paradeigma*, meaning, broadly speaking, an unchanging model. It was used by the philosopher of science Thomas Kuhn (1970) to mean a fixed set of assumptions about the way inquiry should be conducted.

Figure 5.1 Thomas Kuhn, the Big Daddy of paradigms

Kuhn's focus was physics and the way that physicists work with certain fixed methods (which they hate to consider changing), but his ideas have been readily taken up by social scientists, who see a clear relevance of the notion of paradigm to their own work.

The idea of the paradigm is particularly relevant to social scientists because Kuhn suggested that traditional paradigms – familiar models and ways of working – eventually give way to new ones, which are better, more accurate frameworks for thinking about the world under study. But this giving way, he suggested, happens only after much resistance from the old guard who cherish their traditional ways of thinking and working. In short, people don't like change, and scientists – even hard-nosed physicists – are as irrational as the rest of us when it comes to being faced with new thought and new ideas. Eventually, though, acceptance and change is forced on them as evidence gradually reaches overwhelming proportions for the success of the new ways of thinking. He called this process of change *paradigm shift*.

Now, in the social sciences the dominant paradigm for many years was a way of thinking called *positivism* (of which more below), and this has been challenged by a more recently developed framework for thinking called *interpretivism*. So – using the Kuhnian model – it seems as though one paradigm is giving way to another. In fact, the process has been going on for so long (since the 1920s and 1930s) that it is by no means clear that there is a process of paradigm *shift* actually happening in social science. What appears rather to be the case is that the two paradigms, positivism and interpretivism, are coexisting with each other – each recognised as having its own part to play in social inquiry. It depends on what you want to find out: it's horses for courses. One paradigm will be right for one kind of question, the other right for another. In this sense, the paradigm model doesn't quite work in the social sciences, but it does nevertheless provide a useful way of thinking about our main frameworks for thinking – positivism and interpretivism – about the questions that confront us.

Positivism

For positivists, knowledge about the social world can be obtained objectively: what we see and hear is straightforwardly perceived and recordable without too many problems. The things of the social and psychological world can be observed, measured and studied scientifically, in much the same way that physicists study levers, atoms and pulleys.

It was the French philosopher Auguste Comte who, in *A General View of Positivism* (1856), suggested that the most advanced form of thinking was the scientific form – in other words, the science of natural scientists should as far as possible be emulated. Even before this, the Scottish philosopher David Hume had come up with what he called a *principle of verification*. We should ask two questions of any learned work, said Hume (1748/1910):

Figure 5.2 Auguste Comte – the 'father' of positivism

> *Does it contain any abstract reasoning concerning quantity or number?* No. *Does it contain any experimental reasoning concerning matter of fact and existence?* No. Commit it then to the flames: for it can contain nothing but sophistry and illusion.

This was stirring stuff in the eighteenth century, when the predominant world-view was simple: all things are planned for and provided by God. Questions could be answered with the simple 'It is God's will' (to be said slowly, and in a deep voice). Here, with Comte, was someone saying that this wasn't good enough, and that social matters could be studied in

Positivism as a paradigm:

- The social world can be studied objectively.
- The methods of natural science are appropriate in social science.
- General accounts inform the specific.
- The act of trying to know ought to be conducted in such a way that the knower's own value position is removed from the process.

Interpretivism as a paradigm:

- Knowledge is everywhere and is socially constructed.
- All kinds of information are valid and worthy of the name 'knowledge', even things 'of the mind'.
- Specific accounts inform each other.
- The act of trying to know should be conducted such that the knower's own value position is taken into account in the process.

the same way that scientists studied physics and chemistry where there had been such success with scientific method.

We should therefore try to isolate variables, measure the ways that they varied, look at the relationships between the variables, develop hypotheses about these relationships, perhaps manipulate the variables for experimentation to test a hypothesis, and draw conclusions on the basis of these studies. In doing all of this – in following 'scientific method' – we should try to be as objective and as neutral as possible. We should watch from outside as disinterested observers, trying not to 'contaminate' our findings in any way. The world-view underpinning all of this is sometimes called *realism*, namely the view that the world we perceive is straightforwardly the one that is 'out there'. There is not much room for interpretation about it.

Figure 5.3   David Hume

Interpretivism

An alternative view developed. It was that the social world – that is to say, the world in which we are interested as social scientists – is *not* straightforwardly perceivable because it is *constructed* by each of us in a different way. It's not simply 'out there'; it is different for each of us, with words and events carrying different meanings in every case. It cannot therefore be adequately studied using the methods of physics and chemistry, with talk of variables and quantification: an entirely different mindset and set of procedures are needed to inquire into it. This view is called *interpretivism*, and

Figure 5.4   George Herbert Mead – interactionism and interpretivism

started (more or less) with the American sociologist George Herbert Mead (though there were several strands to the line of thinking that we now call interpretivism, and no clear beginning).

The main point about interpretivism is that we are interested in people and the way that they interrelate – what they think and how they form ideas about the world; how their worlds are constructed. Given that this is the case, we have to look closely at what people are doing by using our own selves, our own knowledge of the world as people. We have to immerse ourselves in the research contexts in which we are interested – for example, talking to people in

> **Disinterested:**   Detached, without bias. A piece of academic research is supposed to be seeking the truth without taking sides or coming from a particular angle. Is this ever possible? Probably not, but it's expected that you should be striving to conduct your inquiries as disinterestedly as possible. (Note that 'disinterested' doesn't mean 'uninterested'.)

depth, attending to every nuance of their behaviour, every clue to the meanings that they are investing in something. So we attend to their blinks, winks, hums and hahs, their nods and nose-blowings, as well as listening to the actual words that are coming out of their mouths. The key is *understanding*. What understandings do the people we are talking to have about the world, and how can we in turn understand these?

You will realise that this talk of understanding is at cross-purposes with the method of the positivists. There is no talk of *variables* in interpretivism, because it is considered artificial to fracture the social world into these categories and there is no expectation that you should be objective in your study. It is the opposite, in fact – you should use your own interests and understandings to help interpret the expressed views and behaviour of others. You should be a *participant* in your research situation and understand it as an insider. In doing this, you have to recognise your position – your social background, likes and dislikes, preferences and predilections, political affiliations, class, gender and ethnicity – and how this position (sometimes called 'positionality' – see p. 144) is likely to be affecting your interpretation. So you shouldn't deny this position. On the contrary, you should use it, but in using it you should also be fully aware of it and acknowledge it – aware that it is likely to be affecting your interpretation in particular ways.

Because of these starting points, research undertaken in this tradition is sometimes called 'naturalistic'. In other words, as a researcher you are behaving as naturally as possible in the social world in order to try and understand it properly. You will be listening and watching naturalistically, and in all of this listening and watching you will be using your own knowledge of the world. You will not necessarily be trying to be objective; rather, you will be accepting the centrality of subjectivity. But this is not a second-best to objectivity; it's simply a different 'take' on research. You won't, in other words, be saying 'Well there's not much I can do about a certain amount of subjectivity so I'll have to live with it.' Rather, you'll be acknowledging that, in doing this kind of illumination, our personal selves – our opinions, intentions, likes and dislikes – are an essential part of what we hear and see. So you will start with the assumption that there is no clear, disinterested knowledge – people have feelings and understandings and these affect the ways that they perceive and interpret the world. Not only is it impossible to eliminate these but they are the stuff out of which interpretation is made.

Remember that being objective is not the same as being thorough and balanced. You can be thorough and balanced without pretending to objectiveness. Imagine this scenario: you are interested in the representation of disability in children's comics, with a question of the sort: 'How was disability represented in children's comics in the years 1950 to 2000?' With such a question, you have to use your own knowledge of the world, as I have just discussed: you read, interpret, put into context and so on. And you do this, as far as possible, by using what the great anthropologist Clifford Geertz (1975) called 'thick description'. Thick description refers to understanding a piece of behaviour – a nod, a word, a pause, etc. – in context, and using one's 'human knowing' to interpret it when one describes it. Geertz forcefully notes that in interpreting meanings one cannot be a 'cipher clerk' (1975: 9). You cannot, in other words, simply report things 'thinly' without context. The example he uses is the one originally used by philosopher Gilbert Ryle (from whom he borrowed the idea of thick description) of three boys moving the muscles of their eyes. With one it is a twitch, with another a wink, and with the third a parody of the second one's wink. What turns the twitch into a wink, and what makes the mickey-take a parody? As Geertz puts it: 'a speck of behaviour, a fleck of culture, and *voilà*! a gesture'. The trick is, in reporting your observations, to make clear what is going on in a social situation to turn the twitch into the wink, or into the parody of the wink. How do you know which is which? The interpretative researcher has to tell the reader.

The fact that you read, interpret and put into context in the ways that I have described does not absolve you, though, from the imperative to approach the question in a fair and balanced way. It might be the case, for example, that you come to this question with a particular viewpoint about disability – a viewpoint that says that disabled people are marginalised and oppressed by society. Would this give you licence simply to pick on particularly offensive representations of disability in comics and to ignore positive images of disabled people that you find there? Opinions differ on this, and some advocate research that is 'emancipatory'. They advocate research that principally makes a case – research that is, in other words, campaigning. I do not share this view. My own opinion is that there are many legitimate kinds of activity in life and that *research*, as an activity, is governed by some fundamental ground rules, which include a duty of balance, fairness and thoroughness. Research, in this respect, is different from campaigning.

A good example of interpretative research is to be found in James Patrick's (1973) *A Glasgow Gang Observed*. Here, the author, a young sociologist, infiltrated himself into a gang of young men in the Maryhill district of Glasgow. By becoming a participant in the gang's activities, Patrick (a pseudonym, wisely, since he didn't want subsequently to be knifed) paints a fascinating (and entertaining) picture of the way that the gang worked and its motivations, intentions and modus operandi. It helps us to understand gangs, but there is no pretence that this is a representative picture, or that all gangs are like this. In researching this way, Patrick is not pretending to be objective: on the contrary, he is using all of his personal self to help him infiltrate, engage with and understand what is going on among the young men.

One of the attractions for researchers in the applied social sciences, and I include practitioner-researchers in this group, is the humility of interpretative research – the fact that it makes no grand claims about generalisability or causation. What it does instead is to take from the local experience and illuminate and influence the local experience: it helps to influence the practitioner-researcher's own developing practice.

Paradigms and research approach

Actually, paradigms are not straightforwardly 'views about the world' as I perhaps implied earlier. Rather, they are positions on the best ways to think about and study the social world – the world in which we are interested as social scientists. Table 5.1 indicates how these paradigms differ in respect of what they say about how research should be conducted.

Table 5.1 Paradigms: positivism and interpretivism (loosely adapted from Oakley, 2000)

	Positivist	Interpretivist
The researcher aims to ...	predict and explain, usually generalising from carefully selected samples	understand the particular, contributing to building a framework of 'multiple realities'
The researcher uses (for example) ...	survey, experiment, structured observation	unstructured observation, case study, unstructured interview, participant observation
The researcher aims to be ...	independent, an outsider	an insider, interacting with participants
The researcher looks at ...	things that can be quantified and counted	perceptions, feelings, ideas, thoughts, actions as heard or observed
The researcher analyses ...	variables, decided on in advance of fieldwork	emergent patterns
The design of the research is ...	fixed	flexible
Other words sometimes used (often inaccurately) to sum up these approaches ...	scientific, quantitative, nomothetic	naturalistic, qualitative, idiographic

What planet are you on?

How can you use this knowledge of paradigms in your own research? Actually, if you look at any write-up of social research in an academic journal or in a research report for a commissioning body you will not find mention of positivism or interpretivism. It is taken as 'given' that there are different ways of looking at and thinking about the social world and that these will have structured the research. However, in a dissertation or thesis from a research project at university you will have to show that you understand the broad principles that guide the way that social research is conducted – the ways that questions are answered and data are gathered and analysed. This does not mean that you should have a section on positivism or interpretivism, but it does mean that you should explain the principles that are guiding your research.

What does this mean? Well, positivism and interpretivism are such different ways of thinking about research that one could liken them to being on different planets. To borrow an image, positivists are from Mars and interpretivists are from Venus. On Mars everyone counts everything and talks in numbers, but on Venus they don't know what numbers are (no one has ever seen one) and they just talk to each other non-stop, everyone always asking each other about how they are and how they feel: 'How are you? What do you mean by that? Really? Tell me more.' In fact, the Martians have a joke about the Venusians: 'How many Venusians does it take to change a light bulb? Answer: 19 – one to change the bulb and

18 to share the experience.' (And the Venusians have a joke about the Martians: 'How many Martians does it take to change a light bulb? Answer: 0.83, plus or minus 0.4, depending on the mean palm size of the Martian cohort.' This sends the Venusians into hysterics.)

Writing about paradigms

Now, if you are a positivist writing about research on Mars, you don't begin every sentence with 'Here on Mars …', just as on Earth newspapers do not begin every story with 'Here on Earth …'. It's just part of the background noise. We *know* that we are on Earth and have Earthly experiences every day. We don't need to say it. In the same way, you don't need to say that you are working in a positivist or an interpretivist tradition. You just have to be aware of it. It's part of the air you breathe when you do a particular kind of research.

And, as a student, you have to demonstrate your awareness. This presents something of a dilemma for student researchers, who do realise that they have to show that they know about these things but without having a rather gross reference to them in the text. (Some students write pages about positivism or interpretivism, which is unnecessary and distracting.) It's a bit like the dilemma you feel when you are on your driving test and you feel you should *show* that you are looking in the rear-view mirror by making an exaggerated movement of your head. Though you want to do this, a good examiner will be watching for your eye movements – you don't in fact need to extend your neck to giraffe-like proportions to convince the examiner that you are looking in the mirror. And you don't usually need to explain about positivism and interpretivism in your dissertation. But what you *do* have to do is to be aware of the ways that they are structuring your research.

How can you demonstrate your knowledge of them without the giraffe syndrome? The key is in the argument you make for the approach that you take in your research, though the need for this argument will be more or less pronounced depending on the question(s) that you ask. The key to all research – whether you are thinking as a positivist or an interpretivist – is describing, interpreting and analysing, and what you need to do is to say why you think it is a good idea to describe, interpret and analyse in this way or that. In making this argument, you may make reference to positivism or interpretivism and this may need to be more or less extended. So your methodology chapter will begin with the reasons why your questions have led you to the approach you have decided to take in answering those questions. In explaining these reasons you may begin by saying something such as:

My questions call for straightforwardly descriptive answers and I shall provide these answers through an examination of government statistics and
from my own structured observations.

or

My questions stem from a wish to understand the reasons for Shaquille's
persistent failure and 'blocking' in maths.

In both instances, you would then go on to say how you proceeded from these starting
points to your choice of approach and method. In the first case, it would be possible to
move from the statement about an examination of government statistics to an examination of those statistics relatively unproblematically. (There is no need to say that
statistics have been collected in a positivist paradigm.) However, you may want to
spend more time on explaining the reasons for choosing to use structured (rather than
unstructured – see p. 217–19) observation. In the second case you will need to explain
how you are going to understand Shaquille's difficulties – by asking him questions
about what he is doing when he is calculating, by watching his behaviour, by relating
his difficulties to your own when you were a child studying maths, or whatever. In
doing this, you will wish to outline the background to an approach that accepts as valid
the thoughts, imaginings and empathies that are involved here. And in so doing you
will draw on methodological literature that discusses such an approach. You may also
give examples of such an interpretivist approach to understanding behaviour, such as
Oliver Sacks's (1996) *An Anthropologist on Mars* (the Mars connection is coincidental).

So, getting back to paradigms and how they structure our thinking for our
research, I think the best and simplest way of distinguishing one kind of describing, interpreting and analysing from another is to remember the epithet I earlier
gave from Hume: *Does it contain any abstract reasoning concerning quantity or
number? ... Does it contain any experimental reasoning concerning matter of fact
and existence?* It was 250 years ago that Hume came up with this 'principle of
verification'. This was before the word 'positivism' was coined, but it led indirectly
to Comte's positivism and it serves us well now, for it can lead to the continuum
in Figure 5.5. This, I hope, is a way of not getting trapped in a mindset that says
that we have to be either positivist or interpretivist. Rather, it's horses for courses.

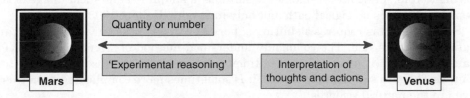

Figure 5.5   Positivism or interpretivism

I don't want to extend the analogy too far, but of course Earth is midway between
Mars and Venus, and here in the real world we use all kinds of reasoning to come to our
conclusions about the evidence that we collect. It is not a question of one *or* the other.

But is it science?

Much of the debate about positivism and interpretivism hinges around whether a study can be called scientific. In fact it is very difficult to define what a 'scientific' study is. Chemists work differently from biologists who work differently from physicists, who work differently from doctors, who work differently from astronomers (you get the idea), yet few people would have difficulty in agreeing that they are all scientists. Imagine for a moment the work of palaeoanthropologists – the scientists who try to understand how our human forebears evolved. They work by collecting fragments of bone and other material and piecing together stories – plausible accounts – of the way that this pre-human may have led to that one. They use information from a whole range of sources in doing this. For example, they use knowledge from geology about the age of rocks in which materials are found; they use carbon dating; they even use knowledge from psychology and physiology. The palaeoanthropologist Louis Leakey described how he worked out that a particular pre-human, for whom he had a skull, had quite advanced language facility by looking at the roots of the specimen's teeth. It transpires that a particular physiological construction – a little depression in the jaw-bone called the *canine fossa* – can be shown to be associated with the production of speech: the little dip makes room for a muscle used in language production. None of this work – depending on inference and intuition – is formally experimental, yet few would doubt that it is science.

In the same way, much of what we do in social research is a mix of forms of inquiry: an idea from here, a hunch from there, a searching for evidence – then a putting together of hunches, ideas and evidence and a 'Eureka!' There is no formal method to follow that will lead you to the right answer. It is always a matter of finding the right information and using your head.

> There is no single way of being scientific. You should be open-minded about the methods that you use to answer your research questions.

Starting points can come from anywhere: from a need, from curiosity, from serendipity, from surprise. The philosopher Paul Thagard (1998) has offered the diagram in Figure 5.6 to explain the relationship of these beginnings of inquiry to forms of questioning that lead to discovery. There is no formal route that could be branded 'Scientific Method®'. As Einstein put it, scientific method is no more than trying to find, 'in whatever manner is suitable, a simplified and lucid image of the world ... There is no logical path, but only intuition' (Holton, 1995: 168).

Sometimes, this requires a shifting of perspective as far as our ideas about causation are concerned. The commonly understood method of science is to look for causes, and this is certainly one legitimate avenue to follow in social science too. But, as Thagard's diagram indicates, it is sometimes more complicated than this – even in the natural sciences.

This complexity is no less true of the social sciences. The world-famous sociologist Howard Becker suggests that the complexity is such in social research that the notion of 'cause' is almost a misnomer (Becker, 1998: 60–1). He suggests that we should see ourselves searching for *narrative* rather than cause:

Assume that whatever you want to study has, not causes, but a history, a story, a narrative, a 'first this happened, then that happened, and then the other happened, and it ended up like this.' On this view we understand the occurrence of events by learning the steps in the process by which they came to happen, rather than by learning the conditions that made their existence necessary.

Jerome Bruner (1997: 126) puts it this way:

The process of science making is narrative … we play with ideas, try to create anomalies, try to find neat puzzle forms that we can apply to intractable troubles so that they can be turned into soluble problems.

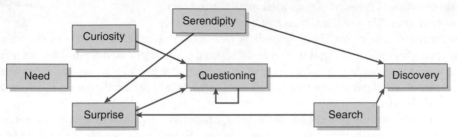

Figure 5.6 Ways to discovery (Thagard, 1998)

If the question demands description, one avenue will be signposted; if it demands illumination, another; or if it demands inference, yet another. It's the same in any field. Police officers investigating Dr Black's murder will seek evidence not just at the simple physical scientific level – was there blood on the lead piping, and whose was it? – but also evidence about motives – did Mrs Peacock stand to gain in some way from Dr Black's demise? How *well* did they know each other (exaggerated wink)? Was she a beneficiary in his will? So they will need not just to send material to the labs for DNA analysis but also to question Mrs Peacock skilfully and observe her demeanour for signs of lying. Likewise, the research team at FastFood Inc., when developing Speed, its new sparkling drink, will want not simply demographic statistics to see which groups of the population seem to be growing or declining, but also rich information from small groups of people – focus groups – about the image portrayed by artwork on prototype cans of Speed.

All kinds of evidence will be needed and employed, and we need to piece it all together. In Bruner's terms, we need to play with ideas; in Becker's, to view the story. Of course, there is always the danger that we may put two and two together and make five. Our 'Eureka!' may be wrong, and there is a real danger of this in the social sciences. This is why it is essential to understand the importance of humility in your claim to have found something out – why it is important to think reflectively and critically.

The Q words – qualitative and quantitative

'Quantitative research' refers to research using numbers, and 'qualitative research' refers to that which does not use numbers. To characterise these 'types' crudely by paradigm, I could say that positivism lends itself to quantification, while interpretivism lends itself to words, thoughts and images: it is qualitative.

I've tried to avoid the Q words in this book because I think that their use makes for unnecessary and unwelcome oppositions between different kinds of research. It is absolutely the case that qualitative and quantitative research differ, and that they are governed by different assumptions and ground rules. But it is not the case that they are incompatible. Indeed, they complement each other. Nor can social and educational research be divided neatly into one or the other type, for much analysis can depend on plainly descriptive words or numbers – words where there is remarkably little in the way of interpretation going on, and numbers doing no more complicated a job than counting. Such analysis eludes the divisions of the Q words and the positivism–interpretivism continuum, employing both words and numbers and slipping effortlessly between the one and the other.

> Quantitative and qualitative research are not in opposition to one another. Rather, they can complement each other.

To create a stark division between qualitative and quantitative sometimes engenders a cart-before-the-horse mentality. Sometimes people are tempted to think of types of research first (quantitative or qualitative) and then think of a research pathway that will lead into one of these. This is entirely wrong: your research approach should be the servant of your research question, not its master. Always start with your research question, and think of ways of answering it. This may lead you to a design frame where you use numbers, or it may lead you to one where you use words. Figure 5.7 shows the research questions we looked at in the last chapter and indicates how they may lead to various forms of inquiry employing both words and numbers.

The point is not to 'do' a quantitative inquiry or a qualitative inquiry with any of these questions. Rather, it is to ask yourself how this or that form of inquiry will best address the question. As you can see, a mix of forms of inquiry is in all of these cases probably appropriate. And you can probably also see that to label the counting that goes on in any of them 'quantitative' is misleading, since the word 'quantitative' implies some special method involving the use of statistics. Some kind of simple statistics may indeed be involved with each of them, but this doesn't make the study 'quantitative'.

This is why I find the use of the quantitative–qualitative division unhelpful. Not only does it imply that the question is subservient to the method, but also it suggests that there is some arcane, God-given set of rules saying that one set of methods will not mix with another. Certainly, we have to use whatever methods we are using properly: there are good and less good ways of using words and numbers. This does not mean, though, that each cannot play its part in answering the question. (I discuss the mixing of methods further on p. 183.) The important thing

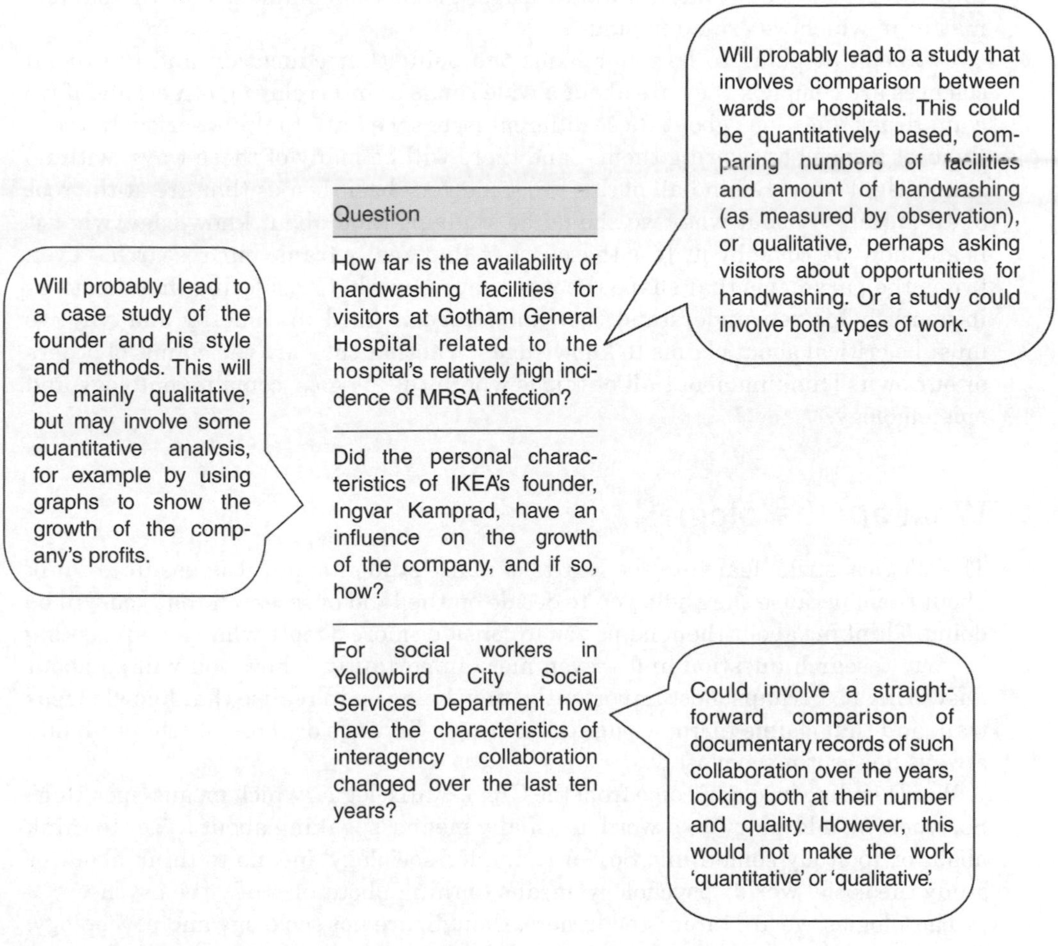

Will probably lead to a study that involves comparison between wards or hospitals. This could be quantitatively based, comparing numbers of facilities and amount of handwashing (as measured by observation), or qualitative, perhaps asking visitors about opportunities for handwashing. Or a study could involve both types of work.

Will probably lead to a case study of the founder and his style and methods. This will be mainly qualitative, but may involve some quantitative analysis, for example by using graphs to show the growth of the company's profits.

Question
How far is the availability of handwashing facilities for visitors at Gotham General Hospital related to the hospital's relatively high incidence of MRSA infection?
Did the personal characteristics of IKEA's founder, Ingvar Kamprad, have an influence on the growth of the company, and if so, how?
For social workers in Yellowbird City Social Services Department how have the characteristics of interagency collaboration changed over the last ten years?

Could involve a straightforward comparison of documentary records of such collaboration over the years, looking both at their number and quality. However, this would not make the work 'quantitative' or 'qualitative'.

Figure 5.7   Different questions lead to different routes of inquiry … using words and numbers

is that you use the design frame that is right for your question, and this is why I have organised the next chapter into *design frames* rather than invoking any quantitative–qualitative division.

Thinking critically – how the 'ologies' help

One of the most frequent reasons for the marking down of a project (or indeed any piece of work in the social sciences) is that a student has not demonstrated an ability to *think critically*. This is about your ability to think-about-thinking and always to be sceptical about claims to knowledge, given the complexity of the subject matter in which we are interested.

I've been at pains to hammer home the point that education and the social sciences are complex: they are about a wide range of interrelating issues, and if we want to ask questions about these different issues we have to think seriously about the best ways of answering them – and there will be many of these ways, with no single 'right' way. Behind all of this are some very basic issues that are at the root of all inquiry   about what we should be studying, and about knowledge, what it is and how we come by it. It is these issues that really frame our research – even frame the paradigms that shape the way that we work. Considering these matters in depth helps you understand that knowledge is hard to come by and why we must be critical about claims to knowledge – whether they are the claims of others or our own. Thinking about all of this is where the 'ologies' come in: ontology and epistemology.

What are the 'ologies'?

The 'ologies' strike fear into the hearts of many students, but it is useful to think about them because they help you to decide on the kind of research that you will be doing. Thinking about them helps you to consider more deeply what you are asking in your research question and – even more importantly – how you will go about answering it. Perhaps most importantly, they help you to realise that knowledge is frail, and that claims to knowledge, in your own findings or those of others, should always be scrutinised closely.

Words ending in 'ology' come from the Greek suffix 'logia', which means 'speaking'. So, when we add 'ology' to a word, it usually means 'speaking about ...', or to think about or to study something. So, for example, 'sociology' means to think about or study the social world; 'psychology' means to think about or study the psyche.

The 'ologies' we are interested in here, though, are not sociology and psychology. They are rather more unusual ones, and are usually associated with philosophy. They are *ontology* and *epistemology*. Some people would say that we spend too much time bothering about these. They would say that it is only because social scientists are so unsure of their status that they spend so much time gazing at their navels about how they know what they know – and surrounding themselves with all sorts of fancy-sounding words (such as epistemology and ontology) that are difficult to understand. The more unsure you are of your academic credentials, after all, the more likely you are to puff yourself up with all the paraphernalia of science.

This is *partly* true of the social sciences and their use of jargon, but *only* partly true. Some of the navel-gazing is actually necessary, because the issues we confront as social scientists really are knotty ones.

That 'knottiness' – in other words, the difficulty of framing the key questions of the social sciences – is what the 'ologies' are about and where they can help out. They are about the fundamental issues, the basic questions. *What* is there to study? How can we *know* about it? How do we find what we are looking for?

Ontology

Much of the confusion about what methods we should use in educational and social research comes from head-scratching about the nature of the world. What *is* it that we are studying? This question is not so difficult for physicists, since it is clear that they study electrons and neutrons and Higgs bosons. No one disagrees. It's similar for biologists: they study life processes in things that are alive. But for social scientists there is a problem, since we are studying people, on their own or together, and people do strange, unpredictable things, gather together in peculiar ways, act irrationally, learn and change. Is it their observable behaviour that is the focus of our deliberations, the way that they gather together, or what? As social scientists we can become especially concerned with ontology because it is not at all clear what kind of world we should be studying.

The trouble is that when you start looking at people and the things that they do, one of the major issues that confronts you is how those things are perceived by us: how those things 'come to life' and how we should look at them. For example, when people are in any kind of relationship with one another – whether as teacher and student, as life partners, as friends, colleagues or anything else – it is undeniable that they create to a greater or lesser extent some kind of 'chemistry' that comes from shared understandings and outlooks (or the lack of these). Now, how do we begin to understand what this 'chemistry', this meaningfulness and mutual understanding, might be? In other words, *what* is it that we are looking at?

Ontology is about this question of what we are looking at. In philosophy, where we borrow the idea from, ontologists have posed questions such as 'What is existence?' and 'What are physical objects?' These questions are clearly not social scientists' focus in their everyday work. But in the broadest possible sense they do have central relevance because there are various kinds of 'existence' and 'objects' or phenomena in which we could be said to be interested in the social sciences. An awareness of the issues of ontology makes us wary, for example, of what is sometimes called a *correspondence view of knowledge*, meaning an assumption that what you see and hear corresponds to facts 'out there' in the real world. This is more or less the view held by the person in the street: what you see is that which is there, and what happens in your head more or less corresponds with what is in the 'real world'. In fact, this turns out to be a lot more complex an issue than you might assume, even for quite straightforward matters, but it is multiplied hugely when we are talking about things to do with human behaviour and interaction.

So, the issues to be encapsulated in the word 'ontology' concern the kinds of things that we assume to exist in the world, and how those things should be viewed and studied. Is the social world in which we are interested best seen as comprising simple *variables*, or matters such as the *interaction* among people? Should we start our inquiries with theories of social behaviour or should we aim to develop our own theories as we progress?

For example, if a boy is biting the other children in the class, how should we look at this problem? Should we treat the issue as a natural scientist might, concentrating on what we can see (the biting) and the variables we can manipulate (perhaps rewards or punishments) to influence his behaviour? Or should we see the problem as a complex of social interactions wherein meanings are made out of the expectations, connections and interactions that occur in the artificial environment of the classroom? Or could we see it in both of these ways?

This is where thinking about ontology helps in the construction of research. It helps us to understand that there are different ways of viewing the world – of viewing what there is to study. In other words, things may not be as simple as they at first appear, and there are different ways of seeing and understanding a problem or an issue. You will understand, if you have read the section above on paradigms, that it is different ontological positions which lead on to the different paradigmatic positions.

> Ontology is about *what* you are looking at – the kind of events that exist in the social world. Epistemology is about *how* you look and find out about these.

Epistemology

If ontology is the study of what there is or what exists in the social world, *epistemology* is the study of our knowledge of the world. How do we *know* about the world that we have defined ontologically? Epistemologists ask questions such as:

- What is knowledge and how do we know things?
- Are there different kinds of knowledge?
- Are there good procedures for discovering knowledge?

Rumsfeld on knowing

If all of this stuff about existence and knowledge is making no sense at all, cheer yourself up with the reassuring thought that you are not alone. In 2002, Donald Rumsfeld, the US Secretary for Defense, gave a now famous news briefing. In talking about weapons of mass destruction, he brightened a gloomy world when he came out with this statement:

> There are known knowns. There are things that we know we know. There are known unknowns. That is to say, there are things that we now *know* we don't know. But there are also unknown unknowns … there are things we *do not* know we don't know. So when we do the best we can and we pull all this information together and, and we then say well that's basically what we see as the situation that is really only the known knowns and the known unknowns, and each year we

---

discover a few more of those unknown unknowns and ... and I, I ... it, it sounds like a riddle ... (Department of Defense news briefing, 12 February 2002)

How true. And it makes a lot more sense when written down than it did when he said it. His brief speech on knowing illustrates some of the difficulties of describing what we know and how we come to know it.

In education, we are interested in all of the knowns and unknowns of Mr Rumsfeld's speech. And one thing that the speech correctly suggests is that nothing is certain. If there is one single thing that you need to absorb from the whole debate about ontology and epistemology it is that knowledge is a frail thing. You can't be *certain* of anything. The main consequence of this for your research project and how you write it up is that you should always make it clear that you understand why it is hard to know something – that you understand why you should be tentative and not over-confident in your conclusions.

Let's look a little at that frailty – at why it is hard to know something, or at least to be sure that we know it. Put differently, why do we have to be careful about asserting something to be true? In Chapter 3 I made the point that you should always avoid phrases such as 'this proves' and 'this shows' and instead use words such as 'this indicates' or ' the evidence suggests' or 'points towards' or 'implies'. You should use phrases such as 'tends to' or 'one might conclude that' instead of bolder ones. Remember again that maxim from the great biologist J. B. S. Haldane (who appears rather dapper in his blazer in Figure 5.8), 'the duty of doubt'. Haldane concluded his famous essay *Possible Worlds* (Haldane, 1928: 224) with the words 'science has owed its wonderful progress very largely to the habit of doubting all theories.'

Figure 5.8 Haldane, who spoke about 'the duty of doubt'

It's all very well to be doubtful and tentative, but what would social scientists say to epistemologists about how they know? ...

How can we know something in the social sciences?

We know things because we *experience* them: we see them, hear them, touch them. *Empiricism* is the word given to the idea that knowledge comes from experience. To know something *empirically* is to know it from experience.

But how do we get from seeing, hearing and touching (experiencing) to knowing something? To explain the process of moving from experiencing to knowing

Wolcott (1992) draws a diagram of a tree, wherein the experience is absorbed by the tree's roots, to be transformed into the knowing that comes via various analytical strategies. Those analytical strategies employ *reasoning* of one kind or another, and there are taken to be two main ways of reasoning that lead us to knowledge.

First, there is *inductive reasoning*. With inductive reasoning we proceed on the basis of many observations gathered from experience to derive a general principle. So, if you see lots of swans and they are all white, you may come up with the general principle that all swans are white.

The sun has risen this morning, and has from the beginning of the time, so you may infer that the sun rises every morning.

The more observation the better and, clearly, the more observations you take, the more sure you can be that your general principle is true. Inductive reasoning's central point is that lots of similar experience leads to general principles.

But there is a big problem with the confidence that comes from this kind of inductive reasoning. This is that just because your observation is always that something is the case, it doesn't automatically follow that this will continue to be the case. For example, when Europeans first went to Australia they discovered that swans could be black as well as white. And while the sun has risen every morning, we now know that there is a variety of astronomical horrors that could end up with it not happening tomorrow. So, our knowledge from induction is not perfect, and never can be. This is particularly so in the social sciences where we very rarely, if ever, find clear-cut evidence of this kind.

Second, there is *deductive reasoning*. Deductive reasoning concerns argument. An argument proceeds on the basis of statements (or premises) which are assumed to be true, to conclusions which must be true if the premises are true. Problems arise, of course, because of assumptions that the premises are true when they are not or when facets of a line of reasoning appear to be connected when in fact they are not, as the deliberations below reveal.

To love is to suffer. To avoid suffering one must not love. But then one suffers from not loving. Therefore to love is to suffer, not to love is to suffer. To suffer is to suffer. To be happy is to love. To be happy then is to suffer. But suffering makes one unhappy. Therefore, to be unhappy one must love, or love to suffer, or suffer from too much happiness. I hope you're getting this down. (Woody Allen)

Mars is essentially in the same orbit ... Mars is somewhat the same distance from the Sun, which is very important. We have seen pictures where there are canals, we believe, and water. If there is water, that means there is oxygen. If oxygen, that means we can breathe. (Governor George W. Bush, 8 November 1994)

Inductive and deductive – they are both forms of reasoning. So, we know things because we think about them and *reason* about them. *Rationalism* is the word given to the idea that knowledge comes from our reasoning. That reasoning depends on both inductive and deductive strategies.

I hope I have explained that these processes of reasoning are far from perfect. Scientists, whether natural scientists or social scientists, try to improve processes of reasoning by being methodical in the way that they seek and acquire experience – seek and acquire evidence. Natural scientists, physicists and chemists, are able to control their experience using carefully contrived experiments and manipulating variables methodically in those experiments. However, in the social sciences it is far more difficult to do this – and, indeed, all sorts of questions arise (as I indicated in the section on ontology) about what exists to be experienced. Knowledge here is said to be *provisional*, and by provisional we mean that it is taken to be the best in the circumstances, but may always be superseded if other information or insights come to light.

As with paradigms, you will not be expected to include dedicated sections on epistemology and ontology in your thesis. They may be mentioned in the discussion of the approach to your research but, as with the non-discussion of paradigms (see p. 112), the trick is to reveal your awareness of their importance with subtlety. Epistemology and ontology are not, after all, at the centre of your inquiry; the only reason why they concern us is that you should appreciate their significance in *shaping* your inquiry – their importance in moulding the nature of your work. You have to show that you haven't stumbled bleary-eyed into the first set of methods you have come across. Rather, you have understood that knowledge is construed in different ways and that there are different ways of coming to knowledge. So you may include sentences such as, 'I recognise the competing world-views that frame social inquiry, and in this recognition I have chosen to ...'. Or, if you want to be more explicit – perhaps for master's, and certainly for doctoral research – you could expand this. You might begin a discussion with something such as:

In considering an inquiry into the topic of stress in nurses, I am faced with two alternatives about the nature of my research. I can make assumptions about the world that faces me being divisible into quantifiable elements that I can measure and manipulate. Or, rejecting the validity of the ontological assumptions on which such division is based, I can see the social world in which I am interested as fluid, as constructed by individuals in myriad ways, as not amenable to quantification ...

This would lead on to a discussion of stress being examined in fundamentally different ways given differing ontological, epistemological and paradigmatic stances. But the discussion of ontology, epistemology and paradigms is always secondary to the topic: you'll notice that in those three sentences there is only a passing reference to 'ontological assumptions'. The topic is the important thing, and what you have to show is that there are different ways of looking at it and studying it.

Critical awareness (again)

I discussed the importance of critical awareness on p. 69. Having looked at all of the rabbit-holes you can stumble into (to continue the *Alice in Wonderland* analogy) when thinking about something and trying to know about it, it is worth restating the significance of criticality and scepticism. But this uncertainty about knowledge should not leave us dithering in a heap of anxiety. Doing research is about finding out and trying to know things in the best possible way. While the important thing to remember about inquiry is that knowledge is tentative and provisional, we should stay optimistic. Remember the three Bs:

> *Be* doubtful.
> *Be* sceptical.
> *Be* critical.

And don't forget the fourth B:

> *But* remember that doubt is nothing on its own. It is a prelude, a stimulus to action.

From purposes to questions to approaches to data gathering

Having looked at research approaches, paradigms and ways of thinking and knowing, let's go right back to the beginning of the chapter and think again now about research design. All the time during a research project you should be considering how the various elements of your research fit together: *purposes*, together with *questions*, together with *literature review*, together with *approach*, which leads on to decisions about design frame, methods and *analysis*.

Figure 5.9   Knitting it together

Each part should be informing the others (see Figure 5.9). How has the purpose (e.g. evaluation, or improving your practice, or describing) led you to a research question? And how has the research question led you to a particular approach or approaches? As your findings emerge you may wish to ask further, subsidiary questions, or you may wish to go back to your literature review to see if light can be cast upon an unexpected aspect of your findings.

In social and educational research there is always this toing and froing between one element and another. You will constantly be revisiting and revising your views, and this is perfectly proper and to be expected, for it means that there will be a logic and a progression to the shape of your research project. This logic needs to be evident to the reader, so you need to be able to show how it is emerging.

What does all of this mean for you and the way that you proceed to your design frame, methods and analysis? It means that you have to think about the inter-relationship of these issues in relation to your project. Figure 5.10 sums these up.

If we look at Figure 5.10, the process of going from questions to approaches can perhaps be illustrated with some examples. In Chapter 1 I talked about differ-ent kinds of research question to try to clarify the different trajectories on which research could be set by different kinds of question. These were questions that demanded description, interpretation, deduction or inference. As the book has pro-ceeded you will have realised that it isn't quite as simple as this. A question that looks as if it will require only description in the answer may be a lot more complex, for description can happen in a wide variety of forms. You can describe in words or in numbers. You can describe one situation or many. Let's imagine that you are interested in hospital education services for children who are chronically sick. You could pose questions such as the following:

1 How many children are educated in hospitals in England, how have trends changed in postwar years, and what are the possible reasons for this?

2 What is the experience of children educated in hospital today?

3 What are attitudes to hospital-educated children when they return to school?

4 If a rest period is introduced into the hospital school day at mid-morning, what will be the consequence on children's lunchtime behaviour?

Question 1 leads you into a project that is unequivocally concerned with descrip-tion and descriptive statistics. You will be seeking answers in official statistics and looking to relate these statistics to social movements, events and changes in policy. *Question 2* leads you to examine children's experience. You can choose how you try to gain access to this experience and how you interpret it, but inter-pretation will certainly be involved. You might choose to observe the experi-ence of children by placing yourself in a hospital education setting, or you might ask the children themselves or their parents or staff. *Question 3* leads you to consider attitudes – the attitudes of children in ordinary mainstream schools – when children return from sometimes long

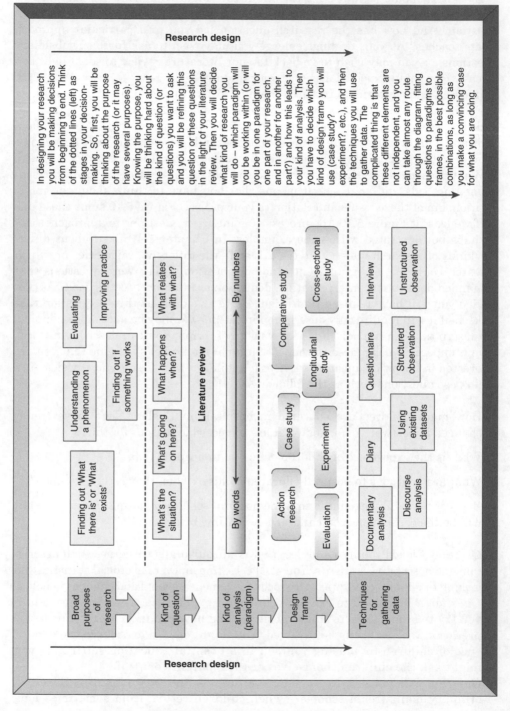

Figure 5.10 Process of research design

stays in hospital. This could be done by interviewing individual children or a group of children in a focus group, or it could be done by giving a question-naire to children, or even by observing a class. Whatever, some kind of judge-ment about their attitudes will be required from the researcher: interpreta-tion will be needed.

Question 4 involves some kind of assessment of consequence: 'What happens when?' While this could be answered narratively, in words, it is more usual in this kind of question to try to be able to say 'This does (or doesn't) seem to be associated with this' – not only are they related, but x seems to be causing y. For this, some kind of measure of y may be helpful.

So, particular kinds of question lead to particular kinds of study. However, the relationship is by no means one-to-one: you cannot map one approach and one method to one kind of question, even though sometimes certain kinds of question will lead more obviously to one route than another. At each stage choices will be required from you – and, rather inconveniently, there are no right or wrong answers when it comes to research design. It's a question of thinking intelligently about it, and then accounting for the choices that you have made.

Let's take a more detailed example of a research study in the context of Figure 5.10. Which route through the diagram would be taken from beginning to end, and what kinds of choices might be made?

Designing research: an example

Angharad is a newly qualified teacher in a rural primary school in North Wales where most of the children are bilingual in English and Welsh. A small minority of the children are fluent only in English, while the other children are familiar with what is called 'bilingual code-switching' – in other words, regularly and unthinkingly switching between two languages in which they are fluent. This is not discouraged in the school, though Angharad realises from her reading that the practice of allowing this has aroused controversy in the education community generally – some believing that the different languages should be kept separate to avoid confusion.

Angharad is aware that the group of five English-only speakers in her Year 3 class is becoming isolated; they are increasingly playing together and there are signs that they are not being integrated into the group and are even beginning to be bullied by some of the bilingual children. Angharad's observation here has emerged out of curiosity and interest: she has become curious about the behaviour of the children, and her reaction is to try to find out whether her perception (a) is an accurate one of what is actually happening (in other words, is she imagining it, or is there more evidence for it than just her gut feeling?), (b) is common in her school and in other schools locally, nationally or internationally where bilingual-ism happens, and (c) that if the situation is as she perceives it to be, whether there is anything that she can do about it.

Purposes ▷

There are two simple purposes in her research, then. The first purpose (related to (a) and (b)) stems centrally out of curiosity (emerging, in turn, out of concern for the isolated children) – curiosity to know whether her feelings are accurate. The second purpose (c) stems out of a desire to improve her practice if it is the case that the monolingual children's experience at school is becoming more separate and segregated from mainstream activity.

Prima facie questions ▷

Two kinds of prima facie question emerge from this. The first leads to a 'What's the situation?' question, while the second leads to a 'What's going on here?' question.

Literature review ▷

Her literature review will focus on bilingualism and code-switching not only in Wales, but also in the US where there is a substantial literature on code-switching in Chicano and Puerto Rican communities. What do school staff in these communities do? Do they have special procedures and policies? Are these similar to those operating in schools in the UK?

Revised thinking in light of literature review ▷

Her literature review will lead her to be better informed about the issue of bilingual code-switching and to realise that positive action could help her to resolve some of the issues that have emerged for the children in her class. Before doing that, though, she would need first to assess properly the level and extent of any problems that existed, and second to understand the likely consequences for the monolingual children. The latter had to be seen in the context of the school's and the local authority's policies on code-switching, and whether anything could realistically be done to influence code-switching or the consequences of it.

Revised questions ▷

Her first question involves some fairly simple data gathering about what is happening, for the question seeks to describe something: to state the current situation. If Angharad believes that she can make observations of the classroom to verify (or otherwise) her informal observation, these may involve both structured and unstructured observations: the former assuming that there are things that she can count and the latter relying more on impressions, gathered more systematically in a diary. Her second question is rather more complex and involves (i) the collection of documentary data from the school and the local authority, and (ii) information from the children themselves on how they are being affected.

Design frame and data gathering ▷

She then decides that her design frame (of which more in Chapter 6) will be a case study. She also decides on methods for gathering data within this frame (Chapter 7).

Mapping this process through our design trajectory would produce something like the series of routes shown in Figure 5.11.

Overview

I've tried to show that much discussion in social research agonises over the purposes of research and what research can and cannot do. What are we trying to

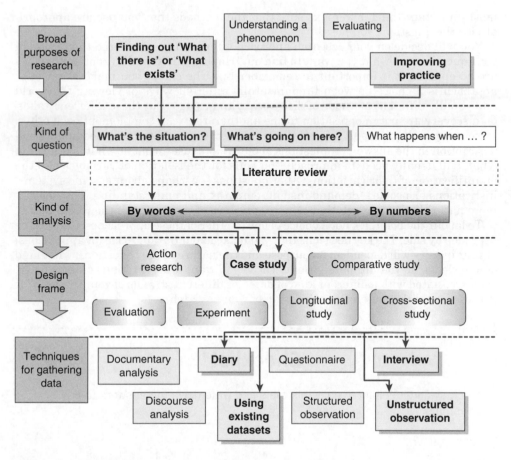

Figure 5.11   Angharad's course through the design maze

study? What counts as knowledge? Can social research explain things? Or does it just help our understanding? How is explanation different from understanding? Is descriptive research without numbers of any value? How far are the methods of *natural* scientists (such as chemists and physicists) appropriate in *social* science? Who can define what science is anyway?

These, among others, are the big questions of social science, and many million words have been written about them without anyone coming to any firm conclusions. Reading about research method in the social sciences leads you to words such as 'epistemology', 'positivism', 'structuralism', 'interpretivism', 'postmodernism', 'quantitative' and 'qualitative', each of them describing different frameworks within which these issues are thought about.

Don't worry about these rather frightening words. More important is an understanding that there is an increasing awareness of the need for different approaches in answering the questions of the applied social sciences, particularly if there is a practitioner focus to these questions. The positive side of this as far as you are concerned is that a broad spectrum of research activity is perfectly acceptable. The most important thing is to make sure that the methods that you use are appropriate for the questions you pose.

You will decide on your research approach after having considered the nature of your question and what you want to find out. Having said that different approaches are acceptable, it is important to remember that the choice you make about your approach is a choice between fundamentally different ways of viewing the world and equally different methods of discovering knowledge. But these different 'takes' on discovery are not in opposition to one another: they can complement each other. Different puzzles demand different thinking strategies. Questions needing formal description in the answer, or questions about what causes what or what is related to what, will usually need an approach that calls for the isolation of variables and the quantification of their variation. Other questions – perhaps about specific systems, institutions or people – demand insight, empathy and understanding. They need a more naturalistic approach that takes cognisance of the person of the researcher.

To labour the point, it's not a choice of one or other of these approaches; they can be used side by side. The key decisions that you make about the approach (or approaches) of your inquiry will depend on its purpose and the nature of your questions: what kind of knowledge do you ultimately want? Or do you want different kinds of knowledge, each associated with a different kind of data, for different strands of your research? It is these issues that determine the design of your research.

Checklist ✔

You may find it helpful to copy this table and write down the answers to the questions.

Have you …

	Notes		
1 … thought about how your research question may lead into a particular *kind* of research?			☐
2 … made a list of what you will need, practically and personally, to complete research of a particular kind?			☐

Further reading

Brookfield, S.D. (1995) *Becoming a Critically Reflective Teacher*. San Francisco: Jossey Bass.
A thoughtful book on reflective teaching, encouraging readers to question the implicit assumptions they hold.

Crotty, M. (1998) *The Foundations of Social Research*. London: SAGE.
Nicely written overview of the interpretivist approach.

Etherington, S. (2004) *Becoming a Reflexive Researcher: Using Ourselves in Research*. London: Jessica Kingsley.
About the realities of bringing yourself to research. Contains sections on heuristic inquiry, keeping a reflective research journal, autoethnography and more.

Fuller, S. (2007) *The Knowledge Book: Key Concepts in Philosophy, Science and Culture*. London: Acumen.
An A–Z of key concepts, refracted through Fuller's refreshingly unusual mind.

MacIntyre, A. (1985) *After Virtue: A Study in Moral Theory*. London: Duckworth.
See Chapter 8 of MacIntyre's book for his devastating critique of the social sciences.

Oakley, A. (2000) *Experiments in Knowing: Gender and Method in the Social Sciences*. Cambridge: Polity.
Ann Oakley is a feminist scholar, and this book includes her take on gender bias in social science. She looks at the historical development of methodology in the social and natural sciences and argues that they have been subject to a process of 'gendering'. Arguing, like so many others, that the divide between quantitative and qualitative should be played down, she says that we should not play down experimental ways of knowing in the social sciences.

Pring, R. (2000) *Philosophy of Educational Research*. London: Continuum.
Excellent – especially on the invalidity of a quantitative–qualitative divide in inquiry.

Sacks, O. (1996) *An Anthropologist on Mars*. London: Picador.
A lovely collection of essays. Sacks is in fact a neurologist, not an anthropologist, and the people he talks with and observes (e.g. people with autism and Tourette's) are particularly interesting for those researching with people who are in any way different.

Savin-Baden, M. (2004) Achieving reflexivity: moving researchers from analysis to interpretation in collaborative inquiry, *Journal of Social Work Education*, 18 (3), 365–78.

Schön, D. (1983) *The Reflective Practitioner: How Professionals Think in Action*. London: Temple.
This is the key text on reflective thinking and practice.

Seale, C. (2003) *Social Research Methods: A Reader*. London: Routledge.
A fine collection of classic papers on method, including pieces from Wright Mills, Durkheim, Flanders, Feyerabend, Kuhn, Geertz and others.

Thomson, A. (2005) *Critical Reasoning: A Practical Introduction*. London: Routledge.
This is industrial strength critical thinking, but clearly explained. If you can use and understand this, you are up in the premier league of critical thinkers.

Wei, L. and Moyer, M. (2008) *The Blackwell Guide to Research Methods in Bilingualism and Multilingualism*. Oxford: Blackwell.
Take a look at this if you are interested in the kind of research Angharad is doing.

6
METHODOLOGY PART 2: THE DESIGN FRAME

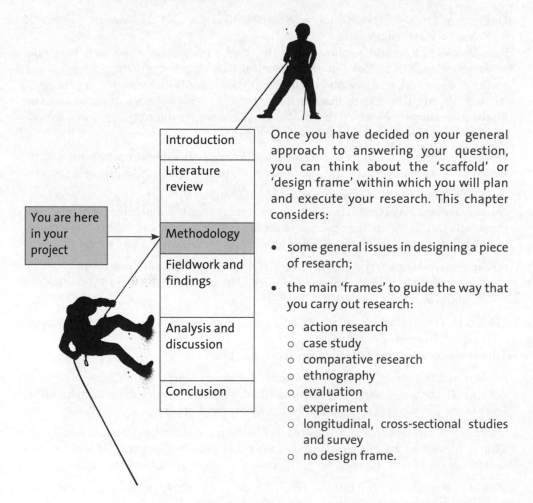

Introduction

Literature review

You are here in your project

Methodology

Fieldwork and findings

Analysis and discussion

Conclusion

Once you have decided on your general approach to answering your question, you can think about the 'scaffold' or 'design frame' within which you will plan and execute your research. This chapter considers:

- some general issues in designing a piece of research;

- the main 'frames' to guide the way that you carry out research:

  o action research
  o case study
  o comparative research
  o ethnography
  o evaluation
  o experiment
  o longitudinal, cross-sectional studies and survey
  o no design frame.

Design is about plan and structure, and as Figure 5.10 in Chapter 5 indicates, the whole programme of your research, from purposes to execution, constitutes the design. One particular part of the sequence of decisions you make will be about what I am here calling the *design frame*. I have called it this because it constitutes the most important element in the way that your research is structured: it's like a chassis that supports your research. The design frame provides the superstructure for your research – connecting purposes with questions with the ways in which data can be collected – though it does not *prescribe* how the data will be collected.

I will be concentrating on seven types of design frame here. There are others, but these seven are the most common structures used in small research projects. They are:

- action research
- case study
- comparative research
- ethnography
- evaluation
- experiment
- longitudinal, cross-sectional studies and survey.

I shall also look at research that is not structured by one of these 'frames', though it will, of course, be designed.

It is important to reiterate that these frames are not designs for research in themselves. The design itself is the plan for research that you adopt from the beginning of your project. The reason I have called these design *frames* is that they provide the defining structure within the design. By choosing one or more of them you are consolidating decisions that you have made about the purposes of your inquiry, the kind of research that you are doing and what you want to achieve from it.

The design frames are scaffolds within which to structure what you do. But it is important also to say that these design frames are not in any way similar as structures, nor are they mutually exclusive. They can exist in combination. So, for example, action research could take shape in most of the other forms, or a case study could include a survey. This will become clearer as we look at the frames themselves.

The idea of research design *per se* – the idea that you plan research at the beginning and carry on according to the blueprint you have drawn until the end – is a bit of a hangover from the days when social research was expected to be as similar as possible to natural scientific

> The design frame is like a scaffold that holds your research in shape and helps to structure it. Many different kinds of design (or 'scaffold') are possible. The design frame you choose will be the one that best helps you to answer your research question.

research. As such, it would be mainly experimental and it would come complete with very specific instructions on procedures, methods and apparatus, with the idea that anyone could come along after you and repeat the experiment you were doing. The key idea behind all of this was *replicability*, or in other words the ability for someone else to repeat what you were doing. If, after many repeats of your experiment, many others had the same finding as you, having followed the same design and procedure, the scientific community could be sure that the finding was secure.

Nowadays, social scientists working in an applied field such as education, social work or criminal justice are acutely aware of the difficulties of conforming to these kinds of expectations for our research. For a start there are now recognised to be difficulties, sometimes insuperable, of managing a social situation in the same way as a chemistry experiment, but there is also now less certainty that there is one best way of organising research. As I tried to show in Chapter 5, if we are trying to research something in the social world we don't necessarily even have to adopt the position of neutral, disinterested observer. By contrast, we can be open, involved interpreters of events, responding and changing as new information appears.

The latter point is particularly relevant as far as 'research design' is concerned, since it implies that there should be far less rigidity about such design than had hitherto been expected. This ties in with the expectation of a recursive plan (rather than a linear plan) that I talked about in Chapter 1. The design, it implies, should not be set in stone, ready to be replicated exactly by the next researcher. Given that this is the case, some have spoken about *emergent design* – in other words, letting the design 'happen' as you find out more about the situation in which you are interested. This idea of emergent design is an important one for social research in the interpretative tradition, and though the word 'design' is still used, it really turns the idea of 'design' on its head, since something that 'emerges' cannot be 'designed'. We should perhaps look for a new word for the process.

However, I'm not going to do that now, since 'design' is the word we are stuck with and everyone knows what they mean by it – or at least they think they do. The trouble with using 'design' is that it implies all of the traditional features of experimental design that I have talked about (e.g. specification of sample, apparatus and so on), and these features carry with them other expectations. There are, for example, expectations about sample size (the bigger the better), reliability (you have to be sure of getting the same result if you do the same again) and validity (you have to be sure that you are finding out what you set out to find). But these are not the ground rules for interpretative research.

Yes, I said *not*. It is *not* expected that you can generalise from interpretative research: your 'sample' gives you insights rather than generalisations. So your 'sample' is small – even as small as one. Be happy with that. In fact the notion of the sample is a misnomer in interpretative research since your informant (or whatever) is not a sample from a wider population. They have integrity in their own right. It is *not* expected that if someone else does the study they will make a finding which is identical to yours. Quite the contrary: someone else will almost certainly find something very different from you, and this is to be expected. They will be interpreting with their personal history, interests, predilections and idiosyncrasies, you with yours.

So, the word 'design' should be interpreted with caution in social research. In certain kinds of research it will be more fixed; in others less so. Expectations about it in one kind of research will not always apply in another.

Some general issues in design

As I have just tried to indicate, the word 'design' is something of a misnomer and leads people to have cast-iron expectations about the structure of research, ignoring the tenets of different types of research – the presuppositions that ground it. Given these different types of research, there can be no expectation that the ground rules and methods of one kind of research will be appropriate in another. It is as well to be aware of this since a major error committed in many dissertations is the use of one set of expectations with a form of research that does not carry these expectations. It is with this warning that I discuss now some general issues in designing a research project.

Sampling

The notion of sampling really belongs in experimental research (see p. 163) and research that seeks relationships among variables. There is the assumption that you are taking your group or groups for your research from a manageable sample which is representative of a larger population. A population in experimental design means something rather more than the one we speak about in everyday parlance (e.g. 'The population of the USA is 315 million'). It means the total number of all possible individuals relating to a particular topic which *could* (if we had all the money and resources we wanted) be included in a study. So, there is a population of teaching assistants, a population of school-aged children, a population of people on benefits, a prison population, and so on. Assuming that the sample is truly representative of this wider population, the findings of your well-designed research can then be generalised to the population.

Of course, the sample may not be representative: there may be *selection bias* of one kind or another. There are many ways in which one can ensure that the sample is representative of this wider population. One is by taking a *random sample*. This is just what it says on the tin: it is a sample that is taken – by a random process, in the same way that names could be picked from a hat. However, it is not good enough for the sample *just* to be randomly taken. If you took as a random sample

> **Selection bias:** A distortion of evidence arising from the way that the data are collected. It usually refers to the selection of people in a sample, but can also refer to bias arising from the ways in which other kinds of data are selected.

of university students the first dozen people you found in the bar on Wednesday night, your sample would be susceptible to various sources of distortion – how do you know that bar-dwellers are representative of the student population generally? It may be that those who go to the bar are less likely to go to the library, or that they tend to represent one ethnic or religious group more than another. That is why this kind of sample (the first dozen in the bar) is called a *convenience sample*, and why a convenience sample has many problems associated with it if you are expecting to generalise from it. To take a true random sample, you would have to ensure that you were drawing a large enough subset of the population so that the chance of getting a distorted picture was reduced to the minimum. You may have noticed that pollsters from market research organisations, when they are looking at voting intentions, take a sample of around 1,000 people; they have calculated that only with this many are they likely to gain a satisfactory sample.

A way of improving a sample's representativeness is to *stratify* it. In taking a *stratified sample* you ensure that the sample you are taking reflects in important ways the characteristics of the actual population. So, supposing you were interested in the views of heating engineers, you could ensure a simple form of stratification in the sample you collected by matching the sample with facets of the (whole) population of heating engineers nationally. You could make sure that your sample mirrored known features of the population – say, with regard to highest qualification. You can see the profile of heating engineers' highest qualifications in Figure 6.1: you would try to match this in your own sample. You could also stratify for the population's age and gender profiles.

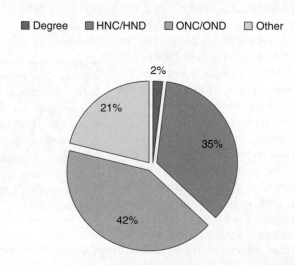

Figure 6.1 Stratify your sample according to known features of the population

What's wrong with the idea of samples?

Professional researchers have extended the notion of sample to all kinds of study, not just experimental research and research concerning the collection of data from groups of individuals. So, sometimes people will speak of a 'sample' in relation to a case study where only one case is being studied. But this is a quite unnecessary extension of the use of the word 'sample' and is clearly ludicrous. For even in a colloquial definition, there is the expectation that a sample will be in some way representative. *The Chambers Dictionary* gives as its definition of sample the following:

> **sample** *säm'pl, n.* a specimen, a small portion to show the quality of the whole.

So, even in everyday usage, 'sample' carries the meaning that the sample is in some way reflective of the whole. But often when the word 'sample' is used in social research it carries none of this 'reflective of the whole' notion. So, a *snowball sample* – which involves the respondent telling the researcher who the next respondent might be, and that respondent doing the same, and so on – does not pretend to any kind of representativeness. Likewise, a *purposive sample*, which involves simply the pursuit of the kind of person in whom the researcher is interested, professes no representativeness. For this reason, these kinds of 'samples' are sometimes called *non-probabilistic* samples, because they do not lend themselves to the kind of design on which inferential statistics using probability estimates are used. Personally, I think it would be easier if they weren't called 'samples' at all.

As I indicated earlier, this carrying of experimental meaning of 'sample' to other kinds of research is accompanied by dangers since it carries with it the quiet assumption that all of the other paraphernalia of experimental research goes along with it. This should not be the case.

> In experimental research, 'sample' refers to a subset that is representative of a larger population. In interpretative research it does not carry this connotation.

Sadly, this mixing of tenets and ground rules has sometimes been deliberate rather than merely accidental, and of course the confusion transmits itself to you as a student – and you have no idea what to make of it. It's only someone who is as old as I am who can realise what has happened. What has happened is that when interpretative research was trying to establish its credentials as authentic 'social scientific' research forty or fifty years ago, researchers went to great lengths to ape the language of traditional experimental and relational research. They did this to boost the status of interpretative research.

So Glaser and Strauss (1967), for example, drew a distinction between what they called the *theoretical sample* and the *statistical sample*. By a 'theoretical sample' they meant the amount of sampling that would have to be done in order for the researcher to be sure that no more categories were being encountered as they went through more and more data. They say: 'As he sees similar instances over and over

again, the researcher becomes empirically confident that a category is saturated'
(Glaser and Strauss, 1967: 61).

If this sounds a little vague, it's because it is, with the word 'empirically' serving
no purpose at all, and thrown in just to make things sound more scientific. (When
do you think, 'Ah! I am now empirically confident!'? When do you feel that warm,
gooey glow of empirical confidence?) If you are interested, I have explored elsewhere
(Thomas and James, 2006) the reasons why interpretative researchers sometimes
seem to think that they need to parrot the language of experimentalists. My feeling
is not only that it is unnecessary to do this (particularly in relation to the sample), but also that it leads to misunderstanding about the nature of interpretative
research. Sadly, the feeling that one has to use the language and methods of experimentalists is a relic of the days when interpretative research was felt to be not quite
good enough. Even more sadly, it leads inexperienced researchers to inappropriate
research designs.

Variables

Things that we want to measure in the social world *vary*. (If they were always the
same – didn't vary – it would be pretty pointless measuring them!) So, *variables* are
measurable attributes of things that change. Age changes, so it is a variable. Scores
on tests vary, so they too are variables. Anything that can be counted could be a
variable: age, class size, time spent sitting down, hair length, reading age, level of
stress, number of words written on a page, and so on. We can also treat what could
be called 'on–off' matters as variables. Thus gender, of which there are of course
only two varieties, can be a variable. The amount of a variable is called its *value*.

Reliability

Reliability refers to the extent to which a research instrument such as a test will
give the same result on different occasions. Really, the idea of reliability has been
imported into applied social research from psychometrics – the 'science' of testing
people's individual characteristics such as ability, attainment and personality. In
my opinion, psychometrics is where the notion of reliability should have stayed. It
is far too heavily drawn on, particularly by student social researchers, who spend
too much time thinking about it and writing about it in their reports. Because it is
something quite concrete (complete with bullet-pointed sub-varieties) in the rather
difficult area of methodology, students sometimes fall on it with eager relief – 'Ah,
here's something I can get my teeth into!' – and spend two or three pages writing
about the sub-varieties of reliability in a wholly irrelevant way.

Certainly if you are collecting data you want your measuring instruments to be
consistent from one time to the next. In other words, if you are giving a test to a
group of children and then give it again soon after, you would expect it to provide
much the same result each time: this is called *test-retest reliability*. Or if two different people gave the same test to the same group, you would expect the test to
provide very similar results each time: it should have good *inter-rater reliability*.

Or you may devise some kind of measure of classroom activity, such as being 'on task' (see the example of Karen on p. 166). If this is the case, you will want to know that the measure you are using is accurately assessing the feature or activity on which you are focusing.

Of course, it is as well to be aware that biases can occur in the use of any instrument – such as teachers giving a test 'helpfully' because they like the new teaching programme which is being assessed by the test. But if teachers were craftily or unconsciously introducing bias in this way it would not be a technical matter; it would be a matter for intelligent appraisal. We should be alert to matters such as this (e.g. giving a test 'helpfully') and try to minimise their occurrence. The compiling of types of errors and biases into technical taxonomies (observer error, observer bias, subject error, subject bias, etc.) diverts attention from the real subject of the research, and it suggests that there are technical 'fixes' to the problems of any kind of individual or social assessment. There aren't. Worse, the idea that these fixes may exist may even distort the construction of instruments, so that they may be 'reliable' but in fact tell us nothing useful.

It is possible to use formulae to help you to establish a coefficient of agreement across times and/or observers which will give a figure representing the reliability of the instrument being used. However, in my experience, in applied social research done by students at undergraduate and postgraduate levels, these are rarely if ever used – nor do they need to be in most cases. It is far more important that you pay attention to whether the instrument is doing what you want it to do and isn't picking up something irrelevant or something that is simply easy to measure (such as 'out of seat' as an indication of being 'off task' – but are pupils necessarily 'off task' when they are out of their seats?). Does it matter if, given on two occasions, the same instrument says something rather different? Surely it is almost bound to, given the nature of people (as distinct from the nature of nitrogen).

As in the case of sampling, there is a confusion that sometimes exists between different kinds of research, with an assumption that reliability should apply in all kinds. It shouldn't. In interpretative research you are interpreting on the basis of you being *you*, interviewing someone else being *them*. Who you are – your 'positionality' (of which more below) – will affect this interpretation, and you would not expect someone else to emerge with the same interview transcripts as you. So reliability is, in my opinion, irrelevant in interpretative research.

Validity

There are two meanings to validity in social science research, but before giving those, I should preface my comments by saying that everything that I have said about reliability applies also to validity: it is a concept imported from psychometrics and from experimental design; it is discussed far too often; and it can distract you from the proper purpose of your research.

> Reliability and validity are important only in certain kinds of research. Don't let consideration of them derail your progress.

What are the two meanings? I have separated these meanings because, as with reliability, some students appear to latch on to the notion of validity and beyond this latching fail to understand the basic differentiation of types of validity (partly because in test construction several subtle differentiations are enumerated). The two types I am enumerating here are *instrument-based validity* and *experimental validity*. Unfortunately, the types have become hybridised and confused in such a way that it is now nigh on impossible to understand what validity means. Here is my simplified version.

Instrument-based validity

With a measuring instrument such as a test, validity is the degree to which the instrument measures what it is supposed to be measuring. *Construct validity* is the Big Daddy of instrument-based validity – the sun around which all the other little instrument-based validities spin. Construct validity is the extent to which the results of a test (or another instrument) correlate with the theoretical construct for which it is seeking to act as an assessment. So, do the results from the test for *x* correlate with the actual *x*? If, for example, someone devises a test for extraversion, scores on this should largely parallel judgements made by a psychiatrist making judgements about extraversion – the latter being taken to be an unimpeachable assessment of this personality trait (and this is of course in itself questionable, but we won't dwell on this). All the other forms of validity you will find are offshoots, really, of construct validity. There are, for example, *content validity* (does it cover all of the necessary content?), *predictive validity* (does a test in intelligence, say, predict the kinds of outcomes for how intelligent people are supposed to fare?), *face validity* (does it look as if it's doing what it should be doing to the person being tested – has it, in other words, got street cred?) and *ecological validity*. They all really are facets of construct validity and there is no real need to try to disaggregate them in your mind unless you are constructing a psychometric test.

Again, the taxonomy of types here is an example of social scientists becoming more interested in the methodology than the subject, and the existence of such a complex taxonomy of types in my opinion distracts from an intelligent case-by-case appraisal of an instrument's use. For example, an IQ test could be constructed that had high marks for construct validity, but this would disguise to the lay reader the extent to which the concept of IQ is itself challenged as a notion – a construct. It's the danger of technical considerations taking precedence over others.

Experimental validity

There are many things that happen in psychological and social life that can mess up an experiment. The extent to which the design of an experiment attends to these and eliminates them is reflected in its 'internal validity'. (Why 'internal'? Don't ask me, ask Campbell and Stanley (1963) who came up with the term.) Chemists (lucky them) can pressurise some nitrogen in a bell jar and see how much it contracts to demonstrate Boyle's law. They don't have to worry about the nitrogen getting older, or having been exposed to the test before, or deciding to quit the experiment for family reasons, or being a particular kind of nitrogen that doesn't like bell jars. No such luck for social researchers. If we construct an experiment we have to keep all of these things (and more) in mind. If an experiment is somehow constructed (designed) in such a way that it manages to eliminate all of these threats to the conclusions being taken seriously we can say that it has good internal validity.

One particularly important threat is that of mistaking causal direction. Is the wind caused by trees shaking their leaves? Are eggs the right size for eggcups because of good planning by hens? I have explored the latter elsewhere in relation to how research on reading difficulty is interpreted (see Thomas, 2002), and it is of course always necessary to consider direction of causation. What causes what? To you and me it's daft even to suggest that the wind is caused by mass leaf-shaking by trees, though a visitor from another planet which experienced no wind, not even a gentle breeze, might be tempted to explore the proposition. It becomes more difficult, though, when an association is found between something like skill in auditory memory and early reading success. It is easy to run away with the idea that the memory is the cause of the reading skill. In fact, though, it may be that reading 'trains' the auditory memory, and that better reading therefore is actually the cause of the better memory.

However, as is so often the case, the problem is not technical. The problem is usually *not* that no one has considered the possibility that y may be causing x rather than x causing y, but rather that they do not *want* to consider the possibility, for any one of a variety of reasons. (The sinister implications of this are discussed very nicely by Gerald Coles (2000) in *Misreading Reading: The Bad Science that Hurts Children*.)

Experimenter effects

Always be wary of the potential of introducing 'experimenter' effects. They are effects caused by you, the researcher. They go under various names – principally, Hawthorne effect and experimenter-expectancy effects. It is important to remember that effects of this kind can occur when you are doing your research and you should be aware of them as you plan your work and discuss your findings. They take various forms in different kinds of research, but I will give a brief account of two particularly important kinds.

The Hawthorne effect

The Hawthorne effect is about a change in people's behaviour which happens because an interest is being taken in them. The interest seems to spark enthusiasm, and the extra energy injected into the research situation may have positive consequences of various kinds. The effect was named after the Hawthorne Works, a factory near Chicago which made electrical parts for telephones. In 1924 the US National Research Council had sent two engineers to run experiments there in the hope that they would learn how improving lighting on the shop-floor influenced workers' productivity.

They did indeed discover that improving light levels improved productivity. But not only this, it transpired that *any* change – the maintenance of tidy work-stations, moving benches around, clearing floors, and even *reducing* light levels – all had the same effect. This iconic study was written up in the literature by Roethlisberger and Dickson (1939). The discussion which followed the Hawthorne research centred around why the improvements in productivity happened, and whether they were due to the alterations in work arrangements (in this case the light level, placement of benches, etc.) or the interest being taken in the workers. It seemed as if it was the latter.

Imagine a rather different scenario from the Hawthorne one, where the change introduced by the researchers is rather more blatant: imagine a local authority is interested in the idea that improved ventilation and air conditioning may improve the concentration and wakefulness of the residents in its senior citizens' homes. The local authority arranges for a small-scale evaluation of the idea in one of its homes, planning for new ventilation to be installed there, and arranging at the same time for the behaviour of the residents to be monitored.

Picture the scene: two cheerful young mechanics come into the home to fit the ventilation apparatus. They joke with the old gentlemen and flirt with the old ladies, whistle and sing and call to one another and generally banter about what a power of good the new apparatus will do the residents. All this is accompanied, before, during and after, by the presence of a friendly research assistant who watches the residents carefully and asks them all how they are feeling. I'd feel more wakeful and alert. Wouldn't you? So how would an investigator know that it was the ventilation equipment that had been responsible for any measured increase in alertness? Answer: they wouldn't. An investigator would have to design their experiment to eliminate the experimenter effect, which is more easily said than done. At the very least, they would have to be aware of the effect and acknowledge its potential contribution to their findings.

The experimenter effect is a fascinating phenomenon and is one that we should always remember, both in constructing our own research and in reading that of others.

Experimenter-expectancy effects

Experimenter-expectancy effects are rather different; in fact, they represent almost the obverse of Hawthorne effects. They are brought about by the expectations of the researcher. By gestures, tone of voice, or the actual questions that you ask or the words that you use you may convey your expectations about your findings to your research participants, who will then, consciously or unconsciously, conform to the lead you appear to be giving. Social scientists always have to be wary about *leading* participants in this way.

Generalisation and generalisability

In everyday life, when we make judgements about the future – predictions – these are usually on the basis of generalisation from experiences we have had in the past.

Events that repeatedly occur in certain circumstances enable you to generalise – to say to yourself that these events will tend to occur in these same kinds of circumstances in the future. You notice that when there are no clouds it doesn't rain, so you make a reasonable generalisation about the low likelihood of precipitation when there are no clouds in the sky. While such generalisations serve us well most of the time, they do not match up to the expectations that science has when it seeks to offer laws and theories – which are also based on generalisation but, one might say, generalisation-plus. Scientists cannot proceed *simply* on the basis of common-or-garden generalisation. As the great philosopher Bertrand Russell (1956: 91) put it, the person who makes the claim that *unsupported bodies in air fall* 'has merely generalized, and is liable to be refuted by balloons, butterflies and aeroplanes'.

What Russell is saying here is that while generalisation is important, it has to be more than a mere rule of thumb based upon everyday observation of life's patterns. Science's generalisations have to have a bit more oomph about them than that. Good generalisations – generalisations that provide accurate predictions – are at the cornerstone of scientific progress. It's just that we have to find ways of making our generalisations more than the 'mere' generalisations Russell was talking about.

And it is even more difficult to make sensible, accurate generalisations in social science than it is in physics or chemistry. Social phenomena are, you will have probably noticed, characterised by the involvement of *people* and the problem is that people don't behave like pulleys. In the things we are interested in as social scientists, the people – our focus of interest – are actually involved in the phenomena being studied. People have interests and enthusiasms; they predict events, get bored, have rivalries and friendships – in the way that pulleys rarely do. So these vagaries and idiosyncrasies of people actually influence the findings of social research. It may be that, for instance, the positive results of an experiment can be put down to the enthusiasm of the people involved in the trial rather than to the exciting pedagogic innovation that inspired the experiment. If we then generalise on the basis of the results of the experiment our generalisation will lead us into troubled waters.

An example of this arises in the interest which has recently surrounded the use of 'synthetic phonics' for teaching children how to read. A number of small-scale studies in Scotland (see Johnston and Watson, 2003) had reported on remarkable advances in the reading and spelling of children who had received a 'synthetic phonics' programme, and there was much ensuing interest from media and government. The Secretary of State for Education, Ruth Kelly, at the time when interest was at its peak commented, 'I am clear that synthetic phonics should be the first strategy in teaching all children to read' (see http://news.bbc.co.uk/1/hi/education/4818516.stm). The trouble was (and still is, since government are still enamoured of the 'strategy') that people were generalising from insufficient evidence. The limited sample was prey to all of the problems that arise because of the enthusiasm and energy that are usually invested in the introduction of an innovation. A much wider, systematic review of the evidence (see Torgerson et al., 2006) in fact showed that no statistically significant difference in effectiveness could be found between synthetic phonics instruction and analytic phonics instruction.

If we leave aside the problem of generalising from insufficient evidence for a moment (and it's a big problem to leave aside), there is a more direct problem of the representativeness of your sample: how well does your sample *represent* the population? As I noted above in discussing sampling, the whole idea of taking a sample is that it is a sample of a wider population, and if your sample does not represent this wider population the extent to which you can generalise from it is only very limited.

Remember that generalisability is of importance only when you want to generalise. If you are conducting a case study with only one subject, it is more or less meaningless to worry about generalisation (though people do worry about it, I can assure you). You cannot generalise from one case. The Germans have a phrase, *Einmal ist keinmal*, which means, roughly speaking, 'What happens only once might as well not have happened at all.' I personally wouldn't go quite that far, but I would agree with a watered-down version of this, namely that we can learn no general lessons from things that happen only once. But how many more do we have to study before we can say that we can generalise? This depends on a great many factors, not least the adequacy of your sample as a representative sample.

As with so much in social science, there are no hard-and-fast rules about generalisation. Many would no doubt go along with the short-story writer Damon Runyon and his comment in 'A Very Honourable Guy': 'The race is not always to the swift, nor the battle to the strong. But that's the way to bet.' In other words, one's generalisations may be far from perfect as ways of judging the future, but one can, to varying extents, rely on them as rules of thumb in ordering our lives or in interpreting the findings from our research.

Positionality

In interpretivist research there is an assumption that knowledge is situated in relations between people. This is sometimes called *situated knowledge*. With this assumption taking the foreground, the person doing the research takes a central role in the interpretation – in the discovery of this situated knowledge. The researcher therefore has an undeniable *position*, and this position affects the nature of the observations and the interpretations that they make. There is an acceptance in this of the importance of the person – their likes and dislikes, their backgrounds and their pastimes, their vested interests and expectations. The researcher is an active, not passive, agent in acquiring knowledge of the processes, histories, events, language and biographies of the research context. Because of the importance of the nature of the relation between the researcher and research participants, the researcher's biography – including class, gender, ethnicity, ideas and commitments – needs to be made explicit.

There is also the assumption that in doing research you are in some sense serving a certain set of needs, and these needs are not necessarily unequivocally good or altruistic. They will not necessarily be about the good of education (in the widest sense) or the child. They may be self-serving or benefiting a particular group. This should be made explicit.

The explicit acknowledgement of this may present some dilemmas. Let's imagine that you are a newly qualified teacher having recently completed your PGCE and you wish to study now for a master's in teaching and learning for which you have to complete a research project. You discuss it with Zena, your Head of Year, and she suggests that you use your research project to evaluate the school's new inclusion policy. You already know from staffroom discussion that the policy is thought to be a joke – devised to keep Ofsted and the local authority happy but serving little purpose in practice. You are therefore faced with a predicament. Given that you intend to undertake an interpretative study, how would you construct your eventual write-up, for the university will be expecting a discussion of positionality – of your interests, uncertainties, allegiances, and so on – while Zena and the school management may expect something entirely different, something that pretends a cleaner, more dispassionate and supposedly 'objective' assessment of what they assume to be 'the facts'. So, for you, this idea from Zena is non-viable as a potential research project because you would have to make all of this explicit in the write-up. The problem here is about the conflict between your integrity as an interpretative researcher and the expectations and interests of the school.

In presenting interpretative research you should accept your subjectivity and not be ashamed of it or afraid of it. Given that it is central, your dissertation or thesis should be written as if you realise the underpinning principles that guide the conduct of this kind of research. An interpretative study will therefore be reported in an entirely different way from an experimental study. You should begin – right at the beginning, in the introduction – with a full discussion of positionality: of *yourself*, why you are interested in this topic, what your personal circumstances are, and so on. You will always write in the first person, saying, for example, 'I believe that ...' rather than 'The researcher believes that ...'. This may seem obvious, but it is a common mistake for students conducting interpretative research – research that demands that they put themselves at the centre of the analysis – to report their work as if they have just conducted an experiment and to omit any information about themselves. If you do this kind of research, readers need to know who you are and where you stand, metaphorically as well as literally.

Triangulation

Triangulation is a term that has been borrowed from surveying and geometry, where it refers to the use of fixed reference points organised in triangles. By knowing an angle and the length of two sides of a triangle, the third can be accurately calculated and distances can be checked and cross-checked.

In social science the term is used simply in a metaphorical way, based on its origins in geometry and surveying. There is no intimation that triangles should be involved, or that things have to be done in threes. Rather, the term is used to indicate that

> **Positionality:** Saying who you are and 'where you are coming from'.
>
> **Triangulation:** Looking at things from different angles and using different methods for looking.

viewing from several points is better than viewing from one. Given the instinctive uncertainty – the critical awareness – that should be the hallmark of the good social science researcher, another viewpoint or another analytic method may make you decide to reject an explanation that you had come up with from your first analysis of findings. Or it may encourage you to have more confidence in the explanation you proposed on the basis of your first analysis. For this reason, using several methods, or viewing things from several directions, is sometimes built into a piece of research at the beginning. Suppose, for example, that you were interested in the kinds of pop music enjoyed by arts and science students, hypothesising that arts students would enjoy 'softer' music than science students. To test this you might take 20 pop groups, and divide them into soft and hard – with Arcade Fire in 'soft' and ZZ Top in 'hard'. Is there any difference in the way that arts and science students react to each? Triangulation would be about looking at their reactions in different ways: you might

- give a questionnaire, asking students to rate their likes and dislikes;
- play them extracts from each type of music, watching for their body language;
- interview a sample from your questionnaire cohort, to take ideas gleaned from your questionnaire further.

This is an example of what the research methodologist Norman Denzin (1978) would call *methodological triangulation*, where more than one method is used to collect data. However, Denzin outlined several types of triangulation, including *investigator triangulation* where more than one person is involved in interpretation and analysis, and *theory triangulation* where more than one theoretical framework might be involved in its interpretation. I would add to Denzin's categories *design frame triangulation*. In other words, you would be triangulating if you used both a case study and a longitudinal study together in the same piece of research.

Opinions differ on the need for triangulation. Some interpretative researchers argue that a piece of interpretative research has value and completeness in itself. It doesn't need any verification from other kinds of research. It has integrity as a singular inquiry. The argument for the integrity of the singular case, singularly done, is a powerful one. But the argument for corroboration, for the need for alternative kinds of evidence, each corroborating the other, is to my mind even more powerful, and triangulation is really simply about corroboration. I discussed the importance of corroborative evidence on p. 22.

The design frames

Action research

Action research is research that is undertaken by practitioners (e.g. teachers, social workers, nurses or doctors) for the purpose of helping to develop their practice.

It is usually done at the same time as perform-ing that practice. The central aim is *change* and the emphasis is on problem-solving in whatever way seems most appropriate. It is flexible in design: the assump-tion is built in firmly at the beginning that as the research proceeds you will go back to revisit your aims, assumptions, beliefs and practices, think about all of these critically and then revise them.

It may be done by an individual or a group, per-haps in collaboration with a consultant such as a uni-versity tutor. For this reason it is sometimes called 'participatory action research'. In other words, the assumption is that it is different from the way that traditional social research has sometimes been con-ceived: that is to say, as research done *by* researchers *on* subjects. It is research primarily done by the 'subject' or practitioner, with the aid of others.

Figure 6.2   Kurt Lewin

The idea of action research came from the great social psychologist Kurt Lewin (Figure 6.2). In his paper 'Action research and minority problems' (Lewin, 1946), he was critical of social research, saying that 'research that produces nothing but books will not suffice'. He describes action research as 'research leading to social action' using 'a spiral of steps, each of which is composed of a circle of planning, action, and

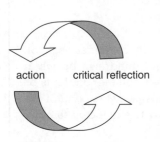

action   critical reflection

Figure 6.3   The basis of action research

fact-finding about the result of the action' (see Figure 6.3). The basic idea is of a continual refinement of your thinking, built upon a foundation of reflection about the problem and ways of going about solving it. The process is shown in Figure 6.4.

So, action research is a bit like a coil or spring, where you are continually moving forward up the coil by reflecting on action and changes that you have made.

Much has been written about action research over the years and there are many different ideas about the

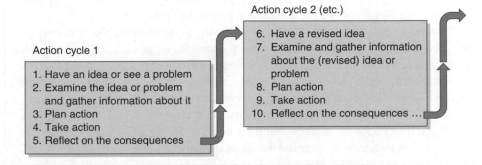

Figure 6.4   Action research: a spiral of steps

way that it should or should not be done. My own view is that there are four basic ideas at the core of action research: that it …

1 is research done by practitioners, at their own behest – not someone else's;
2 is primarily about developing practice and empowering practitioners;
3 involves a commitment to change and to action based on reflection;
4 involves moving forward, always building on what you are discovering, using the process of planning, reflection and re-planning (shown in Figure 6.4).

Beyond this, it can take almost any form that you wish it to take. Indeed, Jean McNiff and her colleagues (McNiff et al., 2003) suggest that action research is more of a 'form of dialogue' than a technique, and that it is about practitioners thinking for themselves and making their own choices, asking themselves what they should do and accepting the consequences of their actions.

For me, this sums up the spirit of action research. Beyond this, it may take almost any form. For example, you may wish to do a small experiment within an action research frame. It may involve a case study. Or you may undertake action research that involves some kind of evaluation.

Example 6.1

Emily is a newly qualified teacher of history in an inner-city secondary school. One of her Year 9 students, Rashid, is surly, disengaged and withdrawn, but when challenged can be aggressive and even physically violent to other students or to staff. At the end of last term he had refused to hand in a pen at the end of the session and when confronted pushed Emily out of the way to exit the classroom. For this he was temporarily excluded from school.

In working with her local university for a postgraduate qualification, Emily decided to do an action research project based not only on Rashid but also on challenging behaviour from other students. The action research framework involved trying to develop her practice in such a way that confrontational incidents would occur less often. The plan is shown in Table 6.1.

A number of issues arose for Emily in doing this; for example, with regard to point 2, some rethinking was necessary about the nature and causes of challenging behaviour. In point 3, some innovative ideas came from separate discussions with her Head of Year and her university tutor. The latter suggested trying to make a special relationship in some way with Rashid and, capitalising on a brief moment when Rashid had shown an interest in one of her lessons on evacuated children in the Second World War, Emily asked her uncle, who had been an evacuee, if he would email Rashid about his experiences – which

Table 6.1 A circle of steps

Action research steps	Questions/issues/actions (in brief)
1. Defining the problem	The incidence of confrontational behaviour from students and one student in particular.
2. Examine the idea or problem and gather information about it	Is it a problem just for Emily? How far is it a problem of her making? Is it the school's problem or the student's problem? Read around the area of challenging behaviour; ask colleagues what they have done in similar circumstances with Rashid and others.
3. Plan action	Define what you mean by 'challenging behaviour'; keep a record and a diary of incidents of challenging behaviour; when does challenging behaviour occur, in what circumstances; plan ways of developing relationships with the students (challenging and unchallenging); list action to be taken if it occurs.
4. Take action	Take the action planned in step 3.
5. Reflect on the consequences	Examine records and diary. Consider the effects of the action taken. What was effective? What wasn't? Discuss with colleagues, advisor, consultant and/or tutor. Move to the next action cycle.

he was glad to do, sparking up an unlikely web friendship. Still on point 3, her Head of Year helped Emily to devise a list of appropriate and inappropriate behaviours to take when physically challenged by a child.

Having completed this 'circle of steps' and reflected on the consequences in the final step, Emily was then able to move on to the next circle of steps, having seen what worked and what didn't work. Rashid certainly responded to the efforts Emily had made on his behalf and began to act, if not with enthusiasm, with more courtesy, respect and a new-found gentleness. She considered a number of possible actions, having completed the first circle of steps. She considered, for example, how far the action she had taken with Rashid was relevant and generalisable to other students in her class. She therefore decided to run a number of small focus groups with three or four of her students in each, and various focus materials comprising newspaper and magazine articles for discussion. With these, she would try to do with the others what she had done with Rashid – find something of interest and use this to help develop a relationship with the students.

Part of her reflection was also to realise that the special relationship she was nurturing with Rashid as part of the research was extra-special, even with the focus groups she had subsequently planned. Given that this might create additional difficulties with other students in the class, she included as her move to the next circle of steps some special activities also with other children in the class – for example, taking a group of the quieter and more able children to a local museum at the end of term.

Case study

A case study involves in-depth research into one case or a small set of cases. The case may be a child, a hospital ward, a period in time, an event, a business, a social services department ... the list could go on. The aim is to gain a rich, detailed understanding by examining aspects of the case in detail. The data you collect can be from different facets of the question you are examining, and these data – perhaps from numbers or from interviews or informal observations – may be combined to tell your finished story. This combining of methods is often important in a case study: it can include as many different methods and procedures as necessary for understanding what is going on in a particular situation. So a case study is like an umbrella, covering a whole range of inquiry activity.

There is no intimation in the case study that you will be generalising from this case to others. How could you? It's one case. In other words, you are not studying this case in order to understand others. You are studying it in order to understand it in itself. For the research methodologist Martyn Hammersley (1992) this choice of one case (or a small number) is made with a trade-off in mind. You are choosing this very restricted sample in order to be able to gain greater detail, but at the expense of being able to make useful generalisations to a broader population.

It's important to note that you don't study a particular case just for the sake of studying it. The case is not simply a story: it has to illuminate some theoretical point; it has to be a case *of* something. In some way it (the case) then explicates the 'something'. Wieviorka (1992: 160) puts it this way:

> For a 'case' to exist, we must be able to identify a characteristic unit ... This unit must be observed, but it has no meaning in itself. It is significant only if an observer ... can refer it to an analytical category or theory. It does not suffice to observe a social phenomenon, historical event, or set of behaviors in order to declare them to be 'cases.' If you want to talk about a 'case,' you also need the means of interpreting it or placing it in a context.

Let me give an example: suppose you were interested as a political science student in the notion of 'a just war' – the idea that some wars are justified ethically: World War II is the one that is usually cited in this context, and several well-known pacifists such as Bertrand Russell came to revise their views on pacifism in the light of this war and the evils it sought to defeat.

Case study research comprises two parts:

i a **subject**, and

ii an **analytical frame**, or **object**.

Now, we could use World War II as a case study *of* a just war. Whereas 'World War II – a case study' in itself would not be a true, social science case study, 'World War II – a case study of a just war' *would* be. In the latter case you are using World War II to examine and illuminate the notion of a just war. You are looking at the features of this war that made it a 'just war'.

Elsewhere (see the 'further reading' section for this chapter), I have used Wieviorka's distinction to note that there are two essential parts to a case study: the *subject* and the *object*. The subject is the case itself (in my example, World War II), while the object is the analytical frame (the notion of a just war) which the subject is in some way exemplifying and illuminating – analysis of 'the just war' is made possible by examination of World War II. Table 6.2 gives some more examples.

Table 6.2   The subject and the object of the study

Subject ...	As a case study of ...
Mrs Smith's geography class	A good class
Editorials in the *Daily Globe* for the six days in the week beginning 5th March	A newspaper proprietor's influence over the content of editorials
Dilby Ward at Midtown Children's Hospital	An effective children's ward
Aleksandr the meerkat	The exemplary use of personality and storyline in advertising

> This right-hand column is the **object** of the case study, which the **subject** (in the left-hand column) explicates.

So, a case study is like one of those capsules with two halves – and each half, each ingredient, is necessary for the other half to work, as shown in Figure 6.5.

Choosing a case study subject

Taking forward this idea that a case study has a subject and an object, how do you identify the subject? There are three main reasons for choosing a particular subject for your case study. You may choose it because you know a great deal about the

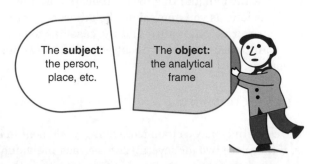

The **subject:** the person, place, etc.

The **object:** the analytical frame

Figure 6.5   Two parts to a case study

case in question and you want to understand some feature of that subject. Or you might choose it because it provides a particularly good example of something – it may not be one with which you have direct, personal experience but it may be iconic or well known and there may be a great deal of information available on it. Or the case you choose may reveal something interesting because it is remarkably different from the norm. I call these three options:

- Local knowledge case studies
- Key case studies
- Outlier case studies

Whichever you choose, you will choose it because of the subject's ability to act as a lens or template through which you are examining the object. Remember that the object is the purpose of your study: the subject is, in a sense, just a vehicle you are using to 'get at', to 'take apart', to explicate the object. Table 6.3 gives some examples of how the different kinds of case study subject will take shape.

Table 6.3 Different kinds of *subject* and how they give rise to different kinds of *object*

Subject type	Subject	Because ...	Object
Local knowledge	Your own class	You know a lot about it	The distortion of the curriculum by national testing regimes
Key	Hostos-Lincoln Academy, New York	It is a well-known example of success	High achievement among students from homes with low incomes
Outlier	The state of Kerala in India	It is different from other low-income states and countries in having low infant mortality	Economist Amartya Sen's 'support-led' approach to improving social conditions

What kind of case study

I don't want to make this too complicated, and you are fine to proceed with a case study as long as you appreciate the difference between the subject and the object – in other words, you realise that the case has to be a case *of* something. However, if you want to think further about potential *kinds* of study you can consider a range of options.

Single or multiple

The case study may contain more than one element in its subject, and if this is so – that is, if there are two (or several) cases – each individual case is less important in itself than the comparison that each offers with the others. For example, a study might be conducted of two schools' different capacities for making effective use of a visiting education support service. By contrasting the schools' 'biographies' – their histories, catchments, staff relationships and other characteristics – light would be thrown on the relative dynamics affecting the reception and use of the support service. The key focus would not be on the nature and shape of relationships *per se* in one school, but rather on the nature of the difference between the one and the other and what this might tell us about the dynamics that were significant in this difference.

The boundary and the shape

The choice about single or multiple studies determines what follows in the shape of the case study. Single studies, containing no element of comparison, will take essentially three forms, wherein features of the subject are bounded by time in some shape or form. The case inquirer notices change as it happens and seeks its antecedents and its consequences. We have to find the 'sequence of steps', as Becker puts it (1992: 209), and understand cause in relation to time, with 'each step understood as preceding in time the one that follows it'. In doing this we conjecture not only about how one thing is related to another, but also about how cause and effect change with time as other elements of a situation also change.

I suggest (drawing on other commentators) that the varieties of time-use lead to three kinds of study: **retrospective**, **snapshot** and **diachronic.**

- The retrospective study is the simplest, involving the collection of data relating to a past phenomenon of any kind. The researcher is looking back on a phenomenon, situation, person or event or studying it in its historical integrity.

- With the snapshot the case is being examined in one defined period of time: a current event; a day in the life of a person; a month's diary of a marriage. Whether a month, a week, a day or even a period as short as an hour, the analysis will be aided by the timing of events as they happen. As the snapshot develops, the picture presents itself as a whole over a defined timeframe.

- The diachronic study shows how changes may have happened over time, revealing how and why those changes may have happened.

For multiple studies the researcher considers additional features of the situation. How can the different subjects be used for comparison? There are two principal means of doing this: first by straightforward comparison between clearly different examples – a *simple comparative* study. Second, comparison may be of elements within one case – comparison, in other words, of nested elements. With *nested* studies the breakdown is within a larger unit of analysis – for example, wards (the nested elements) within a hospital (the larger unit). A nested study is distinct from a simple comparative study in that it gains its integrity, its wholeness from the wider case. For example, with the wards within a hospital you might be looking at, say, three wards within one hospital, but if the one hospital had no significance other than its physical housing of these three wards then the cases would not be seen as nested. The elements are nested only in the sense that they form an integral part of a broader picture.

A further subdivision may be drawn in the multiple study, and this is between parallel and sequential studies. In the first, the parallel study, the cases are all happening and being studied at the same time, while with the sequential study the cases happen consecutively (one after another) and there is an assumption that what has happened in one or in an intervening period will in some way affect the next. Figure 6.6 summarises the choices made in undertaking single or multiple case studies.

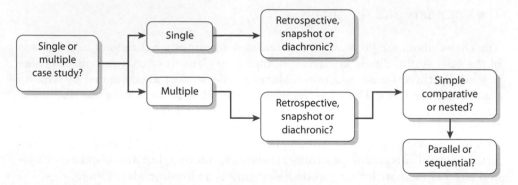

Figure 6.6   Choices in undertaking single or multiple case studies

I examine these types of case study and the choices you make in doing them in much more detail in my book *How to Do Your Case Study* (Thomas, 2011).

Example 6.2

Robin is in his second year of teaching as a Year 6 teacher in a primary school. Last year, in the run-up to the SATs, he noticed some disturbing signs of unease and anxiety among his pupils: more absence and illness and a general sense of disquiet that he couldn't put his finger on. For his project as part of a university course, he decided during the next round of SATs to undertake a case study of his class, focusing in a detailed way on the attitudes and responses of pupils and teachers to these assessments. Starting with the notion of a link between these changes in behaviour and the national testing programme, he knew that his case study would relate the one to the other.

Since the government's regime of testing affected him most directly in Y6 (since this is age at which the SATs are given), Robin knew that of all the teachers in the school it was his own views on the impact of the assessments that were most relevant and important. He was particularly concerned about the emotional impact on the children, so in the six weeks leading up to the SATs he kept a diary of his impressions of the behaviour of the children and his own feelings over that time. He committed to spending 15 minutes at the end of each day writing the diary, which would produce 30 diary entries (6 weeks × 5 days) for subsequent analysis. He also committed to focusing on five children in his class, whose work and demeanour he would monitor closely but informally over the same period. He would for specified periods observe the children informally. He would take notes about the children's work, their attendance and their punctuality and he would make a point of talking to each of them briefly

---

at least once a week, asking about their work and about how they were feeling. He would then keep an audio diary of his impressions of these encounters and the children's comments.

Although the SATs affected his class most directly, Robin had a suspicion that the culture of assessment made its effects felt through the age range, so he decided to interview all of the other teachers in the school for their opinions on the influence that SATs had had, even if only informally, on their own work and the attitude of children to learning.

Robin's analysis concentrated on drawing themes from the data, for example about anxiety in the children and the formalisation of style of teaching by himself and other teachers. He related these themes to the form in which expectations about success in the SATs were communicated to teachers by government departments and their agencies, and the implicit or explicit messages that accompanied these expectations.

In terms of the analysis of case studies that I have given above, we could say that Robin's case study is

- a local knowledge case study
- a single case study
- a snapshot case study.

Classic examples of case study are in Stephen Ball's (1981) *Beachside Comprehensive* and Colin Lacey's (1970) *Hightown Grammar*, which each give a detailed analysis of what goes on in one school over a period of time, and James Patrick's (1973) *A Glasgow Gang Observed*, giving a detailed narrative of what went on in the gang from the point of view of a young man infiltrating it (I discuss Patrick's work more on p. 110). These were doctoral studies, and most dissertation work will not be expected to go into any way near such detail as these authors did in their work. However, they are enormously useful to read – in the work of both Ball and Lacey for examples of the kind of data gathering that can be done and the way that case study work can be linked intelligently to national policy, and in Patrick's work for the style of involvement and reporting discourse that he uses, which is as good as reading a novel.

Ethnography

If you do an ethnography you are working right in the middle lane of interpretative research (see p. 108). This is as interpretative as it gets. Confusingly, this design frame may be called 'case study method' but as we have just seen, case study can cover a much larger range of study methods than merely this one.

The term 'ethnography' comes from a field of social research that emerged in the early part of the twentieth century as a branch of anthropology, the study of humankind and its cultures. Ethnography evolved as a response to what was considered to be an inappropriate way of studying other cultures or communities, which had before the 1920s been treated almost as scientific objects of study by anthropologists. Writing was often judgemental, wearing the moral spectacles

> Ethnographers study a situation from within. They try to become part of the situation they are studying, to understand it like the other 'players'.

of the Western viewer. And if you are interested, look at Stephen Jay Gould's (1996) *The Mismeasure of Man* to see how some anthropological 'scientists' used to do their work by comparing the size and shape of the skulls of different races. Displacing this style of work, the new ethnography aimed to get to the heart of people's understandings of life through fieldwork *with* people rather than supposedly objective study *on* them. James P. Spradley, a great exponent of ethnography in the middle of the twentieth century, put it thus:

> Field work ... involves the disciplined study of what the world is like to people who have learned to see, hear, speak, think, and act in ways that are different. Rather than *studying people*, ethnography means *learning from people* ... Instead of collecting 'data' about people, the ethnographer seeks to ... be taught by them. (Spradley, 1979: 3)

Spradley draws on the example of a young American ethnographer, Elizabeth Marshall, who, interested in the culture of the Kalahari Bushmen, went to the Kalahari with her family in the 1950s. Marshall describes her meeting with a young woman:

> Presently she smiled, pressed her hand to her chest, and said: 'Tsetchwe.' It was her name.
>
> 'Elizabeth,' I said, pointing to myself.
>
> 'Nisabe,' she answered, pronouncing after me and inclining her head graciously. She looked me over carefully without really staring, which to Bushmen is rude. Then having surely suspected that I was a woman, she put her hand on my breast gravely, and, finding that I was, she gravely touched her own breast ...
>
> 'Tsau si' (women), she said. (Cited in Spradley, 1979: 3–4)

You can glean from this brief example of Marshall's writing that the purpose of the ethnographer was to understand from within, treating the people with whom she is working with respect, as different but equal. It is typical of the style of reporting of ethnographers, who work through *fieldwork*, which Spradley (1979: 3) describes as 'asking questions, eating strange foods, learning a new language, watching ceremonies, taking field notes, washing clothes, writing letters home, tracing out genealogies, observing play, interviewing informants, and hundreds of other things'. (Note, though, that 'fieldwork' now means something much more general: any empirical work of any nature.)

He goes on to note that for Tsetchwe to turn the tables and go to a small Wisconsin town to try to understand its culture would involve her doing everything that Elizabeth had to do, which first and foremost would mean ditching a belief in *naive realism*, which is to say the belief that '*love, rain, marriage, worship, trees, death, food*, and hundreds of other things have essentially the same meaning to all human beings' (Spradley, 1979: 4, original emphasis).

Ethnographers have to try to forget the meanings that these phenomena have for themselves in order to understand their significance in the other culture. This is hard of course and it means, usually, a long immersion in the cultures they are studying – learning new languages and learning about unfamiliar customs and practices – to try to understand how sense is made out of these and how meaning is invested in them. In order to make this sense, ethnographers have to use their own resources as people: as Bob Burgess (1982: 1) puts it, 'The main instrument of social investigation is the researcher.' As an ethnographer, there is no attempt to deny your own personal knowledge or to put it to one side, though you might be expected to take an entirely new perspective on the scene that confronts you. In the sense that the person of the researcher is central to the process of research (and you are not in any way attempting to be 'objective'), you must *use* your knowledge of people, social systems and structures and how they relate rather than rejecting this knowledge, but use it in a way that enables you to 'see outside yourself'. You can do this by, for example, using Geertz's thick description (discussed on p. 109). In other words, look to see what turns the twitch into a wink or the parody of a wink. Use your understanding of people to understand this situation that you are focusing on, and tell the reader how you are doing it.

Another facet of the positioning of *yourself* as an instrument of investigation is that you are a participant in the situation that you are observing and studying, which is why the term *participant observation* is often associated with this kind of research. You are not, in other words, trying to be detached or invisible, but rather engaged, fully involved, and gaining insights from this engagement. Participant observation is not limited to observation, pure and simple, though. It consists of watching, certainly, but also conducting interviews, listening to conversations, keeping a diary, taking notes and much more – anything that will help you to record and understand what is going on.

For an interesting (and short) example of the ethnographic genre, see Clifford Geertz's (1977) 'Deep play: notes on the Balinese cockfight', which is available online if you type 'Geertz deep play notes on the Balinese cockfight' into your favourite search engine.

Ethnography is now a well-accepted way of doing certain kinds of applied social research. In fact, some of the most influential research in education has been ethnographic in character. However, doing a small ethnographic project presents some major differences from the classic studies of which I have given examples. For a start, unlike the professional anthropologists cited here, you are unlikely to be entering a culture which is *unfamiliar* to you. Rather, you are likely to be entering a very familiar situation; in fact, the situation in which you are interested may be one with which you are intimately connected, perhaps as an employee or a regular visitor. Second, you will not have the time for the deep immersion of the professional anthropologists – but this may not be as necessary because of the familiarity you already have. This in itself has pluses and minuses: you may know the 'stage' and be an accepted 'actor' on it, but this means that you have to work extra hard to see it in a fresh light.

Though your immersion in the world of your study will be different in these important respects from the immersion of the 'classic' anthropology, beyond this the rationale behind ethnographic work is the same, and is about participation, engagement, thick description and understanding.

Example 6.3

Qualifying as a teacher three years ago, Amy is now head of maths in a large inner-city comprehensive school, but she wishes eventually to move into learning support. As part of a master's degree in education she decides to do her dissertation research on the way that support works in the school. She wishes to understand how students see support, and what support can offer them. In particular, she asks whether there are any ways that the support department in the school can enhance its offer to its students.

She decides that her research project will be an ethnography of support: how it works and how it is viewed and understood by students and staff. She negotiates with the Head of Learning Support to use some of her regular non-contact time to work as an assistant in the Learning Support Department. She asks to be treated as a teaching assistant for these periods, and ensures that she will be working only with classes with whom she has no dealings in her maths teaching. Her sessions of involvement with the department will include attendance at meetings and work with two classes per week as a participant observer: one science class and one languages class.

She prepares for this by planning carefully to observe each of the environments into which she goes. She decides not to take notes as she does this, as this will affect the way that the students and staff react to her during the sessions. However, she will write a diary immediately (or as soon as possible) after every session. She will also conduct unstructured interviews with both teacher members of the learning support staff as well as two of the teaching assistants associated with the department. The interviews will give free rein to these staff to express their views about the operation of support. On top of this, she will interview four students – two from each of the classes that she is working with. Further, on her movements around school, she will keep an eye and an ear open for comments or actions that in any way give clues as to the way in which learning support is viewed in the school. Is it seen genuinely as a way of including all students, or merely as a way of dealing with students who are seen to be 'special needs'?

An excerpt from Amy's diary is as follows:

I make my way to Xanthe's class again, a little late, having been talking to the head of support. I haven't spoken in detail to Xanthe yet about the team teaching idea. Last week's meeting with her was too tense to broach the topic. When I come in this week the situation seems rather similar. Xanthe is taking the class from the front and the children are messing around as they were last week. Xanthe holds up a small glass tank with a funnel upside down over something (a small plant, I think) and compares it with another similar set of objects. The children have to compare the two sets and say how they are different:

CHILD: There's more water in that one.

CHILD: One's all dirty – yeugh.

The session is to show that carbon dioxide is taken up by plants:

CHILD: That dirt's carbon dioxide!

Explanations are again punctuated with inconsequential intrusions:

CHILD: Anyone got a rubber!

These become so intrusive that Xanthe eventually loses her temper and raises her voice. This has some effect on the students, who temporarily quieten down. She capitalises on this by saying:

TEACHER: Right we'll have two minutes of complete silence – not a word.

The children respond to this: they are now clear about the rules and what is expected of them. Again I feel redundant – not only redundant, but worse that I am compounding the situation by my presence, and perhaps that Pauline the teaching assistant is in a similar position. She must feel some degree of inhibition about doing what comes naturally to her to quell the sorts of problems that she is experiencing. Again, there is no way that I feel I can intervene in the immediate situation without making things worse …

(Continued)

(Continued)

Amy analyses her findings using a variety of methods (some of which are described in Chapter 8). Her main aim in the analysis is to understand how learning support is viewed and understood in the school, so she is careful to try to see through the eyes of her informants, with that view moderated and influenced by her own reflections as recorded in the diary. Each element, though discrete, goes to inform each of the others and in her discussion she integrates and synthesises the analysis from each.

Possible question for Amy in undertaking the ethnography:

How will she be able to use this diary when it makes comments that are implicitly critical of a colleague?

Evaluation

Evaluation research is probably the most common kind of research done by professional researchers in education and the social sciences, being undertaken to assess how effective a programme of activity has been. When done by professional researchers it is often carried out as a form of what is sometimes called 'contract research': a university researcher is contracted and paid to provide an independent assessment of some new initiative. A government department, for example, may pay a university research team to look at how effective the policy of employing greater numbers of teaching assistants has been. The pattern is given by Pawson (2006) and corresponds roughly to Figure 6.7.

As you can see from Figure 6.7, evaluation research is different from action research, since there is – in the usual form of evaluation – no assumption that what is being studied feeds back in any systematic way to the activity, intervention or initiative being evaluated. (In action research, remember, there is the assumption that what is being discovered during the research actively feeds back and contributes to the development of the programme of change.) Only after the evaluation has been completed may the person contracting the evaluation decide to continue with the programme, modify it in some way or completely 'pull the plug' on the innovation – depending on the findings of the evaluation. Ultimately, it may be the case that enough pieces of evaluation are conducted in different places and in different circumstances and by different teams for there to emerge a body of research about the particular kind of innovation or

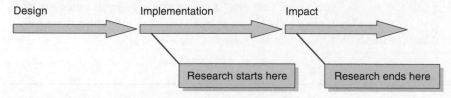

Figure 6.7   Evaluation research (from Pawson, 2006)

programme in question. This body of work can then be drawn together and examined in a systematic review that will inform the development of future practice.

While evaluation research of the kind I have just described is often large in scale, it is quite possible to set up evaluation on a smaller scale for an undergraduate or postgraduate research project. Here you will be looking to assess the impact, effectiveness or other consequences of some newly introduced programme, usually within the frame of an institution's set of policies or of some initiative that you or colleagues have personally introduced. The change is introduced and the evaluation examines the consequences.

Ideally, an evaluation will look at what happens *before*, *during* and *after* an innovation is introduced, with as long a period of examination as possible in each of these three phases. In practice (and certainly this is the case for student project work), evaluation may begin only during the period of implementation, or even after this, though this is of course not ideal.

Given that an evaluation focuses on before-and-after elements, there may be a temptation to think that it has to collect data relating to pre-specified variables – things that you can count – so that it is possible to tell whether there has been a measurable increase or decrease due to the intervention. Certainly this may be the case – for example, reading ages could be taken before and after introducing a new system of reading in groups, and if the evaluation took place over a long enough period it may be possible to draw some conclusions about the effectiveness of that new system. However, an evaluation may collect almost any kind of data that those who are involved in the implementation find acceptable as indices of effectiveness.

Example 6.4

Gemma is studying for a BA in Education and English and is on a placement in a primary school – a placement which her university expects to provide Gemma with information for a double-module research project. Knowing that the school is implementing a new policy for playground supervision, she decides to make the implementation of the policy the subject of her research. The school is completing the policy and just preparing for implementation as Gemma is able to start her research.

After negotiating with her class teacher and the head teacher, she decides to undertake a three-part evaluation. First, at the beginning of term she will collect some data about playground behaviour before the implementation of the policy. Second, she will examine the implementation of the policy itself. Third, at the end of term she will collect data about playground behaviour again, subsequent to the completion of the formal process of implementation.

Several constraints from the 'real world' could have affected the data that Gemma could have collected here, but she capitalised on the fact that she was just in time to collect some 'before' data before looking at the process of implementation.

(Continued)

(Continued)

Gemma devised a checklist for observing in the playground which she used in the first and third phases (in other words, in the before and after phases). The checklist, which she would complete at set times during two weeks of observation before and after, included recording observed incidents of physical aggression from child to child, incidents of verbal abuse and other incidents of teasing or aggression. She would record the circumstances of these. At the same time she would record the circumstances surrounding these incidents and briefly interview staff on duty during each of the periods of intervention, asking also for reflections on the effects of the policy on the circumstances in question. She would emerge with data about 'critical incidents' backed up with (or 'triangulated with') informed comment from staff.

For the assessment of the implementation (i.e. the second stage) Gemma undertook interviews with staff – three teachers, three teaching assistants and three midday assistants – about how they felt about the policy, how they had been involved in devising it, how easy it had been to conduct it in practice and how optimistic they were about change. She interviewed six children – one from each year group – asking some basic questions about the policy (to find out how much they knew about it) and whether they felt it was altering playground behaviour.

Her analysis focused on bringing together the different kinds of data in each of the three phases, and then trying to understand how the implementation had happened in the context of the total evaluation. In other words, understanding how and why there was a fall in the incidence of difficult and bullying behaviour at playtimes but not at dinnertime. Her conclusion – properly tempered with caveats about the limitations of the data – was that the policy worked better when implemented by teachers and teaching assistants than it did when implemented by midday assistants, who had not been involved in the writing of the policy.

Possible questions for Gemma after the evaluation:

Were there enough participants involved in the research to find out what was going on?

How could play-fighting be distinguished from aggression in the observation?

Were there enough 'data points' to be sure that the evaluation was reliable?

Should the evaluation have taken place over longer periods before and after the implementation?

Experiment

As we noted in Chapter 1, one important branch of research is that which seeks to find out whether, or to what extent, one thing causes another to happen. This is in fact often the aim in social research – in other words, trying to see if x causes y – but the different design frames are differently suited to answering such questions. Experiment is taken by some to be the most reliable way of determining that such causation is occurring.

In everyday parlance, 'to experiment' can just mean to try something out, and 'an experiment' can simply mean an investigation of some kind. In science it means something more precise: it means a test done under controlled conditions to prove or falsify an idea or conjecture. However, in social research it means something even *more* specific:

- it is about demonstrating cause and effect;
- it concerns the extent to which we have to control the conditions in the situation of interest to demonstrate that cause–effect relationship.

The reason why it is difficult to say that x causes y in social research is that there are a very large number of factors and issues at play in any social situation. If you change one of these factors and claim that the change you have made has been responsible for the improvement (or deterioration) in another factor you are likely to be challenged by someone saying 'How do you know that it wasn't a, b or c (and not x) that caused y to change?' Using the same example I gave earlier, if a teacher introduces a new scheme of reading and she can show that the reading age of the children in her class rises following the introduction of the new scheme, how can she know that it is the reading scheme that has caused the improvement in reading? Couldn't it perhaps be that the children would have improved anyway – even with the old reading scheme? And if the improvement looks dramatic so that the teacher says 'This extraordinary improvement can only be put down to the new scheme', couldn't the improvement perhaps be attributed to the new energy that the teacher is giving to her teaching, given the stimulus to her interest provided by the new scheme?

Experiment seeks to rule out the possibility that factors such as this (and many others) could be responsible for the change. In its simplest form it seeks to isolate two variables – the one that you assume may cause change (e.g. the reading scheme), and the one that you are assuming may have change effected on it (the reading age in the example that we have been using) – from the myriad variables that might be at play in a situation. In sciences such as physics or chemistry an experimenter holds everything else – every other variable – constant in order to be able to say that any change made to the first variable has *caused* any measured change in the second.

But in social science we can't be sure that x has caused y, because the thing we are interested in measuring (e.g. reading age) has an annoying habit of changing

Table 6.4 The classic experiment

	Pre-test	Treatment	Post-test
Experiment group	Take first measure	✓ give treatment	Take second measure
Control group	Take first measure	✗ no treatment	Take second measure

anyway, irrespective of what is being done to it. This is why, in social scientific experimental research, we have to do something such as bringing in an extra group, as alike as possible to the first group, and giving them everything that the first group was given so that we can eliminate sources of variation – every source of variation, that is, except the one we are deliberately varying. So, an experiment in a social science situation usually involves two or more groups being treated in exactly the same way, save one, namely the manipulation of the first variable. Any difference that then exists between the two groups after the manipulation is made to happen by the experimenter is taken to exist because of the experimental treatment. This classic form of the experiment is usually shown as in Table 6.4.

A lot can go wrong in all of this (see the discussion of experimental validity on pp. 140–1), not least due to the effect of the myriad confounding variables that might affect the result of an experiment. These confounding variables include the galaxy of minor and major things of everyday life that cannot be factored into any social situation: power failures, the colour of the paint on the walls, the morning's argument with the spouse, and so on. The philosopher Alasdair MacIntyre (1985: 99), in his devastating critique of social science, puts it this way: 'There is at the outset no determinate, enumerable set of factors, the totality of which comprise the situation.' He suggests that social science will always either be ignorant of the potential effects of the indeterminate set of factors or will fail to notice the most important of them. He gives the example of the potential importance of the length of someone's nose. He noted that a historian had suggested:

> A control group serves as a basis of comparison in a piece of research. The control group receives no experimental manipulation.

> that the cause of the foundation of the Roman Empire was the length of Cleopatra's nose: had her features not been perfectly proportioned, Mark Antony would not have been entranced; had he not been entranced he would not have allied himself with Egypt against Octavian; had he not made that alliance, the battle of Actium would not have been fought – and so on. (MacIntyre, 1985: 99)

But keeping these caveats about validity in mind, what are the practicalities?

The way that an experimenter states the expected outcome of manipulating the first variable is via a hypothesis. An example of a hypothesis is: 'Raising children's self-esteem in Year 5 will raise their attainment in English.' You can measure self-esteem with tests, and you can measure attainment in English with tests, and when you have completed your experimental study you can see whether your hypothesis is true. (You may come across the term 'null hypothesis', particularly in psychological studies, but I feel there is no need to complicate things with this, which seems to me to be an example of social scientists making things more complicated than necessary.)

It's important to understand some jargon about experiment, and I've been trying my hardest to avoid it until now, but you will need it if you decide to do an experiment and read any further about this design frame. It is given in Table 6.5.

Table 6.5 Experiment jargon

Independent variable	*which means*	the variable you change (e.g. the reading scheme)
Dependent variable	*which means*	the variable you are examining (e.g. reading age) to assess the effect of changing the independent variable
Experimental error	*which means*	uncontrolled sources of variation that occur during an experiment

Figure 6.8 is a greatly simplified representation of the process of an experiment, and experimenters have to set up experiments very carefully (ensuring, for example, that the groups are as alike as possible) to maximise the probability that the conclusions they draw about x causing y are correct. There are many opportunities for going wrong in all of this – in the setting up of an experiment or in interpreting its conclusions statistically. Going wrong can mean that you may assume your hypothesis is correct when it is not, or that you assume your hypothesis is false when in fact it is correct. These errors are usually summed up in some more jargon – Type I and II errors.

- Type I Error: this is when you accept your hypothesis as true, but in fact it is false.

- Type II Error: this is when you reject your hypothesis as false, but in fact it is true.

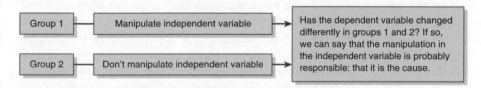

Figure 6.8 What an experiment consists of

We'll examine some of the ways in which the results from an experiment might be analysed and interpreted in Chapter 8.

There are many different sub-frames to the experiment as a design frame (to the extent that there is a whole branch of methodology called 'experimental design'), and it is beyond the scope of this book to examine them. One distinction that is worth making is that between 'true' experiments and 'quasi' experiments. The former include the random allocation to groups of the research participants, whereas the latter do not do this – perhaps using 'natural' groupings, such as those provided by local authority education groupings. If you wish to take this further, look at the 'further reading' section at the end of this chapter.

Example 6.5

Karen completed a PGCE last year after doing a first degree in psychology and is now studying for a master's in teaching and learning. The major part of this comprises a research project that will be written up into a 20,000-word dissertation. Her topic for this will be the organisation of the adults in her class of Year 5 children. She has one teaching assistant permanently and two parent volunteers every morning. Management and organisation of this kind of assistance was not part of her PGCE curriculum, so Karen reads the literature and finds that there are a number of ways of thinking about how extra assistance of this kind can be deployed. One method of organisation called *room management* (see Cremin et al., 2005) involves giving each adult a set of very specific tasks to do (such as predominantly helping individuals or predominantly helping groups), wherein those tasks constitute a named role. The roles can be changed from session to session; the main thing is that each individual knows which role they are supposed to be fulfilling.

Karen thinks that this new method of organisation holds some promise, and hopes that it will provide some structure for her work with other adults in her class. Rather than simply trying it out and proceeding on a gut feeling about whether the new system of organisation seems to be working, she does a small experiment. This involves a particular kind of experimental design, where instead of using two groups (an experimental and a control group), there is one group (Karen's class) examined under two circumstances, or *conditions*, where the only change is to the system of organisation in her class. This particular kind of experimental design is called a *repeated measures design* and is particularly suited to small-scale study. In the first condition she and the other adults are working normally; in the second condition the only change is that they are using the 'room management' system of organisation. To assess the effect of this change Karen decides to use the children's engagement with their work – in other words, looking to see whether they are doing what they are supposed to be doing: certain behaviours, such as sitting and writing, will count as 'on task', while others, such as wandering around the class, will count as 'off task'. By drawing up a list of on-task and off-task behaviours and observing for these systematically Karen can keep a count of what is happening in the class under the two conditions.

The experiment requires organisation that will take many features of the situation into consideration. Karen first has to plan when the observations will take place under the two conditions. Because the two conditions must be identical apart from the change in the system of organisation, she has to ensure that the same kind of work is being done by the children and the same people are there with her class in both periods of observation. They have to be at the same time of day and even, if possible, on the same days of the week, for these are also sources of variation which could plausibly make a difference. Then she has to train the assistant and parents in the room management system and schedule the sessions. She also has to arrange for observation to happen to test the effect of the system on the dependent variable, children's engagement or 'on-taskness': she organises this by asking another parent who regularly assists in the classroom to video the sessions and she subsequently goes through the video with a checklist looking at each child in turn for a set period to work out an on-task percentage figure for each.

Each child's overall engagement (or 'on-taskness') is then plotted for the two occasions, producing the chart shown in Figure 6.9. Using some simple statistics, Karen is able to show that the differences between the two occasions are statistically significant (this is discussed further in Chapter 8). Simple 'eyeballing' of the chart (i.e. just looking at it intelligently) also shows a number of interesting things. Because Karen ranked the children's engagement from lowest to highest in the first condition, she can see how those who are at the lower end of the scale – that is to say, those children who find most difficulty attending – are affected by the introduction of room management. The chart clearly shows that most of these see their engagement improve markedly over the two conditions.

(This example is loosely based on Cremin et al. (2005).)

You'll realise from all of this that an experiment, done well, requires the tight control of variables. One of the things we need to be aware of with experiment of the kind in Example 6.5 is that situations such as these are frail and unstable and difficult to control exactly. The American psychologist Jacob Kounin (1970) wrote a classic text about this instability, and it has profoundly influenced our understanding of what happens in classrooms. The insights it has offered are as relevant today as they were when his book was written. Kounin's breakthrough was to see

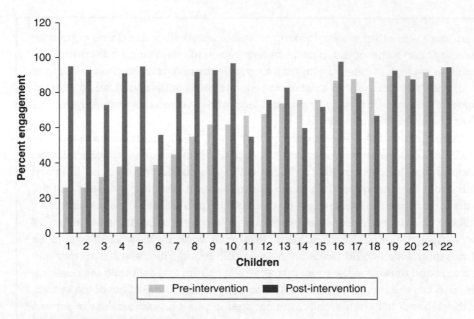

Figure 6.9 Children's overall engagement

the classroom as an environment with an ecology, rather in the way that a habitat for plants and animals is an ecology. An ecology is a dynamic environment: if foxes are blighted, rabbits do well. Or, to put it more prosaically, if you squeeze an environment in one place it bulges somewhere else. Seeing the classroom in this way – as an ecology – Kounin said, helps us to understand why we cannot simplistically expect to be able to impose changes without there being some unexpected consequence. We should always be aware of this when we try to manipulate social situations as tightly as is necessary for the running of an experiment.

The next example of an experiment (Example 6.6) reveals a rather simpler assessment of the effect of an innovation. It is enlightening especially because it was done before applied social science had really been thought of as a discrete field of study, and, indeed, almost before social science itself had been conceived. It shows that groundbreaking research can be undertaken without any thought about paradigms and epistemology (and see also 'No design frame' on p 181).

Example 6.6

Margaret McMillan was a social reformer at the end of the nineteenth century who did a great deal of work in the industrial North of England and in London. She spent several years in Bradford, which had grown exponentially as an

industrial town of 'dark satanic mills'. The accepted practice was for children
to be routinely involved in all kinds of heavy and dangerous work: they were
ill cared for and malnourished.

McMillan said that children at school in the 1890s were 'worse than anything
described or painted … children attended school in every stage and state of
physical misery' (Steedman, 1990: 108). Deciding to do something about this, she
worked with Bradford's school medical officer to undertake research that would
provide evidence of the need for, and benefits to be reaped from, better-fed children. She set up an experiment in which one group of children was fed breakfast
and lunch every school day, while a control group continued without. The findings
are reported in Figure 6.10. The results are so clear and so well presented that
they need no additional explanation.

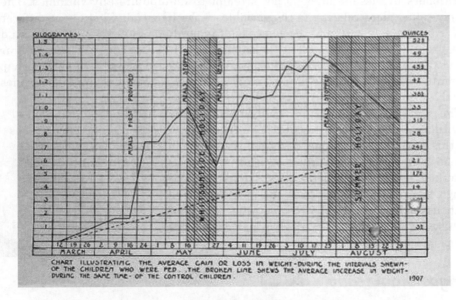

Figure 6.10   Margaret McMillan's chart giving the findings of her experiment
(reproduced by kind permission of The National Archive)

Despite the fact that it could not have been informed by all of the twentieth-
century discussion about methodology and paradigms, this little experiment
constitutes a simple but stunningly effective piece of research. It is perhaps
most helpful not as an example of a simple experiment (though it *is* helpful

(Continued)

(Continued)

in this respect), but rather as an example of a well-thought-through piece of research: it identifies an important issue – malnutrition in children – and it offers a simple solution which it tests. Thus, it goes from idea, to implementation, to collection of data to analysis. The end product gave firm evidence of the benefits of providing free school meals to children and its consequence was the 1906 Education (Provision of Meals) Act in England and Wales.

Longitudinal and cross-sectional studies – and surveys

Both *longitudinal* and *cross-sectional studies* make use of data relating to large numbers of individuals or groups. Unlike researchers undertaking experiments, researchers in these studies do not attempt to manipulate any variables. They simply collect data relating to the variables – the longitudinal study at different points in time in relation to the same set of individuals; the cross-sectional study for subsets of a population all at the same time – in a 'snapshot'. These data are then examined for trends or differences relating to one or more variables, perhaps examining possible reasons for observed relationships between and among these variables.

The *survey* is an important method *within* the longitudinal and cross-sectional design frames and for this reason I am giving it special attention in this section. In fact, the survey is rather more than a method, and rather less than a design. It is not a design frame in itself, but there are clearly defined methods such as questionnaires and interviews that are used within the survey. I shall examine these issues in a moment.

> Longitudinal and cross-sectional studies make use of data relating to large numbers of individuals or groups. The survey is an important method that they use.

Longitudinal study

This involves the study of a group of individuals or cases *over an extended period*, regularly examining them for the effect of time on the variable or variables of interest. Because time is the crucial factor, it is unlikely to be used in a short research project of the type done in an undergraduate dissertation – there simply isn't enough time for you to collect data at intervals sufficiently far apart in time for any meaningful difference to be detected. However, for certain topics, a master's degree and certainly a doctoral degree may provide sufficient time to sample enough points in time to provide meaningful data.

One of the decisions to be made in a longitudinal study is how far apart the data collection points should be. If changes and developments are happening quickly, frequent data collection is necessary, and vice versa.

You may come across the terms *cohort study* and *panel study* in relation to longitudinal research. A cohort is a group of people who share some characteristic or experience. These people can then be followed up at regular points in time. A panel study is similar to a cohort study and the terms are sometimes used interchangeably, though a panel study usually refers to a smaller group wherein individuals can be picked out for further questioning if necessary.

Because longitudinal studies by definition take place over a long period of time, one of the problems associated with them is attrition, or the loss of members from the group being studied. This attrition may be important in some cases, as those who drop out – for example, those who move away or become untraceable – may share particular characteristics of interest to the research, and the data may become skewed for this reason.

> **Skew:** Occurs when the data being collected in your sample vary in a particular way from the data that actually exist in the complete population. This may happen because, for example, you are only questioning people who are easy to question. These people may form a particular subgroup, with views very different from the general population.

A major example of a longitudinal study is in the Millennium Cohort Study, which is examining all 20,000 children born in the UK in 2000–1, looking at the health and well-being of children and parents in the context of a broad range of socio-economic data. The children and their families are observed at regular intervals, illuminating links between different aspects of human development.

Example 6.7

Graeme is a social worker who has a particular responsibility for counselling and supporting the parents of children who are born with inherited illness or disability. With a view to furthering his qualifications in this area, for the past three years he has been gathering data in a structured way from his own work and that of colleagues in different parts of the UK. He enrols as a part-time MPhil student on a two-year university course entitled 'Psychosocial Aspects of Genetic Healthcare', explaining to his tutors that he intends for his dissertation to use the data he has already collected relating to 127 families, adding to that data and eventually analysing the data over the two-year progress of the course. These 127 families will form the *panel* for this study: the children are at different ages and with different inherited conditions but share the feature of inherited illness, and the group is small enough for subsets of it to be asked supplementary questions as the data emerge and themes begin to develop.

(Continued)

(Continued)

Through his professional organisation, the British Association for Social Workers, Graeme has secured a small amount of funding for the research for the purpose of helping to involve the colleagues who are assisting him in collecting data. He promises to involve them in the analysis of the research and to run an invited seminar at the conclusion of the data collection but prior to its analysis. He believes that the seminar will give him insights into how the data should be analysed.

From questionnaires he and his colleagues ask the families to complete, Graeme will eventually have data about the inherited condition, disability, illness and school circumstances of the children, and will have records on the family circumstances of the 127 families, though he expects some attrition as time passes.

Graeme decides that he will focus in his research on the stresses in the family created by inherited conditions. Because it is a longitudinal study and not a snapshot his focus is on the changes and developments in these stresses that happen over time – do they get more or less intense, or do they change in character? His data collection instruments therefore have to be constructed in such a way that they will be sensitive to stress and the ways in which it might change as time unfolds. They should also seek to garner information about the ways in which stress is ameliorated or lessened over time – or the ways in which it increases – and what sorts of influences contribute to the decrease or increase in stress for families.

Graeme's questionnaire, which he pilots with three families he knows well, asks about family stress (self-rated) and reasons for it, with questions about income, professional support for the family, availability of help from friends, family and community, the presence of siblings and their ages, and similar issues. As would be expected, what appears to emerge most clearly from the data is that level of stress seems to be connected most prominently to the seriousness of the inherited condition. It did not show a clearly observable trend over time in Graeme's sample, but this was because data were collected on individuals at different stages since their diagnosis. Because the data are being collected at identical points in time (September to October in 2007, 2008, 2009 and 2010), for some of the children collection took place soon after diagnosis and then at points thereafter, while for others (with whom Graeme and his colleagues had been involved over a longer period) it took place well into their involvement with the family and some time after diagnosis.

In order for trends to be discerned it was necessary to 'disaggregate' the data – to 'pull it apart' – so that it was possible to put individuals into four separate bands, grouped by time since diagnosis. By doing this Graeme could discern that stress started at a high level and fell off rapidly with the input initially of high levels of support but that stress gradually rose again over intervening months and years as supporters seemed to lose interest. Looking at the panel as a whole, the level of stress appeared in its ongoing nature and severity to be ameliorated most significantly by the existence of strong family support rather than professional support, and this observation gave Graeme and his colleagues much food for thought at their seminar at the close of the project.

As this longitudinal study is not an experiment, and the array of variables is not being held constant with only one manipulated (as would be the case in an experiment), it is not possible to say what causal relationship may or may not be involved in any of the observed relationships. All Graeme can do is to make intelligent guesses as to the meaning of the observations he makes about these relationships, and this is a perfectly legitimate thing to do.

> **To pilot:** Means to conduct a much smaller study (a pilot study) to prepare for a larger one. It is done to refine or modify research methods or to test out research techniques.

Questions for Graeme:

What are the ethical issues arising from this kind of study?

Graeme wondered about the ethical justification in adding to the stress of already stressed families by regularly asking them questions, but concluded from his pilot study that it was probably the case that most families valued the interest being expressed in them. Nevertheless, he was keen to avoid putting additional pressure and ensured that each family opted in to the research, and could opt out at any time if they wished.

Were there enough data points at which data were taken?

Cross-sectional study

Here a group or groups are studied at the same time – as a snapshot. One variable may be looked at, providing a descriptive picture, or two or more variables, offering the possibility of seeing a relationship among them. Alternatively, you might *at one moment in time* study equivalent groups – for example, of children at different ages. The key thing is that the observations are all made at the same moment in time, with a group whose members share some characteristic.

An example of a cross-sectional study was the Office for Standards in Education (Ofsted) report *Early Years: Leading to Excellence* (http://www.ofsted.gov.uk/

resources/early-years-leading-excellence). This looked at 84,000 early years and childcare providers, examining the quality of childcare provision made by each alongside the local authority within which that childcare was provided. It found that in the 30 most deprived local authorities, 53 per cent of childminders provided good or better childcare, compared with 60 per cent in the rest of England, with some stark comparisons between best and worst: in Hackney (East London), 29 per cent of childminders were judged to be good or better, compared to Wokingham in Berkshire where the proportion was 81 per cent. What can this tell us? Clearly the local authority is not the *cause* of these differences (even if some politicians will try strenuously to make that case), though it may be the case that in more deprived areas the pool of well-educated people available to work in childcare is smaller than that in a more prosperous region. In this case the grouping provided by the local authority is perhaps misleading since it implies an association between quality of childcare and the administrative authorities themselves, rather than the more amorphous geographical regions in which they are situated.

Example 6.8

Working as a nurse, Sangheeta is a part-time MSc student in healthcare. She is interested in the effects of smoking on young women who are still at school, and as part of her work decides to conduct a cross-sectional study of all the girls in Year 10 in schools of the small unitary local authority (LA) area, Gotham City, within which the hospital at which she works is situated. Having gained the agreement of the Gotham City LA to approach the schools in the city, and having in turn secured the agreement of nearly all the secondary schools to involvement in her research, she visits each to administer a survey to Y10 girls asking about smoking habits and other features of their health and behaviour. In the questionnaire she devised, she asked, for example, for the girls' own self-assessment of how fit they thought they were, including questions on breathlessness and coughing, and on how well they thought that they were doing in their schoolwork compared to the rest of the girls in the year group. She also asked them for their opinions on when girls usually have their first baby.

This provides Sangheeta with descriptive data (e.g. numbers of cigarettes smoked per day for each girl, a self-rating out of 7 on fitness, a self-rating on coughing, etc.). She is able to present graphically the data she receives from the 860 girls to whom she has given questionnaires. The self-ratings on coughing and breathlessness and the self-rating data on fitness and attainment in schoolwork are in the graph shown in Figure 6.11.

She finds that among girls who smoke the average age they expect a woman to have her first child is 25, while for those who never smoke it is 27. She presents this in prose form, since a table or graph is unnecessary.

The population being studied here was intended to be the entire population of Y10 girls in Gotham City, and to all intents and purposes that aim was fulfilled, though two schools did not take part in the study and some girls were absent on the day of the questionnaire. Sangheeta argued that this population was probably representative of the wider national population, and in that sense acted as a sample for this wider population to whom she argued her conclusions could apply. She argued that any relationships that were noted, while they might vary in extent in the wider population, would be unlikely to occur only in the Gotham City sample.

Some simple statistics (examined further in Chapter 8) showed significant differences between the smoking and non-smoking groups. In reporting

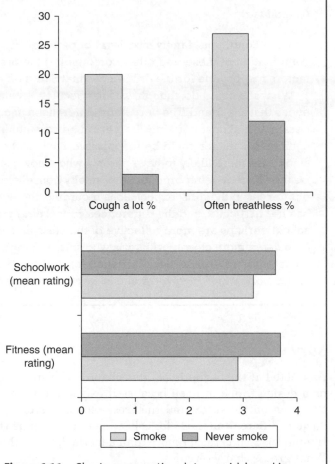

Figure 6.11   Charts representing data on girls' smoking

these, however, Sangheeta had to make sure that she made no over-ambitious claims for her analysis. It is not possible to impute causation from the associations found in a cross-sectional study – or indeed from any associations. It would not be possible, in other words, to say that smoking had *caused* the greater breathlessness, lower perceived attainment, etc. The associations that were discovered could be due to entirely different factors. For example, there may be personality differences between smoking and non-smoking groups which have their consequences both in a tendency to smoke (or, perhaps, just to *say* that they smoke) and in a tendency to answer more 'daringly' in questionnaires. Or there may be differences in parental income levels between smoking and non-smoking teenagers, with associated differences in

(Continued)

(Continued)

housing conditions, family size, level of parental supervision, and so on. Any combination of these and other confounding factors are quite plausibly the factors responsible for the differences that Sangheeta discovered.

What she could do, though, was to speculate intelligently about the differences that she found. The very large differences in coughing and breathlessness could almost certainly be attributed to smoking (though even here a confounding factor could be responsible, such as the fact that teenagers who smoke are more likely to have parents who smoke, and their coughing could be the effect of being brought up in smoky households). On the other hand, the differences in the girls' expectations regarding the age of a woman when she has her first child, and the differences concerning perceived achievement at school perhaps are more reflective of the class and social conditions that are associated more closely with girls who smoke. Sangheeta was able to discuss these possibilities and this discussion formed the basis for the next element of her work, which involved some in-depth case studies with individual girls.

Survey

As I noted at the beginning of this chapter, the survey cannot really be thought of as a design frame in itself because it exists in different design forms (principally the longitudinal study and the cross-sectional study), and yet it holds within it various different methods for collecting data (such as the interview and the questionnaire). So it is rather more than a method, but rather less than a design frame. What are its characteristics?

In a survey you are collecting data from a varied number of respondents (i.e. people who are responding). They may be responding in a questionnaire or in an interview, or they may be completing some kind of diary entry (we shall look at these in Chapter 7). The data can be many and varied. As I have noted in discussing longitudinal and cross-sectional design frames, these data are collected to describe some feature of the social situation in which they exist, and these features of the situation are not manipulated, as they would be in an experiment. Once these descriptive data have been collected they can be examined for the existence of relationships between and among them.

Example 6.9

As is the case in any design frame, the methods used to collect data in a survey will affect the findings that are made. A good example of different methods involved in collecting survey data arose in an argument over the size of the audience for *Coronation Street*. The Broadcasters' Audience Research Board (BARB) has a panel (see p. 171) from whom it finds out what programmes people are watching on TV. The method BARB uses to do this is a 'peoplemeter', which is a device given to all 5,300 households in the panel, who press buttons on the meter to tell BARB what they have been watching. The 5,300 TV sets in the panel are a representative sample of the 20 million or so in the UK, and on the basis of the button-pressing, BARB is able to estimate how many people watched particular programmes. On 25 January 2002, BARB estimated that 11.2 million people had watched an episode of *Coronation Street*. However, another organisation, Carat, undertook a telephone survey of a sample of viewers and estimated the audience for the same episode to be 14.5 million (see http://news.bbc.co.uk/1/hi/entertainment/tv_and_radio/1793556.stm for the full details).

Figure 6.12 BARB and Carat came up with 14 million and 11 million respectively as the audience for *Coronation Street*

Questions that might be asked about the difference and why it existed are many, and include:

- Was Carat contracted by anyone to undertake the survey?

- Might BARB's figures eliminate those who recorded the show to watch later?

Because the panel used in this survey provided both a snapshot and an ongoing picture of TV-watching over time, it could be called either a cross-sectional study (at a particular time, as in this *Coronation Street* case), or a longitudinal study, providing a developmental picture of TV audiences over time (see www.barb.co.uk).

Comparative study

Usually, the term 'comparative study' refers to the comparison of a social situation in one country with that in another. In the broader social sciences it can be used to mean any kind of comparison, but in applied social science and education it nearly always refers to international comparison, and that is the way that I shall discuss it here. Comparative study deserves a special mention as a design frame because it faces particular challenges, and it meets these with a particular range of methods used with a well-developed set of considerations.

For the purposes of applied social research, then, comparative study is about cross-national, cross-societal and/or cross-cultural comparison. Clearly, a range of issues arises when such contrasts are made because differences in language, customs, value systems, lifestyles and institutions exist across these comparisons. Partly, the existence of these issues creates the need for special attention and the need for a special design grouping.

Comparative research will examine issues such as:

- contrasting patterns of development across different societies;

- how specific or how general forms of social and institutional structures are between different societies – how they are the same and how they are different;

- cultural determinants of difference across societies.

> In social research, *comparative study* refers to cross-national comparison with the aim of gaining insights from the comparisons.

Often this kind of research is very large in scale, with cooperation between and among countries, using large research teams and involving high levels of coordination and cooperation. Combinations of methods will be used involving survey, secondary analysis of national datasets, interviews and expert knowledge.

But comparative research is also quite feasible on a small scale, such as that found in your own project, particularly if the researcher has intimate knowledge of both the cultures concerned. The problem that arises on the small scale is that often the research undertaken is of two national or cultural situations, where the researcher – using a participant observation approach and relying on insider knowledge of the two situations – has, in fact, insider knowledge of only one of the cultures involved. If this is the case, it is not possible to make the rich comparisons that would be expected, depending on a fine-grained understanding of what is happening in each. There may be a richly textured understanding of one situation but far less understanding of the other.

Actually, although I note that potential problem, on a small scale a comparative study is sometimes less beset with problems than is the large-scale study. For example, where a large study is seeking to make comparisons across countries in, say, levels of attainment, the only sure way of ensuring comparability is to use the same measuring instruments in different places. But to do this, these instruments (tests or whatever) will be have to be translated from one language to another and cultural references in some way also translated. These translations are fraught with problems. The administration of these tests then has to be coordinated across two or more countries, and this is of course a very expensive business. Where identical measures are not used, the measures that are used for comparison will have been devised locally with different purposes in mind, and with different coding and standardisation procedures. The data may not have been collected in any way systematically. These issues can render meaningless any comparison between national datasets or even the comparison of data from simultaneously given but different assessment instruments.

Small or large scale, what should a comparative study be aware of?

- *Equivalence of the comparison situations.* How far is it possible, for example, to make valid comparisons between Ruritania and Lilliput in their moves to inclusive education? A study may try to focus on these differences, but maybe the differences between the societies are of such proportions that a comparison is meaningless. Ruritania may be well on the path to an inclusive education system, having turned all of its special schools into inclusion services, while Lilliput has never even had any special schools and its primary schools routinely have classes of 60 or more students. To attempt to effect any comparison here would be meaningless (though that hasn't stopped people from trying to do it).

- *Equivalence of measuring instruments.* How, for example, can we ensure equivalence in the framing and interpretation of questionnaire items?

- *Language.* Differences in language may invalidate even seemingly straightforward comparisons. For example, the Swedish words which seem to be nearest to the English word 'community' (*lokalsamhälle* or *närsamhälle*) do not capture the sense of *identity* meant in the English word 'community' (when the word is used in a social science context). They mean 'local society' or something closer to 'neighbourhood'. Even the same word in two English-speaking countries means something different: in the UK education context 'integration' means the teaching of children with special needs in the mainstream school, whereas in the US it means something much more general and does not have the UK meaning at all.

- *The integrity or 'realness' of the geographical unit being studied.* Is it possible to say that you can validly compare the whole of Ruritania and the whole of Lilliput when these countries contain great regional differences? Researchers should be aware of what exactly it is they are comparing, finessing out and making explicit the cultural, religious, historical and individual differences that may exist regionally.

Why are comparative studies useful?

- New insights can be obtained. Educational and social thought can develop in an insular way in particular environments and the recognition that another country or region does things differently can offer new avenues for ideas and for development.

- Potential explanations may occur for the existence of particular developments in behaviour, in understanding or even in institutional growth or decline in a particular place, based perhaps on historical or cultural differences.

- They give us a window on our own unspoken and unquestioned cultural expectations, when these are seen against the backdrop of the expectations and practices of others.

- The problematic differences that occur during analysis of different cultural situations can themselves provide insights. For instance, using the example of the meanings of the word 'community' in different languages, can this provide clues also to the growth of cultural practices and traditions? For example, might the words for 'community' in English, Swedish and French mean something different because of the different ways in which industrialisation and urbanisation happened in those countries?

Example 6.10

Hakan is from Turkey and is studying on a government scholarship for a master's degree in social inclusion at a UK university. Impressed by Robert Putnam's (2000) book *Bowling Alone* (in which he reads that in Scandinavia someone finding a wallet in the street is far more likely to return it than someone who finds a wallet in England), he decides to compare notions of social capital and altruism in England and in his native Turkey. He chooses to focus the research project for his dissertation around altruism and its relationship to social capital and the existence of professionalised support systems in the two countries. How far can the existence of altruism be related to the kind of social capital spoken of by Putnam (1995: 73), who suggests that social capital is the connectedness among people in a society, the 'social networks and the norms of reciprocity and trustworthiness that arise from them'. Reviewing research about social capital in 35 countries, Putnam had noted that across those nations, social trust and civic engagement – from voting in elections to trusting people on the street – were strongly correlated, with a general trend to decline in such phenomena over the years, especially in the US.

Hakan's starting point is a prima facie question about whether professionalised support in different societies may serve to distance people from the natural ties that exist for them with others in their communities. Do highly funded social and healthcare services in which professionals take on the role of the supporter enable community members to withdraw from processes of engaging with others? There is some suggestion in the literature that Putnam reviews for his book that this may be the case, and if it *were* the case it would go some way to explaining the comparatively low levels of social capital noted in the UK *vis-à-vis* certain other European countries.

Hakan realises that he cannot realistically set up any large-scale comparison involving questionnaires and interviews, though he may be able to compare existing datasets relating to the two countries if they exist in a form that would enable meaningful comparison. His main empirical work, however, would be illuminative. He would make observations and record interviews in two situations – doctors' surgeries and school playgrounds – in the two countries. In the doctors' surgeries he has a feeling, based on some preliminary informal discussions with friends, relatives and colleagues in the UK, that a strong and highly specialised system of state-funded healthcare, existing in a long tradition since the set-up of the National Health Service, may have enabled an abdication from personal interest and responsibility among some of those who work in that system. There may have developed a sense of 'the system will provide', enabling a feeling that personal responsibility for helping others can be allowed to take a back seat. Following discussions with relevant people, he decides to focus on health centre receptionists and observes them at their work in one surgery at the same time as conducting some interviews with patients in the waiting room. He does the same in his home town in Turkey.

Because this is a series of short case studies, albeit in a comparative context, the same considerations apply to Hakan in the conduct and interpretation of his work as would obtain in the conduct of any case study (see the section above on the case study). Briefly, this means that he cannot draw any hard-and-fast generalisable conclusions from his work, nor can he make any solid imputations about causation. What he can do is to look at each situation he encounters with an intelligent eye, asking questions and interpreting as he proceeds on the basis of those answers. Do his observations seem to be confirming the assumptions that were made in the prima facie research question, and if so how should interviews proceed on the basis of this? Being a comparative study, the analysis will always pivot on the social, historical, religious and other cultural differences between the two countries – their institutions and their beliefs, and how these frame both the emergence of healthcare services and how these operate.

A useful resource for comparative research is the World Health Organization (WHO) statistics, which can be found at www.who.int/whosis/whostat/EN_WHS08_Full.pdf.

No design frame

Sometimes a piece of research is so straightforward that a *frame* itself is not actually necessary. The frame itself – the scaffold which holds things in place – is helpful only if the research is of a certain type, a type that demands certain kinds of discipline before it can be said to be legitimately done. The experiment proffers the obvious example: there is a set of rules about how the design should be executed in order that we can say that the conclusions being drawn have any kind of validity.

Or the scaffold may be needed, as in the case of action research, to offer a template for an inquiry that seeks to fulfil a certain purpose – the purpose of improving practice. The scaffold labelled 'action research' offers to you the collected wisdom of all those who have thought about and done this kind of research before and it suggests to you ways of proceeding, avoiding their mistakes and benefiting from their successes: it guides you in this direction, and ushers you away from another.

However, first-class 'frameless' research also exists. In fact, examples of such frameless research exist everywhere. With certain kinds of questions all that is important is that the best methods of collecting data are used in response to the research question, and the most appropriate methods are used to analyse those data once they have been collected. Indeed, some of the most important pieces of social research can be identified from long ago – from before the time when social scientists talked about research design, methodology and paradigms. A famous example exists in Florence Nightingale's advocacy for better living and treatment conditions for the soldiers fighting in the Crimean War in the middle of the nineteenth century. Nightingale did not agonise over the type of design frame she would use in making her case. Rather, she identified an issue and proposed a solution based on the collection of simple statistics showing the causes of death amongst soldiers and the months in which they died. She thought carefully about how to present her statistics and decided to use the 'coxcomb' diagram shown in Figure 6.13. Although the graph is now famously inaccurate, it served its purpose in broadly revealing the relative importance to be attributed to particular causes and the blame to be assigned to the living conditions of the troops.

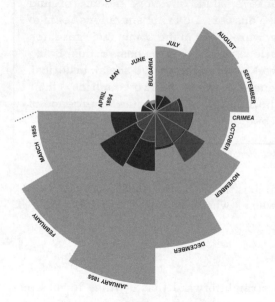

The point of saying this is, once more, to play down the significance of method as if it is all-important. It is to stress, by contrast, the importance of thinking about your question and the best way to answer it. Certainly, good design is essential in any inquiry, but that doesn't mean that you have to feel straitjacketed by ideas of 'correct' procedure. See the design frame as a way of helping you – of helping you to connect your question to appropriate methods: it shouldn't chain you up in irons. The celebrated sociologist C. Wright Mills (1959/1970: 224) in his advice to new social researchers put it this way (in the gendered language of his time, for which, apologies):

Figure 6.13   Florence Nightingale's chart showing how many soldiers died in each month and their causes of death

Be a good craftsman: Avoid any rigid set of procedures . . . Avoid the fetishism of method and technique. Urge the rehabilitation of the unpretentious intellectual craftsman, and try to become such a craftsman yourself. Let every man be his own methodologist; let every man be his own theorist; let theory and method again become part of the practice of craft.

Can I mix design frames and methods?

Yes, it's absolutely fine to mix design frames and methods. In fact, it is to be applauded. There is absolutely nothing wrong in using, say, a survey, an experiment and a case study all in the same research project (though you wouldn't physically be able to fit them all in, given the time you have available for your project). As I keep pointing out, in doing your research it's horses for courses: different elements of your research, related to different questions, will almost certainly need different methodological responses from you. Some people talk about using a 'mixed method design' as if this were some daring, imaginative innovation; but to me it seems the most obvious thing in the world to mix methods. To go back to the example of the police officers at the murder scene, it would be very odd if they said 'No, sorry, we have made a policy decision only to collect interview data. We will *not* be collecting DNA under any circumstances.' The Chief Superintendent would be up before the Home Secretary pretty sharpish. It would be expected that every shred of evidence and every conceivable analytical tool should be used in the investigation, with appropriate caveats about the strength and weakness of various kinds of evidence and the ways that pieces of the story meshed together. It would then be for the jury to decide how convincing a case had been made. It is the same for your research and your dissertation.

It is *not* all right, though, to mix the assumptions for one kind of design frame with another. You cannot, for example, use the assumptions behind the construction of an interpretative case study for the construction of an experiment. These design frames stem from different paradigms: one is about interpretation and illumination, while the other is about description and inference, usually involving quantification of information. Unfortunately, the failure fully to realise this causes many student researchers (and some professional ones) to follow methodological paths that are not only unnecessary but also misleading, as I have tried to show in the discussion of sampling, reliability and validity, above (see also Hammersley, 1996; Bryman, 1998; Pring, 2000; Gorard and Taylor, 2004).

Postmodernism

You may find the word *postmodernism* raised in discussions of research methodology. Postmodernism is neither a design frame nor a method. Rather, it is an approach to knowledge and inquiry, and it has relevance both for the 'Can I mix methods?' and the 'But is it science?' questions.

Postmodernism has different meanings across the arts and humanities. In the social sciences it refers to the view that there is no *one* way of understanding things, and no *one* way of doing inquiry. 'No one has the one right answer', is the motto of postmodernists. They're sceptics, and proud of it. For social scientists, postmodernism is essentially a critique of the arrogance and confidence of modernism – the latter being nothing but a set of post-Renaissance delusions, postmodernists would say. The delusions emerge from a misplaced belief in the certainties promulgated by rationalism and scientific progress, combined with what is sometimes called a 'Whig view of history' (Butterfield, 1931/1973). The latter is an optimistic view of progress-upon-progress in human affairs.

It's a view that can be summarised in Frank Spencer's famous assertion 'Every day in every way, I am getting better and better!'

Well, the postmodernists – despite, incidentally, all being avid followers of *Some Mothers Do 'Ave 'Em* – would disagree with poor Frank in his endorsement of the Whig view. Everything isn't getting better and better. Behind the postmodern critique is the view that the systems of thought that have evolved in the modern world – categories for thinking in psychology, sociology, history, philosophy and elsewhere – carry with them no necessarily right way of organising our inquiries. These frameworks for our thought are hopelessly ambitious, postmodernists would say, and fail to acknowledge the intricacies, complexities and sheer contingency of the social world. True, false: who knows? The social world is indeterminate and unpredictable and it is intellectually dishonest to pretend that we can explain it in terms of 'meta-narratives' – the grand explanatory schemes and theories of modernism.

For the social sciences a number of philosophers have shaped the postmodern critique. Heidegger challenged the distinction between the objective and the subjective. Wittgenstein came to the view that language cannot be dissected and analysed – meaning is in the context of what we say, not in the actual words. Kuhn and Feyerabend challenged the notion that there are 'correct' (rather than just useful) scientific theories. Foucault explained how knowledge and power are interrelated and how certain forms of explanation (or 'discourses') are simply those that are convenient to people who hold power. Rorty notes that all explanation, even scientific explanation, is merely a kind of convincing and for the time being useful narrative.

People claim to be postmodernists or, just as likely, vehemently reject postmodernism, but I find this slipping into camps rather too simple. We are all postmodernists now, to the extent that we are all far more sceptical than we would have been fifty years ago about the truth claims promoted by certain kinds of inquiry. You'll notice in my ten-second review of postmodernists in the previous paragraph that the lines of thought that they have set off have had quite an influence on the way that we go about inquiry today. The mood now is of caution and criticality. This does not, however, mean that we have to go to extremes and deny that obvious things can be true: I am sure that I am sitting at a table, even if I can't prove it to the satisfaction of an irritable philosopher. We shouldn't disappear critically into our own navels.

If you are persuaded by the postmodern critique, how does this affect the way that you do research? I think in the real world it means that you fail to be impressed by complex explanatory theories that seek to explain too much. It means that you are ultra-cautious about the claims of method to offer answers to complex social questions or questions about individual motivation and psychology. An interesting idea related to a postmodern perspective comes from the sociologist Claude Lévi-Strauss (1962/1966). He suggested that we should in social inquiry forget the idea that there are right or wrong ways of going about it. Rather we should use *bricolage*, which is the French word meaning something akin to 'do-it-yourself'. If we use *bricolage*, we are *bricoleurs*, or DIYers. The intimation behind this is that we should reject the assumption that highly ordered methods get us somewhere in education and social scientific inquiry. We should be less self-conscious about our methods and use what seems best for answering our research questions: there are no right or wrong methods. Derrida (1978: 285), who is often thought of as a postmodernist, discusses Lévi-Strauss's *bricolage* as follows:

> The *bricoleur*, says Lévi-Strauss, is someone who uses the 'means at hand', that is, the instruments he finds at his disposition around him, those which are already there, which had not been especially conceived with an eye to the operation for which they are to be used and to which one tries by trial and error to adapt them, not hesitating to change them whenever it appears necessary, or to try several of them at once ...

The first practical step is retrospective: a *bricoleur* will, Lévi-Strauss says,

> turn back to an already existent set made up of tools and materials, to consider or reconsider what it contains and, finally and above all, to engage in a sort of dialogue with it and, before choosing between them, to index the possible answers which the whole set can offer to his problem. (Lévi-Strauss, 1962/1966: 19)

The sociologist Howard Becker (1998) suggests something similar (though I don't think he would readily call himself a postmodernist) and he calls these different ways of proceeding *tricks*. A trick is, in short, a device for solving a problem and offering ways around existing discourses of explanation. He divides his tricks into those of *imagery*, *sampling*, *concepts* and *logic*. While Becker's book is not one for the novice researcher, it is certainly a refreshing antidote to recipe-driven research. It is all about using your intelligence. It's about throwing away the textbooks (but not this one, obviously) and *thinking*; it's about training yourself to think and using your own resources. While I doubt that Becker is an avid follower of *Star Wars*, I am sure he would endorse Obi-Wan Kenobi's advice: 'Go with the Force, Luke.'

The key for those persuaded by the scepticism of the postmodern critique is to 'think outside the box' when it comes to inquiry. Think laterally, and beyond the confines of the existing categories of research. In my book *Education and Theory* (Thomas, 2007) I give some examples, such as 'thought experiments' and Plato's Socratic dialogues. A useful example in education is to be found in Jones and Brown's (2001) 'reading' of a nursery classroom.

How to structure and write your methodology chapter

Your methodology chapter is the place where you explain everything that I have addressed in this chapter and the previous one. As such, it has to do a lot of work in a relatively short space. It has to show how you have related your research question to the methods that you decided to employ in answering it. However, it is also the place for some basic details about your work, such as who your participants are, and, if you are undertaking an interpretative study, who *you* are. It also needs to say how you collected data and how you analysed them, and I cover these issues in the next two chapters of this book. Table 6.6 summarises the usual structure of a methodology chapter.

Table 6.6　The structure of the methodology chapter

Headings in your methodology chapter	
Design	Here, you justify the approach you have taken. Why have you decided to adopt an interpretivist stance or an objectivist stance? Why have you adopted a particular design frame such as action research or case study or experiment? Account for the decisions you have made. (There's no need to go overboard on epistemology or ontology, though. Your understanding of these will help *you* to make the best choices about method. Your understanding of epistemology is for *you*, not your reader.)
Participants (including you)	Did you try to take a representative sample? Say how it was collected. Or did you, by contrast, look at a single person, giving a day-in-the-life case history? If so, account for why you chose this person. If you are working in an interpretivist frame you will need to have a subsection on your own *positionality*.
Ethics	Spell out how you have been addressing ethical issues since you started considering them (see Chapter 2) and explain what steps you have taken to ensure that you are working within ethical guidelines.
Data gathering and materials used	Explain your use of data-gathering tools such as tests, questionnaires, interviews, a diary, images (see Chapter 7). Explain also your choice of analytical tools such as thick description, software or particular statistical tests (see Chapter 8). If appropriate, outline how *triangulation* has played its part.
Procedure	Explain what you asked your participants to do. Explain how and when you used your instruments for data gathering and analysis. What steps were taken, and in what order?

Your methodology chapter will evolve as you proceed through your project. As you can see from Table 6.6, it contains elements from the beginning to the end of your endeavours. As well as saying *why* you chose this or that design route, you need to say what you actually did methodologically. It's also the best place for a discrete section on ethics, as I discussed in Chapter 2, because you can raise the ethical concerns you have addressed in the context of your participants.

Given the evolutionary nature of your methodology chapter, it's a good idea to draw up a file that contains its skeleton elements – design, materials, procedure, ethics – and to add to this and refine it as your work proceeds, rather than expecting to write it all in one go.

Overview

In designing your research you have to consider the approach that you wish to take (see Chapter 5) and the implications this has for the way that you think about the entire structure of your research, including the methods you use, the way you identify your participants and issues such as how far you will be able to generalise your findings to other situations. You may decide to employ a design frame that helps you structure your research.

The design frame is a superstructure that governs the way that your research proceeds. There are a number of such superstructures available, and each is associated with particular purposes, particular kinds of questions and sometimes particular approaches to knowledge. Different design frames can be used together in a research study, and each can complement the others – yet sometimes no design frame as such needs to be employed.

The design frames themselves – action research, case study, comparative study, ethnography, evaluation, experiment, longitudinal study and cross-sectional study – are not incompatible. They may nest inside each other or sit alongside each other. But each has its own procedural ground rules and it is important to understand why these exist and how they influence the structure of your inquiry.

Checklist ✔

You may find it helpful to copy this table and write down the answers to the questions.

Have you …

		Notes	
1	**… thought about whether yours is the kind of research in which *variables* are measured?**	If so, identify the variables. Otherwise, outline the interpretative context of your research	☐
2	**… thought about *sampling*?**	What sort of sample?	☐
		If you need a sample, how are you going to identify it?	
		Or is it more a question of identifying participants?	
3	**… considered the various design frames which may structure your research?**	Are any of these particularly suitable in your circumstances?	☐
4	**… drawn up a 'Design and methodology skeleton chapter' file in Word, which contains the following subheadings: design, participants, ethics, data gathering and materials, procedure?**	Add to this skeleton framework as your project proceeds	☐

Further reading

General issues in design

Bryman, A. (2001) *Social Research Methods*. Oxford: Oxford University Press.
An authoritative, wide-ranging coverage of methods used in social research.

Gorard, S. and Taylor, C. (2004) What is triangulation? *Building Research Capacity*, 7, 7–9.
A useful overview of triangulation.

Research Methods Knowledge Base: http://www.socialresearchmethods.net/kb/samppro]b.php.
A conventional exposition of design, giving a good overview of experimental design and probability.

Thomas, G. (2011) The case: generalization, theory and phronesis in case study. *Oxford Review of Education*. 37 (1), 21–35.
In this article I discuss generalisation more fully, especially in the context of case study.

Winter, G. (2000) A comparative discussion of the notion of 'validity' in qualitative and quantitative research. *The Qualitative Report*, 4 (3–4). Available at: www.nova.edu/ssss/QR/QR4-3/winter.html.
Winter provides a full and interesting discussion of validity.

Action research

Carr, W. and Kemmis, S. (1986) *Becoming Critical: Education, Knowledge and Action Research*. London: Routledge.
An academic treatment of action research.

McNiff, J., Lomax, P. and Whitehead, J. (2003) *You and Your Action Research Project* (2nd edn). London: Routledge.
McNiff and her colleagues have written several books on action research and all are good, practical manuals.

Case study

Hammersley, M. (1992) *What's Wrong with Ethnography*. London: Routledge.
Includes a high-quality, academic discussion of case study.

Ragin, C.C. and Becker, H.S. (eds) (1992) *What is a Case? Exploring the Foundations of Social Inquiry*. Cambridge: Cambridge University Press.
There are some excellent essays on case study in this book, notably Becker's own and the chapter by Wieviorka.

Stake, R.E. (1995) *The Art of Case Study Research*. Thousand Oaks, CA: SAGE.
Stake writes well about the constitution of case study.

Thomas, G. (2011) *How to Do Your Case Study – A Guide for Students and Researchers*. London: SAGE.

Here, I have tried to guide the case inquirer through the process of doing a case study, looking at the different avenues open.

Thomas, G. (2011) A typology for the case study in social science following a review of definition, discourse and structure. *Qualitative Inquiry*, 17 (6), 511–21.
This is a more academic treatment of the topic, looking at a number of definitions down the years and proposing a typology that sets different kinds of case study in context. I suggest that case inquirers as they proceed with their studies have a variety of methodological routes open to them.

Ethnography

Becker, H.S., Geer, B., Hughes, E.C. and Strauss, A. (1961) *Boys in White: Student Culture in a Medical School*. Chicago: University of Chicago Press.
A study, mainly by participant observation, of a class of new undergraduates as they progress through medical school.

Geertz, C. (1977) Deep play: notes on the Balinese cockfight. In C. Geertz, *The Interpretation of Cultures*. New York: Basic Books. Available at http:// www.si.umich.edu/~rfrost/courses/Matcult/content/Geertz.pdf (accessed 7 September 2008)
A classic case study that reads more like a story than a piece of ethnography, and this is a tribute to the quality of Geertz's writing.

Evaluation

Pawson, R. and Tilley, N. (1997) *Realistic Evaluation*. London: SAGE.
A particular 'take' on evaluation, but a widely used one.

Experiment

Cremin, H., Thomas, G. and Vincett, K. (2005) Working with teaching assistants: three models evaluated. *Research Papers in Education*, 20 (4), 413–32.
See this paper for an example of a small-scale experiment. It gives the full details of the study on which 'Karen's' case study is based in this chapter (Example 6.5).

http://foodheroesandheroines.wordpress.com/tag/margaret-mcmillan/.
This gives details of Margaret McMillan's experiment on school meals.

Longitudinal and cross-sectional studies

Ruspini, E. (2002) *An Introduction to Longitudinal Research*. London: Routledge.
A useful overview, giving detailed examples and discussing problems well.

Comparative research

Phillips, P. and Schweisfurth, M. (2008) *Comparative and International Education: An Introduction to Theory, Method and Practice*. London: Continuum.
Covers methodology and some of the issues that arise from comparative research.

See also journals such as *Compare* and *Comparative Education*: look them up on the Internet – they will contain recent discussion of important issues.

Mixing methods

Gorard, S., with Taylor, C. (2004) *Combining Methods in Educational and Social Research*. Maidenhead: Open University Press.
Usefully discusses the use of more than one method and the divide that has unhelpfully come to exist between quantitative and qualitative research.

Postmodernism

Stronach, I. and Maclure, M. (1997) *Educational Research Undone*. Maidenhead: Open University Press.
See especially the first chapter for a discussion of what it is all about.

7

THE RIGHT TOOLS FOR THE JOB: DATA GATHERING

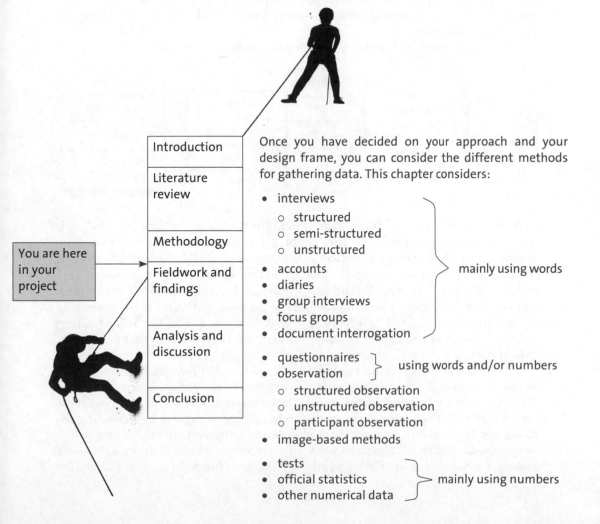

Introduction
Literature review
Methodology
Fieldwork and findings
Analysis and discussion
Conclusion

You are here in your project

Once you have decided on your approach and your design frame, you can consider the different methods for gathering data. This chapter considers:

- interviews
  - o structured
  - o semi-structured
  - o unstructured
- accounts
- diaries
- group interviews
- focus groups
- document interrogation

mainly using words

- questionnaires
- observation

using words and/or numbers

  - o structured observation
  - o unstructured observation
  - o participant observation
- image-based methods

- tests
- official statistics
- other numerical data

mainly using numbers

Tools and methods

I have been talking about design up to now. Design itself is not much use without a construction to follow it. A chair *designed* by Thomas Chippendale would be nothing without the subsequent *construction* of the chair, and for this Mr Chippendale needed *tools*: saws, hammers, chisels, screwdrivers, scissors, lathes and so on.

It's the same with research design. Once you have decided how you are going to approach your question and the broad design frame that you will be using, you can make up your mind about how you are going to collect your data – make up your mind about the tools that you will use: the instruments and techniques with which you will gather information. It shouldn't be the other way round. You shouldn't, in other words, come up with a tool first and then try and find a way of using it. The psychologist Abraham Maslow (1966: 15–16) said 'I suppose it is tempting, if the only tool you have is a hammer, to treat everything as if it were a nail', and his cautionary words should be heeded – we shouldn't let our methods dominate. They shouldn't have precedence over our questions, or we end up in a world where research tells us only certain kinds of things, and our understanding can be correspondingly distorted.

Let's have a recap on how the research process has progressed …

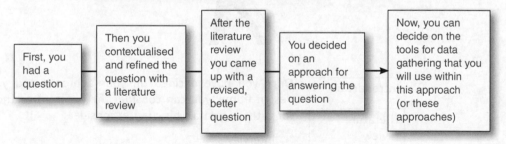

A method is a way of doing something, often with an intimation that it is being done systematically. In this chapter I shall outline a number of data-gathering methods which are ways of getting hold of data systematically. By 'systematic' I don't mean rigidly and formally, with tight, standardised procedures (though this *may* be the case). Rather, I mean done in a considered, thought-through way. These methods may be used with the approaches and design frames explained in Chapters 5 and 6. Some of these methods collect data mainly comprising words; some convert information into numbers; some collect both words and numbers.

Just a note about vocabulary: already in this chapter I have talked about tools, methods, techniques and instruments, using the terms almost interchangeably. This is a little confusing, I realise, especially as textbooks sometimes conjoin these terms also with the terms of research design. I'll try to explain by extending the metaphor I used before. Screwdrivers, chisels and hammers are undeniably tools – not methods. But they have to be used with a method: watching an inexperienced person wield a saw is an almost painful experience. You need to understand how to use the saw – find a good sturdy base, hold the wood on it with your foot, gently make a starting groove holding the wood firm, push down hard with the saw, and pull back lightly. Until you have learned this, the saw is as good as useless. So, tool and method go together. This is even more the case with social research: tool and method are almost bonded together, to such an extent that it is sometimes difficult to separate them out – the method *is* almost the tool in itself. This is why the terms are sometimes used together. So, you can think of this chapter being about tools, or methods, or techniques, or instruments.

Be creative

Right at the beginning I must say that you should not feel constrained by the tools that I will outline in this chapter. There is room for your creativity and imagination in the techniques that you adopt to collect data. The ones outlined under the subheadings in this section are some of the most commonly used methods for gathering data, but the list is neither definitive nor exhaustive. I spoke to a student recently who had been really creative in the way that he had thought about collecting data. He was collecting life histories from veterans of special schooling – people who had attended special schools in the 1930s and 1940s – to ask how they thought special schooling had affected their lives. Apart from the conventional method of interviewing these people, he also drew timelines on two pieces of A4 paper glued together lengthways (see Figure 7.1) on which he drew important historical events relevant to this lifespan which he could talk through with his research participants.

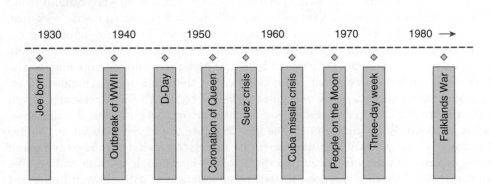

Figure 7.1   A timeline for stimulating memories

The events on the timeline would serve to jog memories and help put things in the right place. He could leave these long pieces of paper with the participants for them to look at on their own and to discuss with friends and relatives. Though I know this method for gathering 'data' is not unique to my student, it will not be found in any of the general textbooks (or none that I have seen, anyway). This doesn't stop it from being a first-rate, home-made technique for both stimulating the production of information and helping to ensure its veracity.

So, in gathering the data you can be as imaginative as you want, and you should not feel constricted by the tools outlined in the sections that follow. Many of the considerations raised in these, though, are relevant for any research involving people, and it is worth reading through the general advice accompanying each of these for pointers on the conduct of work with people. The watchword is imagination concerning the tools that you use, and you can get help here from friends and relatives: ask them for their ideas, or have a brainstorming session (see p. 17). Check with your tutor the ideas with which you emerge.

Data-gathering tools mainly for use with words

Interviews

An interview is a discussion with someone in which you try to get information from them. The information may be facts or opinions or attitudes, or any combination of these. There are three basic subtypes of interview: **structured** interviews, **unstructured** interviews and **semi-structured** interviews. Each involves the interviewer in face-to-face contact or telephone contact with another person, namely the interviewee. (Incidentally, 'respondent' and 'informant' are words that are sometimes used instead of 'interviewee'.)

A great deal is provided by this personal contact: you are another human being (I'm just guessing here), and interviewees will respond to you, in bodily presence, in an entirely different way from the way that they would have reacted to questionnaires that came through their letterboxes, or to emails. This is a ready-made support for you: most people want to help and give their opinions (as long as the topic is not in some way sensitive for themselves, their colleagues, friends or family), and they will usually be energised to help by your physical presence. If you take the trouble to schedule a visit you can be more or less guaranteed a response. Most importantly, though, you will be able to relate to interviewees while you are talking to them; you will be able to hear and understand what they are saying and use gestures or words to encourage them to say more (or less). You will be able to watch and listen for nuances of their behaviour which will give you important clues about how they feel about a topic. Because of the primacy of the personal contact, your appearance, demeanour and tone are important – how do you want to be seen? As 'one of us' (i.e. like the interviewee)? As a person in authority? As a neutral observer? ... Or what? Your decision should influence the way that you look, sound and behave.

However you decide to present yourself, it is good practice of course to try to put the interviewee at ease before the interview proper begins – to talk about the weather, about your journey, about anything inconsequential that will break the ice. This is sometimes called 'establishing rapport'. Its nature, of course, varies with the nature of the interviewees and your relationship with them. Remember, though, that establishing rapport is not simply a mechanical process to be gone through; it is a process of actually making contact – of proving that you are human – and this can be far more difficult in some cases than others. With children it can be particularly difficult, and because of this interviews with children are often best avoided unless you know them well. I can remember doing a piece of research for a government department in which I conducted a series of interviews with half a dozen or so 13-year-olds in a special school for children with behaviour difficulties. From memory, I think the most extended response I received was 'Dunno', despite my heroic attempts at establishing rapport.

With the element of personal contact being so important, you will have to ask yourself before the interviews begin what it is that you are trying to get from your interviewees and how the personal contact will help. Does your design (i.e. your purposes, questions, approach and design frame) mean that you will be interpreting what your respondents say for illumination of the research scene? Or does it lead you to want straightforward 'facts'? If the former, you will be trying far harder to 'read' your interviewees' behaviour – their mannerisms, gestures, hesitations, glances away – and you will be recording these (in your head or on a notepad) as carefully as their words. You will be using these clues to make informed guesses about what interviewees might really mean beyond the actual words that they are using.

> 'When *I* use a word,' Humpty Dumpty said in rather a scornful tone, 'it means just what I choose it to mean – neither more nor less.' (Lewis Carroll, *Alice Through the Looking-Glass*)

Humpty Dumpty was right: words do change their meaning, depending on context – and meaning goes *beyond* the words, so that we can often 'read' what another person means, irrespective of the words they use. So, sometimes when I say 'Yes', I mean 'No' and I guess that those around me can tell I mean 'No' by my manner and demeanour: I may say it sarcastically or hesitantly; I may be lying and avoid eye contact (not that I lie often, obviously). When I answer open-ended questions I may seem to be skirting around or fudging the issue. This is where being in a face-to-face interview is invaluable, in divining these quite subtle behavioural or linguistic giveaways to the meanings people might really hold.

In recording what people are saying, you have a choice: you can take notes there and then (or very soon afterwards), or you can electronically audio-record for subsequent transcription. It depends on how faithfully you feel you need to record every word that is said,

> **Transcript or transcription:** A written form of something that was originally in *spoken* words. So, if you have interviewed someone and have made an audio recording of the interview, then played it back to yourself and typed it all out, the typed-out form is called the 'transcript'.

though of course an audio recording doesn't pick up the behavioural cues that I have just noted, so an accompanying set of notes can be useful as well. It can be very helpful to have an accurate record of an interview, especially if you are doing interpretative research, and if you feel this will be necessary then ensure that you are set up for electronic recording (and practise at home first, because it is easy to get things wrong). Whatever methods you use to record, you will need to explain these methods briefly to the interviewee and what is being done with the data – how it is being stored, analysed and subsequently destroyed (see the discussion of ethics in Chapter 2).

Telephone interviews are bound by the same considerations as face-to-face interviews, but you miss the contextual and behavioural detail, not to mention the commitment of your respondents.

Structured interviews

A structured interview is a meeting with another person in which you ask a pre-determined set of questions. Beyond this set of questions there is very little scope for further follow-up – little scope for pursuing an interesting comment from the interviewee. The idea behind the structure is that there is a degree of uniformity provided across the different interviewees you meet. The interviewees' responses will be recorded on a form that will probably mix different kinds of response, both open-ended and closed.

Open-ended and closed questions

An open-ended question is one that allows respondents to reply in whatever way they wish. For example, you may ask interviewees 'What are your feelings about the National Lottery?' and they can give vent to whatever opinions or prejudices they wish, taking as long as they like. It is your job then to record this information as accurately as you can (or need to) for subsequent analysis. Closed questions are those that demand a particular response, such as 'Do you approve of the National Lottery? Yes or no', or 'How comfortable are you with the idea of the government raising money by the National Lottery? Very comfortable, comfortable, no opinion, not comfortable, very uncomfortable'. Respondents have to respond in the way that the closed question format demands. They can't say 'Well, it depends what you mean by "comfortable"' or 'I have mixed opinions.'

A structured interview has a limited number of strengths. First, compared with other kinds of interview, it can be administered relatively easily and quickly. Second, interviewees' responses can be quite easily coded. Beyond this, though, the structured interview has not very much in its favour. Remember that you are interviewing in order to get something other than an assured response: you want to be reaching something that comes from the person-to-person contact that goes beyond mere ticks in boxes. The face-to-face interview gives you an opportunity to gain an understanding of the interviewee, and this ready-made strength of the interview situation is not being used with a structured interview. While you can note the respondent's general demeanour in response to your questions, you don't have an opportunity to follow up these signals with further questions if you limit yourself to the format of a structured interview. Because there is no great advantage in the structured interview to giving it in a face-to-face manner, it may as well be given in written form – in other words, in a questionnaire (see p. 207).

Unstructured interviews

An unstructured interview is like a conversation. There is no predetermined format to the interview beyond your general interest in the topic. You don't meet your interviewee with a pre-specified list of questions. The idea behind the unstructured interview is that interviewees should be allowed to set the agenda. *They* should be the ones who are determining the important issues to be covered. This is of course what is wanted in interpretative research: in this kind of research you are looking for your respondents to set the scene and let *them* tell *you* what the issues are. You, the researcher, go in with an open mind and it is important that the 'frame' set for the research allows the interviewee scope to do this.

Beyond this desire to let the interviewee lead the way, there are variations on a theme of just how unstructured the interview should be. If your respondent goes completely off the topic then you would wish to bring them back to it in some way. However, this would need to be done sensitively, since it may be the case that this is the way that they talk – going 'off message' for a while before they return to the topic. Or they might like to tell a story when they are talking, and the unstructured interview gives them a chance to do this. Sometimes an interviewee will use the opportunity of a 'sympathetic ear' to give vent to a particular point of view or to use you almost as an unpaid counsellor.

Within reason, you should try to be understanding here. Not only has this person given you their time but they may be offering you something of great relevance in doing so. If it seems the case in this sort of circumstance that something of a delicate or sensitive nature is being disclosed you should clear with your interviewee after the interview that they are happy for the specific information to be used and in what kind of disguise – you could reveal it only as a general comment, perhaps, or it may be acceptable to your interviewee to quote from them in an anonymous way on which you can agree.

How should you prompt the interviewee without setting the agenda yourself? There are degrees of strength of prompt: you may simply say 'Can you tell me more about that?' or offer something stronger such as 'How did that make you feel?' or 'What happened next?' However, if you really are interested in what the interviewee has to say you would avoid a question such as 'Does that make you feel angry?' This really would be putting words into the interviewee's mouth.

Semi-structured interviews

The semi-structured interview provides the best of both worlds as far as interviewing is concerned, combining the structure of a list of issues to be covered together with the freedom to follow up points as necessary. Because of this combination it is the most common arrangement in most small-scale research. However, this does not mean that it is always the best, given your purposes and your design frame: one of the other arrangements may be better suited to your needs. If, for example, you really are interested in interpreting your interviewees' comments and if you are a participant observer in the situation that you are researching, an *unstructured* interview would be a better choice.

I say this because too many students (in my opinion) opt for the semi-structured interview as the most straightforward and seemingly obvious choice, where in fact it can lead them to do a different kind of research from that which they set out to do. If you really do intend to do an ethnographic piece of research, entering your research environment as a participant observer, you are trying to understand how the 'players' in that research are playing their roles – depending on the meanings that they construct within that environment. If this is the case, if this is what you want to do, then the semi-structured interview is too rigid a tool to be working with. It's like asking your respondent to be an artist and giving them a painting-by-numbers kit with which to do it.

In order to get the best of both worlds afforded by the semi-structured interview, you will need an *interview schedule*, which is a list of issues which you want to cover. These issues don't have to be in the form of questions; rather, they provide merely an aide-memoire of the important points for discussion. However, you are not forced by the procedure to go through these points in order, or to keep in any way formally to a set format for the interview. Rather, they are a reminder of what you intend to cover.

If, for example, you find that your interviewee has provided a response to your second point while addressing your first issue, there is no need subsequently raise this as a specific question, unless you feel that there is more you wish to know. In fact this is the hallmark of the semi-structured interview: if you wish to know more, then you ask about it. Prolong the discussion on that point.

Your interview schedule, drawn up prior to the interview, is a framework of issues, leading to possible questions, leading to possible follow-up questions, leading to 'probes'. Probes are encouragements to interviewees to proceed with aspects of their answers; these may be verbal – for example 'Go on …' – or non-verbal, a tilt of the head or a nod or a raising of the eyebrows (but preferably not all three at once).

Let's take an example of how that might be done. Supposing you were a probation officer studying for a master's degree in forensic psychology and were interested in perceptions of victimisation among young offenders from black and minority ethnic groups. You decide to conduct interviews with young men in a young offender institution which you occasionally visit. The questions you choose are based around experiences of dealings with the police, with teachers

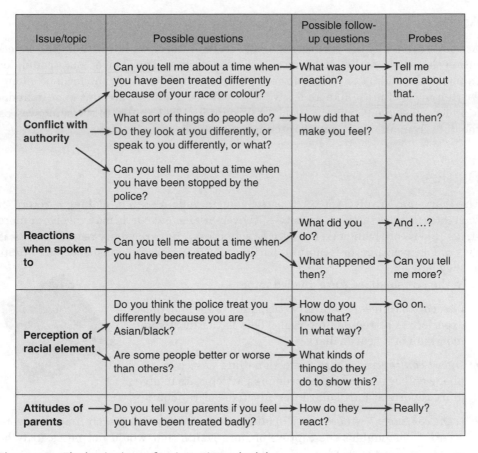

Figure 7.2   The beginnings of an interview schedule

and with others such as shopkeepers and how far there is a perception among your interviewees of victimisation because of race. You begin by asking questions about the situations in which conflict has occurred, about the young men's reactions when spoken to, the attitudes of their parents to the police. Your schedule looks like the one in Figure 7.2.

This schedule of issues, questions and probes is just a guide from which you can deviate as necessary: it's a structure to help you conduct the interview; it is not a straitjacket. In other words, you should feel free to ask different questions or supplementary questions as the need arises. You may find that one particular element of the interview is yielding particularly interesting comments and if this is the case you may wish to spend nearly all of the interview in this area. This is the essence of a semi-structured interview – namely that the structure reminds you of your aims and themes, but it does not constrict you.

Accounts

Accounts are really the products of unstructured interviews but without the expectation that these will have been collected via an interview. The account could, for example, depending on your informant, have been provided in the form of a long, written piece of prose like an essay, or it could be a similar account kept in audio form for subsequent transcription. An account will be handled in the same way as the data from an unstructured interview.

Diaries

The diary may involve you, or a participant in your research, making a record of thoughts, feelings, actions, responses, conversations, etc. Or it may involve a more structured record being taken of specific activities. A research diary records events as they unfold over time, or it captures participants' experience of unusual or rare events as they happen.

In the jargon, diaries are divided into:

- *interval-contingent*, where participants report on their experiences at regular intervals. This is the most common kind of research diary.

- *signal-contingent*, where some signalling device (e.g. a phone call or text message) prompts participants to give diary reports at particular intervals (fixed or random).

- *event-contingent*, where participants provide a diary entry each time the event occurs. This enables the capture of rare events that would not necessarily be caught by fixed or random interval assessments.

Some people will be more fulsome in accounts in a private disclosure of the kind given in a diary than they would be in a face-to-face interview. This is often the case with children and young people, as long as they have the writing skills. If they don't have such skills, you could consider the use of an audio diary. You may even wish to use a video diary, where expressions, gestures, sighs, grimaces, frowns, tears even, may be recorded – features of the situation that would be missed in a written or audio diary. If you think that this is the case, then a video diary is worth the extra effort.

If you are using a diary as part of an interpretative study, you will probably want to write up your diary immediately after your session in the field, recording an assortment of facts, opinions, views, interpretations, snatches of remembered conversation and so on. You can keep it in written form or in audio recording to be transcribed subsequently.

Below is a section from a diary I took for a piece of research I was doing on the role of the governor in school. (It was eventually aborted, probably wisely.) Being on the governing body myself, I could be a participant observer.

Wed. 21 March. Full governors' meeting …

The head teacher's report is a model of boredom, covering nothing that could remotely be said to have anything to do with the strategy or the direction of the school. There's something on some exchange students from Germany (who are 'very attractive' according to head teacher – seems an odd way to describe the students), something on staff, something on drugs with a cut-out from the local paper saying that drugs are a problem, as if we didn't know they were a problem – and as if we needed a cutting from the paper to tell us. Nothing about the strategy of the school. Just something to keep the head teacher talking for 20 minutes. We listen politely. No: more than politely. Everyone here seems to acquiesce in this, as though that's what they're here for – a bunch of people who have been put on the planet for the purpose of listening to the head spout forth about mundane happenings at the school. They seem to think that they are here as a hybrid of guardian and trustee – to make sure that good is done and no one on the staff gets up to any mischief, and I suppose there's some justice in this. This is perhaps what the original purpose of the governors was.

The irony was that (as I distantly remembered it) old-fashioned governors – fierce old ladies and retired colonels – probably did serve something of this function. This new breed, though, has had its remit changed to that of strategic arrowhead and holder of the legal responsibility. But this doesn't quite seem to have got through to your common-and-garden governor who still sees herself (or more likely, himself) as guardian/trustee. But the problem in this new mixed-mode governor is that they are not remote like the old fierce ladies and the colonels. They have gone native. They're there, wanting to be liked by the head teacher and the deputies, wanting to get invited to the opening of the new building, wanting to be wanted, as we all do. Maslow was right; it's the fundamental human need and is almost crushingly over-powering. Because the need to be wanted is so powerful, no one says to the head teacher 'Shut up you boring fart; this is not only irrelevant, it's also incompetently presented and incoherent. Please desist immediately.' No – instead we all listen, all 20 of us in complete silence apart from the occasional polite titter at the bad jokes, and at the end the chair says 'Thank you P for that very full and informative report.' Me too. I want to be liked too. So I nod my head weakly and smile in the direction of the head teacher when he finishes and hope he notices me.

You will see from this diary that it is more than simply a record that this happened, then that happened, then that happened, etc. Rather, it is a record not only of events but also of my interpretations. In line with the expectations of ethnography it is a set of my own interpretations of events – interpretations concerning the roles of governors and how they constructed their own identities in the committee meeting and on the board generally. Why did they think they were there? What did they think they were doing? What did the head think he was doing, and how did he construct ideas about the roles of governors (if indeed he had any ideas at all – about anything)? *Not* to make these interpretations (and you don't have to be as unkind as I have been here) is one of the most common weaknesses of the research diary or its analysis. Taken as part of an ethnography, a diary is not simply a record of events.

Alternatively, a diary can be more structured, collecting data about specific events or activities. In a small study I undertook as part of my PhD, I asked 100 primary school teachers to keep a diary in the format of a timetable. It was about the people who worked alongside them in the classroom, how long they worked and what they were doing. I had done a questionnaire previously, asking about the general categories of person who might be working, which turned out to be parents, teaching assistants, sixth-form students, volunteers, etc. I also wanted to find out about the type of activity, the group size being worked with and the length of time these people were working in the classroom. This was a lot of information to collect and it was an important consideration that information about the associations among these people and their activities be preserved without in so doing generating a form that would be intimidatingly complex and time-consuming for busy teachers to unravel.

I decided on a diary for each of my informants, with the familiarity of a timetable format used as a means to gaining the maximum possible information in the minimum possible time for the teachers. As it worked out, they seemed to like the familiarity of the format, which made it simple to complete, and I obtained a 60 per cent return rate (which is very good for a request for involvement of this kind sent by post). In fact, simplicity is the watchword for any request of this kind: if it looks hard to complete, the bin beckons.

The diaries were completed for one week of the winter term. Teachers coded the type of people working with them in the classroom (6 options), the type of activity (15 options), the group size being worked with (5 options) and the length of time worked. They were asked to put the initials of the participants alongside the codes, and using these it was possible to determine the number of times a particular individual within a category worked during the week. Most of the data were handled in terms of sessions of help, a session being an uninterrupted session or consecutive sessions (i.e. only interrupted by break or lunch) undertaken by one individual. The diary would be returned to me in the form of a timetable like that in Figure 7.3. Teachers would also add codes representing the kind of activities undertaken. On the reverse side they could add day-by-day comments of their own choosing – thoughts, feelings, ideas, regrets, missed opportunities, etc.

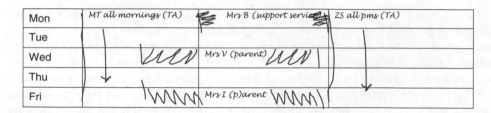

Figure 7.3　Diary kept in the form of a timetable

So, like any data-collection method, a diary can take a number of forms, with the emphasis on the collection of data over time.

Group interviews and focus groups

Group interviews warrant a discussion separate from individual interviews since a particular way of behaving overcomes a group and you need to be aware of this if you are interviewing more than one person at the same time (and, yes, for these purposes two people constitute a group). People behave differently in groups: particular individuals may become more talkative or less talkative; some people take the lead, while others follow; some will tend to be 'stroppy', others helpful. And there are particular ways a whole group will behave, differently from individuals. So, for example, there is an inclination for a group to display what is called a 'risky shift phenomenon', a tendency well established in social psychology. This is the likelihood that a group will make a riskier decision than an individual. If you asked a set of groups a question such as 'Would you have a person with a criminal record to stay in your house?' and then asked an equivalent number of people but as individuals, you would probably find a riskier decision (i.e. more likelihood of saying 'yes') in the groups. There's safety in numbers, and this maxim applies even if decisions are being made about wholly imaginary happenings.

So before you set up the group interview you need to establish why you are doing a group interview rather than a set of individual interviews. Is it to save time? If it is, then you must be aware that you will be getting different responses from those you would have obtained from the same people interviewed individually. Aside from any tendency to 'risky shift' and other phenomena associated with groups, the group may be dominated by one or two voices and these may not be at all representative of the general opinion. There are, of course, legitimate reasons for wanting to interview a group, and these will concern the group psychology itself. Do you want to find out how a group (i.e. *as* a group) will behave or move in response to an imaginary event? Do you want to *compare* the group attitude with a set of individually assessed attitudes within the group, perhaps to judge the impact of the power or influence of one or two group members? It is factors such as these for which you can legitimately use a group interview.

The term **focus group** has come to be used interchangeably with **group interview**, but the two kinds of group are different in important respects. In group interviews the emphasis is on the researcher taking a lead role, asking questions and being in control of the discussion – rather in the way that an interviewer is leading the discussion in a structured or semi-structured interview. So the researcher asks questions and respondents answer. But in focus groups (which emerged, incidentally, as a technique from marketing research), the researcher plays the role of **facilitator** or **moderator**. If you are running a focus group your aim is to facilitate or moderate discussion *among participants*, not between yourself and the participants. The idea is that you take a marginal rather than a pivotal role.

In the focus group, participants, usually eight or so, who have a relevant characteristic or feature of their lives in common will be brought together in an informal setting to discuss the topic in question. As in an unstructured interview with an individual, the idea is to get at the understandings, beliefs and values of the participants. And in the same way that in an individual unstructured interview the aim is to let the *individual* take the lead in setting the direction of the discussion, so in the focus group the aim is to let the *group* take the lead. As facilitator, your role is to stimulate discussion, and you may do this with your comments or you may prepare a range of *focus materials* for the group to discuss. These are materials – for example, objects, artefacts, photographs, drawings, newspaper clippings, short videos, audio recordings – that help the group focus on the topic of interest. If, say, you were interested in the views of parents on testing, you might collect some examination papers, some photographs of young people in a hall sitting an examination or a video of a news programme showing students' reactions on the day that A-level results are published. You might set off discussion following such a video with the starter: 'Reactions?'

Given that you need your wits about you to facilitate effectively in a group such as this, it is common practice in professionally conducted research to use an observer to record information about context, environment and participants' behaviour. In small-scale research it will not usually be possible to get help in this way, so it may be helpful to record proceedings using audio and/or video.

Document interrogation

Gathering data from documents represents an entirely different proposition from gathering data from people. Essentially, the knack is to find the right documents, read them and think about them.

Because of the sheer variety of documents and documentary interrogation, it is difficult to give general advice. I can, however, give an example from a piece of research that I did for a government department (Tarr and Thomas, 1997). In this, I was asked to look at schools' special educational needs (SEN) policy documents, which schools were obliged to produce by law, to see how far the documents met the expectations of statutory guidance. The research involved obtaining the policy documents from a representative sample of schools, examining what was in them and cross-checking this against the government's guidance on the contents of a schools policy document of this kind. So, there were two forms of documentary interrogation involved here – interrogation of the schools' policy documents and interrogation of government advice published in different documents – and my job was to check one against the other to see how schools were meeting expectations.

My colleague and I first read the government documents to garner information that we considered would be important for writing a school policy on special needs. There were two such documents containing such information: the Education (Special Educational Needs) (Information) Regulations; and the Code of Practice on special educational needs. Our main task was to distil from these documents a list of issues that a policy had to cover. This was a difficult task, because the criteria to be met appeared in different forms in these two documents. We were eventually able to group the criteria under 15 main headings, each of which had several subheadings. The main headings are given in Table 7.1.

Table 7.1 A checklist derived from government guidance: main categories which should appear in each SEN policy

1. Principles and objectives held by the school
2. SENCO's name and role
3. Strategic management and target setting
4. Admissions
5. Specialisms
6. Resource allocation
7. Identification, assessment and review procedures
8. Curriculum: strategies to include all children
9. Integration strategies
10. Complaints: how parents can complain and how complaints are dealt with
11. INSET and staff development: plans for teachers and assistants
12. External support: sources and LA agreements
13. External relations: liaison arrangements
14. Parents: how a working partnership is ensured
15. Transition: between schools/to adult life; SEN register; LA pro-formas

We then had the job of looking at schools' policies. We asked the head teachers of 252 schools from nine local authorities (with a stratified sample of secondary, primary and special schools) for a copy of their SEN policies. Of those approached 181 obliged, providing a 72 per cent return. Each policy received was examined against the criteria in the checklist. First, did each policy cover every point in the checklist? There was no magic way of finding this information other than through stapling a checklist to each policy, reading each one from cover to cover, and ticking (or not ticking) the checklist point by point as we judged that criteria were (or were not) covered.

While we were doing this we also had to judge *how well* each policy addressed each of the criteria in Table 7.1. Again, this was a question of intelligently reading the policies. Did they merely mention (or fail to mention) each point on the list? Did they elaborate on the issue? Did they explicate fully? The answers were a matter of judgement, and while it may have been possible to make these judgements more objectively (e.g. by counting the number of words given over to an issue), we decided against this course of action, believing that it would provide a less valuable picture than our own assessment from reading. (It might be possible for one school to say more in 25 words than another said in 250.) Essentially, there was no substitute for reading and thinking.

From the overall sample of schools, 18 policies were then selected (two from each local authority) for detailed examination. The more detailed examination involved comparing the policies with the corresponding local authority policies (which also had to be read), assessing readability, accessibility and length. To assess readability, the documents were scanned using optical character recognition (OCR) software. They were saved into Word, which we then asked for readability statistics.

You will note from this example that there were few technical tricks or special procedures available for interrogating the documents. Given the ease with which documents can now be downloaded (particularly government and other policy documents), a key shortcut is in some basic document interrogation using computer software. This is easy if the document is in Word, but a bit trickier if it is in PDF. If the latter, you can, after checking copyright, copy the whole thing and then paste it into Word. (*Tip*: To copy a whole PDF file, press Ctrl+A, which selects the whole document; then Ctrl+C, which copies it, then switch to a blank Word document and paste it into that with Ctrl+V.) If you are not able to download the relevant document in word-processing or PDF format, the one technical trick that is widely available now is through electronic scanning. Most scanners now are provided with OCR software which will do the 'reading' (but sadly not the thinking or understanding) for you. When you scan your text your software should give you the option of enabling the text to be 'read' as text (as distinct from simply taking a picture of the text). It will then save this into a word-processing file, and once this is done there are a number of ways in which your computer can help you to analyse the text, and these forms of analysis are covered in Chapter 8. Unfortunately, though, there is no substitute for intelligent reading in the interrogation of documents.

Documents occur in many and varied shapes and forms and we can be creative in their location and interrogation. Again, there is no sense to be had in a separation of types of inquiry into 'scientific' and 'non-scientific' here – it's a question of 'Where can I find the information, and how can I use it intelligently to come up with answers to my questions?' Science, whether it is astronomy or social science, is eclectic in its attitude to evidence – and documents, whatever their provenance, are invaluable. The great astronomer and scientist Edmund Halley back in the eighteenth century used documents to predict the return of his comet. Coady (1994: 13) notes that Halley relied

> upon earlier testimony in identifying his famous comet and predicting its return at seventy-five-year intervals. It was while Halley was studying the comet of 1682 that he noticed the similarities between it and two other bright comets reported by earlier astronomers in 1531 and 1607. Noting the intervals of approximately seventy-five years he predicted the return of the comet in 1758 – which proved correct.

Seek documents relevant to your research topic on the Internet. As I write, it has been announced that court records are to be published online in order to make more transparent the sentencing of law-breakers. Such records will be invaluable to the social scientist.

Data-gathering tools – for use with words and/or numbers

The data-gathering tools I have outlined so far are used mainly with words. In this section I will describe tools that will collect words or numbers or both – or they may commonly convert the words into numbers in some way.

Questionnaires

The defining characteristic of a questionnaire is that it is a *written* form of questioning. Beyond this, that is to say, beyond being in written form, the questions may be open or closed (see the box on p. 196). You may be collecting facts (e.g. 'How many cups of tea have you drunk today?') or attitudes (e.g. 'Do you think parents should be stopped from smacking their children?'), or you may use a questionnaire as part of an assessment procedure to assess something such as personality. To extend the analogy of data-gathering instruments as tools, the questionnaire is a versatile tool and is used in a number of different kinds of research design. It can be tightly structured, but can also allow the opportunity for a more open and discursive response if required. Questionnaires may be read out by interviewers (either face-to-face or by phone) or sent to respondents for them to complete themselves; they may be sent by post or email or may be presented online.

There are some basic considerations in constructing a questionnaire:

1 Keep everything short. If possible, limit your questionnaire to one side of A4. The number of people who respond to a questionnaire will decrease in proportion to its length. Make the questions as succinct as you can.

2 Be clear about what you are asking. Only ask for one piece of information at a time. I made the silly mistake recently in a short questionnaire of asking for two pieces of information in one sentence. This confused the respondents, who latched onto the first part of the question and ignored the second.

3 Be precise. Because the only source of clarification is on the piece of paper in front of your respondents, you have to be clear about what you are asking. So, instead of asking, for example, 'How often do you read academic journals?' you would be better to ask 'Do you read academic journals?' and then give a choice of options, such as 'more than once a month, once a month …'

4 Collect all necessary details. It is frustrating to look at a returned set of questionnaires and say to yourself, 'Oh, I wish I'd asked about …'. For example, it may be useful to have information on the form about gender, or years of experience in the profession. Sometimes, these factors, while they may not have seemed important at the outset, become important after your

'eyeballing' of your data (see Chapter 8). They can add an additional dimension for very little extra work, particularly if you are analysing your responses statistically.

5   Be aware of 'prestige bias'. Most people want to look good: to appear clever, nice, rich (or, in the case of students, poor), educated, ethical, and so on. The phenomenon that makes us want to appear any or all of these things can lead to 'prestige bias' in the responses to questionnaires. Be aware of this in the way that you pose questions and interpret the responses.

Prestige bias can occur in a different form if your respondent assumes any kind of 'right answer'. If you were to ask university students, for example, about their use of the library they might well feel that it would be helpful to them in some manner (even if the questionnaire is anonymous) to answer in a way that would indicate more frequent rather than less frequent use. When I ask students to complete an evaluation questionnaire at the end of a term's teaching, for example, I am aware (because they tell me) that students think that I look for similarities between handwriting on the evaluation and handwriting on other samples of work. Slim as they must realise the possibility is that I pore for hours over their written responses looking for this kind of similarity, it clearly nevertheless is something that goes through their minds, and probably has an effect on their responses. You should be aware of the possibility of this kind of bias when you construct your questions and in the way that you distribute and manage the collection of responses. Don't just tell people that it is anonymous, but make it clear how anonymity will be achieved and respected.

Kinds of question and kinds of response

I have already noted the difference between open and closed questions (see the box on p. 196). You can think of **open questions** in a questionnaire in the same way that you think about unstructured interviews, diaries and accounts. They are bound by the same considerations, in that you are aiming to get at the central concerns of an issue as your respondents see them. In a written questionnaire, though, where there is little in the way of stimulus (as there would be in an interview), you will have to give more of a prod to jog the mind of your respondent. It will be no good asking 'Is there anything else you would like to say?' as an open question at the end of a questionnaire, since a good proportion of your respondents will be overcome with the well-known phenomenon of mind-emptying – certainly familiar to me in many and varied situations from the doctor's surgery to the job interview, where my memory is suddenly and inexplicably flushed clean of all those desperately important matters that I had been anxious to discuss.

Open questions may be simply a question such as 'How would you describe your manager's management style, in two or three sentences?' Or you may structure them differently, for example:

- If I had to sum up the culture at my place of work in a word or phrase, it would be …

- I am/am not enjoying my work because …

Closed questions can be organised in a number of ways, depending on the kind of answer required. Let's have a look at some of those ways.

Dichotomous questions

'Dichotomous' means 'two-way', and the dichotomy is usually 'yes' or 'no'. For example:

Have you ever applied for a post of responsibility?	Yes	☐
	No	☐

These can often be screening questions. In other words, you may use the question to separate respondents into groups, who can then be questioned separately. If they haven't applied for a post of responsibility (in this example), why not? Your subsequent questions to this group will pursue this theme. And if they have applied, what happened? A separate route of questioning can be used for this subset.

Multiple-choice questions

These contain two or more answers where respondents can be told either to tick one box or to tick as many boxes as needed. For example:

In an emergency, which of the following would you feel confident in teaching to a Year 7 class (tick as many as you like):

Maths	☐	
English	☐	
A modern language	☐	
Science	☐	
History	☐	
Geography	☐	
Other	☐	Please specify _____

Depending on the purpose, the form of the multiple-choice question will change, of course. If you were interested in respondents' knowledge rather than their beliefs and there was only one right answer, you would restrict the number of choices to one.

Be aware that this kind of question can be useful where it relates to a fact, such as the number of years of experience of a respondent in the profession. Rather than simply asking for a bald figure, putting figures into bands can make it unnecessary for the respondent to spend time working out an exact answer (in which you probably are not interested anyway) and the bands (e.g. fewer than 7 years, 7–19 years, 20 years or more) provide a useful grouping for any subsequent analysis.

Rank order questions

Here, respondents have to rank items (i.e. put them in order) on a list according to some criterion – best to worst, most able to least able, degree of difficulty, and so on. Within this ranking, you can either ask for a limited number of choices (e.g. first, second and third), or require respondents to rank the whole list.

For example, as a dietetics student, you may be interested in the success of diets according to a range of criteria, from ease of use to ultimate effectiveness in terms of weight loss. As part of the research you ask a sample of experienced dietitians to rank ten popular diet regimes on different criteria – from their ease of use to their effectiveness in real-life situations. You first ask them to rank according to ease of use, with an instruction as follows:

> On the basis of your experience with patients, please rank these diets for their ease of use in practice. Please rank them in order, with 1 for the easiest to use, and 10 for the most difficult.

Atkins diet	☐
Cambridge diet	☐
Dukan diet	☐
Jenny Craig diet	☐
LighterLife diet	☐
Rosemary Conley diet	☐
Slim-Fast diet	☐
Slimming World diet	☐
South Beach diet	☐
WeightWatchers diet	☐

Following this, you would ask for other rankings, using different criteria for judgement – criteria such as cost and ultimate success in effecting weight loss.

(*Tip:* always pilot a questionnaire such as this with critical friends. The points they raise (perhaps something like, 'What do you mean by "ease of use"?') will help you to refine the wording of your questions or instructions.)

Rating scale questions

These require the respondent to rate some experience, attribute, attitude, etc., along a continuum. You may, for example, wish to ask adults about their experience of testing and assessment when they were at school:

> Remembering back to when you were at school, would you say that your experiences of formal assessment and testing were

> Very positive   ☐
>
> Positive   ☐
>
> Neutral   ☐
>
> Negative   ☐
>
> Very negative   ☐

The respondent will tick only one of these boxes.

Constant sum method

The constant sum method requires the respondent to distribute 'points', usually 100, to a set of answers. It's as if you give respondents 100 counters to pile up in any of the category boxes as they deem fit. For example, suppose you were interested in parents' perceptions of a good teacher. You might come up with a taxonomy (i.e. an arrangement of ideas) that contains a number of features which might be associated with good teaching: kind, thoughtful, generous, etc. Using the constant sum method, you ask your respondents to divide their points among these features:

> What for you are the important characteristics of a good teacher? You have 100 points to distribute among the characteristics outlined below. You can distribute the points entirely as you wish, but the points must add up to 100:

> Kind   ☐
>
> Thoughtful   ☐
>
> Generous   ☐

Good communicator   ☐

Good listener   ☐

Well organised   ☐

Caring   ☐

Considerate   ☐

The constant sum method is best done with you, the researcher, present.

One of the advantages of this method is the attribution of a 'strength of feeling' weighting to various answers, revealing the relative importance attributed to the different options, so you may be able to see, for example, that 'Kind' is felt to be twice as important as 'Well organised'. This allows some statistical manipulations of the data that would not be possible with other questionnaire data-collection methods.

Matrix or grid questions

Matrices (grids) provide a series of questions, which all have the same answer scale. For example, if you were interested in canvassing parents on what constitutes a good teacher, you might ask them to suggest how important each of these criteria were, all on the same scale of 1 to 5.

Importance ⟶

1 2 3 4 5

Caring   ☐ ☐ ☐ ☐ ☐

Efficient   ☐ ☐ ☐ ☐ ☐

Reliable   ☐ ☐ ☐ ☐ ☐

Kind   ☐ ☐ ☐ ☐ ☐

Understandable   ☐ ☐ ☐ ☐ ☐

Helpful   ☐ ☐ ☐ ☐ ☐

It is necessary to make clear to respondents the 'direction of travel' of the numbers being used in this kind of scale. I have used an arrow in this example, but you may wish to make this doubly clear by, for example, adding words such as 'high' or 'low' at each end, or adding a graphic such as a smiley. (*Tip*: smileys and other useful graphics such as ☜ and ✓ can be found in Word under the Wingdings font. From the Insert menu, click on 'Symbol', then on 'More Symbols', then scroll down under 'Font' to Wingdings, scroll through the pictures, click on the one you want, and press Insert.)

Scales

Scales, that is to say sets of items and responses, appear in some of the question formats above. However, there are a couple of kinds of well-known scale that are worth mentioning as easily used tools: the Likert scale and the semantic differential scale.

The Likert scale

The Likert scale was thought up by the psychologist Rensis Likert primarily for measuring attitudes: respondents indicate their levels of agreement to statements provided by the researcher relating to that attitude, belief or characteristic. The respondent, rather as in rating scale questions, responds to each item on a five-point or seven-point scale, usually with answers from strongly agree, agree, neither agree nor disagree, disagree, strongly disagree. To remove the tendency for some people to over-choose the middle option, this middle option is sometimes removed, making a four-point scale. The latter is used in the Rosenberg Self-Esteem Scale, where the first three items are:

	Strongly agree	Agree	Disagree	Strongly disagree
1. On the whole I am satisfied with myself.				
2. At times I think that I am no good at all.				
3. I feel that I have a number of good qualities.				

Here is part of a questionnaire using a three-point Likert scale that colleagues and I (Vincett et al., 2005) used as part of a larger piece of research with children in Essex schools:

	Yes ☺	A bit 😐	No ☹
My teacher likes to listen to my ideas.			
My teacher helps me with my work.			
I think my teacher's classroom rules are fair.			
If I have a problem I can tell my teacher.			
Sometimes my teacher lets me choose what work to do.			
My teacher tells me when I have done something well.			

A Likert scale can be used in any situation where belief or attitude is to be measured. The important thing to remember is that you are asking for agreement or disagreement with a *statement* that you provide. (The Rosenberg and other scales can be accessed via http://eib.emcdda.europa.eu/html.cfm/ index3676EN.html.)

The semantic differential scale

Using opposite-meaning adjectives such as 'kind/cruel' or 'exciting/boring', the semantic differential scale requires the respondent to rate something on a seven-point scale in relation to those adjectives. You may be interested in the assertion that rap music encourages sexism and violence among young people. Rather than simply asking 'Do you think that rap music encourages sexism and violence among your age group?', you could use the semantic differential scale to draw a more 'textured' picture of respondents' thinking, and look at interesting differences where they occur between subgroups within your sample. For example:

> Thinking of [name of rap singer's] music and its lyrics, how would you rank it along these criteria? Put a tick in the appropriate box on each row.

Exciting								Boring
Kind								Cruel
Generous								Tight
Selfish								Altruistic
Active								Passive
Racist								Non-racist
Fair								Unfair

Because the semantic differential is a little out of the ordinary for many respondents it is probably best done in a questionnaire format with you present. If you did not intend to be present, at the very least you would need to give an example of an already completed (but irrelevant) one to explain what needs to be done.

Questionnaire structure

Give some thought to how to arrange the questions. For example, don't start with difficult questions, or open-ended questions: leave these until the end, since they require thought and may put off a respondent from bothering. Remember that you are dependent entirely on their goodwill. Start with something easy such as a 'How far do you agree with ...?' question. This will ease them into the questionnaire and whet their appetite to carry on. Most people, after all, do like to give their opinions: you just have to make it easy for them to do it.

Remember that not all of your questions will be relevant to all of your respondents, so make sure that you include *filters* if necessary, for example: 'Have you ever written for a professional journal? Yes ☐ No ☐. If Yes, please go to Q 5. If No, please go to Q 9.' You can use arrows and boxes to make it clear to respondents where they should go next.

Especially if the questionnaire is sent by post, it is a good idea to include a personalised covering letter or some kind of introductory page explaining briefly the purpose of the research and why it is important. This should include information about confidentiality, publication and ethics (see pp. 47–8), and who is responsible for the research. Don't forget to thank the respondent profusely at the end of the questionnaire.

Because a questionnaire is out of your control once it is sent out, it is important that it should be unambiguous in its interpretation. To make sure that you get things right you should always pilot a draft questionnaire on a small group of people who can give you feedback.

Questionnaires online

If you want to conduct a survey online there are a number of web-based services available. One of the best known is SurveyMonkey at www.surveymonkey.com. This lets you construct your own questionnaire free for a survey of up to 100 respondents. It guides you very helpfully through the questionnaire construction process and then offers you a way of 'posting' your survey, as shown in Figure 7.4. The whole process is easy and presents your respondents with a professional-looking interface. Do test out a pilot survey first, though, with two or three friends.

☉	Create a link to send in your own email message or to place on a webpage The simplest and fastest way to collect responses. We generate a link for your survey that you can just copy and paste.
☉	Upload your own emails and have us send a survey invitation You can upload your emails, and we will send a survey invitation on your behalf. You can customize the message that is sent, and track who responds in your list.
☉	Create a popup invitation for your webpage We give you the code to generate a popup invitation on your own webpage.

Figure 7.4   SurveyMonkey's offer for 'posting' your survey

If you want anything more complex than a basic questionnaire or if you want to send it to more than 100 people you will need to pay for the SurveyMonkey service or for another one like it. The one that my university department uses is the Bristol Online Survey (BOS). This provides, as they describe it, 'a fully integrated

Web environment for the design, delivery and analysis of online surveys'. It doesn't require any technical knowledge and will give you instant feedback on the survey as it progresses. Data can be downloaded into Excel, and you can set up your supervisor, your colleagues or fellow students to view results. There is also support provided. The downside is that it comes at a price (£500), but your university will almost certainly subscribe to a service of this kind, and if yours does you should have free access: ask your supervisor. If, in the unlikely event of your university department or faculty not subscribing to such a service, BOS will consider on a case-by-case basis appeals from individuals for a reduced-cost provision.

	Yes	No	Not sure	Further comment
a. We intend to discontinue the Editorial as a feature of each issue of BERJ. Do you agree that this is an appropriate change?	☐	☐	☐	

Figure 7.5　Example question on BOS

Figure 7.5 is an example of a question from a survey that I put together on BOS. It was to members of the British Educational Research Association about their views on the Association's journal. You'll note that the questionnaire provides 'buttons' for users to click on. If the people you wish to survey have access to the Internet, then this really is the preferred method of questionnaire distribution, saving a great deal of time in distribution, collection and analysis. It should help also in boosting response rate, obviating the need for envelopes, stamps and other paraphernalia. Figure 7.6 is an example of the output, ready-organised for you.

1.a. We intend to discontinue the Editorial as a feature of each issue of BERJ. Do you agree that this is an appropriate change?			
Yes:	▓▓▓▓▓▓▓	38.7%	120
No:	▓▓▓▓	23.5%	73
Not sure:	▓▓▓▓▓▓	37.7%	117
1.a.i. We intend to discontinue the Editorial as a feature of each issue of BERJ. Do you agree that this is an appropriate change? – Further comment			
View All Responses　There are too many responses to display on this page and so all the responses to this question are available on a separate page.			

Figure 7.6　BOS output

To contact BOS go to www.survey.bris.ac.uk, and if your institution does not subscribe you can direct it to www.survey.bris.ac.uk/support/sign-up-instructions. There is also a facility for a demo account.

Observation

Observation is one of the most important ways of collecting data in social research. Observing means watching carefully, and you can do this careful watching in some very different ways, depending on the approach to research that you have decided to take. For our purposes here, the basic difference is between a kind of observation in which you systematically look for particular kinds of behaviour and one in which – remembering back to Chapter 5 – you watch as a spy or a witness, informally (but methodically) recording important facets of the stage on which you observe.

The first kind of observation, where you watch for particular kinds of behaviour, is called *structured observation*. The second kind, where you get on the stage, take part, record from the stage and watch from there, is called *unstructured observation*.

Structured observation

In structured observation you are making assumptions that the social world is viewable through a prism that enables the breakdown of social activity into quantifiable elements – bits that you can count. Like a prism breaks white light into its separate colours, so the prism of the structured observer breaks the social situation down into separate bits.

The first thing that the observer has to do is to define what these bits are to be. They may be individual pieces of action or language, such as a child physically touching another child or a teacher using a particular kind of question. The next thing that a structured observer has to do is to devise some way of counting these elements. This is done in a number of ways.

Duration recording

The observer measures the overall time that a target behaviour (such as 'child out of seat') occurs. You will end up with an overall time, for example 27 minutes in a session of 60 minutes.

Frequency count recording

The observer records each time the target behaviour (e.g. the teacher's use of praise to the whole class) occurs. You will end up with an overall number, for example 4 times in a session. (This is also called 'event sampling'.)

Interval recording

You decide on:

- an interval (3 seconds, 10 seconds, 20 seconds, or whatever – depending on the complexity of what you are looking for);

- target individual(s); and

- categories of behaviour (e.g. on-task, off-task).

You will end up with data which can be processed in a number of ways. The most usual way of processing it is to count up the number of times that the target individual has scored in, say, the behaviour category of interest and then to express this as a percentage of the total number of possible observations.

For example, if your interval is 10 seconds, it means that you are going to be making 6 observations a minute and therefore 360 per hour. Out of these 360 possible observations you may have only seen the child being on task on 36 occasions – if this were the case then you could express this as $36/360 \times 100 = 10\%$ on task.

> **Nature of structured observation**: Defining, counting – characterised by non-participant observation.
>
> **Data gathering**: Various methods of recording particular behaviour: duration, frequency, interval recording.
>
> **Instruments**: Various checklists (e.g. Flanders Interaction Analysis)

Time sampling

You may come across the term 'time sampling'. This simply refers to the fact that you are selecting intervals out of the total time available for observation and then only observing during the selected periods (e.g. the first half hour of the morning, over a period of five days). It is not therefore a data-collection method in itself but may be used with any of the methods listed above.

Figure 7.7 is an example of an actual piece of recording undertaken by teachers in their classes in a piece of research I undertook with colleagues into classroom organisation, where the various kinds of organisation were called 'learning zones' (Vincett et al., 2005).

There are some well-tried and tested schedules for structured gathering of classroom activity. One of these is the classic but still widely used Flanders Interaction Analysis (see Flanders, 2004). It is about classroom talk and consists of a schedule of categories which a researcher will use to examine how language is being used in the classroom:

A   **Teacher talk**

1   Clarify feeling constructively
2   Praise or encourage
3   Clarify, develop or make use of ideas suggested by students   *Response*

4 Ask questions

5 Lecture

6 Give directions   *Initiation*

7 Criticise

B **Student talk**

8 Student talk in response to the teacher   –   *Response*

9 Student talk initiated by the student   –   *Initiation*

C **Silence**

10 Silence or confusion

The researcher checks every three seconds which of the categories is relevant and marks it on a list similar to the one in Figure 7.7.

Structured observation was extensively used in a major piece of classroom research known as the ORACLE project (Galton et al., 1980). It is worth looking at this if you intend to undertake structured research.

Pupil	1 min	2 min	3 min	4 min	5 min	6 min	7 min	8 min	9 min	10min
Claire										
Naz										
Laura										
Kate										
Elise										
Tom										
Nico										
Joe										
Ghazala										
Hannah										

Figure 7.7 Structured observation

EVALUATING LEARNING ZONES: PUPIL ENGAGEMENT
Collecting data

Engagement refers to the extent that pupils are 'on task' during any teaching period. It provides a useful measure of how well organised and industrious the class is. One reason for this choice in our research is that this measure has been successfully used in other research into room management and zoning procedures. It proves to be a robust and useful measure of classroom activity. There is research to show that engagement rates relate solidly to achievement.

If using this method to evaluate an intervention, such as Learning Zones, a base-line measurement would be used prior to beginning to use these models, and then again once the models have been used for several weeks. If the intervention is successful, there should be an improvement in on-task behaviour.

Instructions for collecting data

Identify ten pupils for data collection – a mixture of boy/girl, different abilities.

For a period of twenty minutes complete the pupil engagement tally for the ten pupils.

Every minute look at each pupil quickly in turn and note whether they are on or off task. Put a tick if the pupil is on task and a cross if not.

For each pupil calculate the percentage of time on task (number of ticks divided by total number of tallies × 100). For example if a pupil obtains sixteen ticks out of a possible 20, then 16/20 × 100 means the pupil was on task for 80% of the time.

Unstructured observation

Consistent with the tenets of interpretivism (see p. 108), unstructured observation is undertaken when you are immersing yourself in a social situation, usually as some kind of participant, in order to understand what is going on there. Ethnographers, with whom this kind of observation is usually associated, often discuss social life as if it were a stage, or a set of stages, on which we act out roles. Unstructured observation will be geared to understanding how these roles play themselves out on the stage of life.

Often this kind of observation is called *participant observation* because it is associated with researchers becoming participants in the situations they are research-

ing. I have already discussed participant observation on p. 157, but as Burgess (1982) points out, the term 'participant observation' is a little confusing since it connotes much more than simply observation. It entails talking to people, watching, reading documents, keeping notes and anything else that enables you to understand a situation.

A distinction is sometimes drawn between different kinds of observation that all occur within the participant observation frame.

Burgess (1984), for example, outlines three types: complete participant; participant as observer; and observer as participant. These represent, if you like, different 'levels' of participation. With the first, complete participant, the assumption is that you are an integral part of the situation you are studying, as with the school governor diary I described on p. 201, or as with James Patrick's (1973) 'participation' in the Glasgow gang he describes. 'Membership' is probably a better word than 'participation' in these examples. With the last, observer as participant, there is no attempt at involvement in the situation. And this is all, of course, within the ethnography fieldwork tradition.

Personally, in practice I find it difficult to disentangle where one kind of participation begins and another ends in this kind of classification, and I am not going to offer a taxonomy which implies that researchers should have to slot themselves into one notional type rather than another. Rather, for me there is simply a continuum of observation (see Figure 7.8), with structured at one end and unstructured at the other, and, while each extreme end tends to be associated with particular approaches to research, there are no hard-and-fast rules about which to adopt. As I have been at pains to point out throughout this book, the central consideration in choosing approaches, methods and tools is their quality of fit for the purposes and questions in your research. It is these that should always be at the front of your mind.

So, the continuum of types of observation and types of participation or involvement given in Figure 7.8 shows a number of potential forms of combination. You *can* do structured observation as a participant, but this would be unusual. Likewise, you *can* do unstructured observation as a non-participant, though the latter does not quite fit the frameworks of research design offered by textbooks. Nevertheless, it is a combination commonly adopted, particularly by students, who perhaps are attracted by the apparent straightforwardness of the unstructured approach to observing, but who perhaps feel that the exigencies of life will interrupt a full ethnographic involvement.

At its worst, though, this sort of unstructured observation is unstructured by *anything at all* – even by a view about how we can find out and how we can

> **Nature of unstructured/ participant observation**: Not breaking down the situation; becoming part of it; seeing the situation as a whole.
>
> **Data gathering**: Interviews, introspection, reflection, direct observation.
>
> **Instruments**: Watching, keeping a diary, audio recording, interviewing, introspection, taking photographs and videos and examining documents.

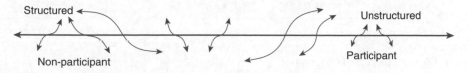

Figure 7.8 A continuum of observation and participation

know – and it can end simply as a catalogue of quotations and observations, with little in the way of cement to give it integrity, interest or meaning. So, while unstructured observation may seem to be an easier way of observing than using structured observation, in fact it requires a great deal of preparatory work and devotion to become part of the situation you are observing and it needs sensitivity, commitment and thought to analyse the findings meaningfully.

Having issued this dire warning about the unconsidered use of unstructured observation, what can I suggest should be done? I can give Figure 7.9 as an example from a piece of research that I undertook for the children's charity Barnardo's (Thomas et al., 1998). As part of this research I undertook some observations in mainstream classrooms to try to understand how well some children with physical disabilities who had formerly attended special schools were becoming included in the mainstream. My observation was unstructured, though I was not a participant

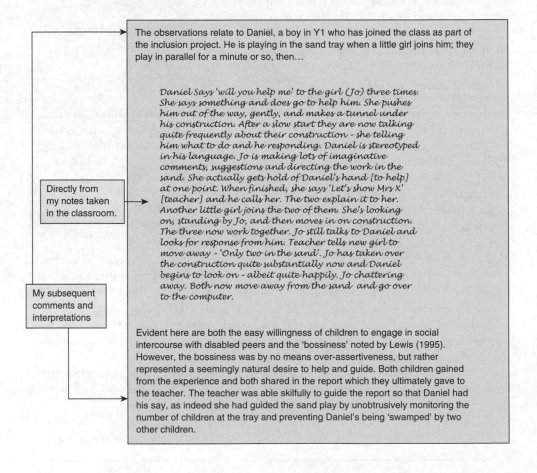

The observations relate to Daniel, a boy in Y1 who has joined the class as part of the inclusion project. He is playing in the sand tray when a little girl joins him; they play in parallel for a minute or so, then…

Directly from my notes taken in the classroom.

Daniel Says 'will you help me' to the girl (Jo) three times. She says something and does go to help him. She pushes him out of the way, gently, and makes a tunnel under his construction. After a slow start they are now talking quite frequently about their construction - she telling him what to do and he responding. Daniel is stereotyped in his language. Jo is making lots of imaginative comments, suggestions and directing the work in the sand. She actually gets hold of Daniel's hand [to help] at one point. When finished, she says 'Let's show Mrs X' [teacher] and he calls her. The two explain it to her. Another little girl joins the two of them. She's looking on, standing by Jo, and then moves in on construction. The three now work together. Jo still talks to Daniel and looks for response from him. Teacher tells new girl to move away - 'Only two in the sand'. Jo has taken over the construction quite substantially now and Daniel begins to look on - albeit quite happily. Jo chattering away. Both now move away from the sand and go over to the computer.

My subsequent comments and interpretations

Evident here are both the easy willingness of children to engage in social intercourse with disabled peers and the 'bossiness' noted by Lewis (1995). However, the bossiness was by no means over-assertiveness, but rather represented a seemingly natural desire to help and guide. Both children gained from the experience and both shared in the report which they ultimately gave to the teacher. The teacher was able skilfully to guide the report so that Daniel had his say, as indeed she had guided the sand play by unobtrusively monitoring the number of children at the tray and preventing Daniel's being 'swamped' by two other children.

Figure 7.9   Unstructured observation

in the situation. I think my answer to the question that I posed just now about 'What should be done if you can't be fully involved as an ethnographer?' is that my notes were bound by the same considerations as the ethnographer's, even though my involvement in the activity of the class was minimal.

I hope it is clear that I have in my notes attempted 'thick description' (see p. 239), for example in my comments about the teacher's intervention. That intervention was skilfully and tactfully made to prevent the developing bond between Daniel and Jo unravelling with the intrusion of another child, who would almost certainly have offered Jo more enticing conversation opportunities. Through my observation I was trying at the same time to interpret – using my understanding of situations like this to enable this interpretation. The subsequent comments and interpretations attempted to capitalise on and develop the notes taken in the classroom, tying in the latter with commentary I had garnered in my literature review.

Gathering image-based data

Now that digital photographs and videos are more or less free and disposable, image-based methods provide a powerful extension to data collection. Data may be collected in photographs, videos, films, graffiti, drawings, cartoons and so on.

The most widely used forms of image-based research are:

- *Photo elicitation*, which Prosser and Loxley (2008) describe as 'the use of photographs (whether researcher-created, respondent-created or found) in a research interview to stimulate a response'.

- *Graphical elicitation*, where respondents are encouraged to talk via some object, a picture in a book, a photo or a drawing. They may be asked to draw a sketch or construct a mind map which charts ideas which may be difficult to articulate. Prosser and Loxley suggest, for example, that if you were exploring respondents' relationships with others such as family members or friends, you might ask them to draw a diagram in which they:

  o place themselves at the centre of the diagram;

  o let the physical distance between them and the other characters reflect how close the relationship is;

  o let the size of the shape representing a person or group vary with their importance to them (e.g. a big circle around important people/groups, smaller around less important people/groups);

  o show the connections between relationships by an arrow/line, and its nature by a brief label;

  o show the personality of key people or the character of a group by the use of colour or symbols such as pictures or shapes.

There are a number of advantages to the use of images in small-scale research:

- You can more easily include the person or persons on whom the research focuses. While observation pure and simple is always from researcher to researched, image-based methods offer the reciprocal relationship as well: the researched can set the agenda and the research can be more inclusive.

- You can capture a social scene far more quickly than you can with notes. The captured scene will enable you to freeze the scene in time for your subsequent analysis at leisure.

- The scene can be captured discreetly, with little input from you, ready for your subsequent interpretation. Not only is it more subtle than, say, interviewing, but it can also break the ice. As Schwartz (1992: 1) put it, his camera was 'an excuse to start up a conversation, and the longer I made photographs, the more people I met'.

- You can adapt your method to your research study 'process'. You may, for example, wish to repeat photographs of the same situation over a range of times and dates.

- These methods blend really easily with other methods. Prosser and Loxley (2008) describe a study about city gentrification which combined photography, ethnographic fieldwork, grounded theory, shooting scripts, analysis of detailed field notes, over a period of 16 years.

- Photos (or other images or videos) can be used to excite a response. This can be particularly useful with children, with whom it is often difficult to engage if you limit yourself to words.

- Prosser and Loxley also point to the ambiguity of an image and its almost haphazard capacity to kindle a response – in your informants or in you yourself – that may be quite unexpected.

Prosser (1998) gives an excellent overview of data collection using images and ways of interpreting the data collected.

Data-gathering tools – mainly for use with numbers

I said at the beginning of this book that *experience* is at the heart of empirical inquiry, with experience in this context meaning our perception of the world around us. Words and numbers are our messengers about the experience we draw on in empirical inquiry. As messengers, words and numbers do not themselves constitute direct experience. Rather, they stand in the place of experience: they *represent* experience.

I begin with this point while talking in this section about the use of numbers because there can be the tendency in social research to treat numbers as if they are in some way superior as envoys of truth – that they are in some way cleaner, more objective vehicles for the carriage of knowledge than are words. This is partly because they tend to be associated with certain approaches to research (see Chapter 5) that in the popular mind accompany the methods of the natural sciences.

But this notion of clean, simple efficiency in the transport of knowledge is misleading, for in social research numbers are only as reliable as the concepts that underlie them. I can try to explain what I am talking about here by reference to the notion of intelligence and its translation into a number in the form of an intelligence quotient (IQ). In the popular mind IQ represents a robust and stable measure of a straight-forward concept: intelligence. As such, it has entered the public consciousness as an unproblematic representation of an uncomplicated mental faculty.

But intelligence is now widely critiqued as a concept – it is lying in the gutter of social scientific thinking (see, for example, Gould, 1996; Devlin et al., 1997; Klein, 1997; Dickens and Flynn, 2001; White, 2006) – and if the undertaker hasn't actually been called yet, we can at least say that the last rites are about to be read any time now. However, you wouldn't guess this from looking at magazines and television programmes, which are replete with IQ tests: you can test your own IQ, test the family's IQ, test the nation's IQ – even test the dog's IQ. This peculiar resilience is down to the allure of a simple figure which seems to carry the imprimatur of science.

The IQ story is just a brief health warning about the risks in using numbers in social research, which doesn't mean that *all* numbers are automatically suspect. Some numbers are perfectly straightforward, though of course there are always possibilities for counting things in different ways and for measurement error. Where you should be automatically wary and instinctively suspicious is in the attribution of numbers to complex ideas (as in the IQ example) and in the use of complex statistics. Again, they may represent satisfactory analyses of quantified phenomena, but we should always be aware that the more complex something is the more chance there is of something going awry or of the wool being pulled over our eyes. I shall look further at this in Chapter 8, where I shall also look at some of the features of the kinds of numbers we can use in social and educational research in preparation for a discussion of some basic ways in which these numbers can be used for analysis.

Measurements and tests

The word 'test' has a general meaning of 'check'. In using a test you are checking the extent of something, whether this be learning of some topic at school, or the level of cholesterol in the bloodstream. The results of a test will nearly always be in numerical form. In healthcare, tests will nearly always be of the simple meas-urement form, whereas in education they take more varied forms, being formal or informal measures of some attribute, personal feature or attainment. They exist in simple, home-made measures, and also in complex and well-standardised forms. Test construction and standardisation is a large and separate field of study and it is beyond the scope of this book to examine it in any detail, so I shall confine myself to some general comments about tests and how you may collect data from them.

Tests can be formal or informal, norm-referenced or criterion-referenced.

In its simplest form, a home-made test assesses something that has been taught, or a level of pre-existing knowledge. The teacher may devise a spelling test or a tables test, and give marks out of 20, say. In the same way, for a small research project you may devise a test to assess the extent of learning.

Tests can be divided into those which are **norm-referenced** and those which are **criterion-referenced**. A norm-referenced test compares the person being tested to a sample of their peers. A criterion-referenced test simply assesses whether someone is able to meet some criterion, irrespective of how well other people perform on the test. The purposes of norm- and criterion-referenced tests differ: the norm-referenced test aims to compare individuals, one against others, while the criterion-referenced test merely says whether or not 'person A can do x'. Intelligence tests and most reading tests are examples of norm-referenced tests, since they seek to tell testers how well testees compare next to other people. A driving test is an example of a criterion-referenced test, since there is no comparison going on with the cohort of other people doing the test. It doesn't matter how many people can or can't do the three-point turn – if you can do it, then you get your box ticked and you have passed this part of the test. It is quite easy to devise a criterion-referenced test yourself.

When using norm-referenced tests, testers are more interested in differentiating among a sample – in comparing this child with others, or in comparing one group with another. In order to make accurate comparisons of this kind, a procedure known as standardisation is used in the construction of norm-referenced tests. This involves constructing the test under particular specified, repeatable conditions with large samples from a population (of, say, 11-year-olds) and, in turn, it is expected that the test will be administered and scored in practice under those same conditions. A good test is one that is reliable and valid, these words in test construction having rather more specific meanings than those they carry in research design generally. Broadly speaking, reliability refers to the test's ability to measure something consistently, while validity is a measure of how well it is assessing what it is supposed to measure. You can usually be confident that in most commercially produced tests reliability and validity will be satisfactory.

Many standardised tests – of attainment in reading, maths, non-verbal ability or a wide range of other faculties – are now available online; see, for example, www.gl-assessment.co.uk/.

Official statistics

Official statistics can form the basis of first-rate research yet are used surprisingly little in student projects. It's almost as if most student research still exists in the pre-Internet era. If you can therefore show that you have drawn relevantly from these statistics your project will be viewed all the more favourably. There is a variety of websites from which you can easily download data of extraordinary detail and richness. This can nowadays be manipulated in your own spreadsheet remarkably simply (I'm using Excel in the examples here).

The procedure for getting hold of the data for your own manipulation is straightforward. Don't forget to check for copyright first. Then, once you have opened the relevant PDF or website page, you can drag your cursor over the table you are interested in, copy it and paste it into Excel for subsequent analysis. This is how you do it:

- Select the material you want (choose the cursor tool in Adobe if it does not at first appear).

- Copy it (Ctrl+C).

- Open Excel.

- Make sure the top left-hand cell is selected in your Excel spreadsheet.

- Go to Edit, and click 'Paste special'.

- Click on 'Unicode text' in the dialogue box that appears. Click on OK.

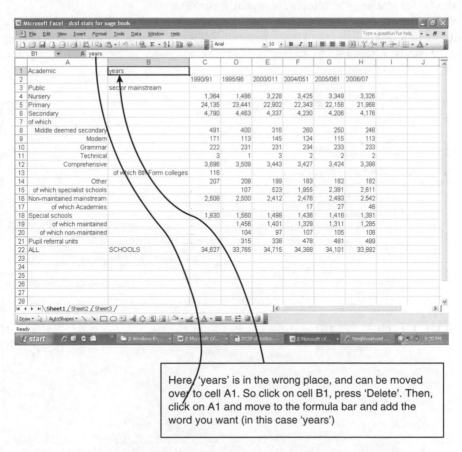

Here, 'years' is in the wrong place, and can be moved over to cell A1. So click on cell B1, press 'Delete'. Then, click on A1 and move to the formula bar and add the word you want (in this case 'years')

Figure 7.10 A spreadsheet of 'Number of schools, by type of school – time series' taken from official statistics (DCSF, 2007): tidying up

- Put your cursor over the little clipboard sign that appears at the bottom of your pasted material. Click on the little arrow that appears to the right of it (labelled 'Paste options').

- Click on 'Use text import wizard'.

- Click on 'Finish' (or answer each question in turn if you can make sense of them).

While Excel makes a good job of copying the table, certain cells will probably be out of place, and you will have to spend 15 minutes or so tidying up the table so that material is in the right place. For example, if a row of cells has been shifted one column to the right, drag your cursor over it so that it is selected. Then click on the heavy border around the selected material and drag it to the right position. You will end up with something like the spreadsheet in Figure 7.10. Something will inevitably still be wrong. For example, if you want to add or delete text (which may be in the wrong place), click on the cell you want to change, and go to the box at the top of the page to alter it, as in the figure.

Figure 7.10 is from the very first table of the Department for Education's statistical bulletin, and I have just taken it as an example. I'll say some more about how this kind of data can be *analysed* in Chapter 8. However, for now, let us look at how you can

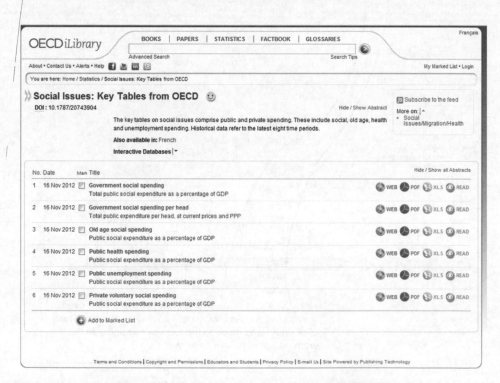

Figure 7.11   The OECD website – excellent for comparative research

transfer this to your Word document. Click on the top left cell (A1) and drag down until you reach the bottom-right one (H22). Copy (Ctrl+C), move to Word, place the cursor where you want the table and paste (Ctrl+V). You can then edit as you wish.

Another excellent statistics resource, particularly for those undertaking comparative research, may be found at http://stats.oecd.org/source/ or http://stats.oecd.org/wbos/ Index.aspx?usercontext=sourceoecd, which provide a wide range of statistics gathered by the Organisation for Economic Co-operation and Development (OECD) (see Figure 7.11).

The Neighbourhood Statistics website of the Office for National Statistics gives a mass of information, for example about census data, including accommodation types, numbers of cars, country of birth, distances travelled to work – and much more – related to people and regions in the UK (see Figures 7.12 and 7.13). It is especially useful if you wish to relate your data to general statistics for a region or nationally. It can be found at www.neighbourhood.statistics.gov.uk/dissemination/.

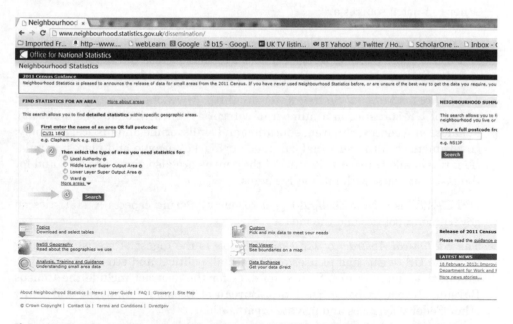

Figure 7.12 The Neighbourhood Statistics website of the Office for National Statistics

Emma Smith's excellent website at www.secondarydataanalysis.com gives access to these and a broad range of other UK, US and international data websites. The US sources, for example, lead you to administrative records, archives and gateways including FedStats and public opinion research, census records, and longitudinal and cohort survey data.

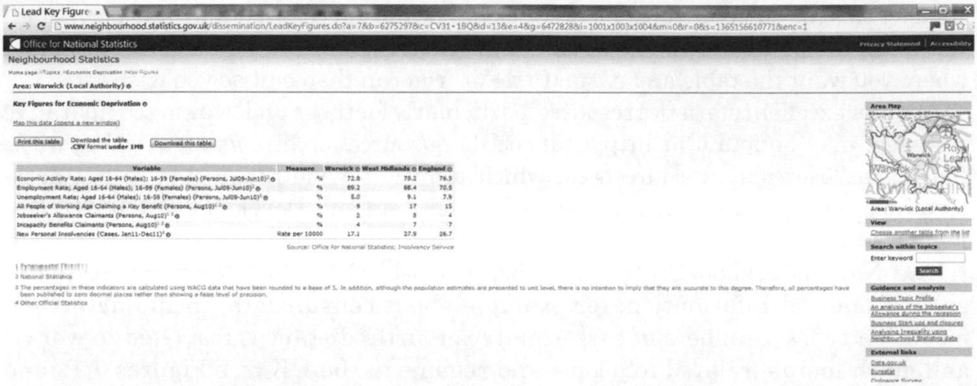

Figure 7.13　Neighbourhood statistics unpacked

Other top-notch sources are:

- *FedStats* (http://fedstats.gov) is an American government website giving statistics on regions of the US, data from a range of agencies such as the Bureau of Justice and the National Institute on Drug Abuse, and an A to Z of topics.

- The *Office for National Statistics* website (http://www.ons.gov.uk) gives a broad range of UK statistics in a number of categories. These include the following: business and energy; children, education and skills; crime and justice; economy; government; health and social care; labour market; people and places; population; travel and transport. Results of the census are also given for 2011 and for the last 100 years, with interactive maps.

- *OFFSTATS* is a New Zealand-based resource offering especially statistics on government, politics and the media.

- The *Statistical Abstract of the United States* is the digest of statistics coming from the US census and focuses on the social, political and economic organisation of the United States. Sources of data for the abstract include the Census Bureau, Bureau of Labor Statistics, Bureau of Economic Analysis, and many other Federal agencies and private organisations.

- *UNdata* (http://data.un.org/) is the United Nations collation of country data services, with particularly useful areas on crime and education. The latter includes links to a broad range of other databases including those of UNESCO and the OECD.

- The *World Factbook* is produced by the CIA (yes, *the* CIA – the Central Intelligence Agency). As it describes itself, it 'provides information on the history, people, government, economy, geography, communications, transportation, military, and transnational issues for 267 world entities'. It is very useful for making international comparisons.

Overview

I've looked at a wide range of data-gathering tools and methods, some that concern the collection of numbers, and some the collection of words. Some collect both. As Angharad's 'itinerary' on p. 128 in Chapter 5 indicates, these are tools that can be employed in a variety of ways with the design frames of Chapter 6. The techniques associated with these tools can be quite specialised, but it is important not to get hypnotised by these complexities. At the end of the day, these are tools that help you to gather data associated with the design path that you have followed.

Checklist ✔

You may find it helpful to copy this table and write down the answers to the questions.

Have you ...

	Notes	
1 ... thought about the different kinds of data you can collect?	What kinds of data are these? Write them down here	☐
2 ... decided on the method (or methods) you will use to collect data?	What is this? Write it down here	☐
3 ... begun to think about how you will analyse these data in the context of answering your research question?		☐

Further reading

Interviews and accounts

Barbour, R. and Schostak, J. (2005) Interviewing and focus groups. In B. Somekh and C. Lewin (eds), *Research Methods in the Social Sciences*. London: SAGE. A brief but useful account.

Diaries

Altricher, H. and Holly, M. (2005) Research diaries. In B. Somekh and C. Lewin (eds), *Research Methods in the Social Sciences*. London: SAGE.
Short and to the point.

Bolger, N., Davis, A. and Rafaeli, P. (2003) Diary methods: capturing life as it is lived. *Annual Review of Psychology*, 54, 579–616.
This is a thoroughgoing academic review. All the information you would ever want on diaries, and more.

There is an excellent, practical webpage on the use of diaries at http://sru.soc.surrey.ac.uk/SRU2.html.

Focus groups

Bloor, M., Frankland, J., Thomas, M. and Robson, K. (2001) *Focus Groups in Social Research*. London: SAGE.
A comprehensive overview.

Parker, A. and Tritter, J. (2006) Focus group method and methodology: current practice and recent debate. *International Journal of Research and Method in Education*, 29 (1), 23–37.
A good up-to-date account treated with academic rigour.

Questionnaires

Oppenheim, A.N. (2000) *Questionnaire Design*. London: Continuum.
Regarded as a classic text on the subject, and deservedly so.

Observation

Structured observation
Croll, P. (1986) *Systematic Classroom Observation*. Lewes: Falmer Press.
A good, balanced overview.

Unstructured observation
An excellent outline of participant observation is given at www.infed.org/research/participant_observation.htm

Image-based methods

Prosser, J. and Loxley, A. (2008) Introducing visual methods: ESRC National Centre for Research Methods review paper. Available at: http://eprints.ncrm.ac.uk/420/1/MethodsReviewPaperNCRM-010.pdf (accessed 4 November 2012).
An easily accessed and thoroughgoing overview offering practicality and rigour. It covers everything from respondents with cameras to photo elicitation and graphical elicitation.

Prosser, J. (ed.) (1998) *Image-Based Research*. London: Routledge.
The bible of theory and practice on this subject with contributions from a range of experts. It is more technical and discursive than Prosser and Loxley (2008).

Tests

http://www.gl-assessment.co.uk/
Includes access to tests and various online assessments.

Official statistics

Smith, E. (2008) *Using Secondary Data in Educational and Social Research*. Maidenhead: Open University Press.
An invaluable sourcebook for official statistics and how you can use them.

8

HOW TO ANALYSE THE INFORMATION YOU GATHER

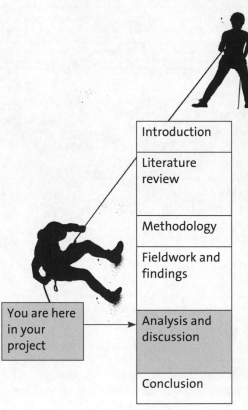

Introduction	
Literature review	
Methodology	
Fieldwork and findings	
You are here in your project →	Analysis and discussion
	Conclusion

Following the collection of your data, you need to analyse them. Your data may be in any of a variety of forms, and the methods for analysing the data will vary. This chapter considers:

- analysing words – the constant comparative method (coding, sorting and patterns);

- analysing numbers – understanding what numbers are saying and making your numbers meaningful to others (eyeballing, descriptive and inferential statistics, significance);

- understanding what your analysis tells you – discussing your findings in the context of previous research and developing theory.

You are now analysing the data that you have collected, in whatever form. There is a wide array of analytical methods for handling the data that you have gathered, and I can only look at a small sample of them here. I will look at some of the most commonly used methods, but will also try to explain some of the principles of data analysis that underlie these and other methods.

As in every other chapter of this book, I stress here the importance of the coherence of your story. Your analysis should fit the approach you have taken in your research. If there are different elements to your research, each structured by a different approach, the analysis relating to each element should be appropriate.

Analysing words

When you have gathered data in words – and you don't intend in any way to convert those words into numbers – you are seeking to use those words in descriptive or illuminative analysis of the situation in which you are interested. You are seeking understanding and insight, adopting the assumptions of interpretivism.

Constant comparative method

The basic analytic method of the interpretative researcher is *constant comparison*. Sometimes called the 'constant comparative method', it stands behind every technique in this paradigm. The constant comparative method involves going through your data again and again (this is the *constant* bit), comparing each element – phrase, sentence or paragraph – with all of the other elements (this is the *comparative* bit). There's nothing more complicated than that, though there are different ways of going about the constant comparative method, many of which are outlined in texts such as Miles and Huberman (1994). Some of these are useful; others, in my opinion, make things appear to be more difficult than they really are.

From the constant comparison you mark your data up with **codes** – abbreviations, names, marks and/or colours – that describe its important facets. You eventually emerge with **themes** which capture or summarise the contents of your data. The process is described in more detail in Figure 8.1.

These themes or *categories* are the essential building blocks of your analysis. Remember that the aim in using an interpretative approach is to emerge with the meanings that are being constructed by the participants (including you) in the situation.

There are various ways in which you can *map* your themes to show the *interconnections* between them. This mapping is often the weakest part of students' use of interpretative data. While the identification of themes is important, students sometimes go little beyond this and do not manage to explain how ideas are related to one another. The two methods I shall outline here for mapping of themes are **network analysis** (Bliss et al., 1983) and my own adaptation (Thomas, 1992) of **construct mapping** (Jones, 1985). I shall illustrate these methods by drawing on my own use of them.

Network analysis

In network analysis you aim to show how one idea is related to another using a network, which is a bit like a tree, with a *trunk* that forms the basic idea and *branches* coming off the trunk representing constituent ideas. This is useful where there is a core theme which you consider comprises a range of sub-themes. Network analysis shows how themes are related to one another in a nested arrangement, with each branch holding a range of other ideas. In this sense it provides a hierarchical organisation of the ideas contained in your data.

One of my own uses of network analysis was in a piece of research where I was interested in the role of teaching assistants (TAs) in the classroom. How did TAs construct ideas about their role? I interviewed a range of TAs, transcribed our interviews and then went through the procedure in Figure 8.1. This enabled me to boil down the general commentary on *role* to two basic themes – about pedagogy (i.e. teaching) and about affective (i.e. emotional, personal) concerns. These were the basic ways in which TAs seemed to be thinking about how their place, their value, their contribution

1. Read all of your data: interview transcripts, diaries, notes from unstructured observations, etc.

2. Make an electronic copy of all of your raw data. Mark it 'RAW'. You now have two copies: your raw data and your working data files. Keep them separate and keep the 'RAW' one somewhere safe.

3. Now read through your *working* files. As you are reading, underline, mark, label or highlight parts that you think are important. (This is the process of *coding*.) As you proceed, you will get an impression of important ideas or subjects that are recurring. We can call these your *temporary constructs*. Make a list of these.

4. Read through the data again, using the list of temporary constructs from your first reading to check against. Draw up a grid with the temporary construct on the left, and page references to where the construct is evidenced on the right. Make notes and observations on the grid as you do this. You will get quite a long list – Table 8.1 shows an abbreviated example.

5. Eliminate any temporary constructs that do not seem to have been reinforced in the rest of the data. Don't delete that actual data itself, though – it may form an important counter-example against the general themes that are emerging. Highlight these counter-examples in a different colour on your working data records, and keep a separate list of them.

6. From the second reading, come up with *second-order constructs* that seem to be making a good 'fit' with your data. These second-order constructs should make a good job of summarising the important themes in your data.

7. Look through once more, refining these second-order constructs now as marker-posts for the organisation of your data. Once you are satisfied that these capture the essence of your data, label these as your *themes*.

8. Think about the themes. How do they seem to be connecting together? What matches with what? Are there any unanimous areas of agreement? Are there any contradictions or paradoxes?

9. Find ways of *mapping* your themes (see below under *network analysis* and *construct mapping*).

10. Select good quotations or sections from your work to illustrate the themes.

Figure 8.1 The constant comparative method

Table 8.1   Examples of notes and observations

Temporary construct	Page numbers and notes
Territory	Diary, pp 15, 17, 19. Interviewees: Sara pp 3, 4; Geoff pp 4, 6. Big issue for Geoff - got q. emotional
Threat	Diary, pp 1, 7, 9, 15. Interviewees: Sara pp 7, 9; Geoff pp 5, 6

their sense of self-worth were constructed. I was able to break down these two basic themes into sub-themes, as in the summary diagram in Figure 8.2.

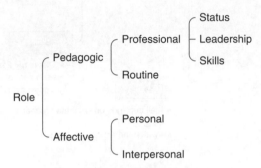

Figure 8.2   Summary network of themes and sub-themes

Having satisfied myself that this summative network of themes and sub-themes adequately summarised the data of the TA interviews, I went back to each of those interviews looking for examples of each of these themes and sub-themes in the interviewees' comments. For each interviewee, I was then able to come up with a network analysis of the interview. An example of one of these, together with my commentary, is given in Figure 8.3.

Construct mapping and theme mapping

While network analysis provides a hierarchical arrangement of ideas and themes, *construct mapping* puts those themes in sequential order from the interview and uses lines and arrows to make the connections between the ideas and themes. I have called it 'construct mapping' here out of respect for the person, Sue Jones, who developed the idea out of George Kelly's (1955/1991) personal construct theory. Jones (1985) devised a method for drawing on Kelly's notion of bi-polar constructs governing the way that we all see the world. In fact I found this theoretical lens too complex and adapted the construct mapping for my own purposes to a method I shall call **theme mapping**.

Theme mapping begins, as does most qualitative analysis, with the constant comparative method (see Figure 8.1). Once you have established your themes you go through your working data files and look for good quotations that illustrate those themes. Then, in the order that those quotations appeared in the interview, you can put them into boxes on the page. The page now becomes your 'map'. You may also find other quotations that in some way complement or contrast with these quotations. Put

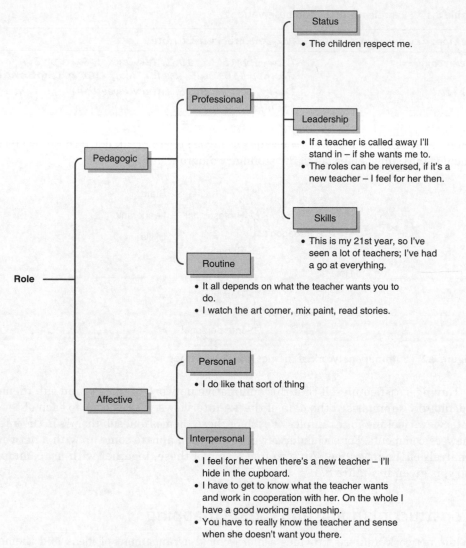

Status
- The children respect me.

Professional

Leadership
- If a teacher is called away I'll stand in – if she wants me to.
- The roles can be reversed, if it's a new teacher – I feel for her then.

Pedagogic

Skills
- This is my 21st year, so I've seen a lot of teachers; I've had a go at everything.

Routine
- It all depends on what the teacher wants you to do.
- I watch the art corner, mix paint, read stories.

Role

Personal
- I do like that sort of thing

Affective

Interpersonal
- I feel for her when there's a new teacher – I'll hide in the cupboard.
- I have to get to know what the teacher wants and work in cooperation with her. On the whole I have a good working relationship.
- You have to really know the teacher and sense when she doesn't want you there.

Commentary: An individual with the confidence to define her role for herself, given her long experience. A certain amount of conflict arises precisely because of this experience and the esteem in which she is held: professional constraints work to elevate her status, a process which she evidently has to try and minimise. Affective factors are important in helping to define the role, though she has to rely on 'sensing' that the teacher may not be at ease in her presence.

Figure 8.3 Network analysis

these in boxes on the 'map' too. Now label the boxes with the names of the themes and draw dotted lines if ideas seem to be connected between themes, and solid lines with arrows where one theme (the theme towards which the arrow points) seems in some way to account for or explain the theme at the other end of the arrow.

The example I give in Figure 8.4 is a theme map following the analysis of some interviews I conducted with support teachers for children with special educational needs. Rather than withdrawing children to work with on their own, these teachers had recently changed their way of work to be in the classroom, working alongside the class teacher. I was interested in their perceptions and feelings concerning their role in the classroom. Did they feel useful? Were there tensions, and if so, of what kind? How did the other teacher react to them? How did the children view them? And so on. From my interviews and from my own diary working as a support teacher I emerged with a number of themes relating to these questions. These were: status and self-esteem, territoriality, threat/suspicion, interpersonal factors, ideology/professional, communication, organisation, school policy and role clarity. You will see that seven of these nine themes are flagged in the interview theme map in Figure 8.4.

Aside from anything else, the theme map gives a kind of mini-representation of the interview, because the illustrative quotations are given in the order that they have appeared in the interview.

Tip: when drawing a diagram of this kind use the Text Box facility in Word. Go to the menu bar near the top of the page, click on 'Insert' and then click on 'Text Box'. (In Word 2007, now click on 'Draw Text Box'.) Then use the cross-cursor to draw a box in which you will be able to write text. Also, by clicking on the edge of the box you will be able to drag it around to where you want.

Grounded theory

Many people say that they are using a *grounded theory* approach when what they mean is that they are using the constant comparative method (see Figure 8.1). In fact, many of the assumptions behind grounded theory – for example, about grounded theory enabling prediction – seem inappropriate and outdated now, and I have explored this elsewhere (Thomas and James, 2006). Lincoln and Guba (1985: 339) make a similar criticism, suggesting that constant comparison is the kernel of grounded theory worth preserving. Indeed, the nuts and bolts of grounded theory procedures are unnecessarily complex and I advise you to avoid them. Stick to constant comparison.

What *is* nice about grounded theory is that it offers a neat encapsulation of the essence of interpretative inquiry – in that you let the ideas (the 'theory') emerge from your immersion in a situation rather than going in with fixed ideas (fixed 'theory') about what is happening. But the inventors of grounded theory (Glaser and Strauss, 1967) did not contrive this idea *de novo*: it has always been at the heart of interpretative inquiry. Some people speak about grounded theory as if it is synonymous with interpretative inquiry – or even as if all of interpretative inquiry depends on it. It isn't, and it doesn't.

Thick description

I noted *thick description* in Chapters 5 and 6 when talking about interpretivism, case study and unstructured observation. I include thick description here, in a discussion of how to analyse, because it is, in a sense, both a form of data gathering *and* a form of analysis. When you are doing the thick description you are also doing the analysis.

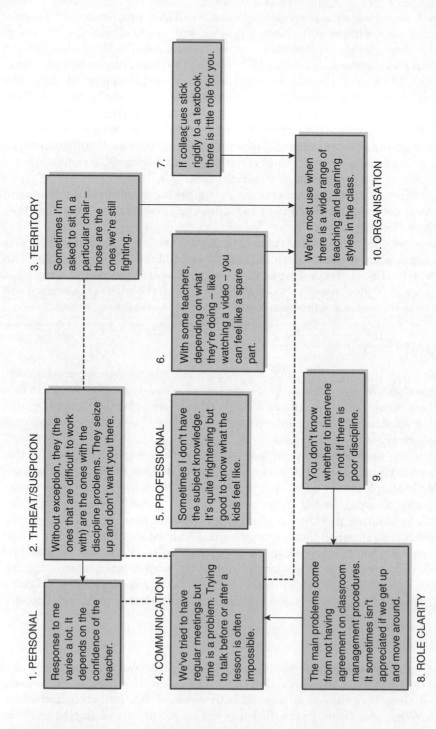

Figure 8.4 Theme map of an interview with a support teacher

The text inside the figure boxes reads:

3. TERRITORY

Sometimes I'm asked to sit in a particular chair – those are the ones we're still fighting.

7.

If colleagues stick rigidly to a textbook, there is little role for you.

10. ORGANISATION

We're most use when there is a wide range of teaching and learning styles in the class.

6.

With some teachers, depending on what they're doing – like watching a video – you can feel like a spare part.

2. THREAT/SUSPICION

Without exception, they (the ones that are difficult to work with) are the ones with the discipline problems. They seize up and don't want you there.

5. PROFESSIONAL

Sometimes I don't have the subject knowledge. It's quite frightening but good to know what the kids feel like.

9.

You don't know whether to intervene or not if there is poor discipline.

1. PERSONAL

Response to me varies a lot. It depends on the confidence of the teacher.

4. COMMUNICATION

We've tried to have regular meetings but time is a problem. Trying to talk before or after a lesson is often impossible.

8. ROLE CLARITY

The main problems come from not having agreement on classroom management procedures. It sometimes isn't appreciated if we get up and move around.

You are doing this by intelligently reflecting on the scene, imagining, putting yourself in another's shoes, 'seeing' what the other person is doing. You are doing this with the knowledge you have not only of people, but also of life and of the contexts that people inhabit – the stages on which they act. If you opt to do this kind of thick description, it helps to know something of the situation that you observe.

A good example of this making use of your ready-made knowledge – the knowledge of being human – is found in the great sociologist Erving Goffman's (1956) book *The Presentation of Self in Everyday Life*. In this, Goffman unpacks a storehouse of examples of how people behave in social life as if they were on a stage, always conveying some meaning with their behaviour. In doing this, he is employing thick description. He describes a man walking down the street who trips on a loose kerbstone. The man doing this, observes Goffman, will invariably turn round to look at the offending stone. He does this, Goffman says, not out of any profound interest in the kind of phenomena that trip people up, but in order to *convey* something to any onlooker who might have seen him trip and humiliate himself. He is saying, with the turn and the look, 'I am not the sort of fool who habitually trips over things – what kind of extraordinarily disguised danger could have led me to stumble?' In other words, the turn and the look have a meaning. It is these meanings that you have to look for in thick description.

I attempted thick description in my diary of my own time as a school governor. In the passage below, you can see how I was using my knowledge not just of social situations, but also of social behaviour and of professional contexts.

Noticing of the development of a club, with 'solidarity'.

The club is all-male.

Comment on Head's weakness.

Lastly we talk about the member of staff whom the Head has been having trouble with. He says that she is now taking it to her trade union. I report that the teacher governor had approached me in the car park; feel almost that I am betraying confidences, but I'm sure that it's not inappropriate to be saying this here. However, there is the warm, cosy feeling of the men's club again here in this sub-group: odd little comments reinforce the view that it's a difficult world – us against them and the feeling that if you support me I'll support you and we'll all have an easier life. I don't often think in gender-ist terms but there is a male–female difference here, I'm sure. The view that women are bickerers, complainers, petty is never explicitly articulated, but unless I'm being unusually over-sensitive today I think I sense the feeling that as men we ought to have solidarity in maintaining a level-headedness; in maintaining the momentum of the status quo; in preventing anyone from rocking the boat – and certainly not rocking it ourselves. But perhaps this is all delving a bit too deeply and imagining plots; if the reports of my children are anything to go by the teacher in question is 'absolutely horrible' and ought to find another career rather than simply having her duties taken away. The ambivalence of management in this case, manifested by bringing the issue to governors, is probably just weakness: cock-up rather than conspiracy.

Sadly, my own thick description contains none of the creativity of Goffman's. However, what I hope that I have been able to show here is the willingness to try to understand what is going on in a social situation; to try to use my knowledge of it, and *not* attempt to be some kind of neutral bystander.

Discourse and content analysis

Discourse analysis is the study of language in social use and, confusingly, is spoken about in different ways in different branches of the social sciences. Psychologists think of discourse as the language that goes on between people, tending to focus on small units of language such as the choice of individual words and intonations ('micro-analysis'). Sociologists, by contrast, tend to think of discourses as forms of language use that define social relations, and particularly power relations between and among people ('macro-analysis'). You'll understand from these very different starting points that there is no one method to discourse analysis. The term *content analysis* is sometimes used when the analysis refers to written text rather than the spoken word.

Fairclough (1995) describes what he calls a 'critical discourse analysis' which is useful for us in the applied social sciences because it combines both psychological and sociological traditions. His outline of it is shown in Figure 8.5. Fairclough puts it this way:

> a piece of discourse is embedded within sociocultural practice at a number of levels; in the immediate situation, in the wider institution or organization, and at a societal level; for example, one can read an interaction between marital partners in terms of their particular relationship, relationships between partners within the family as an institution, or gender relationships in the larger society. The method of discourse analysis includes linguistic *description* of the language text, *interpretation* of the relationship between the (productive and interpretative) discursive processes and the text, and *explanation* of the relationship between the discursive processes and the social processes. (Fairclough, 1995: 97)

For simplicity's sake, take it that the general method in 'gutting' an interview or some other sample of language use is broadly the same as in the constant comparative method (see Figure 8.1). The difference is in the focus of the discourse analyst. Rather than being at the first level on ideas, it is on the use of particular words, phrases, idioms, similes, metaphors, kinds of rhetoric, and so on. How are these used to construct notions such as 'education', 'health', 'order', etc.? In each case the discourse analyst will look to see how notions are constructed by the choice of words and language forms used in a discourse, whether that be an interview transcript or a document.

So, the difference of emphasis that the discourse or content analyst will put on the process outlined in Figure 8.1 is on the particular words and phrases used.

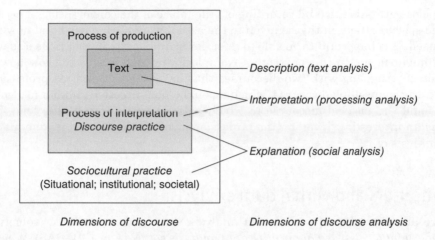

Figure 8.5   Fairclough's 'critical discourse analysis'

Discourse analysis thus stresses the *coding* aspect of the analysis of an interview or a text, paying more attention to the choice and use of words and phrases. Given that the actual words and how they are used play more of a part than they do in an ethnographic use of constant comparison, it is more important that you are aware of your protocols for recording. A good example is given by Fairclough of a transcript of a conversation between a doctor and patient:

```
 1  Patient: but she really has been very unfair to me. got ⌐no
    Doctor:                                               ⌊hm
    Patient: respect for me at ⌐all and I think . that's one of the
    Doctor:                    ⌊hm
 5  Patient: reasons why I drank so  ⌐much  you  ⌐know  ⌐—
    Doctor:                          ⌊hm         ⌊hm   ⌊hm
    Patient: and  ⌐em
    Doctor:      ⌊hm   are you you back are you back on it have you started
    drinking  ⌐again
10  Patient:  ⌊ no
```

                                                        (Fairclough, 1995: 98)

You'll notice a number of features of this transcript:

- The lines are numbered (every five lines) for ease of reference when referring back to the text in a subsequent analytic discussion

- There are devices used to indicate a gap or pause or discontinuity in the conversation. In this case a single dot ('.') is used. For longer pauses a dash is used.

- Brackets [are used to indicate 'overlaps' between one person and another in the conversation.

This close attention to (and recording of) the fabric of the conversation is because of the special attention that is given to the actual words being used and how they are used. It is important to be able to refer, for example, to interruptions and what they might mean. In this particular example Fairclough is able to show how the doctor is struggling with two discourses that he sees governing his professional work: the counselling discourse, which has to be non-directive ('hmmmm', 'go on', etc.), and the medical discourse in which he is expected to take the lead. This forms an interesting 'lever' on the professional role of the GP for anyone making an analysis of it.

Computers and verbal data analysis

There are a number of verbal data analysis programmes available (sometimes called *computer-assisted qualitative data analysis software*, or CAQDAS). Whether or not you use these depends on the amount of data that you have to process. Nothing, of course, substitutes for your intelligent reading of your data, and this to my mind is the main danger of software in qualitative data analysis: it leads you to the false belief that something else is going to do the hard work for you. My one trial of CAQDAS left me disappointed and I have never used it again. It left me believing that there's no substitute for a good set of highlighters from W.H. Smith, a pen and paper, and a brain. You can also use Word for a large number of operations, such as word count (clicking on the status bar opens the Word Count dialogue box), or the readability statistics that are provided as part of the spelling and grammar facility (press the F7 button and go to the bottom of the dialogue box, press Options, then tick the box offering readability statistics). You can also use the Find facility (Ctrl+F) to find strings of text or important words that you have identified.

Although I have not been very positive about CAQDAS, it may work for you, particularly if you have a very large amount of data to analyse. Well-known packages are *NVivo* and *Atlas.ti*, and your choice should depend largely on the one favoured by your institution – you should then be able to draw on the institutional licence, and be able to find someone who can give you support in the software's use. (You'll notice that both *NVivo* and *Atlas.ti* have silly idiosyncrasies added to their brand titles to try to make them look more technical. This is one of my main bugbears about research method and design – that people try to make it look more technical and complex than it really is. It happens both here and in statistical analysis and you should be doubly sceptical about any brand name or statistical test name that is (a) unpronounceable, or (b) makes no sense.)

Sociograms

A *sociogram* is a useful way of *mapping relationships* among children (or, less often, adults). It involves asking them who they would like to sit next to, who they would like to work with – or the opposite: who they would *not* like to sit next to, and so on. The posh name for this is *sociometry*.

For the standard sociogram you will give each child a piece of paper on which they write their own name and the two names of their choices. You then map these to the sociogram, eventually producing a chart like that in Figure 8.6. For each choice you draw an arrow indicating the direction of choice. So, for example, Stacy on the far left chose Hannah and Lara. If a choice is returned, or *reciprocated*, the arrow becomes double-headed.

Features that may emerge from the sociogram are:

- *isolates*, with no choices from other individuals;
- *reciprocated choices*, where individuals choose each other;
- *one-way choices*, where one person chooses another but this choice is not reciprocated;
- *cliques*, tight-knit groups of three or more whose choices are all made within the group (e.g. Kylie, Alison and Ellie);
- *clusters*, which are more general groupings (e.g. the fairly significant one around Robbie, Simon and Ben);
- *stars*, who have a large number of choices (e.g. Ella and Ben);
- *power-brokers*, who have choices from the stars but not necessarily many others.

The sociogram given in Figure 9.6 is taken from research I undertook for Barnardo's on the inclusion of children with physical difficulties in mainstream schools. The children in one primary school class were asked to say in confidence who they would like to sit next to or play with. The 'included' student is Luke. In each of the classes I studied it was interesting that in general an unremarkable pattern of relationships emerged for the 'included' students. Even where the students had severe disabilities they emerged as well integrated socially into their classes. For several of the 'included' children reciprocated choices are made. Interestingly, Luke is the only child crossing the gender barrier.

There is a basic freeware program for drawing sociograms available at www. phenotyping.com/sociogram/. This lets you enter your names and then draw lines between them. Although you cannot draw the arrows to show direction of relationship, these could be added afterwards by hand. Although a bit clunky (and you may find a better one by using your favourite search engine), what the program does offer is the chance to move people about so that you can show clusters more easily without having lots of crossing lines. You could then, once you have the clusters clear in your mind, transfer to freehand drawing or drawing in Word (using text boxes).

Sociometry involves some significant ethical issues. You should think hard about how you phrase questions and how you present the material to those participating

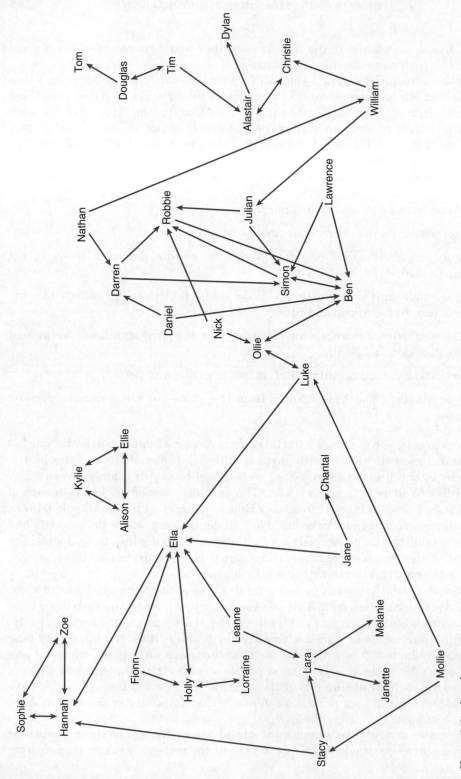

Figure 8.6 A sociogram

in your project. You must assure your research participants absolute confidentiality and anonymity and take great care not to allow participants to see others' papers. Pseudonyms must of course be used in any write-up.

Analysing numbers

I'm fully aware that some people who study in the social sciences don't like numbers. After all, you came into the area – teaching, psychology, social work, nursing, medicine, dentistry, probation, or whatever – because you want to work with people. You find people interesting, and numbers somehow don't fit into the people scenario.

You should, though, bear a few things in mind. First, statistics are not as hard as you might think. Second, they actually can be quite useful. Third, if you really can't get to grips with them it's not the end of the world, because it is research you are interested in, not statistics *per se*, and research is about finding out. There are many ways of finding out, and the more complex statistical ways get too good a press in the finding-out stakes: they're not the only way or even the main way; they are just analytical tools. Fourth, if you really can't understand statistics (and you will understand most of the basic methods) don't blame yourself. Blame the statisticians for not explaining them properly.

It's rather like the phenomenon of going into a builder's merchant and the men (it's usually men) behind the counter pretending slightly impatient bewilderment that you don't have any idea that what you need is called a bayonet grit-edged flange. It's the same with most statisticians: they seem almost to delight in the complexity of the names of statistical tests, which are named after letters of the Greek alphabet like 'chi' (Why? Don't ask me), or Russian statisticians like Kolmogorov and Smirnov. If the chi-square test were to have its name changed to the Cuddly Test and the Kolmogorov–Smirnov test were to have its name changed to the Fluffy Test, I'm convinced that fewer people would be put off statistics in the social sciences. And statisticians seem to feel that it is a crime only one notch down from first-degree homicide to simplify their explanations: you are seldom likely to hear a statistician saying 'I'm oversimplifying, but think of it this way ...'. They mix a fascination with the mathematical and logical beauty of the statistic and the expectations that surround its construction with a kind of self-conscious awareness that if it is used wrongly it will be meaningless. Such self-conscious awareness is, in one way, commendable, but it means that whenever they explain something the explanation has so thoroughly to explain every detail of construction and use that it becomes meaningless to anyone without a degree in statistics. What they don't accept in this honest explanation is that these statistics are only crude tools anyway: being exact about the details won't alter this.

Anyway, I digress, partly to try to put you at your ease, but this is perhaps better done by suggesting that you get a glass of wine and sit down in your best armchair and let the words flow over you in this bit of the book. If some of them float slowly enough to stick, then so much the better. You may even be tempted to use numbers.

Even if you are stats phobic, do try to have a look here because even if you don't feel confident enough to use them yourself a basic understanding will help you to interpret published research more intelligently.

Kinds of numbers

Let's start with the numbers that are used in statistics. You thought you knew, roughly speaking, what numbers are, didn't you? 1 is 1 thing, 2 is one more thing than 1 thing, and 3 is ... er ... one more than two things. I don't want to disillusion you about this: most of the time you're fine working on this assumption. But you know the story about physics students when they reach university having to forget all they knew about physics and starting again? It's a bit like that in the social sciences when it comes to numbers. The good news is that the alternative is really easy – and you understand it already (honestly). It's just a question of putting what you already know into the language used by social scientists. Just think of it this way:

- There are categories of things, e.g. the categories of gender (female and male), kinds of disability, types of schools, etc. For ease of working things out in research, these categories may be given numbers (e.g. female, 1; male, 2); these numbers, because they are really just shorthand for names, are called **nominal** or **categorical**.

- Things can be put in order, e.g. top, middle, bottom; 1st, 2nd, 3rd, etc. These orderings can be given numbers: top (1), middle (2), bottom (3); 1st (1), 2nd (2), 3rd (3), 4th (4), etc. Because they are in order, these are called **ordinal** data. Although there is an order indicated here, there is no value implied beyond this. Certainly, one value is larger or faster or better than the next. If your respondent is ranking their fondness for school on a 5-point scale (1 hate; 2 dislike; 3 neutral; 4 like; 5 adore) you know only that 5 is better than 4, or 2 is better than 1; but you do not know by how much.

- There are the 'everyday' numbers that you and I usually think of when we talk about numbers – here we are talking about **interval** data, because the intervals between the numbers are always the same (unlike nominal and ordinal data). So the number of children in a class or the amount earned in pocket money in a week are interval data.

You can probably see why it is not good to mix these kinds of numbers. For example, you can't multiply nominal data. And the distance between ordered numbers is not always the same, so these can't be treated the same as other numbers. It's just a question of putting what you already know into the slots used by statisticians.

A good website which explains all of this in more detail is www.stats.gla.ac.uk/steps/glossary/presenting_data.html.

Now that we have got types of numbers clear (have we? – don't worry if you haven't; you'll still be able to manage), in statistically analysing the data you have gathered there are three principal branches of statistics that will help you deal with most of the methods that I have discussed in this book:

- one branch is about *statistics that describe* – this is the very easy one;

- the next is about statistics that help you understand a relationship – this is also easy;

- the last is about *statistics that enable you to deduce (or infer)* something about a large group from a small one – this is slightly harder (but still understandable).

But before going into these, I have to tell you about eyeballing and about Excel.

Eyeballing

The first rule of analysing by numbers is *eyeballing*.

Eyeballing is having a look at a range of numbers to see what the look tells you. Though it doesn't appear in the statistics textbooks, it is perhaps the most valuable statistical technique, since it forces you to think intelligently about what the numbers are saying, and it discourages you

> Numbers can help you to describe, to understand a relationship or to understand what may be causing what. But much depends on how the numbers are collected and analysed.

from making silly statements about a set of numbers based on a wrongly used statistic. Does a series of numbers seem to be going up or down or staying the same? Does it seem to be fluctuating wildly or is it quite stable? Are there any 'outliers' (data points that don't agree with the others) – are they interesting (in a good or bad way)? Does one set of numbers seem to vary with another set? Your most valuable tool is your eye – not the Kolmogorov–Smirnov test. Use it.

Using Excel to do your data analysis

Beyond eyeballing, you will want to do some actual calculations, and I have limited most of the workings involved in the statistics that follow to Microsoft Excel, since this spreadsheet is bundled with nearly all home computers and you should have easy access to it. Where more sophisticated statistics-handling software is needed I'll say so.

In the analysis of numbers that follows I am assuming a very basic working knowledge of Excel. Having said that, here are a few basic facts that I find students sometimes do not know about Excel:

1 Data entry: data are put in individual *cells* (27 and 15 in my example here).

2 The cells have *references* (e.g. A2, D22).

3 Formulae (i.e. 'sums') are also put in cells, and the formula always must begin with an equals sign. The formula relates to the data references of the cells.

4 When you have finished the data entry and the formula, click on the *tick*. When I clicked on the tick in this example, the answer (42) appeared in the cell.

If you are a complete novice with spreadsheets, hopefully this will get you started. Play around with Excel: it's quite rewarding.

On older versions of Excel, you will find it useful to install the Excel Data Analysis ToolPak, which is not installed with the standard Excel setup. (This is not absolutely necessary for all of the examples below, but it's a helpful tool, and worth looking at.) To find the ToolPak, look in the Tools menu. If you do not have a *Data Analysis* item (usually at the bottom of the list), you will need to install the Data Analysis tools. Here are the instructions from Excel on how to do this:

1 On the *Tools* menu, click on *Add-Ins*.

2 In the *Add-Ins available* list, select the *Analysis ToolPak* box, and then click on 'OK'.

Statistics that describe

Descriptive statistics are about the simplification, organisation, summary and graphical plotting of numerical data. They are easy. I know I've already said that, but they are. They are about questions such as 'How many?' and 'How often?' and will be presented in figures such as pie charts and bar charts. There are also simple statistics such as percentages and averages (technically called 'derived statistics', because they are derived from the descriptive ones). Many dissertations are marked down because the authors make surprisingly little attempt to use these to show the figures in a way which will be immediately meaningful to the reader. If you have a list of numbers, do try to make them meaningful to the reader by using statistics. I'll give some examples and show how you can translate them to a more meaningful form with Excel. *Tip*: don't bury your tables and/or the statistical analysis of them in an appendix. Too many students do this; I have no idea why.

Let's take some numbers – a *frequency distribution* – from a government statistics website (DCSF, 2007). Table 8.2 shows numbers of schools in England and

Table 8.2   Numbers of schools in England and Wales

	1990/91	1995/96	2000/01	2005/06
Nursery	1,364	1,486	3,228	3,349
Primary	24,135	23,441	22,902	22,156
Secondary	4,790	4,463	4,337	4,206

Wales going back over a series of years.

You should be able to copy these numbers directly into your Excel spreadsheet from the PDF (see p. 227 on how to do this). Once they are there and you have edited the figures for the ones you want (let's say as in Table 8.2), paste these figures to a new sheet (see Figure 8.7). Now here's how to turn the table into a bar graph:

1 Select the *area* of the figures (including header rows and columns) by dragging your mouse over it.

2 Click on the *chart tool* icon. (In Excel 2007, click on 'Insert', then on the little coloured icon for 'Column'.)

3 In older versions of Excel, when the dialogue box appears, just click 'Finish' for the chart to be pasted into your worksheet, or, if you want a custom-made chart, where you have been offered the option of presenting the data as, for example, a pie chart, then press 'Next' instead of 'Finish'.

4 When the chart has appeared click on it, press Ctrl+C (copy) and then paste it (Ctrl+V) into your Word document.

Once you have done this, it is up to you to interpret the chart. Why have numbers of secondary and primary schools decreased, for example, while numbers of nursery schools have increased? It is up to you to offer an explanation to the reader.

Let's take another example from the same government statistics website (DCSF, 2007). Table 8.3 is about annual expenditure per student in a range of OECD countries.

Now, using these statistics, you can easily sort them for a very useful analysis. The one I am going to describe can even be done in Word, without recourse to Excel.

Table 8.3 Annual expenditure on education per student, 2004

	Early childhood education	Primary education	Secondary education
Australia	–	5,776	8,160
Belgium	4,915	6,636	7,751
Denmark	5,323	8,081	8,849
Finland	4,282	5,581	7,441
France	4,938	5,082	8,737
Germany	5,489	4,948	7,576
Greece	–	4,595	5,213
Ireland	4,948	5,422	7,110
Italy	5,971	7,390	7,843
Japan	3,945	6,551	7,615
Luxembourg	–	13,458	17,876
Mexico	1,794	1,694	1,922
Netherlands	5,807	6,222	7,541
New Zealand	5,112	5,190	6,299
Norway	4,327	8,533	11,109
Poland	4,045	3,130	2,889
Portugal	4,461	4,681	6,168
Spain	4,617	4,965	6,701
Sweden	4,417	7,469	8,039
Switzerland	3,581	8,570	12,176
Turkey	–	1,120	1,808
UK	7,924	5,941	7,090
USA	7,896	8,805	9,938
OECD average	4,741	5,832	7,276

Source: DCSF (2007).

I notice, from eyeballing, that the UK's expenditure on 'early childhood education' appears high. So I can sort this table to put the countries in order by early childhood spending. I put the cursor anywhere in the table, click on 'Table' for 'Layout' in Word 7) then click on 'Sort' for the relevant variable. The table you will get is shown in Table 8.4.

I find Table 8.4 interesting: the UK is top in early childhood spending! Hooray! It is interesting particularly when you also look at the amount spent on each secondary pupil, which appears – on eyeballing – almost as if it might tend to go down as the expenditure on early childhood goes up. If you make a finding of this kind it is worth exploring further. You might, for example, want to do a bar chart (using the method described in Figure 8.7) of these figures to pursue any such relationship. It's easier to see such a relationship in a graph rather than a table. To take it even

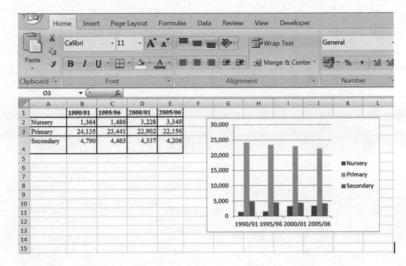

Click on 'Insert' then on the 'Column' icon

Figure 8.7   Turning a table into a bar chart

further you might look to see whether they statistically relate with one another (co-relate, or correlate). I describe how to do this in the next subsection.

Excel offers a good range of descriptive statistics in a variety of charts, which (in Excel 2007) you can access by clicking on 'Insert' on the top menu bar. Then, in the 'Charts' section, you'll see the options of 'Column', 'Line', 'Pie' and 'Bar'. Think about what you want the chart to do for you: Table 8.5 offers some pointers about what each is good for.

You may want to show a *measure of central tendency* – an *average* to you and me. Averages are split into three kinds: the *mean*, the *median* and the *mode*. These different kinds of average are useful for different circumstances. The mean is the 'average' that most of us are familiar with: it's the total amount of the characteristic you are studying (e.g. children's scores on a test) divided by the total number of observations (e.g. the number of children). But sometimes a mean isn't the best way of showing the 'centre'. By eyeballing the figures you may see that the typical value is such-and-such but that this would be misleading if a mean were used. Let's take the example of ten children's scores on a test and assume that they have scored as follows:

$$0, 9 ,9, 9, 9, 9, 9, 9, 9, 9$$

Here, the *typical* value is clearly 9, though one person – who may have been asleep during the test – is going to distort the figures and bring the mean down to 8.1. So, the mean is a bit misleading as a *typical* value. Here, the *median* will be useful because it is the 'middle' figure. If the scores are arranged in order (lowest on the left, highest on the right), the median is the score which falls slap-bang in the middle. In this case, the median is therefore 9.

Table 8.4 The data of Table 8.3, sorted by expenditure on early childhood education

	Early childhood education	Primary education	Secondary education
UK	7,924	5,941	7,090
USA	7,896	8,805	9,938
Italy	5,971	7,390	7,843
Netherlands	5,807	8,222	7,541
Germany	5,489	4,948	7,576
Denmark	5,323	8,081	8,849
New Zealand	5,112	5,190	6,299
Ireland	4,948	5,422	7,110
France	4,938	5,082	8,737
Belgium	4,915	6,636	7,751
OECD average	4,741	5,832	7,276
Spain	4,617	4,965	6,701
Portugal	4,461	4,681	6,168
Sweden	4,417	7,469	8,039
Norway	4,327	8,533	11,109
Finland	4,282	5,581	7,441
Poland	4,045	3,130	2,889
Japan	3,945	6,551	7,615
Switzerland	3,581	8,570	12,176
Mexico	1,794	1,694	1,922
Turkey	–	1,120	1,808
Luxembourg	–	13,458	17,876
Greece	–	4,595	5,213
Australia	–	5,776	8,160

The other measure of the average is the mode. This is the most frequently occurring value. So, in a list that goes 1, 2, 3, 3, 7, 9, the mode is 3.

It is easy to find the measure of central tendency using Excel. Suppose, for example, you have a range of test scores which is: 1, 2, 3, 3, 3, 5, 6, 7, 8. Enter these numbers into separate cells on a worksheet.

Table 8.5 Types of charts and their uses

Chart	
Column charts	Good for • Comparing values • Ranking top to bottom
Bar charts	Good for • Comparing values • Ranking top to bottom Remember: Excel presents the bar chart 'on its side', which may make this a better format than the column chart if there are long labels to read.
Line charts	Good for • Comparing values over time Remember: sometimes it is not correct to draw a line, i.e. there is not always a link between one value and the next.
Pie charts	Good for • Comparing each value with the total value But do think about what you are using it for. For example, it's not worth showing just two values (like 60% female; 40% male) in a pie chart: it's just as easy to read the numbers.)
Scatter charts	Good for • Comparing pairs of values For a class of school children, for example, you may be collecting data on two variables – such as actual age and reading age.

In a nearby cell type
=mode(a3:a11)

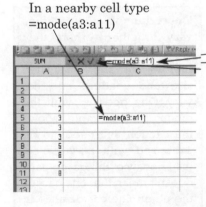

You'll notice the formula appears in the formula bar as you type. Then click on the tick box, and the answer, namely 3, will appear in the place of the formula.

If you want the mean, type
=average(a3:a11)

If you want the median, type
=median(a3:a11)

You might be interested in showing how much *variation* there is in a range of numbers. For instance, our test wouldn't be much use if it produced a range of scores which looked like this: 5, 5, 5, 5, 5, 5, 5, 5, 5, 5 in ten children. (If the score were out of 10, it would probably mean that five of the questions were absurdly easy, and five absurdly hard.) Here the variation between the values is zero. To measure how much variation exists, a statistic called *standard deviation* (SD) is used. Put simply, standard deviation is the average amount by which each score differs from the mean.

To calculate standard deviation in Excel, using our data from the previous example, type **=stdev(a3:a11)** and follow the same procedure. The answer in this case is 2.39.

Statistics that help you understand a relationship between two variables

You may want to look at *two* features of a situation and see whether the two are interrelated: you may be looking at children's scores on test A and test B in order to see if there is any relationship between the two sets of scores.

For example, when I was an educational psychologist visiting a young offenders institution I was required to test the young men's reading. It struck me that their reading was generally very poor, but their self-esteem was also poor, along with their verbal reasoning and other aspects of their make-up. I could have looked (I didn't actually do it, so these are imaginings) at the relationship between reading and self-esteem (the latter as measured by the Rosenberg Self-Esteem Scale, as described on p. 213). To look at the relationship and present the findings in a readily digestible form I could have used a *scatter graph*, where reading age (in months) is presented along one axis and self-esteem along the other axis.

I show my imaginary data and its translation to a scatter graph in Figure 8.8. The self-esteem scores are in column A and the reading ages (in months) in column B.

To get this scatter graph, do the following:

1 Enter your data – in my example in columns A and B.

2 Select the data by dragging your mouse over it, from top left to bottom right.

3 Click on the Chart Tool in earlier versions of Excel. In post-2007 versions, click on 'Insert', then 'Scatter' (under the 'Charts' tab).

4 In earlier versions of Excel, at the first dialogue box, scroll down to XY (Scatter), then keep clicking 'Next' until you reach finish. At each point, you will have the opportunity to customise your graph.

> **Co-variance:** How things vary together – how they co-vary. So in a silly example, we can show that shoe size and reading age co-vary. One goes up with the other. The example shows the caution that needs to be exercised with co-variance: just because things co-vary doesn't mean that one causes the other. The co-variance in this case is of course due to a third variable: maturity, or age. As age goes up so does reading age (in general), and so does shoe size.

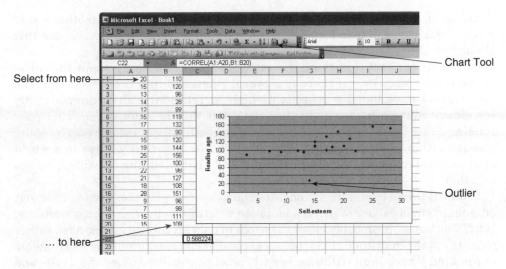

Figure 8.8   The relationship of reading and self-esteem: correlation and a scatter graph

You will see from the scatter graph that the results on self-esteem and reading tend to 'go with' one another. In other words, if self-esteem is lower for one young man, reading also tends to be lower (and vice versa). The important words here are 'tends to'. It isn't a hard-and-fast relationship, as you can see especially from one *outlier*, who has very low reading but reasonable self-esteem. The way we describe the extent of the connection between one variable and another is with the *correlation coefficient*. Correlation tells us the *strength* of the relationship between one variable and another.

When you ask Excel to work out the correlation figure for you, the result will be a number between −1 and +1. The nearer to +1 the result is (e.g. 0.8), the closer is the relationship between the two sets of scores. If the score is 0, there is no relationship; if the score is near −1 (e.g. −0.7), the relationship is inverse, that is, if the score on one variable is high, the score on the other will probably be low.

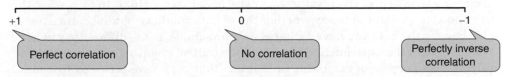

To get the correlation coefficient for the scores in the example, type in a spare cell:

=correl(a1:a20,b1:b20)

Once you have worked out a correlation, it is possible to do two things: first you can work out the level of significance of the correlation (significance is explained in the next subsection); second, you can predict one score from another using a technique called linear regression (see the 'further reading' section for this chapter).

Of course, the fact that there is a relationship says nothing about the cause of the relationship or – if there *is* a causal relationship – the direction of the causation. I have found a reasonably high correlation in the example of my imaginary young offender institution data, but this does not tell me that poor reading *causes* poor self-esteem, or that poor self-esteem *causes* poor reading (though either is a possibility). More likely is the fact that we live in a world of closely interrelated social phenomena and that *all* things of this kind 'go together'.

I found it to be a depressingly consistent phenomenon with these young men that on almost any measure of social adaptation or attainment their scores were low. Why? The 'cause' is probably closer to factors to do with culture and poverty rather than any of the multitude of psychological phenomena measurable by instruments of the kind I have been outlining here. It has been realised since the 1920s and Gordon's (1923) studies of canal boat children in the UK or Wheeler's (1970) similar studies of, and findings about, 'mountain children' in the US that it was (and is) the cultural milieu rather than any psychological characteristic that determines a child's success at school.

It has, in other words, been known for yonks (a technical term) that this is the case. Sadly, it is often the ideas and research methods of social science that propagate the belief that it is ability (and disability) of some kind – not poverty, difference or life experience – that is the principal force at play in determining such success or failure. The lesson? Measurement is useful in many kinds of social research, but when we look for relationships between variables we have to be very wary about imputing reasons for any relationships we discover.

Statistics that help you to deduce (or infer)

These statistics, also known as *inferential statistics*, form a large branch of analytical statistics in the social sciences. They are used particularly where we are trying to interpret the results of an experiment (see p. 163). In fact, what the tests do is to enable you to say whether the results you have obtained are extendable beyond the data you have gathered in your sample: is the difference you have noted between the experimental group and the control group one on which you can rely for this purpose of extension, or is it one that may have occurred by chance in your study?

Most of these statistics tell you something actually quite basic: whether the difference that you find between this set of numbers and that set of numbers is just down to chance or – if you have designed the study well – due to some feature of the situation in which you are interested. You will produce a figure after having completed your statistical test which will tell you the level of chance stated as a one-in-something (say, one in 20, or one in 100). This is where there is often confusion, with many people believing that once the issue of chance has been dealt with in the interpretation of a study's findings, everything else is OK.

It's not: the study must have been designed properly, and this involves thinking about a whole range of design considerations from sampling to wording to control, which I mentioned in Chapter 6. Only when we are sure that these design dimensions have been addressed appropriately can we go ahead and get fussed about whether the findings could have occurred by chance. I mention this only because some beginning (and some experienced) researchers treat the statistical test, well chosen and calculated, as if it is the most important guarantor of a study's worth. It most definitely is not, partly because of *the GIGO principle* – garbage in, garbage out.

The GIGO principle is an important one to remember in any use of statistics, and particularly in inferential statistics which are used in more complex studies where there is more chance of design error. But assuming that everything has been set up properly (a big assumption), the statistic *is* a necessary part of a study which examines the relationships between and among variables, whether or not these involve assertions about cause. I shall run through a few examples of how these tests are used in a moment, but before that will have to look briefly at the importance of *statistical significance*.

Statistical significance is expressed in terms of probability. What is probability? Probability is a numerical description of the likely occurrence of a particular event and it is expressed on a scale from 0 to 1. So something that happens only very rarely would have a probability close to 0, while a very common event has a probability close to 1. So $p = 0$ means it would never happen, while $p = 1$ means it would always happen. The probability of drawing a club from a full pack of cards is worked out by dividing the number of possible outcomes of this event (i.e. 13, because there are 13 clubs in the pack) by the total number of outcomes (i.e. 52, because there are 52 cards in the pack). So, do the math: the probability is expressed as $p = 0.25$. (A fuller explanation of all this is given at www.stats.gla.ac.uk/steps/glossary/probability. html#probability.)

The statistical tests we are talking about here tell us the probability that a finding would have been made by chance. Let's take a simple example: suppose you gave a maths test to 15 boys and 15 girls and you have the children's results in front of you, with a difference between them. The statistical test will then tell you how likely it is that you would find the same (or greater or lesser) difference by chance. The result is expressed in a 'probability figure', such as 'p is less than 0.05'. This means:

the probability is less than 5 in 100 that this result would have been found by chance

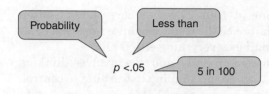

which in the language of statisticians becomes:

$$p < 0.05$$

Another way of putting it is that there is less than a 5 per cent (i.e. 1 in 20) chance that this result would be obtained by chance. Yet another way of saying it is that if you repeated the experiment again and again, only one time in 20 (i.e. 5 times in 100) would you achieve by chance a result like the one you obtained. The probability figure can be made more difficult to 'hit' by changing it to 0.01 (i.e. 1 in 100), or easier, by changing it to 0.1 (i.e. 1 in 10 that it would have been found by chance).

That's all that *significance testing* is about: these figures relating to chance. Important though it is to the interpretation of findings from certain kinds of research design, it's certainly not worth getting in a tizzy about not understanding how to calculate it. However, as is the case in much research study, it is useful to *understand* how published research uses statistics such as these and what they mean, even if you don't intend to undertake a study in which you would wish to calculate them.

I shall examine two of the most frequently used statistics of this kind here: *chi-square* (pronounced kye-square, and sometimes written as χ^2) and the *t test*. I have chosen these as examples, since they have a range of uses in the kind of research in which we are interested. It is worth noting, though, that Excel is a spreadsheet rather than a statistical package, and it is rather clumsy at calculating chi-square. If you want to do a lot of chi-squares it is probably worth investing in a student version of the well-known statistical package *SPSS* (Statistical Package for the Social Sciences). I'll come to SPSS in a moment, after a word or two about chi-square and how to calculate it manually.

Chi-square

Chi-square is used to determine the likelihood that a distribution of *frequencies* would have been found by chance. Supposing we had asked a group of 99 newly recruited police officers about their attitude to stop-and-search procedures, with the options and findings shown in Table 8.6. Chi-square will tell you the likelihood that this range of findings would have been obtained by chance.

Table 8.6   Policemen's attitudes to stop-and-search procedures

Category of attitude	Police officers
1. Keep the law on stop and search as it is	58
2. Make the law easier for us to stop and search	32
3. Make the law more difficult for police to stop and search	9

I have worked out 'by hand' that with a chi-square statistic of 36.42, this is significant at the 0.01 level. Here's how I worked it out in Excel. First, the formula:

$$\text{chi-square} = \sum \frac{(O - E)^2}{E}$$

I laid out my actual data (or 'observed frequency', O) in column A. Then I worked out the 'expected frequency' (E) in column B. (This 'expected frequency' is the number of responses that 'should' be in each category, all things being equal, so in my example of 99 possible responses shared between three categories, it should be 33 in each.) Then I subtracted each column B figure from each column A figure and put the result in column C. I squared the column C figure and put it in D. For column E, I divided the column D figure by the column B figure. Then I *added* all the column E figures *together* (this is what $\sum$ means) to give 36.42, which is the chi-square value. As Brucie says: 'That's all there is to it!' Figure 8.9 shows what it looks like in Excel.

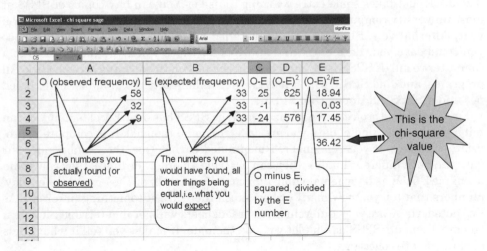

Figure 8.9   Calculation of chi-square

What does the 36.42 mean? Good question. To interpret it, you have to look it up in the appropriate table (see the Appendix on page 296) together with the degrees of freedom for the data. The latter is simply the number of rows minus one. So, in the example, there are three rows, thus the degrees of freedom (df) is 2. Have a look in the table along the row for df 2. If your chi-square value is greater than any of the figures for the row (4.61, 5.99 and 9.21 in this case), then you can say that it is significant at that level. In fact it is greater than the largest of these (9.21), so it is significant at the 0.01 level. In other words there is less than a 1 in 100 chance that this finding would have been made by chance.

Is this worth knowing? Well, if I'm honest, I have to say that any argument I might choose to put on the basis of these data is hardly very much stronger with the significance figure added, though with a more complex range of data it may have been useful to calculate the statistic. In my opinion, the value of this kind of significance figure is more important in fields of study outside the social sciences (such as medicine), particularly where it is possible to control trials more precisely, though there are of course circumstances where it may be useful to us in applied social science. Again, it is the way in which the study is set up that is more important than this significance figure. You must always keep design issues in mind – the words that are used in the question, the people who are chosen, and so on – both when constructing your study and interpreting its findings.

SPSS, crosstabs and chi-square

It is clumsy to work out chi-square on Excel (which is why I have shown how to do it manually above). However, it is quite easy to compute it using SPSS. This program does everything (and more) that a student or professional researcher would wish it to do. It just takes some extra learning to use it. You can buy copies of SPSS at most university computer centres, or download a rental version for 6 months or a year. Alternatively, SPSS is usually installed on pooled university machines, so you could save your data entry and analysis for times when you have access to a computer room. (If SPSS isn't immediately obvious on the opening screen, click 'All programs' and find SPSS, which may, rather unhelpfully, be alphabetically listed not under SPSS but under *IBM* SPSS.)

For small-scale projects, the main advantage SPSS has over Excel is that you can tell it easily what kind of data you are collecting, and then ask it to compute appropriate statistics. If you remember, I mentioned earlier that the numbers of your data can be of different kinds – they can describe an order (ordinal), they can stand for names, such as 0 for female and 1 for male (nominal), or they can be 'everyday' numbers that tell you how many or how much there are of something (interval). As I've noted, these are very different and spreadsheets will get in a terrible muddle if you mix them up. SPSS doesn't let you mix them up. It makes you tell it what kinds of data you are collecting.

Let's take an example. Suppose you are interested in the healthy (or not) lifestyles of students and you wonder whether there is a difference between male and female students in their tendency to adopt a healthy lifestyle. Your data collection depends, in part, on questionnaires given to 20 male and female students in which you ask them, amongst other things, 'Yesterday, did you eat five portions of fruit and vegetables?'

First, you'll have to prepare your data collection sheets on SPSS. You can either collect your data on paper and later transfer it to a computer with SPSS installed or, if money is no object, you can install SPSS on your tablet computer and go out into 'the field' (i.e. the Student Union) and enter the data straight into that.

Wherever you are, once you have opened SPSS, it will come up with the screen shown in Figure 8.10, asking you what you want to do. Click the button that says 'Type in data'. You'll be faced with a page that looks a bit like an Excel spreadsheet,

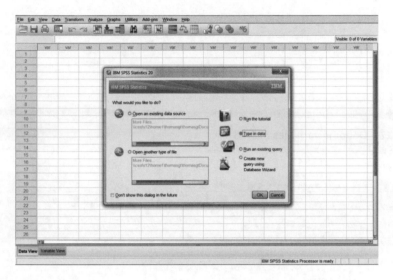

Figure 8.10   Opening SPSS

as shown in Figure 8.11. But there are some very important differences. First of all, you'll notice that at the bottom left of the page there are two rectangular buttons marked 'Data View' and 'Variable View'. To keep things simple, we'll enter just two variables, one called 'gender' and the other called 'fiveaday'. To do this, we'll move from the 'Data View' to the 'Variable View' by clicking on the appropriate button at the bottom left. (You may wish to practise using SPSS by going through the directions I'm giving here on a computer which has SPSS installed.)

In the first column of Variable View – the one that SPSS calls 'Name' – you'll put in your two variable names, namely 'gender' and 'fiveaday' (see Figure 8.12). When you do this, the other columns become filled with information, which you can now change as appropriate. The important columns here are 'Values' and 'Measure'. In 'Values' you are going to call females '0' and males '1' for the gender variable, and for the fiveaday variable you are going to tag 'yes I had five or more yesterday' as 1, while 'no I didn't have five yesterday' you'll tag '0'.

To do this, click in the box corresponding to the intersection of 'Values' and 'gender' and a dialog box will appear, as in Figure 8.13. Here, in the dialog box, enter '0' in the 'Value' space, press tab, and put 'Female' in the next box. Then click on 'Add'. Do the same for 1 and Male, and click on 'OK'. Now click in the box corresponding to the intersection of 'Values' and 'fiveaday' and repeat the procedure, thinking of appropriate names for 0 and 1 for this variable.

Figure 8.11   Opening a data entry page in SPSS

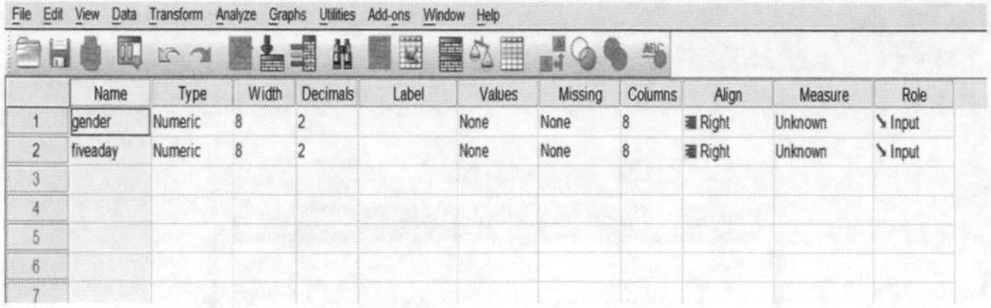

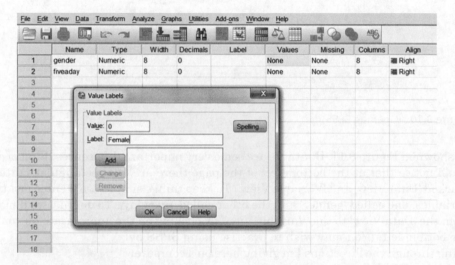

Figure 8.12   Defining variables in SPSS

Figure 8.13   The Value Labels dialog box

Now, click on 'Measure' and for each variable (i.e. gender and fiveaday) click on 'Nominal' when you are presented with the drop-down box. (It's *nominal*, just to remind you, because the 0 and the 1 are like names; they don't actually mean 'no thing' and 'one thing' – here, they mean 'no' and 'yes'.) Now click back on 'Data View' (bottom left) and you will see your two variables proudly standing in the first two columns.

Where were we going to collect our data? Ah yes, the Student Union. You make your way there. A likely candidate is sitting on his own, drinking his beer and scribbling on his phone. You approach. 'Excuse me,' you say, 'would you mind answering some questions about your lifestyle for my research project?' You take his dumbfounded half-nod to be an expression of eager acquiescence and you sit down beside him, handing him the information and consent sheet about your project. Your first question is about gender, though you have already made a good guess at this, so you don't actually need to ask him (unless you want to make it part of your rapport-making banter). You enter a '1' in the first row of 'gender'.

Then you ask: 'Yesterday, did you eat five portions of fruit and vegetables?' He replies: 'Beer has got hops in, hasn't it? They're fruit, aren't they?' (You see, this is what social research is like. Nothing's ever simple.) It transpires, once you have established that beer, sadly, does not count as fruit juice, that he consumed nothing remotely resembling a portion of fruit or vegetables yesterday. So that's a zero then. But remember that this zero doesn't mean 'none'; rather, it means 'no, he didn't eat five portions of fruit and vegetables yesterday'. Someone who ate four portions (i.e. less than five) would also get a zero.

You repeat this for 20 students, trying to get equal numbers of men and women, and you end up with something like the data sheet shown in Figure 8.14.

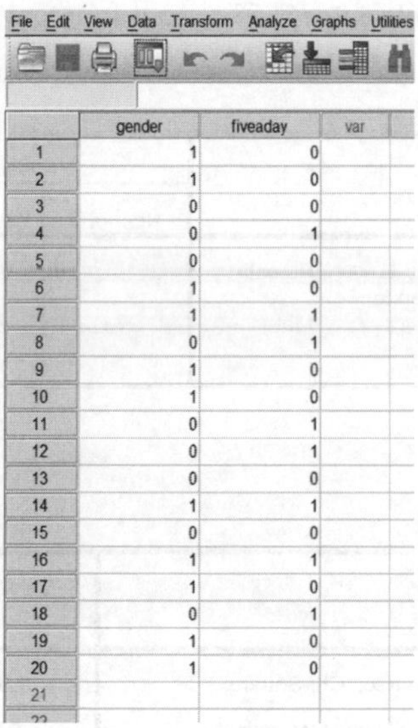

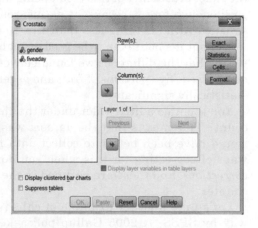

Figure 8.14   Data View sheet after completion

Now you can ask SPSS to do some statistics for you. Click on 'Analyze' at the top of the sheet, then press 'Descriptive statistics', then press 'Crosstabs'. This will 'crosstabulate' the data from your two variables. You'll get a dialog box like the one in Figure 8.15. In the dialog box, click the first arrow 'Rows' for the gender variable, then the next arrow 'Columns' for the fiveaday variable and then click the 'Statistics' button. Then click on 'Chi-square', then 'Continue', then 'OK'.

An 'output' magically appears. Don't worry about all the verbiage at the top. It's put there by statistics geeks to make it all as confusing as possible. (It's a power thing.) What you are interested in is the two boxes labelled 'gender*fiveaday Crosstabulation' and 'Chi-Square Tests'.

I've given these in Table 8.7. The first table shows how gender breaks down according to the fiveaday answers; this 'crosstabulation' represents the counting that SPSS has done for you. The second gives the significance figure. The latter is cunningly disguised by the geeks to be as inconspicuous as possible – look for the cell I've shaded here, in the column labelled 'Asymp. Sig. (2-sided)'.

You'll see that the figure is 0.199. What does this mean? It is the actual significance figure, not the chi-square statistic result, so you need go no further. SPSS has done it all for you. Marvellous – no

Figure 8.15   The Crosstabs dialog box

Table 8.7   SPSS output for crosstabulation and chi-square

gender * fiveaday Crosstabulation

Count

		fiveaday		Total
		No, not 5	Yes, ate 5 or more	
gender	Female	4	5	9
	Male	8	3	11
Total		12	8	20

Chi-Square Tests

	Value	df	Asymp. Sig. (2-sided)	Exact Sig. (2-sided)	Exact Sig. (1-sided)
Pearson Chi-Square	1.650[a]	1	0.199		
Continuity Correction[b]	0.682	1	0.409		
Likelihood Ratio	1.664	1	0.197		
Fisher's Exact Test				0.362	0.205
Linear-by-Linear Association	1.567	1	0.211		
N of Valid Cases	20				

a. 2 cells (50.0%) have expected count less than 5. The minimum expected count is 3.60.

sums, no tables, no nonsense about degrees of freedom. Why isn't it in the form of $p < 0.05$, or $p < 0.01$? It's because SPSS has worked out the *exact* probability. So the exact probability of this result being made by chance is 0.199, which isn't really good enough for us, because it means, roughly, a 1 in 5 chance. You would not be satisfied with anything less than 1 in 10 (0.1). (Well, you and I might in the real world, but it's not taken to be good enough in academic social science.) So we have to say that the difference we found between the women and the men in their tendency to eat five portions of fruit and vegetables a day is too small to be considered statistically significant.

You'll notice a little rider under the chi-square box about 'minimum expected count'. This means that the dataset was too small for a fully reliable result. It would have been better to collect data from more people. However, there are ways of correcting for this when you do your SPSS analysis (using *continuity correction*), and these are outlined in the further reading given at the end of the chapter.

Let's take another example of chi-square, as handled in a rather different way by SPSS. A 2005 Gallup poll asked 1,005 men and women about their

Table 8.8 Belief in the supernatural

	Do you believe that houses can be haunted?	
	Yes	No
Men	145	358
Women	222	280

attitudes to the supernatural. The first question was about whether they believed that houses could be haunted. The findings for this question are shown in Table 8.8.

We can work out, using chi-square, whether there is a real difference (i.e. not a *chance* difference) between men and women in their belief in haunted houses. You'll notice that the counting has already been done for us by Gallup in this example. In other words, we are not entering the data in the same way that we did for the previous healthy lifestyles example; in that one we got SPPS to count the frequencies for us. But here, we (or, rather, Gallup) have done the counting first and now we are asking SPSS just to find the statistical significance of the differences between men and women in their belief in haunted houses. You can follow this route for the data you collect for your own project – for example, the healthy eating data. You may, in other words, choose to count all the data 'by hand' first and then enter it this way.

To do this, you need to present the information in Table 8.8 to SPSS in such a way that it understands what you want. How do you do this? Switch to Variable View and create *three* variables, in the same way that you did in the previous example. Yes, three, not two. We have to create variables that describe 'belief' (where I have called the values labels 'Believ' and 'Dontbe') and 'gender' and then give SPSS the data as they correspond to these. So we need to create the third variable, which I have called 'Freq'. On this example, remember that the numbers you are putting in are 'interval', not 'nominal', which you'll have to make clear in the 'Measure' column. Irritatingly, SPSS calls these interval numbers 'scale',

so you click the 'Scale' option under 'Measure'. We now have to tell SPSS that the numbers in the 'Freq' column represent the number of cases in the various combinations of variables. To do this, click on 'Data' at the top, then 'Weight Cases'. In the dialog box, click 'Weight Cases by' and click the arrow for 'Freq'. You'll end up with a Data View screen as in Figure 8.16.

Now click on 'Analyze', then 'Descriptive Statistics' then 'Crosstabs' and in the

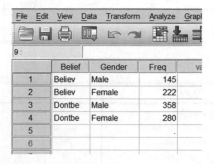

Figure 8.16 Weighted cases

dialog box click 'gender' and press the arrow for 'Rows', then click 'Belief' and press the arrow for 'Columns'. Now click on 'Statistics', then 'Chi-square' and then 'OK'. Phew. You'll end up with the output shown in Table 8.9. (Annoyingly, you can't cut and paste from this, but what you can do is to export the file to a Word document. To do this, click 'File' and then 'Export'.)

And what does the output all mean? As before, the bit you want – the bit about whether the result is statistically significant – is hidden amongst the statistical verbiage. Treat it as a game to find the treasure. Fun – you against the geeks! Or you can just look at the cell I've shaded in Table 8.9, and always look for that bit in your own output data. Here, in this case, the figure, at .000, is less than .05 (much less), so we can say that the difference between men and women in their tendency to believe in haunted houses is highly statistically significant. There's virtually no chance it would have been obtained by chance.

The problem with these tests, as I keep trying to stress, is that one can become hypnotised by the statistics, rather like the hi-fi experts who become so interested in the fidelity of the sound produced by their wonderful equipment that they don't seem actually to hear the music itself. Becoming over-concerned with the statistics can, if you are not careful, distract you from more interesting aspects of the data. For instance, the Gallup poll on belief in the supernatural proceeded to ask some more questions, as summarised in Table 8.10.

What can we do with these fascinating findings? We can continue to go through, looking for the statistical significance of the differences between men and women. This may tell you a bit – but how interesting is it? Well, moderately interesting, I suppose. But there is much *more* interesting stuff here, like

Table 8.9   SPSS output showing crosstabs summary and statistical significance

Gender * Belief Crosstabulation

Count

		Belief		Total
		Believ	Dontbe	
Gender	Female	222	280	502
	Male	145	358	503
Total		367	638	1005

Chi-Square Tests

	Value	df	Asymp. Sig. (2-sided)	Exact Sig. (2-sided)	Exact Sig. (1-sided)
Pearson Chi-Square	25.690[a]	1	.000		
Continuity Correction[b]	25.031	1	.000		
Likelihood Ratio	25.835	1	.000		
Fisher's Exact Test				.000	.000
N of Valid Cases	1005				

Table 8.10   Further aspects of belief in the supernatural

	Believed	
	Men	Women
That houses can be haunted	29%	44%
That astrology can affect people's lives	14%	30%
That people can communicate with the dead	16%	32%
That witches exist	13%	13%

the selectivity people seem to exercise in deciding how much of the supernatural to believe in: we are presented with the fact, for example, that of the 32% of women who believe that we can communicate with the dead, many do not believe that witches exist! How can people reconcile such discordant beliefs? Pondering on issues such as this is what 'theorising' in social science is all about.

The t test

In chi-square, you are comparing frequencies of data and looking to see whether the numbers represented by those data are significantly different. Suppose, though, that you have a comparison of scores to look at – comparing, say, the results of two groups on an examination. Here, the *t test* is useful, and for this we can return to Excel (though you can of course also do it in SPSS).

My example is a piece of research that I conducted with some trainee dentists and their field tutors. The study was to look at whether e-learning or a lecture was better for getting over some boring information about dental practice management and governance, and we were also interested in whether trainees and tutors responded the same or differently to the two methods of teaching (see Browne et al., 2004). I won't try to disentangle the full analysis here. Rather, I have extracted some of the data and performed a *t* test on one group of trainees' and one group of trainers' results after they had been taught by lecture. The Excel workings are shown in Figure 8.17.

The *t* test tells you how likely it is that these two sets of results – those from the trainees and those from the trainers (in columns A and B) – would be found by chance. Eyeballing them, we can see that they *differ* (though not by very much: the mean for the trainees is 9.07 and that for the trainers is 9.69), but we are interested in the magnitude of this difference and how likely it is that the findings would have arisen by chance. Given that the difference isn't very much, I would guess that the scores are not significantly different; that is to say, I would guess that this might just be a difference that could be accounted for by chance factors.

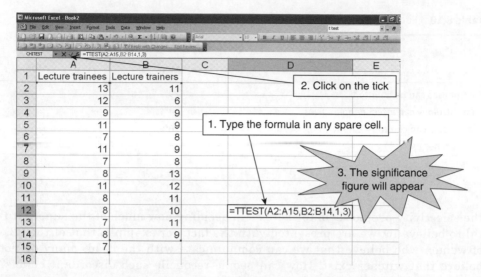

Figure 8.17 Are trainees or trainers better when learning from lectures?

So, how did I do the *t* test? After entering my data in columns, as in the previous example,

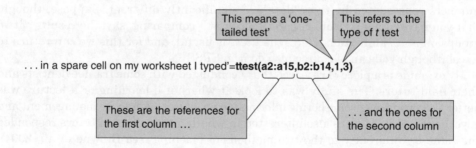

Just a word about the '1' and the '3' at the end of the formula line. The '1' tells Excel that you want it to do a one-tailed as opposed to a two-tailed test. For details on what this means you will need to read one of the texts listed in the further reading for this chapter. The '3' tells Excel that you want it to do a comparison of unrelated groups. Again, for the details of the alternatives, consult the further reading or look at the Help facility for *t* tests in Excel. (However, the latter seems to have been written by someone without the remotest sense that people will (a) be reading it, or (b) will need to understand it. It will therefore probably make you feel suicidal, as it did me, so I don't recommend it if you are not feeling cheerful.)

Once you have clicked on the tick, the result will appear where you typed the formula: 0.21. What does this 0.21 mean? As with the figure that SPSS worked out for chi-square, it is the *actual significance figure*, not the t test statistic result. This time, Excel has done it all for you. In other words, the exact probability of this result being made by chance is 0.21 (or roughly 1 in 5). Again, this is not really good enough for us – there is just too much chance that this finding would have been made by chance. (In other words the probability of it being found by chance is more than 1 in 20, or, indeed, 1 in 10 – or in tech talk $p > 0.05$, or $p > 0.1$.) We cannot therefore take it that there is any statistically significant difference between the trainers and the trainees in their ability to learn from lectures.

There are statistical tests for a variety of different purposes. For example, if you wanted to examine the differences between more than two groups in the example above (say we added a group of probationers to the group of trainers and the group of trainees), then you would have to use an analysis of variance (or ANOVA) instead of the t test. And if the number of people from whom you gather data is rather small it may be useful to use a nonparametric test such as the Wilcoxon rank test or the Mann–Whitney U test. It's beyond the scope of this book to go into the strengths and weaknesses of these and other statistical tests, so if you want to do anything much more complicated than any of the operations I have outlined here you will need to consult a more specialised book and ask for help from a tutor who specialises in statistics.

When you read more specialised statistics literature, be aware that in order to make my explanations here half-intelligible I have taken several shortcuts, not least in my dispensing with the use of the null hypothesis. For further reading, you will need to get your head around this. Be aware when reading explanations based on the null hypothesis that everything is a bit back to front, like trying to work out what 'not unhelpful' means. Good luck.

Discussing your analysis

This discussion is the completion of your research – its fruition. In it, you are coming full circle and returning to your initial questions and the context provided by your literature review. Remember the questions that you posed at the outset and the foundations provided (and the gaps left) by your literature review. The literature review provided a great basis for your thinking, but on its own it's a bit like a gin and tonic without the gin. Your research itself, all of the painstaking work that you have been doing out there in the field, is the gin that gives the kick – the element that makes the whole thing exciting. Your research itself enables you to complete the circuit of questioning, thinking, finding out, rethinking

Discussion occurs in different forms in different kinds of project write-up. It should always tie your findings and analysis with your questions and with the issues you disclosed in your literature review. And like the literature review, it is a synthesis, a narrative, a discussion – not a list.

and answering. Here, in the discussion, you orchestrate all of this – you present an argument to the reader, showing how you have answered your initial questions, revealing how ideas are interconnected, and saying why you have come to the conclusions with which you have emerged.

How is the discussion that integrates the different elements of the report organised? It is in the presentation of findings, their analysis and discussion that there is perhaps the greatest room for variation between different kinds of project write-up. In the most formal social scientific research – that which follows the lead of natural science and traditional social science – there are clear lines that are drawn between these elements of a study. However, in applied social research it is often far more difficult to separate out one part from another. In an ethnographic study the findings *are*, in a way, the analysis. When you are watching and taking notes and then making a 'thick description' you *are* analysing.

And I think this ethnographic principle, in more or less diluted forms, is probably taken to apply now to a far wider range of research. It is, to a greater or lesser extent, the watchword in nearly all social research. No longer is it the case now that you can pretend that you are a dispassionate, objective observer having little or no influence on the research scene that you are observing. Or at least you can pretend, but no one will believe you. It was the assumption that this *was* indeed the case – that you could be disinterestedly separate and objective – that made supervisors once upon a time (when I did my own psychology degree in the late Middle Ages) insist on the formal separation of these elements.

You had to pretend almost that you did not possess corporeal status, and this extended to the abolition of the first person singular: the word 'I' was forbidden in written work. I and my fellow students all had to pretend that we weren't actually embodied – almost as if the words we were writing had been beamed spiritually onto the page via a medium. We had to write in the passive tense, and say daft things such as 'The researcher believes …'. Did this actually make people believe it was objective? Well, it's amazing what people will believe.

And, as part of all this nonsense, it was assumed that *data gathering* could be cleanly separated from *analysis*. Now, though, there is the recognition that data gathering, in some way or another, is always infused with the person of the researcher. There is little point in pretending that this is not the case.

All research in the applied social sciences takes on these assumptions to some extent now: there is the acknowledgement that applied social research is complex – messy, even – often involving a knotty intertwining of ideas, facts and person. The corollary for the presentation of this chapter (about analysis and discussion) and the previous chapter (about data gathering) is that there is a continuum of kinds of organisation of your write-up. At one end, if you are doing a fairly formal study involving, say, an experiment, it is legitimate to adopt a linear approach: the presentation of your *findings*, with little in the way of commentary, will precede the *analysis*, which will precede the *discussion*. The discussion will take place separately, placing your statistical analysis in the context of the wider body of work that has occurred before it.

However, for a more interpretative piece of research you will not want to separate parts in this way, since all the time you will be testing out your emerging findings against your thoughts. All the time you will be validating or rejecting your findings against the body of knowledge that you already possess by virtue of your own experience and your reading. In these circumstances it is inappropriate to impose a strict line between analysis and discussion. One suffuses into the other. The difference between the different kinds of study is shown in Figure 8.18.

Formal linear study	Findings ⟶ Analysis ⟶ Discussion
Mixed study	Findings/analysis ⟷ Discussion
Interpretative study	Findings, analysis and discussion

Figure 8.18   Different kinds of analysis and discussion

Analysis and synthesis

We talk mostly about the analysis of your findings, but analysis is not the whole story. There is also synthesis to consider. How are analysis and synthesis different, and how do they both contribute to your project write-up?

Analysis is about taking things apart. It's from the Greek ἀνάλυσις, meaning 'breaking up'. Whether your focus in your analysis has been on words or numbers, this process of taking apart – in some shape or form – always occurs. After the taking apart, the deconstruction, it is about a process of careful inspec-

tion, to see the relationship of one thing with another: how are they connected? How do they depend on each other? What makes them work together? Are there parts which are incompatible? And so on.

Synthesis is about putting things together and is from the Greek σύνθεσις, meaning 'putting together' or 'composition'. But it is not just about chucking things together willy-nilly. This just makes a junk sculpture. If you just 'brought together' the pieces of a jigsaw you would have a mess. The synthesis bit comes in using your intelligence to make something more of the individual bits than they are on their own.

The process may be quite mechanical, where you are slotting pre-existing ideas together, as in a literature review, though even this requires some creativity and the final slotting together will be idiosyncratic – there will be no single right 'answer'. Or it may be much more creative: you have the raw material, say, of your findings and you choose to put these together in the way that you think best. Which makes most sense? Which seems most interesting? Which is the most convincing narrative?

It is about seeing relationships between ideas and discovering how they are connected, seeing where things fit together (and where they don't).

How do you do this process of integrating the various elements of your project – and integrating analysis and synthesis? It involves recursion (i.e. retracing your footsteps), summary, putting ideas (yours and others') next to each other to see how they shape up together. You should be doing this all of the time anyway in doing your work, but it is here in the discussion chapter that you have to bring it all together and make it meaningful to the reader. To do this, there has to be a continual revisiting of ideas and arguments to see which seem more or less valid. Some ideas may be rejected or put into abeyance. Tell readers about this: tell them about your process of acceptance, rejection and reformulation and the conclusions to which you have come.

Table 8.11 gives some key words and phrases that you might use in discussing your work. You might also wish to look at Frank Smith's (1992) excellent book *To Think* and his list of 77 'thinking words'. Here's how Smith explains the way that the storehouse of words is used:

> Some look back on past events: deduce, explain, recall, reflect, remember, review, and revise. Some project into the future: anticipate, conceive, divine, expect, foresee, imagine, intend, plan, plot, predict, project, and scheme. Others seem mostly concerned with what is going on at the moment (although the present is never entirely free of past or future connotations): analyze, argue, assert, assume, attend, believe, categorize, classify, comprehend, concentrate, conceptualize, determine, empathize, estimate, examine, invent, judge, know, opine, organize, presume, propose, reason, suggest, suspect, and understand. (Smith, 1992: 2)

Table 8.11   Key words and phrases in discussing

Focus	Typical words and phrases	
Remind the reader of the issues, briefly	recap, summarise, revisit, reiterate	Moderated throughout by criticality and tentativeness
Remind the reader of what you were trying to do	explore, investigate, examine, illuminate, look at, research into	
Questions and arguments: your own and others'	ask, posit, argue, aver, suggest, assume, put forward, note, highlight, draw attention to, believe, assess	
What have you found?	disclose, reveal, uncover, suggest that, point to	
Has it affirmed?	affirm, agree, verify, legitimate, validate, support, confirm, establish, uphold, sustain, corroborate, endorse	
Has it contradicted?	contradict, disagree with, oppose, deny, challenge, conflict with	
How have your ideas developed or changed?	develop, redevelop, formulate, reformulate, deduce, speculate, construe, conclude, conjecture, guess, hypothesise	

It is important to reiterate some general rules here, since you will be seeking to weave together facets of your research work – ideas, arguments, findings and assertions – in ways that you have not in other parts of your project write-up. Remember always to be critical and to be tentative, as discussed in Chapter 3. Remember the duty of doubt. Be critical of others, certainly, but only when you have good evidence to be so. Be equally critical of yourself in the way that you have done your research, but make sure this is constructive criticism, noting always what you could have done instead.

Drawing out 'theory'

I noted in Chapter 4 the different meanings of **theory** in social research and the tangles that can arise because of the confusion between these meanings. Here, in your discussion, theory is concerned with one of those meanings in particular – to do with seeing links, generalising, abstracting ideas from your data and offering explanations, connecting your findings with those of others and having insights. In fact, it's about analysis and synthesis.

But in doing this, you don't say 'I am drawing out theory'; rather you provide evidence of the process in your thinking and writing. It is very important that you do this, for the absence of 'theory', as I have noted in Chapter 4, is a major reason for the marking down of a piece of work, particularly at master's level and beyond.

The way that you draw out theory hinges upon your own knowledge of your subject and how your findings sit in relation to this knowledge. Your knowledge, your familiarity with your subject, will in turn depend on your reading and understanding of the existing research and debate. Links and associated ideas will have occurred to you throughout your project, and here, in your discussion, you tie up issues, cement connections and make explicit the clusters of ideas in your own work and that of others. These connections may be to existing bodies of knowledge or models of explanation or even to formalised 'theory' (such as Marxist theory, Freudian theory, behavioural theory or construct theory), or they may be to points of interest or 'trouble', as Bruner puts it (see p. 64), in the literature. You articulate continuing paradoxes, or perhaps offer tentative explanations for differences that continue to exist between your own analysis and that of the literature. All of this generalising process *is* the drawing out of theory.

> Drawing out 'theory' isn't just about making links to 'big' theory (such as Marxist or Freudian theory), though it can be about this if you have framed your project around one of these. More importantly, it is about making connections, identifying issues and offering reasoned explanations.

It's as if your head is a giant sorting machine for the mass of data, yours and that of others, that has been pumped into it during the course of your project. It's all swilling around in there, but it mustn't simply swill out onto the paper in front of you. Rather, your head must provide little crystallisation points to which ideas (little 'theories') can attach themselves. And these little starting points, these tiny crystals, these inspirations, will – if you work hard at it – grow by the accretion of other ideas and insights. In this process is the development of theory.

There follow two examples of theorisation, with 'theory' conceived of differently, but equally validly, in each.

Murder in the family: an example of theorisation

Amerdeep is working for a master's degree in forensic psychology, hoping ultimately to be promoted to the rank of inspector in the police service. Her research project centres on the media's presentation of mental instability and illness in the discussion of serious offending. This involves content analysis of newspaper articles about murder and other serious crimes. One of Amerdeep's main sources in her literature review is a Home Office study entitled *Murder and Serious Sexual Assault: What Criminal Histories Can Reveal about Future Serious Offending* (Soothill et al., 2002). Among the rich data she finds in the report is that shown in Table 8.12.

Table 8.12   Murderers by victim–offender relationship

	N	% with previous convictions
Family	119	62.2
Acquaintance	218	69.7
Stranger – male victim	195	70.3
Stranger – female victim	31	61.3
Total	563	68.0

From Soothill et al. (2002).

Table 8.12 reveals that in around two-thirds of *all* murders, including family murder, in the Home Office study the murderer had a previous criminal conviction. This surprised Amerdeep, whose impression from reading the press was that murder of a family member was something of a different kettle of fish from other murder – that it was a crime of passion, motivated by domestic unhappiness, provocation, self-defence or rage. The popular belief – either created by or just reflected in the press – was of domestic murderers being like you and me: ordinary people impelled under extraordinary circumstances to awful acts. But the Home Office research said something different: that 62 per cent of family murder was committed by someone with a previous criminal conviction – *not* like you and me. Or to put it more accurately, it was committed by a very unusual subset of the population at large: those with a criminal conviction, and in this sense the population of family murderers was similar to the population of all murderers.

Here, in this noticing of something unexpected, was the germ of *theorisation*. It came from an intelligent noticing of a mismatch, an 'angle', a disparity between a common view and the evidence. It enabled Amerdeep to take her analysis beyond mere description and towards discussion of this disparity. Her theorisation involved the integration of a range of 'knowledges':

- her knowledge as a police officer;
- her knowledge as an ordinary member of the public;
- the data she had accumulated as part of her empirical research;
- her reading of the research literature.

All of this diverse knowledge was available to her in making sense of her observation about murder 'in the family'.

That first step – the seed of the idea, the noticing, the point of crystallisation – took place early on in the project, during her reading for her literature review. She had to hold that seed of an idea with her as she progressed through the rest of her literature review and her data collection. In many ways, the observation of incongruity between the literature and a popularly held view altered the course of her research, and this was to be expected (see the discussion of the *recursive plan* on p. 19). This small starting-point, arising from her noticing of something unexpected, gathered other pieces of information to it; it led to new questions; it led to a more targeted search for data that would throw light on it. She could ultimately identify it as one of the major themes of her research.

Given that seed of inquiry, that itch to find out more – the 'trouble' – Amerdeep started thinking, or theorising (see Figure 8.19). She came up with possible explanations for the finding, and sought ways of testing those ideas. For example, was her idea of 'received wisdom' concerning family murderers wrong? To test this out she could do a small impromptu survey of friends and colleagues. And what did the media tend to say about family murder? She would make a special note to examine this in her content analysis. Could it be that the highly detailed Home Office study was leading her astray? What was the sample of murderers used? If it was murderers in prison (as it was), it omitted murderers who were not in prison, and these would surely form a special subset – perhaps overrepresented with family murderers. While murder carries a mandatory prison sentence, it may be that family murderers tend to receive much shorter sentences so the population of them in prison is proportionately smaller at any one time than that of the non-family murderers – and those of them who are in prison may be there because their backgrounds and histories make them more typical of 'normal' prisoners, making them less likely to receive parole, etc. In all of this Amerdeep was reading, asking questions, gathering ideas, 'gutting' other ideas and research findings, questioning explanations, questioning her own beliefs and views, and coming up with new tentative explanations. All of this is theorisation.

(Continued)

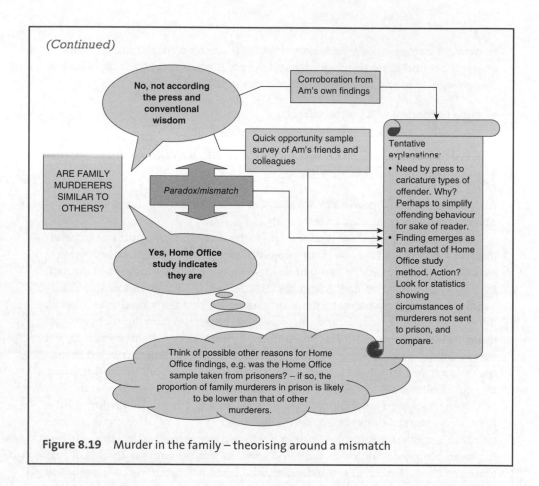

Figure 8.19 Murder in the family – theorising around a mismatch

Laughing all the way to school: another example of theorisation

Michael is studying for a BA in English, psychology and education and has been working during his vacations as a volunteer in a primary school close to his university. He is now able to use the goodwill felt towards him at the school to help him gain access for his double-module interdisciplinary research project. He has an interest in inclusive education and wonders how Year 6 children use humour and laughter to include or exclude other children. He plans to do some informal observations in an ethnographic design frame. He explains this to the staff at the school, who are happy with it, given appropriate assurances of anonymity and of completely unobtrusive observation, and the head teacher requests support for Michael's study in a letter to parents.

On discussing theorisation with his tutor Michael decides that he needs to review the way that others have understood humour and laughter and their role in creating social capital – in forming the social 'glue' and 'oil' that helps groups to stay together. In reviewing the literature Michael comes across some classic works by Freud and Bergson, and out of these he develops a typology that sees humour being used in three ways by groups:

- to relieve tension or stress;

- to assert superiority;

- to introduce new ideas into a community's thinking by highlighting incongruity.

This typology forms the basis for his *theorisation*. He sees connections to inclusion and exclusion certainly in the first two points of the typology – in the ways that certain children may be the object of unkind humour, first to defuse tension in a group by identifying a different 'outsider', and second to strengthen *bonds* in a subgroup by isolating individuals perceived to be inferior. However, he noted that humour may also be used to defuse tension in a harmless way, by not making a joke at anyone's expense – and in fact in the hands of a socially skilled member of the group to deflect attention from individuals at times of tension onto an impersonal feature of the situation.

Michael linked the idea of *social bonds* with Robert Putnam's (2000) notions of *bonding* and *bridging* in social groups. Bonding, said Putnam, is a means of strengthening a group by excluding others, with bridging by contrast being a means of easing in new members. As Putnam puts it, 'Bonding social capital constitutes a kind of sociological superglue, whereas bridging social capital provides a sociological WD40' (Putnam, 2000: 22–3). Michael related his typology to Putnam's bonding and bridging as indicated in Figure 8.20.

This detailed and thoughtful overview of the literature provided Michael with a strong theoretical framework within which to build and conduct his ethnography – the latter involving observations and interviews. By watching especially in his observation for instances of the use of humour and its use in the relief of stress, the exertion of superiority or the highlighting of incongruity, he could first broadly define its use in his analysis and discussion as threatening or benign. He could then in turn interpret specific instances as examples of Putnam's bonding and bridging. This provided an invaluable lens through

(Continued)

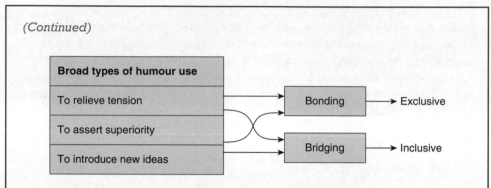

(Continued)

Figure 8.20   Typology related to Putnam's bonding and bridging

which to view examples of humour. Without it, Michael's narrative would have been a flavourless set of illustrations: illustrations of what? There needs to be a structure within which these illustrations can be interpreted. This is not to say that the structure cannot in itself ultimately be questioned and reinterpreted or even discarded: this is all part of the process of 'theorisation'.

You can see, I hope, that what goes under the name of 'theorisation' and 'theory' takes a variety of shapes and forms in different types of inquiry. The important thing is to use your intelligence to try to understand what is going on – to be *making sense* of your findings.

Overview

This is the most interesting part of your project – the part where you get the chance to think seriously about your own findings and what they mean. The analytical frame that you use, whether it is thick description or some kind of statistical method, will provide a rich source of ideas for your thinking. The examples I have given in this chapter are widely used, but remember that there are many others to explore.

Now that you are here, near the end of your project, analysing the results of all your hard work, you can let yourself off the leash a bit, and make wider interpretations and judgements. The kinds of interpretations that you make will be determined in part by the approach or approaches that you have taken, but it is here that you will set your analysis in the context of everything that has gone before, including your literature review. You will be tying strands together, intertwining ideas, weaving a fabric that is sometimes called 'theory'. If done well, this can be a real contribution to knowledge in a particular area. It may be a small area, but you will have enhanced your own understanding and added to that of others. And you will have developed your own skills along the way.

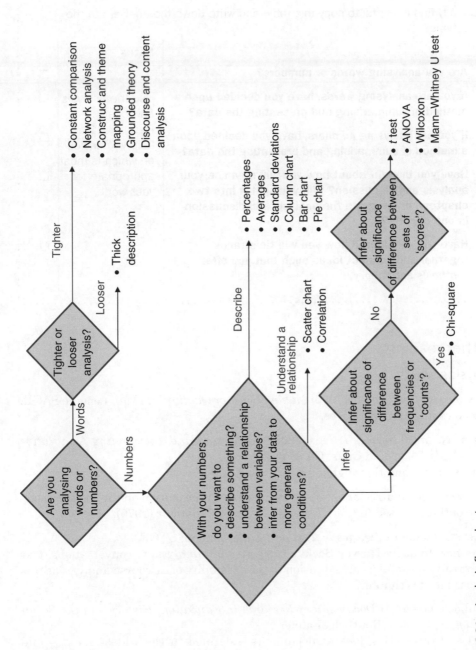

Figure 8.21 Analysis flow chart

··

Checklist ✓

You may find it helpful to copy this table and write down the answers to the questions.

	Notes	
1 Are you analysing words or numbers?		☐
2 If you are analysing *words*, have you decided upon a method of summarising and presenting the data?	Use the analysis flow chart in	☐
3 If you are analysing *numbers*, have you decided upon a method of summarising and presenting the data?	Figure 8.21 to help you decide on which is most	☐
4 Have you thought about how you will organise your analysis and discussion? Will you split it into two chapters, or integrate the analysis and discussion in one chapter?	appropriate for your work	☐
5 Have you considered how you will tie strands together and connect ideas such that you offer *synthesis* and *theory*?		☐

··

Further reading

Analysing words

Coffey, A. and Atkinson, P. (1996) *Making Sense of Qualitative Data*. London: SAGE.
Good on coding and narratives.

Denzin, N. and Lincoln, Y. (eds) (2008) *Collecting and Interpreting Qualitative Materials*. Thousand Oaks, CA: SAGE.
Comprehensive and thoroughgoing.

http://www.hoopandtree.org/sociometry.htm gives information on the sociomatrix – one of these is used in Colin Lacey's *Hightown Grammar* (1970).

Lepper, G. (2000) *Categories in Text and Talk*. London: SAGE.
Shows how to apply Harvey Sacks's *categorisation analysis* to conversations, text and narrative. Useful as an extension to the possibility of discourse analysis as it is discussed in this chapter.

McCulloch, G. (2004) *Documentary Research in Education, History and the Social Sciences*. London: RoutledgeFalmer.
A full and interesting look at documents – defined in the widest sense – and documentary analysis.

Miles, M.B. and Huberman, M. (1994) *Qualitative Data Analysis: An Expanded Sourcebook* (2nd edn). London: SAGE.
One of the bibles of qualitative method.

Riessman, C. (2008) *Narrative Methods for the Human Sciences*. London: SAGE.
I haven't tackled narrative analysis here, but this offers a good introduction.

Ryan, G.W. and Bernard, H.R. (2003) Techniques to identify themes. *Field Methods*, 15 (1), 85–109.
A good summary on identifying themes.

Schwandt, T.A. (2001) *Dictionary of Qualitative Inquiry*. Thousand Oaks, CA: SAGE.
Actually, this is much more than a dictionary.

Analysing numbers

Connolly, P. (2007) *Quantitative Data Analysis in Education*. London: Routledge.
A thorough and user-friendly introduction to the use of statistics in education.

Field, A. (2013) *Discovering Statistics using IBM SPSS Statistics* (4th edn). London: SAGE.
If you want to go further in using statistics, for which you will need SPSS, you can't do much better than this book. Highly detailed. Some funny examples, including lap dancers and ejaculating quails.

Hinton, P.R. (2004) *Statistics Explained: A Guide for Social Science Students*. London: Routledge.
A good spread, though more on social science *per se* rather than applied social science.

Miles, J. and Shevlin, M. (2001) Applying *Regression and Correlation: A Guide for Students and Researchers*. London: SAGE.
Good on correlation.

Salkind, N.J. (2004) *Statistics for People Who (Think They) Hate Statistics*. Thousand Oaks, CA: SAGE.
This is my favourite book on statistics. It has lots of cartoons and is nicely written. It explains (if you really want to know) the difference between one-tailed and two-tailed tests. If you are going to get one book on statistics, I would recommend you get this one.

9
CONCLUDING AND WRITING UP

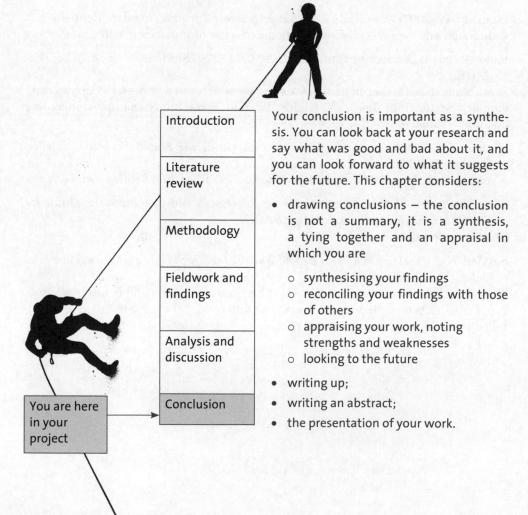

Introduction
Literature review
Methodology
Fieldwork and findings
Analysis and discussion
Conclusion

You are here in your project

Your conclusion is important as a synthesis. You can look back at your research and say what was good and bad about it, and you can look forward to what it suggests for the future. This chapter considers:

- drawing conclusions – the conclusion is not a summary, it is a synthesis, a tying together and an appraisal in which you are

  o synthesising your findings
  o reconciling your findings with those of others
  o appraising your work, noting strengths and weaknesses
  o looking to the future

- writing up;
- writing an abstract;
- the presentation of your work.

You are now coming toward the end of your project – and it's the time when you can draw conclusions. It's also the time when you will probably be doing most of your writing and tidying up, so I shall include some general points in this chapter which in fact apply right through your project work – points concerning audience, the way that you write and the way that you present your work. I shall also say something about the *abstract*, since it is here, at the end of your project, that this should be written.

Writing a conclusion

At the beginning of this book I said that your research project is like a story: it needs a beginning, a middle and an end. You are now at the end, writing the conclusion, and this bit is as important as the beginning. It's important because it performs a set of crucial functions which I'll come on to in a moment, and because, like the introduction, it is the part that will be read most thoroughly by markers and, possibly, an external examiner. They will of course read the whole report carefully and make detailed comments on it, but they will be looking in the conclusion and the introduction for a sense of cohesion and integrity, for a sense of your approach to research, for a sense of your critical awareness and your attitude to knowledge. These are as important as, or more important than, what you have actually 'found'.

The good news is that the conclusion doesn't need to be very long. The conclusion and the introduction are the shortest chapters in your dissertation. Although the conclusion contains elements of summary, it is not *principally* a summary: it should not plod through each of the chapters saying what each was about. The reader has read those and doesn't need to be reminded of them. Rather, it is a synthesis that captures for readers what the research was about and how it has answered the question or questions that you posed at the outset. In doing this it should leave readers with an idea of your understanding of the field and your understanding of research, its benefits and its frailties. In doing all of this it should:

1 *refer back to the introduction*, where you set out the purpose of your research. In the introduction you began to carve out the shape of your project. You sculpted the project around the BIS – around the *background* of the area in which you are interested, an *issue* that you identified to do with that background (you asked 'What's missing?' or 'What doesn't make sense?'), and you promised a *solution* – some kind of answer – which would address the issue you had identified. Now that you have completed your research you can reflect on your solution. How well have you addressed your issue? Have you filled in the information that was missing, or have you helped to resolve a dispute or assisted in addressing some incongruity? Have you thrown extra light on some dilemma or paradox? Here, in the conclusion, you can say whether you have been able to do any of these.

2 *chart the progress of any change* in your questions as the project has progressed. It should say how your interests have changed and note any variation from your original plans caused either by circumstance or by your rethinking about method.

3 *summarise briefly the main findings* and outline in a page or two any dilemmas, questions and paradoxes still existing.

4 *acknowledge your project's limitations and weaknesses*, which you may realise toward the end were quite major. Perhaps you should, in retrospect, have used a completely different approach. Do acknowledge this if it is the case; don't try to paper over the cracks, because the reader will realise it anyway. Say that you recognise in hindsight that you should have used a different method, used different tools or adopted a different form of analysis. You will be credited for your perception and understanding in the examiner's marking. After all, part of the criticality of which academics are so fond consists in the ability to be self-critical and to understand the shortcomings and imperfections that almost inevitably exist in social research.

5 *outline any recommendations* for those who have been participants in your research (e.g. the school that accommodated you) or for policy more widely. However, there is no *need* for a research project to offer recommendations of this kind, and often when students include these they can seem trite and reveal a lack of understanding about the realities of policy and practice. With this in mind it is as well, if you do want to make any kind of recommendation, to include here some discussion about implementation in the real world. Here, the title of a famous article comes to mind: 'The myth of the hero-innovator' by Georgiades and Phillimore (1975). It makes the point that it is extraordinarily difficult to effect change in an organisation and that if you expect or hope to do this you need to devote a great deal of attention to the workings of the organisation, its structure and its politics.

6 *outline points for further research*, or how your research leads to further questions. This may be obvious, but if it isn't try the following:

- *Imagine*. How would things be different if something were changed in 'the system'? Suppose, for example, that you have been researching the curriculum and there were no National Curriculum (you never know, it might happen one day). On the basis of your research, what could you say about such a scenario?

- *Predict*. How is something likely to look or to be in the future, based on the way you have found it to be in your research? If you are doing research, for example on the funding of the health service in your region, how would things look if the National Health Service were to accept 'top-up funding' from patients?

- *Solve*. What tentative solutions can you offer to any broader questions or issues that have been raised in your research? Does it offer any insights on problems that exist today? For example, if you have been undertaking research on the marketing of soft drinks to children, what insights might be offered on the growth in childhood obesity? But remember: be tentative; be modest; think small – your findings may well be relevant, they may be significant, but the hallmark of scholarly research is self-critical caution. Unlike journalists, researchers know – and are proud that they know – that they don't have easy answers. Remember that you are not a journalist.

- *Compare or draw an analogy*. Find the similarities and differences between your topic of interest and a similar subject, or with the same subject in a different time period or place. For example, if you were looking at the relationship of income to quality of healthcare regionally and nationally, could further research offer additional insights by including an international perspective?

Table 9.1 summarises the main issues that need to be in your conclusion and it offers some phrases which you might use in the writing of the conclusion.

Table 9.1 What should your conclusion contain?

Issue	Possible phrases
Briefly summarising	• In this project I have investigated ...
Revisiting the background, issue and promised solution	• The issue of ... is of central importance for our understanding of ... Despite this, little attention has been paid to ... In my research, I set out to ...
Evaluating your actual 'solution'	• The findings of this project reveal that ... • The findings support the idea that ... • This study confirms earlier work by ... and, moreover, suggests that ... • It can be concluded that ...
Limitations	• The project was restricted by ... • The research focused only upon ... • Ethical considerations precluded the use of a control group ... • The use of an interpretative approach enables an understanding of specific ... However, caution should be exercised in generalising these findings to the broader field of ...
Recommendations for further research	• Further work needs to address ... • A cohort study over three years, and involving ..., would address the stability of the findings outlined here • Research on the specific role of ... would be of value in ... • It would be interesting to assess the effects of ... • It would be useful to compare experiences of boys and girls
Implications and recommendations for policy and practice	• Given the range of views around the issue of ..., the evidence from this research suggests that ... • My research implies that policy should tend to favour ...

Writing up

The notion of writing up is something of a misnomer since the advent of word-processors. Now, following the invention of these magical machines, you can keep files of your work as you proceed, and 'writing up' has really become a process of getting things in order. Your files may contain quite different kinds of information and when you have finished collecting data, analysing them and discussing them, it is time to hammer them into shape in the chapters of your dissertation or thesis.

A very rough guide to the typical organisation of a dissertation or thesis write-up is given in Chapter 2. The chapter titles do not need to be identical to those given here and certain chapters may be split into two or three, or, by contrast, conflated. Go with your common sense on this, always keeping your readers in mind: the aim in dividing the work into chapters is to help readers understand where they are. By the same reasoning, you can be imaginative about the chapter titles. For example, a business studies student conducting a project on movement in house prices might divide the literature review into these two chapters: 'Modelling house price variation' and 'Recent empirical evidence on price change internationally'.

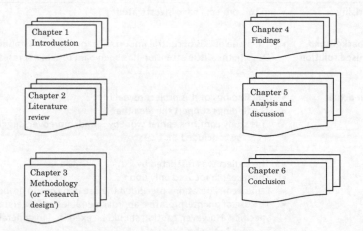

Writing an abstract and finalising the title

At the *end* of your project, you can write your abstract – though it will be placed right at the *beginning*, on the first page after the title but before the contents page. Your abstract should be between 150 and 300 words – enough to fit onto one side of A4. (It is acceptable to use single spacing for the abstract.) You should spend a lot of time thinking about your abstract because it should encapsulate the whole project and it creates a first impression to all of your readers – and it is the abstract that will be recorded electronically. If anywhere, it is here in the abstract that you are writing a summary of the project: it should be a balanced review of your questions, methods, findings and conclusions. Don't make the mistake (which many people do) of not saying what you actually found.

Figure 9.1 shows my own PhD abstract. While a PhD is a lengthier and more complex piece of work than an undergraduate or master's project, the abstract is essentially the same in each. I have put in the thought bubbles by the side my reflections now on this abstract. Looking back on it I think it is not too bad, though it is a little pompous in parts and there is a touch of repetition, which I would, if I were writing it again, remove.

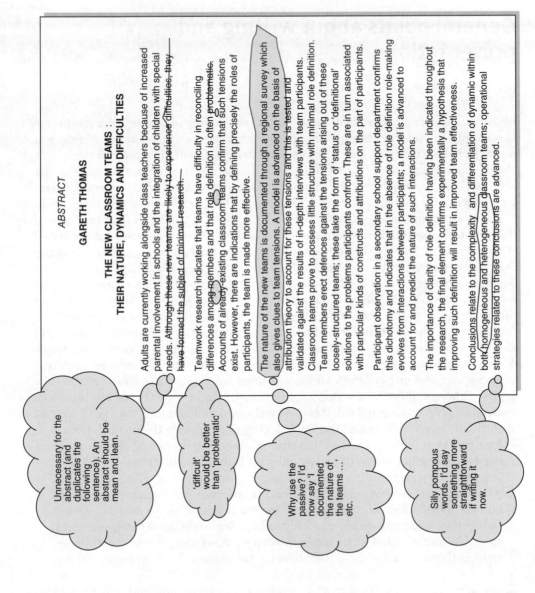

Figure 9.1 An abstract

I have discussed the title on p 24 and noted that you should have a *working title* while you are conducting your research. Now, at the end, you can choose a title that actually encapsulates what your research was about, and it may be rather different from your working title.

General points about writing and presentation

Writing

I have talked *ad nauseam* about being critical and telling a coherent story, and this is certainly the central current through any consideration about the way that you write. But the writing is more than an articulation of your thought and work; it is also a communication of this to others. Writing is about communicating; it is not about trying to sound clever (and this sadly is not a maxim followed by some academics who write for scholarly journals – I have explored this elsewhere: Thomas, 1994).

There are many books on how to write, and you won't have time to read any of them, but in case you do let me point you to one that has helped me: John Whale's (1984) *Put it in Writing*. He gives a number of reminders, such as 'remembering the reader', and 'hear it in your head'. In other words, read it out to yourself in your head (or, even better, out loud). Does it sound right? Does it make sense? Will the reader understand? Whale also suggests that you should sound like yourself, and this is certainly good advice, with the proviso that there is *register* to consider.

'Register' is the accepted form of writing for a particular audience or forum, and to write your dissertation in phone text would be unacceptable, obviously. There is a certain expectation about a degree of formality that has to surround anything as important as a piece of work which will count in a significant way towards your degree. However, this does not stop you from using your own words and sounding like yourself in your writing. Indeed, it is to be welcomed and admired. George Orwell, in his brilliant essay 'Politics and the English Language', makes the point that there is bad writing that finds its roots in imitation of others (i.e. imitating them and therefore *not* sounding like yourself) and actually leads to sloppy thinking:

> [Our language] becomes ugly and inaccurate because our thoughts are foolish, but the slovenliness of our language makes it easier for us to have foolish thoughts. … Modern English, especially written English, is full of bad habits which spread by imitation and which can be avoided if one is willing to take the necessary trouble. If one gets rid of these habits one can think more clearly. (Orwell, 1969)

Given that one of Orwell's targets is academic language (and you will have come across plenty of examples of bad writing in your own reading), his essay is well worth reading. He comes up with a checklist of what to do and what not to do:

1 Never use a metaphor, simile or other figure of speech which you are used to seeing in print. (In other words, avoid clichés.)

2 Never use a long word where a short one will do.

3 If it is possible to cut a word out, always cut it out.

4 Never use the passive where you can use the active.

5 Never use a foreign phrase, a scientific word or a jargon word if you can think of an everyday English equivalent.

6 Break any of these rules sooner than say anything outright barbarous.

It is worth reiterating that your design frame and approach determine to a great extent the register that you adopt in your write-up. The examples of ethnography that I have given show, I hope, that the kind of writing, the register, that you use in this sort of work will be very different from the write-up of an experiment. The former may be more like a newspaper article or even a novel, while the latter will demand more of the structure and strictures of formal academic writing.

One last point:

Q. Can I say 'I'?

A. Yes. 'I' is a good word, though you should try to steer clear of using it repeatedly. The main thing is to avoid using silly constructions such as 'The researcher selected 25 students …' instead of 'I selected 25 students …'. (See also p. 272.)

Non-sexist and non-discriminatory writing

Quite rightly, there is the expectation that your writing should not engender or perpetuate stereotypes of any kind, and there are some basic rules here. Do not use any gender-based language (e.g. using 'he' when you mean 'he or she'). To avoid it, try using the plural, or if that really won't work, use 'they' as a non-gendered singular pronoun. Some people get very exercised about this ('But it's not correct grammar!'), but it has now become an acceptable form of use to avoid sexist writing. Don't use a gendered form if a neutral form is available (e.g. don't use 'headmistress' in preference to 'headteacher').

At the time of writing 'disability' is acceptable, though 'impairment' is preferred by some authorities. 'Handicap' is not acceptable.

In the UK, the term 'black and minority ethnic' (BME) is used by the Home Office to refer to all people who are not white.

Presentation

Draft, proofread and edit; re-draft, re-proofread and re-edit; then re-re-draft, re-re-proofread and re-re-edit … and so on. Get it right. Perhaps I'm oversensitive, but when I am marking and I read something that clearly has not been proofread even once I feel a little insulted. It puts me in a bad mood, and you don't want to put your marker in a bad mood.

Use word-processor tools to check your spelling and grammar, but be aware that they are not foolproof. Words such as 'practice', which in UK English change their spelling depending on their use ('practice' when a noun, 'practise' when a verb), may not be picked up by your spellchecker. So ask someone who is good at spelling to proofread for you. If English is not your first language, ask someone for whom it is if they will read it through for you.

Get your apostrophes right. I know it shouldn't matter to your markers, but sadly it does. When they see *childrens'* it jumps out at them and puts them instantly off their lunch. Given that more than half of students use apostrophes incorrectly, here is my half-page guide. It is not comprehensive: it is based on my experience of the most common apostrophe mistakes made in students' work.

Apostrophes I: it's or its?

Use *it's* only as an abbreviation for *it is*, or, less often, *it has*. For example:

- *It's* a nice day today.
- I'm going because *it's* necessary.
- *It's* [it has] been a long time.

Use *its* for everything else. For example:

- *Its* colour is blue.
- The dog was cross because *its* dinner was late.

(In other words, *its* is an exception to the general rule that a possessive *s* takes an apostrophe.) And note that there is no such construction as *its'*.

Apostrophes II: ownership

The apostrophe shows that something is 'owned'.

Singular nouns – like *cat, tree, Piaget, nut* – take an apostrophe **before** the *s* when you want to indicate ownership. For example:

- *Piaget's* theories have been used for many years in education.
- The *cat's* fur is falling out.

But when those singular nouns have an *s* added to make them **plural** – like *cats, trees, nuts* – they take an apostrophe **after** the *s* to show ownership. For example:

- *Trees'* leaves fall in the autumn.
- Three *students'* ethics forms were sent for scrutiny by the ethics panel.

However, nouns with **special plural** forms – like *people*, *women*, *children* – take an apostrophe **before** the *s*. For example:

- The *women's* group met on Wednesdays.

- *Children's* clothes are not subject to VAT.

There are a few other things to consider – but that's for the advanced course.

Other points

There will be regulations and guidelines about the presentation of your thesis produced by your university department. Clearly you must conform to these, so look them up on your department or university website. Here are a few all-purpose ones:

- *Numbering.* Make sure your pages are numbered. Go to Insert in Word, then click on 'Page Numbers'. The bottom right is the best place for a page number in my opinion.

- *Tables and diagrams.* Label tables 'Table 1', 'Table 2', etc., and the same with diagrams and pictures, which are called 'Figures'. It is best to label these by chapter, so the fourth table in Chapter 3 would be called 'Table 3.4'. Refer to tables and figures by their numbers, not as 'in the following table'.

- *Margins.* Use at least 33 mm (1.25 inches) on the left and 25 mm (1 inch) on the right, top and bottom. Your university may have its own specification, but I've never seen any of my colleagues actually get out a tape measure when marking. The main thing is to ensure that the margins are ample so markers can write in them, with a bit more on the left to allow for binding.

- *Spacing.* University regulations usually specify double spacing, though I'm not actually sure why. I think it is a hangover from the days when typesetters needed to write between lines. I personally prefer single spacing – and there is a green issue here as well – but of course you must follow the guidelines set by your university or department. I think 1.5 spacing would usually be acceptable (and it's what I use whenever ordered to use double spacing).

- *Quotations.* If you use a quotation, make sure you put it in quotation marks. If you use a quotation of 40 words or longer, indent it. Otherwise, keep it in the text. (If it is indented you don't need to put quotation marks around it.)

- *References.* There is a distinction between references and a bibliography. References are the works that you have actually referred to in the text. A bibliography, by contrast, is a list of works that you may have read but not necessarily mentioned by name. In an academic work of this kind it is *references* that you need (see the Harvard method, pp. 83–85).

- *Hyphens and en dashes.* When you type a hyphen between spaces – often as a way of making a parenthetic remark like this – Word autocorrects it into something called an 'en dash'. It looks like this –. It's a bit longer than a hyphen and is a 'proper' dash. The only problem is that when you go back to edit material and want to put in a dash and type the hyphen, Word doesn't 'know' what you are doing, so it just puts in a hyphen. This looks messy. To avoid it, use the en dash direct entry when editing (i.e. press Ctrl and the minus sign on the number pad).

Coda

Coda is a pretentious word meaning 'nearly at the end'. I'm using it because I don't want to end the book on anything as dull as a discussion of the use of the hyphen versus the use of the en dash.

I said at the beginning that research can give you a buzz, and I am sure that you will have felt that buzz. You will have emerged from doing a research project with greatly enhanced skills. You will have acquired detailed knowledge about one aspect of education, healthcare, medicine, business, law, dentistry, social work or whatever, and you will be something of an authority on this aspect of your subject. You may even have insights on policy and practice that will be valuable in local discussions. But perhaps more importantly, you will have acquired knowledge about how to inquire and do research, having developed a healthy scepticism about the claims of research to be able to discover the truth. You will be able to set different kinds of research against each other and against other kinds of inquiry, and evaluate the strengths and weaknesses of each. And, by doing all of this in your own research, you will be able to understand better the research that you read.

I hope you have enjoyed the journey. Good luck.

Checklist ✔

Have you …

1 … written a conclusion based on the issues outlined in Table 9.1? ☐

2 … organised your work into chapters? ☐

3 … sketched out how your work will divide between the chapters? ☐

4 ... decided, finally, on a title? ☐

5 ... written an abstract? ☐

6 ... got hold of your university department's regulations on referencing and presentation and made sure you conform to them? ☐

Further reading

Writing

AERA (1999) Publishing educational research: guidelines and tips. Available at: http://www.aera.net/uploadedFiles/Journals_and_Publications/Journals/pubtip.pdf (accessed 12 October 2008).
This is mainly intended for junior researchers trying to get published and contains some good advice on writing.

Becker, H.S. (2008) *Writing for Social Scientists: How to Start and Finish Your Thesis, Book, or Article* (2nd revised edn). Chicago: University of Chicago Press.
Excellent on writing, and how to communicate rather than sound clever.

Thomson, A. (2005) *Critical Reasoning: A Practical Introduction*. London: Routledge.
See especially Chapters 4 and 5 on writing and reasoning. Good especially on how to summarise.

Wolcott, H.E. (2009) *Writing Up Qualitative Research* (3rd edn). London: SAGE.
Does what it says on the tin, and Wolcott is a good writer to use as a model.

APPENDIX: CRITICAL VALUES FOR CHI-SQUARE

	Level of significance		
df	0.1	0.05	0.01
1	2.71	3.84	6.63
2	4.61	5.99	9.21
3	6.25	7.81	11.34
4	7.78	9.49	13.28
5	9.24	11.07	15.09
6	10.64	12.59	16.81
7	12.02	14.07	18.48
8	13.36	15.51	20.09
9	14.68	16.92	21.67
10	15.99	18.31	23.21
11	17.28	19.68	24.72
12	18.55	21.03	26.22
13	19.81	22.36	27.69
14	21.06	23.68	29.14
15	22.31	25.00	30.58
16	23.54	26.30	32.00
17	24.77	27.59	33.41
18	25.99	28.87	34.81
19	27.20	30.14	36.19
20	28.41	31.41	37.57
21	29.62	32.67	38.93
22	30.81	33.92	40.29
23	32.01	35.17	41.64
24	33.20	36.42	42.98
25	34.38	37.65	44.31
26	35.56	38.89	45.64
27	36.74	40.11	46.96
28	37.92	41.34	48.28
29	39.09	42.56	49.59
30	40.26	43.77	50.89

REFERENCES

Alderson, P. (2004) *Ethics, Social Research and Consulting with Children and Young People* (2nd edn). London: Barnardo's.

Andreski, S. (1972) *Social Sciences as Sorcery*. London: André Deutsch.

Ball, S. (1981) *Beachside Comprehensive: A Case-Study of Secondary Schooling*. Cambridge: Cambridge University Press.

Becker, H.S. (1992) Cases, causes, conjunctures, stories, and imagery. In C.C. Ragin and H.S. Becker (eds), *What is a Case? Exploring the Foundations of Social Inquiry*, pp. 205–16. Cambridge: Cambridge University Press.

Becker, H. S. (1998) *Tricks of the Trade*. Chicago: University of Chicago Press.

Bliss, J., Monk, M. and Ogborn, J. (1983) *Qualitative Data Analysis for Educational Research*. London: Croom Helm.

Booth, W.C., Colomb, G.C. and Williams, J.M. (2003) *The Craft of Research* (2nd edn). Chicago: University of Chicago Press.

Browne, E., Mehra, S., Rattan, R. and Thomas, G. (2004) Comparing lecture and e-learning as pedagogies for new and experienced professionals in dentistry. *British Dental Journal*, 197 (2), 95–9.

Bruner, J. (1997) *The Culture of Education*. Cambridge, MA: Harvard University Press.

Bryman, A. (1998) Quantitative and qualitative research strategies in knowing the social world. In T. May and M. Williams (eds), *Knowing in the Social World*. Buckingham: Open University Press.

Burgess, R.G. (1982) *Field Research: A Sourcebook and Field Manual*. London: Routledge.

Burgess, R.G. (1984) *In the Field: An Introduction to Field Research*. London: Routledge.

Butterfield, H. (1931/1973) *The Whig Interpretation of History*. London: Pelican.

Campbell, D.T. and Stanley, J.C. (1963) *Experimental and Quasi-Experimental Designs for Research*. Chicago: Rand McNally.

Coady, C.A.J. (1994) *Testimony: A Philosophical Study*. Oxford: Clarendon Press.

Coles, G. (2000) *Misreading Reading: The Bad Science that Hurts Children*. Boston: Heinemann.

Cremin, H., Thomas, G. and Vincett, K. (2005) Working with teaching assistants: three models evaluated. *Research Papers in Education*, 20 (4), 413–32.

DCSF (2007) *Education and Training Statistics for the United Kingdom*. London: DCSF. Available at: www.dcsf.gov.uk/rsgateway/DB/VOL/v000761/index.shtml (accessed 22 September 2008).

Denzin, N. (1978) *Sociological Methods: A Sourcebook* (2nd edn). New York: McGraw-Hill.

Derrida, J. (1978) *Writing and Difference*. London: Routledge & Kegan Paul.

Descartes, R. (1647/1996) *Meditations on First Philosophy*. Cambridge: Cambridge University Press.

Devlin, B., Fienberg, S.E., Resnick, D.P. and Roeder, K. (eds) (1997), *Intelligence, Genes and Success: Scientists Respond to the Bell Curve*. New York: Springer-Verlag.

Dewey, J. (1920/2004) *How We Think*. Whitefish, MT: Kessinger Publishing.

Dickens, W.T. and Flynn, J.R. (2001) Heritability estimates versus large environmental effects: the IQ paradox resolved. *Psychological Review*, 108, 346–69.

Fairclough, N. (1995) *Critical Discourse Analysis*. Harlow. Longman.

Flanders, N. (2004) Interaction analysis. In C. Seale (ed.), *Social Research Methods: A Reader*, pp. 111–16. London: Routledge.

Galton, M., Simon, B. and Croll, P. (1980) *Inside the Primary Classroom*. London: Routledge & Kegan Paul.

Geertz, C. (1975) *The Interpretation of Cultures*. London: Hutchinson.

Georgiades, N.J. and Phillimore, L. (1975) The myth of the hero-innovator and alternative strategies for organizational change. In C.C. Kiernan and F.P. Woodford (eds), *Behaviour Modification with the Severely Retarded*. Amsterdam: Associated Scientific Publishers.

Glaser, B.G. and Strauss, A.L. (1967) *The Discovery of Grounded Theory: Strategies for Qualitative Research*. New York: Aldine.

Goffman, E. (1956) *The Presentation of Self in Everyday Life*. Edinburgh: University of Edinburgh.

Gorard, S. with Taylor, C. (2004) *Combining Methods in Educational and Social Research*. Maidenhead: Open University Press.

Gordon, H. (1923) *Mental and Scholastic Tests among Retarded Children*, Education Pamphlet 44. London: HMSO.

Gould, S.J. (1996) *The Mismeasure of Man*. McHenry, IL: Sagebrush Education Resources.

Haldane, J.B.S. (1928) *Possible Worlds and Other Essays*. London: Chatto & Windus.

Hammersley, M. (1992) *What's Wrong with Ethnography*. London: Routledge.

Hammersley, M. (1996) The relationship between qualitative and quantitative research: paradigm loyalty versus methodological eclecticism. In J.T.E. Richardson (ed.), *Handbook of Research Methods for Psychology and the Social Sciences*. Leicester: BPS Books.

Holton, G. (1995) The controversy over the end of science. *Scientific American*, 273 (4), 168.

Hume, D. (1748/1910) An enquiry concerning human understanding. In *English Philosophers of the Seventeenth and Eighteenth Centuries: Locke, Berkeley, Hume*, Harvard Classics Volume 37. New York: P.F. Collier & Son. Also available at: http://eserver.org/18th/hume-enquiry.html.

ICM (2007) *Royal Family and War Survey*. Available at: www.icmresearch.co.uk/pdfs/2007_august_daily_mail_royals_poll.pdf (accessed 10 February 2013).

Jenkins, R. (1992) *Pierre Bourdieu*. London: Routledge.

Johnston, R.S. and Watson, J.E. (2003) Accelerating Reading and Spelling with Synthetic Phonics: A Five Year Follow Up. *Insight 4*. Scottish Executive.

Available at http://www.scotland.gov.uk/Publications/2003/03/16513/18923 (accessed 10 February 2013).

Jones, L. and Brown, T. (2001) 'Reading' the nursery classroom: a Foucauldian perspective. *International Journal of Qualitative Studies in Education*, 14 (6), 713–25.

Jones, S. (1985) The analysis of depth interviews. In R. Walker (ed.), *Applied Qualitative Research*. Aldershot: Gower.

Junghans, C., Feder, G., Hemingway, H., Timmis, A. and Jones, M. (2005) Recruiting patients to medical research: double blind randomised trial of 'opt-in' versus 'opt-out' strategies. *British Medical Journal*, 331, 940. Available at: www.bmj.com/cgi/reprint/331/7522/940.pdf (accessed 26 August 2008).

Kellett, M. (2005) *How to Develop Children as Researchers*. London: Paul Chapman Publishing.

Kelly G.A. (1955/1991) *The Psychology of Personal Constructs*, Vol. II. London: Routledge.

Klein, P. (1997) Multiplying the problems of intelligence by eight: a critique of Gardner's theory. *Canadian Journal of Education*, 22 (4), 377–94.

Kounin, J. (1970) *Discipline and Group Management in Classrooms*. New York: Holt, Rinehart & Winston.

Kuhn, T. (1970) *The Structure of Scientific Revolutions* (2nd edn). Chicago: University of Chicago Press.

Lacey, C. (1970) *Hightown Grammar*. Manchester: Manchester University Press.

Lévi-Strauss, C. (1962/1966) *The Savage Mind*. Chicago: University of Chicago Press.

Lewin, K. (1946) Action research and minority problems. *Journal of Social Issues*, 2 (4), 34–46.

Lewis, A. (1995) Views of schooling held by children attending schools for pupils with moderate learning difficulties. *International Journal of Disability, Development and Education*, 42 (1), 57–73.

Lewis, A. and Lindsay, G. (2000) *Researching Children's Perspectives*. Buckingham: Open University Press.

Lewis, A. and Porter, J. (2004) Interviewing children and young people with learning disabilities: guidelines for researchers and multi-professional practice. *British Journal of Learning Disabilities*, 32 (4), 191–7.

Lincoln, Y.S. and Guba, E.G. (1985) *Naturalistic Inquiry*. Beverly Hills, CA: SAGE.

MacIntyre, A. (1985) *After Virtue: A Study in Moral Theory*. London: Duckworth.

McNiff, J., Lomax, P. and Whitehead, J. (2003) *You and Your Action Research Project* (2nd edn). London: Routledge.

Maslow, A. (1966) *Psychology of Science*. New York: Harper & Row.

Medawar, P.B. (1982) *Pluto's Republic*. Oxford: Oxford University Press.

Miles, M.B. and Huberman, M. (1994) *Qualitative Data Analysis: An Expanded Sourcebook* (2nd edn). London: SAGE.

Milgram, S. (1963) Behavioral study of obedience. *Journal of Abnormal and Social Psychology*, 67 (4), 371–8.

National Commission for the Protection of Human Subjects of Biomedical and Behavioral Research (1978) *Belmont Report: Ethical Principles and Guidelines for the Protection of Human Subjects of Research*. Bethesda, MD: The Commission.

Newman, J.H. (1852/1960) The idea of a university. In M. J. Svaglic (ed.), *The Idea of a University Defined and Illustrated*, pp. 15–16. San Francisco: Rinehart Press.

Oakley, A. (2000) *Experiments in Knowing: Gender and Method in the Social Sciences*. Cambridge: Polity.

Orwell, G. (1969) Politics and the English language. In G. Orwell, *Inside the Whale and Other Essays*. London: Penguin. Available at: http://orwell.ru/library/essays/politics/english/e_polit (accessed 2 October 2008).

Patrick, J. (1973) *A Glasgow Gang Observed*. London: Methuen.

Pawson, R. (2006) *Evidence-Based Policy: A Realistic Perspective*. London: SAGE.

Pólya, G. (1945/2004) *How to Solve It*. Princeton, NJ: Princeton University Press.

Pring, R. (2000) *Philosophy of Educational Research*. London: Continuum.

Prosser, J. (ed.) (1998) *Image-Based Research*. London: Routledge.

Prosser, J. and Loxley, A. (2008) Introducing visual methods: ESRC National Centre for Research Methods review paper. Available at: http://eprints.ncrm.ac.uk/420/1/MethodsReviewPaperNCRM-010.pdf (accessed 4 November 2012).

Putnam, R. (1995) Bowling alone: America's declining social capital. *Journal of Democracy*, 6, 65–78.

Putnam, R. (2000) *Bowling Alone: The Collapse and Revival of American Community*. New York: Simon & Schuster.

Roethlisberger, F.J. and Dickson, W.J. (1939) *Management and the Worker*. Cambridge, MA: Harvard University Press.

Russell, B. (1956) Galileo and scientific method. In A.F. Scott (ed.), *Topics and Opinions*. London: Macmillan.

Ryle, G. (1949/1990) *The Concept of Mind*. London: Penguin.

Sacks, O. (1996) *An Anthropologist on Mars*. London: Picador.

Schwartz, D. (1992) *Waucoma Twilight: Generations of the Farm*. Washington, DC: Smithsonian Institution Press.

Smith, F. (1992) *To Think: In Language Learning and Education*. London: Routledge.

Smith, J. and Heshusius, L. (1986) Closing down the conversation: the end of the quantitative–qualitative debate among educational inquirers. *Educational Researcher*, 15, 4–12.

Soothill, K., Francis, B., Ackerley, E. and Fligelstone, R. (2002) *Murder and Serious Sexual Assault: What Criminal Histories Can Reveal about Future Serious Offending*, Police Research Series Paper 144. London: Home Office. Available at: www.homeoffice.gov.uk/rds/prgpdfs/prs144.pdf (accessed 24 October 2008).

Spradley, J. P. (1979) *The Ethnographic Interview*. New York: Holt, Rinehart & Winston.

Steedman, C. (1990) *Childhood, Culture and Class in Britain: Margaret McMillan, 1860–1931*. New Brunswick, NJ: Rutgers University Press.

Tarr, J. and Thomas, G. (1997) The quality of special educational needs policies: time for review? *Support for Learning*, 12 (1), 10–14.

Thagard, P. (1998) Ulcers and bacteria I: Discovery and acceptance. *Studies in History and Philosophy of Science. Part C: Studies in History and Philosophy of Biology and Biomedical Sciences*, 29: 107–36. Also available at: http://cogsci.uwaterloo.ca/Articles/Pages/Ulcers.one.html.

Thomas, G. (1992) *Effective Classroom Teamwork: Support or Intrusion*. London: Routledge.

Thomas, G. (1994) Write on or write-off? *British Journal of Special Education*, 21 (1), 12.

Thomas, G. (2002) Are eggs the right size for egg cups because of good planning by hens? Where is reading research going? *Educational Psychology in Practice*, 18 (2), 157–66.

Thomas, G. (2007) *Education and Theory: Strangers in Paradigms*. Maidenhead: Open University Press.

Thomas, G. (2011) *How to Do Your Case Study – A Guide for Students and Researchers*. London: SAGE.

Thomas, G. and James, D. (2006) Re-inventing grounded theory: some questions about theory, ground and discovery, *British Educational Research Journal*, 32 (6), 767–95.

Thomas, G., Walker, D. and Webb. J. (1998) *The Making of the Inclusive School*. London: Routledge.

Torgerson, C., Brooks, G. and Hall, J. (2006) A systematic review of the research literature on the use of phonics in the teaching of reading and spelling. Research Report 711. London: Department for Education and Skills.

Vincett, K., Cremin, H. and Thomas, G. (2005) *Teachers and Assistants Working Together*. Maidenhead: Open University Press.

Wacquant, L.D. (1989) Towards a reflexive sociology: a workshop with Pierre Bourdieu. *Sociological Theory*, 7, 26–63.

Wells, M. (2005) Paxman answers the questions. *Guardian Unlimited*, 31 January. Available at: http://politics.guardian.co.uk/media/story/0,12123,1402324,00.html (accessed 26 August 2007).

Whale, J. (1984) *Put it in Writing*. London: Dent.

Wheeler, L.R. (1970) A trans-decade comparison of the IQs of Tennessee mountain children. In I. Al-Issa and W. Dennis (eds), *Cross-Cultural Studies of Behavior*, pp. 120–33. New York: Holt, Rinehart & Winston.

White, J. (2006) *Intelligence, Destiny and Education*. London: Routledge.

Wieviorka, M. (1992) Case studies: history or sociology? In C.C. Ragin and H.S. Becker (eds), *What is a Case? Exploring the Foundations of Social Inquiry*, pp. 159–172. Cambridge: Cambridge University Press.

Wolcott, H.F. (1992) Posturing in qualitative inquiry. In M.D. LeCompte, W.L. Milroy and J. Preissie (eds), *The Handbook of Qualitative Research in Education*, pp. 3–52. New York: Academic Press.

Wright Mills, C. (1959/1970) *The Sociological Imagination*. New York: Holt.

INDEX